VITRUVIUS SCOTICUS

Plans, Elevations, and Sections of Public Buildings, Noblemen's and Gentlemen's Houses in Scotland

WILLIAM ADAM

With an Introduction and Notes to the Plates by

JAMES SIMPSON

DOVER PUBLICATIONS, INC.
Mineola, New York

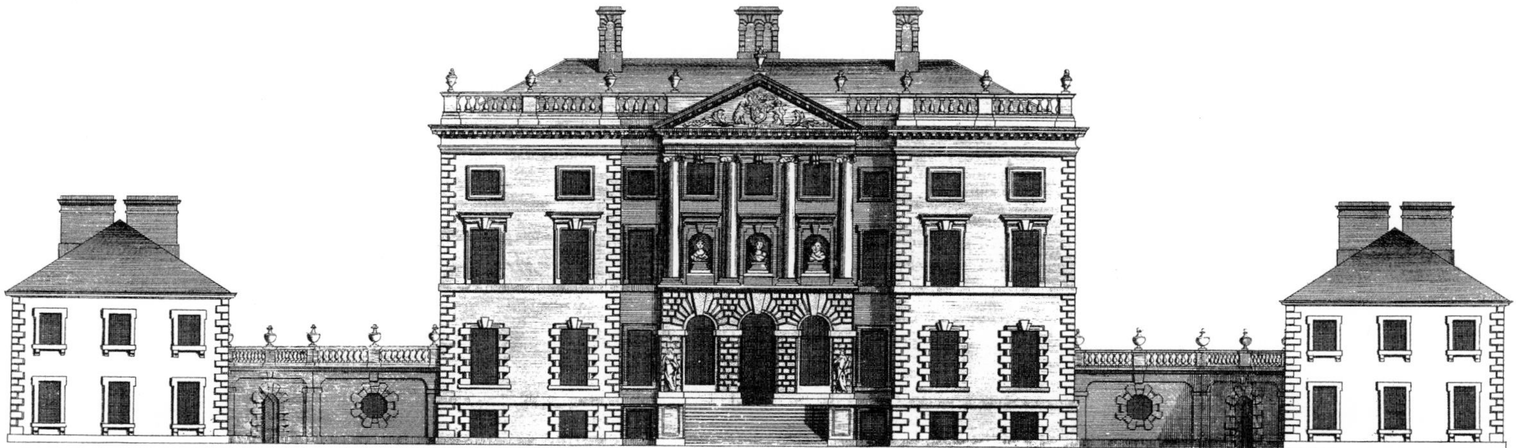

Bibliographical Note

Vitruvius Scoticus: Plans, Elevations, and Sections of Public Buildings, Noblemen's and Gentlemen's Houses in Scotland, first published by Dover Publications, Inc., in 2011, is a reproduction of the work originally published as *Vitruvius Scoticus; Being a Collection of Plans, Elevations, and Sections of Public Buildings, Noblemen's and Gentlemen's Houses in Scotland* by Messrs. A. & C. Black, Edinburgh, in 1812. It includes an Introduction and Notes to the Plates by James Simpson.

Library of Congress Cataloging-in-Publication Data

Adam, William, 1689–1748.

Vitruvius Scoticus : plans, elevations, and sections of public buildings, noblemen's and gentlemen's houses in Scotland / William Adam.

p. cm.

Originally published: Edinburgh: A. & C. Black, 1812.

ISBN-13: 978-0-486-47307-9

ISBN-10: 0-486-47307-4

1. Architecture—Scotland—Designs and plans. I. Title. II. Title: Plans, elevations, and sections of public buildings, noblemen's and gentlemen's houses in Scotland.

NA997.A5A4 2011

720.22'2411—dc22

2010047355

Manufactured in the United States by Courier Corporation

47307401

www.doverpublications.com

CONTENTS

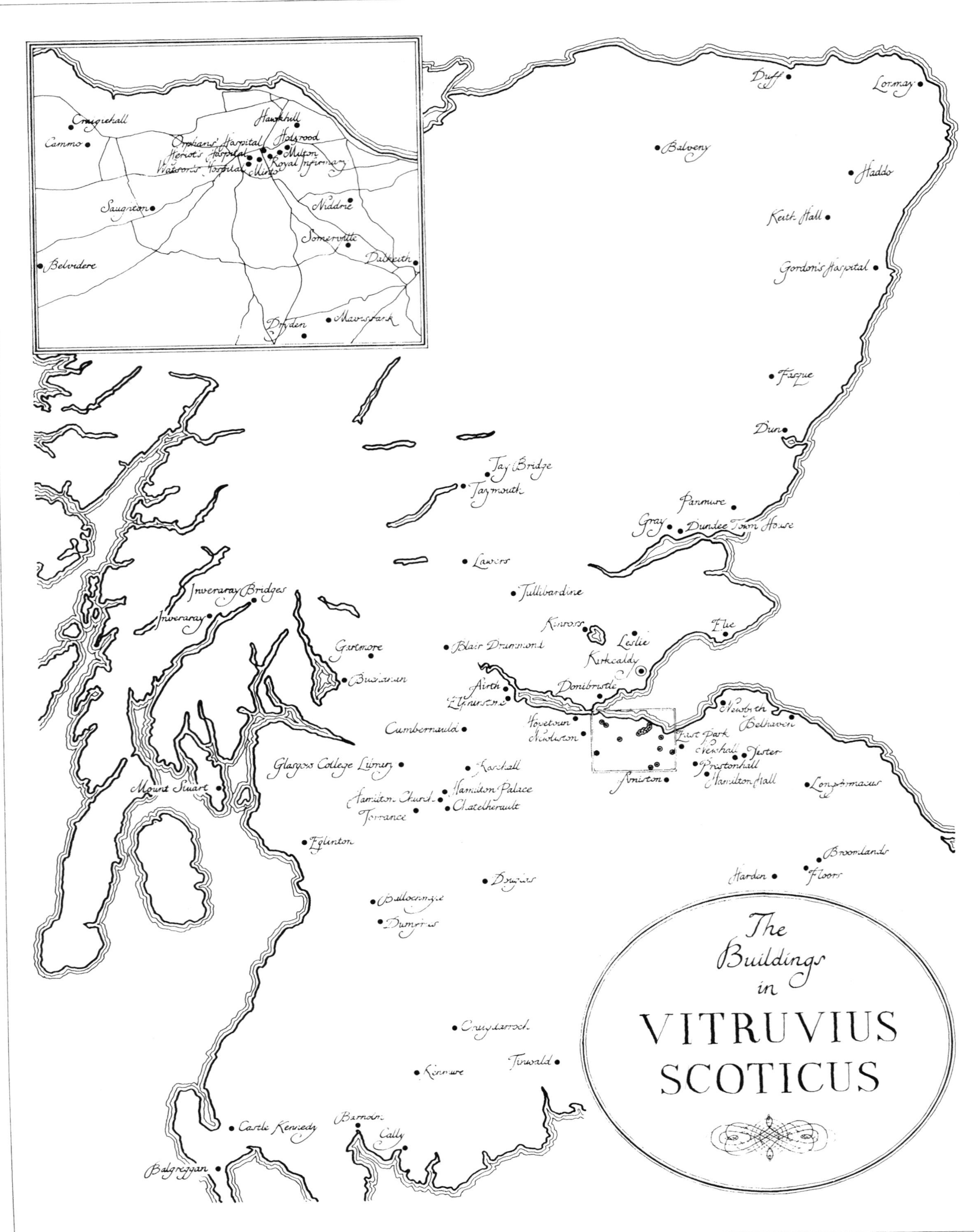

The Buildings in VITRUVIUS SCOTICUS
Craigiehall
Cammo
Hawkhill
Orphans' Hospital
Holyrood
Heriot's Hospital
Milton
Watson's Hospital
Minto
Royal Infirmary
Saughton
Niddrie
Somerville
Belvidere
Dalkeith
Dryden
Mavisbank
Duff
Lormay
Balveny
Haddo
Keith Hall
Gordon's Hospital
Fasque
Dun
Tay Bridge
Taymouth
Panmure
Gray
Dundee Town House
Lawers
Tullibardine
Inveraray Bridges
Inveraray
Kinross
Leslie
Elie
Gartmore
Blair Drummond
Kirkcaldy
Buchanan
Airth
Elphinstone
Donibristle
Newbyth
Hopetoun
Belhaven
Cumbernauld
Niddry
Newliston
East Park
Newhall
Yester
Glasgow College Library
Pristonhall
Hamilton Hall
Arniston
Longformacus
Mount Stuart
Hamilton Church
Hamilton Palace
Chatelherault
Torrance
Eglinton
Broomlands
Harden
Floors
Douglas
Ballochmyle
Dumfries
Craigdarroch
Tinwald
Kenmure
Castle Kennedy
Barnbarroch
Cally
Balgreggan

PREFACE

Vitruvius Scoticus has always been a rare and somewhat mysterious book. I was introduced to it ten years ago by Professor Alistair Rowan, then of the University of Edinburgh, when I was an architecture student at the Edinburgh College of Art, and as a result it became the subject of my final year dissertation. The guidance I received at that time from Mr Colin McWilliam, my tutor, and from Miss Catherine Cruft of the National Monuments Record of Scotland has stood me in good stead ever since. The starting point of any work on William Adam must be the early chapters of *Robert Adam and his Circle in Edinburgh and Rome* and the extent of my debt to John Fleming will, I hope, be obvious.

In the course of the original study my wife and I visited many of the houses illustrated in the book, and without exception we were warmly received; I am most grateful to all the owners who welcomed us. I am also grateful to the owners of private muniments to which we were were given access, and particularly to Mr Keith Adam of Blair Adam and to Sir John Clerk of Penicuik, for without the Adam papers at Blair Adam and the Penicuik papers, most of which are now in the Scottish Record Office, much of great interest and importance would be simply unknown. Thanks are due, too, to the staff of the Scottish Record Office, the National Library of Scotland and the National Monuments Record of Scotland, who never fail to be helpful.

Many individuals have helped me in general ways and with specific pieces of information. Dr Alan Tait of Glasgow University has advised me on several occasions, and the place of William Adam as a landscape designer will be firmly established in his forthcoming book *The Landscape Garden in Scotland*. Mr Tim Connor helped greatly with the complex history of *Vitruvius Scoticus* and added several pieces to the jigsaw; the place of the book in the wider scheme of things will be better understood following the publication of his and Dr Eileen Harris' forthcoming *Bibliographical Dictionary of British Architectural Books*. I am grateful to Mr Howard Colvin for his generosity with information and for lending me the Braco Case Depositions, printed papers relating to the lawsuit, which are a mine of information on William Adam. Mr Ian Mowat has helped me with material relating to John Adam and Mr John Morris with material on the book. Mr Nicolas Allen, Mr Iain Brown, Miss Mary Cosh, Mr John Dunbar Mr Richard Emerson and Mr David Walker have supplied me with information and pointed out my mistakes.

The book itself has been reproduced from the copy in the University of Glasgow Library by courtesy of the librarian, and I acknowledge the assistance of Mr Baldwin, Keeper of Special Collections. The receipt form is reproduced from the original in the Rothes MSS in Kirkcaldy Museum by courtesy of the Curator. The map was drawn by Miss Mandy Palmer and the grid references were computed by Miss Cathy Maxwell.

While I have been preoccupied with drawing together the threads for publication, additional burdens have been placed on my family, on my partner Mr Stewart Brown, and on everybody in our office, not least on my secretary Mrs Cathy Mason. The end would never have been reached without extensive advice and assistance from Mr Ian Gow and from my wife, Ann. It remains for me to confess full responsibility for any errors, opinions and speculation and to hope that *Vitruvius Scoticus* will be, if not less rare, at least less mysterious in the future. Finally, I would like to dedicate this new edition of *Vitruvius Scoticus* to the future of what to me is the most important of all the buildings in the book: to Mavisbank.

JAMES SIMPSON
EDINBURGH
JANUARY 1980

INTRODUCTION

William Adam (1689–1748)

The author of *Vitruvius Scoticus* was born in Kirkcaldy on 30 October 1689, and died in Edinburgh on 24 June 1748, 'generally lamented and deservedly so', according to the obituary in the *Caledonian Mercury*, 'not only by those who knew him but by all who wish well to the Publick. His Genius for Architecture pushed him out of Obscurity into a high degree of Reputation.,[1] His origins were not in fact wholly obscure for the family traces its descent from the Adams of Fanno in Angus; John Adam, William's father, was the second son of Archibald Adam of Fanno and later of Queen's Park, also in Angus. This John established himself as a mason in Kirkcaldy and, when his elder brother's son died unmarried, he succeeded to the little that was left of the family property. He married Helen Cranston, the daughter of a Session Court Judge, and of their numerous children William was apparently the sole survivor.[2]

Little certain is known of the early part of William's life, but he probably attended the Grammar School in Kirkcaldy until about 1704, and it seems likely that he spent some time thereafter travelling and perhaps completing his education in the Low Countries.[3] It also seems highly probable that he was brought up to take on his father's business, which may, given his status and the pattern of subsequent events, have been quite substantial. It has been suggested that John Adam died in about 1710 and that William returned to Kirkcaldy at about this time.[4] In any event, according to his grandson, 'he built there in what is called The Links a house which even now discloses marks of architectural elegance'.[5] Gladney House in Bute Wynd was built in 1711 for William Robertson of Gladney, formerly Bailie to the Countess of Wemyss and after her death 'Tacksman of the Coall in Abbotshall'.

In 1714 Robertson and Adam, then styled 'Masson in Linktown of Abbotshall', formed a partnership, contracted for the lease of clay from Andrew Ramsay of Abbotshall and built a brick and tilework, possibly the first in Scotland and apparently the first to manufacture 'Dutch pantiles'.[6] On 30 May 1716 William turned his business partnership into a family one by marrying Mary Robertson,[7] his partner's daughter, who was then just seventeen.

Information on William Adam's activities at this period remains scarce, but in 1719 he was named in a contract as the supplier of iron and bricks for the construction of the Earl of Moray's new house at Donibristle designed by Alexander McGill.[8] There is at present no evidence to suggest that he was active as an architect on anything other than a local level before about 1720, and such material as there is suggests that he was making full use of his very considerable ability, energy and continental experience to develop and extend the commercial base which he had inherited and on which his architectural career was to be founded. Besides pantile manufacture, he brought a new type of barley kiln from Holland for making barley bree or strong ale[9] and he introduced Dutch ideas on the construction of canals: 'I have seen all the most considerable ones (canals) in both Holland and England', he wrote to Sir John Clerk of Penicuik many years later, 'I can venture to say that I am as much master of the form and disposition of them as of the building of a house'.[10] Interests in coal mining and salt panning went together and may have evolved from the partnership with Robertson, while the trade in building materials and contracting grew naturally and was to flourish in due course alongside the practice of architecture.[11]

From 1716 William lived with his wife at Gladney House on the Links of Kirkcaldy,[12] and in July 1717 their eldest daughter, Janet (Jenny) was born.[13] By 1720 he was thirty-one, firmly established and becoming known far beyond the boundaries of Fife, though not as an architect. On the other hand, all the leading practitioners, including Alexander McGill who was probably the foremost at this time, were mason-architects, and it must be presumed that an ambitious young mason-contractor of the background, education and experience of William Adam had architectural ambitions. A good deal of published material was available, both written and drawn, which could supply all that was necessary to complement a knowledge of practical building, and some of the architectural books which are known to have been in the Adam Library in the 19th century may already have been in William's possession in 1720.[14] His emergence as an architect in the early 1720s and his rapid rise to pre-eminence need not therefore be particularly surprising, but it is nevertheless unfortunate that it is still not possible to date any designs with confidence to the years before 1721. The fact that his earliest known patrons included such eminent men as the Duke of Roxburghe, the Earls of Stair and Hopetoun and Sir John Clerk of Penicuik makes this doubly intriguing.

On 17 January 1721, William Adam, now styled 'architect of Kirkcaldy', signed an agreement with the first Earl of Hopetoun for the enlargement of Hopetoun House in accordance with 'a draught to be fixed on by His Lordship'.[15] On 5 March Mary Adam gave birth at Gladney to their eldest son John,[16] and on 18 May William was at Kelso for the founding of the first Duke of Roxburghe's new house of Floors.[17] By January 1723 he was designing an addition to the old house of Newliston for the second Earl of Stair[18] and a villa for Baron Clerk at Mavisbank;[19] Clerk and Stair were probably the most important of William Adam's patrons, for not only did they commission work themselves and participate to such an extent that Mavisbank must be said to have been designed jointly by Adam and Clerk,[20] but they recommended him to others and sponsored him for several public appointments, with disappointing results at first, but ultimately with some success.

The influence of Clerk and Stair in the mid 1720s is nowhere more obvious that at Dalmahoy, for George Dalrymple shared the Exchequer Court bench with Clerk, and was Stair's younger brother. Colonel Sir James Campbell's military association with Stair may have been significant in Adam's appointment to do work at Lawers, while legal connections through Clerk were probably important in his securing commissions from Robert Dundas of Arniston and David Erskine, Lord Dun. Baron Clerk was himself a widely respected authority on architectural matters, and it may have been on his recommendation that William Adam was retained by the second Earl of Aberdeen at Haddo, which, though designed in the 1720s under Clerk's influence, was not built until the 1730s; moreover at Haddo, as at Mavisbank, the mason contractor was not William Adam, but Clerk's own protégé John Baxter.[21] A certain transition was made therefore between 1719, when Adam was supplying materials to McGill at Donibristle and 1723, when he was supplying plans and supervising the work of another mason.

By the later 1720s William Adam was not only best known as an architect, but in the words of John Clerk of Eldin 'he had established himself the universal architect of his country'.[22] That is not to say that his other enterprises had in any way diminished, quite the reverse: Sir John Clerk of Penicuik, on a visit to Kirkcaldy in 1728 'could not enough admire the enterprising temper of the proprietor who had at that time under his own care near to twenty general projects – Barley Mills, Timber Mills, Coal Works, Salt Pans, Marble Works, Highways, Farms, houses of his own a-building and houses belonging to others not a few'.[23] Not all shared Clerk's admiration, however: 'As for Adams', wrote the Marquis of Annandale in 1724, 'he has so many real, and so many imaginary projects, that he minds no body nor no thing to purpose'![24]

In the course of the 1720s William moved the centre of his activities from Kirkcaldy to Edinburgh. According to his grandson he acquired in 1725 'a house situated close to the southern end of the South Bridge on the West side',[25] but it was only after the birth at Gladney of their third child, Robert, on 24 July 1728[26] that the Adams moved to Edinburgh. Land at North Merchiston may also have been purchased at about this time as a site for a villa.[27] The move is probably best explained by the obvious need to be accessible in the capital to patrons and business colleagues; as the geographical distribution of commissions shows clearly, many more opportunities lay in Edinburgh and the Lothians than in Fife. In time business interests also grew in the Edinburgh area, for though the ties with Kirkcaldy, including the partnership and ultimately full ownership of the brickworks, were maintained, stone quarrying, hewing and carving became centred at the quarry at Queensferry, which was probably first opened to supply the work at Hopetoun, and in 1739 he leased the Pinkie coalfield at Musselburgh from the Marquis of Tweeddale.[28] The City of Edinburgh marked the Adams' arrival in 1728 by electing William a Burgess and Guildbrother 'gratis' for 'services done to the good toune'.[29]

As early as the spring of 1723, Sir John Clerk was promoting William Adam with a view to his appointment as architect for a new Law Court and Record Office under the 'Town of Edinburgh Bill'.[30] However this came to nothing, as did Lord Stair's attempt to secure for him the office of Surveyor of the King's Works in Scotland, previously held by James Smith;[31] application was apparently made to Sir Robert

Walpole in 1727 and the appointment – with, if John Clerk of Eldin is to be believed, a Baronetcy – only fell through because of the King's death.[32] A public appointment did come, however, in 1728, when he became 'Clerk and Storekeeper of the Works in Scotland' and in 1730 he was appointed 'Mason to the Board of Ordnance in North Britain'.[33]

In 1726 William Adam was sufficiently confident of his position to be considering the publication of a book of designs, and Clerk and Stair were at least aware of the project.[34] In the spring of 1727 Adam went to London in the company of Sir John Clerk and at the invitation of Lord Stair, and Adam apparently took with him a set of drawings to be engraved for the book. He joined up with Clerk at Stamford on 24 March and, after failing to gain admittance to Burghley House, they travelled to London together by way of Wimpole Hall near Cambridge, which had recently been enlarged by James Gibbs. They reached London the next day and made their way to lodgings in Suffolk Street arranged for them by William Aikman, the portrait painter and a cousin of Clerk's. Unfortunately Sir John makes no further mention of Adam in his journal,[35] so there is no means of knowing whether or not he met any of the influential people who entertained Clerk. According to John Clerk of Eldin, however, Lord Stair 'invited Mr Adam to go with him to London where he had never been that he might have an opportunity of being introduced to many people of genius and taste and of seeing various buildings both public and private'.[36] Presumably some part of this object was achieved by Adam as well as by Clerk; in any event both subscribed to James Gibbs' *Book of Architecture*, to be published in the following year, and both had their portraits painted by Aikman.[37] Clerk was back at Penicuik by the end of May, and Adam rather later, without apparently having made any arrangements for the engraving of his drawings, for they were subsequently engraved by Richard Cooper, a young engraver who settled in Edinburgh in 1730. The book project remained alive, but for some reason William failed to bring it to fruition.

The architectural practice continued to grow in the late 1720s and 1730s and, as might be expected, the patronage became more diverse and less dependant on the influence of Clerk and Stair. By this time William's own reputation and acknowledged success were more important than personal recommendations in the attraction of new commissions. In 1730 he was remodelling Yester for the fourth Marquis of Tweeddale,[38] building Cumbernauld House for the sixth Earl of Wigton[39] and involved in various projects for the fifth Duke of Hamilton, including the new church at Hamilton,[40] the first of his public buildings. And besides new commissions, work continued on many old ones; Hopetoun, for example, was building more or less continuously throughout William's career. In 1731 Adam was back at Newliston advising Lord Stair on landscape work,[41] for it would appear that he was also building a reputation as a landscape gardener, designing earthworks, waterworks and planting in addition to a number of garden buildings of which 'Chatelherault'[42] is the most renowned. The most important house of this period however was Duff, designed in 1735 for Lord Braco, on the outskirts of Banff, and the commission included garden buildings and possibly landscape work as well; unfortunately the project ended in 1739 in a bitter dispute which took many years to resolve.[43]

Although the country house practice continued to flourish, 1730–40 was the decade of public buildings. Gordon's Hospital in Aberdeen,[44] Dundee Town House[45] and Glasgow University Library[46] were all designed in the early 1730s and in 1733 William's Ordnance Board appointment brought the commission to design and build the bridge over the Tay at Aberfeldy for General Wade.[47] The Edinburgh hospitals – the Orphans',[48] George Watson's[49] and the Royal Infirmary[50] – followed in the late 1730s.

Success brought prosperity, for according to his grandson: 'In the year 1731 William Adam, then in the forty-third year of his age, became possessed of the lands and estate of Blair Crambeth in Kinross-shire, which with the exception of from fifteen to twenty-five acres of infield land around the humble dwelling of its proprietor was a wild uncultivated district of 640 acres of Scotch measure . . . his singular faculty of forecast with an adventurous and sanguine disposition made him attempt improvements in situations which would have intimidated most other men of that period'. From this time a proportion of William's energy and resources was put into the extension and improvement of the estate and into the construction of 'a village of considerable elegance', which 'from his attachment to his wife he named . . . Maryburgh'.[51] At about the same time William was planting his villa estate of North Merchiston 'according to the prevailing taste of his time'. Unfortunately however, neither the mansion house at The Blair nor the villa at Merchiston, both of which appear to have been projected, were built in William's lifetime.

In the meanwhile the establishment south of the Cowgate in what became known as Adam's Square, expanded as the Adams increased in number. Margaret was born on 14 April 1731, but did not survive. James was born on 21 July 1732 and William in 1738;[52] the birthdays of the other five girls, Helen (Nelly), Mary, Elizabeth (Betty), Susannah and Margaret (Peggy) are not recorded, nor are those of two other children, a William and another Margaret, who died in infancy.[53] All the accounts suggest that Mary Adam presided over a warm, stimulating and sociable household, and watched closely over the upbringing of her 'bairns'. John was sent to the Dalkeith Grammar School, where his distinguished contemporaries included William Robertson, for whom the Adam's Square house became something of a second home; in fact it seems to have been a social centre for most of the young men who were to generate the 'Edinburgh Enlightenment': 'The numerous family of Mr Adam', wrote John Clerk of Eldin, 'the uninterrupted cordiality in which they lived, their conciliating manners and the various accomplishments in which they severally made proficience, formed a most attractive society and failed not to draw round them a set of men whose learning and genius have since done honour to that country which gave them birth'. Besides Robertson and Adam Ferguson – Robert's 'particular friend' – John Home, Adam Smith, David Hume, Alexander Carlyle and many others were regular visitors to Adam's Square.[54]

In the 1740s William was as busy as ever and John was playing an increasingly important role in the office and in the general running of the business. Work in progress at this period included alterations and additions at Taymouth Castle[55] for the third Marquis of Breadalbane and a new house in Perthshire for Nicol Graham of Gartmore.[56] But the most important new commission was probably for the twelfth Lord Lovat at Castle Dounie in Inverness-shire where building was to begin in 1745;[57] not surprisingly the project was abandoned. At Inveraray, however, the '45 only delayed the construction of the new castle designed by Roger Morris for the third Duke of Argyll,[58] and when work was resumed, William Adam was appointed to superintend the work. But the main result of the '45 was a sudden increase in the volume of military work; the Ordnance Board accounts for 1746 reveal payments to the Adams for 'workmanship and repairs performed and materials delivered' at Fort Augustus and Fort William, Blackness, Carlisle, Duart, Dumbarton, Edinburgh and Stirling Castles.[59] But the biggest commitment of all was to the construction of Fort George, which was to keep the Adams working every summer for fifteen years.

In the mid 1740s William's health was failing and at Inveraray and Fort George John played an important role from the start; at Hopetoun too John took increasing responsibility, and in 1746 or 1747 Robert began to play a part. In the autumn of 1747 William became seriously ill, and it was John who went to London in the spring of 1748 for important discussions with the Ordnance Board and with Roger Morris and the Duke of Argyll.[60] He took the opportunity of making a country house tour of his own; but when he got back to Edinburgh it was to find his father dying. The *Scots Magazine* recorded the death on 24 June 1748 of 'William Adam, King's Mason, a celebrated architect';[61] his obituary in the *Caledonian Mercury* continued: '. . . his Activity of Spirit, not to be confined within narrow Bounds, diffused itself into many Branches of Business, not more to his own benefit than to that of his native country. As to the latter, 'tis fortunate he has left behind him some promising young men to carry on what he has so happily begun. Their regard for so worthy a Man their Parent, will be to them a more than ordinary Incitement to tread in his steps; for he was a good Artist, but a still better Man'.[62]

John Adam of Maryburgh (1721–92)

On his father's death, John Adam inherited the Blair Adam estate, North Merchiston, Adam's Square and most of his father's other property and business interests. His first act, according to his son, was to double the provision made in his father's will for his mother, brothers and sisters, which still left him with a fortune of some £15,000. He ensured his succession as Master Mason to the Board of Ordnance and to the work which went with the appointment, most notably the construction of Fort George, and then took Robert into partnership so that the proceeds of the government work would be shared equally between them.[63]

John was by nature a practical builder and a conscientious man of affairs; according to his son he 'never relaxed from the most industrious attention to business or deviated from well regulated economy in his style of living. His chief indulgence was . . . in adorning his villa of North Merchiston and in the improvement, chiefly by judicious planting of his estate of Blair'.[64] The architecture of the ten years following William Adam's death must be regarded as the work of a firm in which John was the senior partner, but it is fairly clear that Robert's was the guiding hand in design matters until his departure on the Grand Tour in 1754; Robert was clearly responsible for example for the design of the Adam mausoleum in Greyfriars' Churchyard[65] and for the feathery rococo gothick refronting of the old church at Yester as a mausoleum for Lord Tweeddale, both of 1753.[66] James' influence, even in Robert's absence, seems to have been slight.

The work at Fort George provided valuable experience for the younger brothers in the early 1750s, for there was no better training to be had than in the service of the Board of Ordnance, and Colonel Skinner, the Chief Engineer for North Britain who was in charge of the work, knew his business. But other projects were in hand, most notably the completion of Hopetoun and Inveraray, and the building of Dumfries House in Ayrshire for the fourth Earl of Dumfries. In Robert's absence John produced buildings which were sound and sensible, and austerely masculine, a type epitomised by the villa which he built at Hawkhill in 1757 for the bachelor judge, Andrew Pringle, Lord Alemoor.[67] Lord Milton's house in the Canongate of the mid 1750s,[68] and Ballochmyle, built for Allan Whitefoord in about 1760[69] also come into this category.

In 1758 Robert returned from Italy to London, and James, Jenny, Betty and young William went south to join him. James returned to do his stint at Fort George in 1759, went to Italy in 1760 and finally rejoined Robert in 1763. John visited London himself in 1759, combining the trip with the now customary country house tour which this time included Norfolk. From then on, however, he had sole responsibility for carrying on the Scottish practice, the Ordnance Board contracts and the numerous business enterprises.[70] In the early 1760s, Robert was beginning to have the same success in London that his father had had in Scotland forty years before, and at the same time John was expanding his inheritance in Edinburgh, having apparently doubled it since the time of his father's death. Already, however, marked differences in temperament and attitudes were apparent: 'I see,' wrote James from Italy on hearing that a start on the North Merchiston villa was imminent, 'that John proposes making himself very fine in a new house and is adorning it with all those figures of architecture that are known on the other side of the Tweed, where really I begin to imagine the three arts of painting, sculpture and architecture are as little understood as in Nova Scotia' ![71] In 1764 trouble came from a totally unexpected quarter, and for John things were never to be quite the same again.

From 1753 John had banked with the house of Adam and Thomas Fairholme; in 1761 Adam Fairholme, a friend and contemporary of John's at Dalkeith Grammar School, went to London with the express purpose of speculating in English stocks. In 1764 he failed, burnt his books and fled from England. The situation was compounded for John by the fact that his payments from the Ordnance Board had been deposited with Adam Fairholme in London while he drew on Thomas in Edinburgh. It appeared that he had lost more than £18,000, about half of his total wealth at that time. The Blair and his beloved North Merchiston were put on the market, the town establishment reduced to a third, carriage, horses and servants dispensed with. The brothers in London rallied round and in order to help invited John to become a partner in what his son later described as a mercantile concern 'connected chiefly with the business of building'. Young William was to be the manager, and the firm 'William Adam and Co'. It was then discovered that John had a preferential claim against the Fairholmes as a result of which, after carrying the case to the House of Lords, the £18,000 was recovered; the property was withdrawn from the market and by 1767 John's prosperity was restored. All seemed as before, and so it was for about five years, but there was one difference: John's partnership in William Adam and Co. and his consequent involvement in the 'adventure of the Adelphi', and all that followed.

In 1770 John wished to give up architecture and business and retire to his estate; by this time however, the brothers were heavily dependant on his capital and resisted all attempts to withdraw it. In the meantime the Adelphi scheme was being financed by discounting bills, and when the Ayr Bank failed in the summer of 1772 all was thrown into confusion. John spent time in London in 1772 and 1773 and disaster was avoided with the aid of a lottery; by this time, however, John had advanced no less than £30,000 more than any of the other brothers, money which he wished to put into improvements at The Blair. Things went from bad to worse as the brothers cast around for schemes with which to recoup their losses; there was a saltpetre factory at Sandend on the King's Road, Liardet's patent stucco and numerous other failures. By 1781 John's property was mortgaged to the tune of £36,000; in exasperation he broke off all communication with his brothers and in 1786 the estate was again put up for sale. John felt deeply that his brothers, in whose affairs he had only accidentally become involved, had behaved dishonourably; he after all had a family to support and sons to succeed him while they did not; yet they made very little sacrifice. He gradually gave up all hope of recovery; having left Adam's Square in 1777 and sold the last of the property there in about 1786, he and his wife were living in a small flat opposite Brown's Square, from which they moved in 1789 to share a house in George Street with his recently widowed sister Betty. There, three years later, John Adam died.[72]

John's career was, to say the least, overshadowed by that of his brothers. His own architecture was not undistinguished, but he recognised his own limitations and in 1772 even got Robert and James to make designs for his own house at The Blair. Despite James' somewhat vitriolic observations, the North Merchiston villa was probably a house of some quality and distinction, and its garden – with 'spiral walks and shrubberies and . . . intricacies which gave a great feeling of extent'[73] – was clearly of considerable interest. His business activities were almost as extensive as his father's, he was involved in the design and construction of canals, roads and bridges and of major civic improvements in Edinburgh and the coal, brick and tile interests were continued. Aberdeen granite quarries were acquired and in 1765 John became a shareholder in the Carron Iron Company. If it had not been for the compound failure of the brothers' London ventures, much more might have been achieved both in business and on the Blair estate; and without Robert's dazzling success as an architect, John Adam's own architectural achievements might be more generally recognised.

William Adam of Blair Adam (1751–1839)

John Adam's wife, whom he married on 8 July 1750, was Jean Ramsay,[74] daughter of a merchant in Kirkcaldy. Their eldest son William was born on 21 July 1751 and at the age of twelve he experienced the consequences for the Adam family of the Fairholme failure. He went to Christ Church, Oxford, in 1769 and in the same year his younger brother John died at Eton. He was called to the Scottish Bar in 1773, became a Member of Parliament in the following year and in 1780 was appointed Treasurer to the Board of Ordnance. On the fall of Lord North's administration in 1782 he went to the English Bar. He played a leading part in the impeachment of Warren Hastings in 1788, became a K.C. in 1796 and Attorney General to the Prince of Wales. He became a Privy Councillor in 1815, and in the following year was appointed Lord Chief Commissioner of the Jury Court for the Trial of Civil Causes in Scotland.[75]

With growing indignation William Adam observed his father's embarrassment as a consequence of his uncles' business ventures, and lost money himself in some of the later schemes. While at the Board of Ordnance he secured the post of Carpenter Contractor to the Board for his uncle Robert, but by that time the Company had difficulty in raising the capital to carry on the business. In 1790 he visited The Blair after an interval of six years and was so impressed with the growth of the planting that he persuaded his father to withdraw it from the market. After his father's death in 1792 he took seven years to clear the inherited debts before continuing with improvements and the expansion of the estate.[76] He apparently felt extremely bitter about the way in which his uncles had behaved, and his interest in the publication of *Vitruvius Scoticus* in the years 1804–12 may have been prompted by a desire to promote the memory of his father and grandfather at his uncles' expense. He formed the Blair Adam Club and was a close friend of Sir Walter Scott. He published *The Gift of a Grandfather* in 1836 and died in 1839.

The Book

Vitruvius Scoticus was conceived by William Adam not later than the spring of 1726; but though subscriptions were received from 1727, plates engraved from about 1730 and sheets printed in 1746 or shortly after, the book remained unpublished on William's death in 1748. John Adam revived the project in the 1760s, but it was left to his son William finally to secure publication in about 1812. The number of copies produced was not large, possibly fewer than 150, and the book has always been scarce. The copies were assembled from the sheets printed in the 1740s and later with a new title page and 'List of Plans'; some of the sheets exist in more than one form.

The name *Vitruvius Scoticus*[77] was probably intended from the book's conception. In 1733 the English Antiquary, James West, went to see 'Mr Cowper, Engraver who, with Mr Adams, the architect, is about publishing and engraving all the fine buildings in Scotland to make a *Vitruvius Scoticus*'. Nevertheless in the 1760s it is usually described as 'The Book of Scotch Houses' and William Adam himself referred in his receipt forms only to 'My Designs for Buildings & C.' It is interesting, however, that in a letter to Sir John Clerk of Penicuik dated 5 May 1726 William Adam asked to borrow Palladio and the third volume of *Vitruvius Britannicus*, which he lacked, and continued: 'I have not been able to goe to London yet, by the many Drawings past and now among hands. . . . . . I write My Lord Stair lately, and told him that it was not possible for me to get up this summer that if I liv'd should certainly goe with his Ldsp. the end of this year, and that in the meantime, I'm getting Doubles of all my Draughts to carry with me in order to put them in the Engraver's hands . . .'[78] Forty years later the book then proposed was described as being 'after the manner of Campbell's Vitruvius', and it is difficult not to conclude that *Vitruvius Britannicus* was William Adam's model from the start.

In the end William delayed going to London, with his draughts until March 1727, but whether or not Richard Cooper, who engraved the main series of plates, was in London at that time is uncertain. Cooper is known to have been born in Yorkshire in about 1705, to have trained with John Pine, travelled in Italy and settled in Edinburgh in 1730.[79] There is no reason to believe that any of the plates were necessarily engraved before 1730. The Holyrood plates were dedicated to 'His Royal Highness FREDERICK, Prince of Wales, etc'; Prince Frederick came to Britain in December 1728 and was created Prince of Wales in January 1729. The Heriot's Hospital plates were dedicated to 'Patrick Lindsay Esqr. Lord Provost of Edinburgh' and Lindsay held office from 1729 to 1731 (and again in 1733–5).[80] The Dundee Town House plates were dedicated to Alexander Robertson, who was Lord Provost in 1731 and 1732.[81] The evidence is, therefore, that the engraving was begun by Cooper after his arrival in Edinburgh.

On his return to Edinburgh in the summer of 1727 William began to collect subscriptions with a book of receipt forms, presumably engraved – but probably not by Cooper – and printed during his stay in London. Each form was separated from its counterfoil by a wavy cut through a complex and elegantly worked scroll, so that the two parts could be reliably matched, and the engraved legend was contained within an elegant cartouche incorporating the symbolic tools of the architect's trade, dividers, compasses, rule and square. Form 'No 28' records that Adam 'Received the *17th* day of *Sepr.* 1727 of *the Earle of Rothes, Three Guineas* – being *the* first Payment for *two* Copy'*s* of My Designs for Buildings & C. in 150 Plates which will be delivered in Sheets to the Bearer hereof upon Payment of the like Sum'.[82] Lord Dun was the seventy-second subscriber on 17 November 1727 for a single copy, the 135th subscription was received in March 1728[83] and James Duff of Craigston subscribed for a single copy as late as 1732.[84]

It may be that the subscriptions came more slowly than William expected and it would appear that the total number was only about 150, but whatever the reason there is no evidence that any of the subscribers received their sheets. Nevertheless the project remained alive and Cooper went on engraving at least into the late 1730s apparently completing more than the 150 plates originally proposed. The Royal Infirmary plates, for example, must have been engraved by Cooper after the building was designed in 1738. However, no designs from the 1740s were engraved by Cooper, and it is at least possible that the project lapsed on account of a dispute or disagreement of some sort with the engraver, to be revived either shortly before or shortly after William Adam's death in 1748.

The sheets which were ultimately bound up in 1812 – at least those of the main series of plates – were printed on two kinds of paper, readily distinguishable only by their watermarks. One of these has not been identified, but the other is 'Heawood 1710', made at The Hague in 1746.[85] It would appear, therefore, that about 150 sets of these sheets were printed in the late 1740s, but were still not distributed to the unfortunate subscribers or otherwise published. If the difficulty lay with Cooper rather than with the Adams, then it was removed by his death in 1764.

The three years following the Fairholme failure in 1764 were bad years for John Adam. Nevertheless on 10 August 1765 John signed an agreement with Andrew Millar, bookseller in London, for the publication of a *Book of Architecture of the Public and Private Buildings in Scotland.* According to a memorandum of this agreement[86] the book had been 'composed, designed and engraved' by John and his father, the number of plates had been increased from the original 150 to 160, and 150 copies had been printed on a good French [*sic*] paper. John agreed to supply an explanation and description of the plates after the manner of *Vitruvius Britannicus* by 5 September 1766 and to hand over 750 sets of printed sheets by the following Christmas. John was to surrender the plates and agreed to take not more than 950 copies in all, of which he could take 200 copies for subscribers, any remaining to be sold at a price fixed by Millar. Permission was to be sought to dedicate the book to the King and Millar was to pay John £2,000, which would at that juncture have been particularly welcome. The proposed publication was announced in the *Public Advertiser* on 30 April 1766[87], when it was made clear that the sheets were to be bound in 'two large volumes folio' with a description of the plates in English and French and that the price to subscribers was to be five guineas. Most of the prints 'being already engraved' could be seen 'at A. Millar's and D. Wilson's in the Strand, and at J. Dodsley's in Pall Mall'. Delivery was promised 'on or before March 1767'.

Once again, for reasons which are not now apparent but which may have been financial, the book failed to appear. However, an entry in Gough's *British Topography* of 1780 describes the 1766 proposal and further states that 'Most if not the whole of Mr Adam's designs were engraved, several re-engraved on a more elegant plan, some proof impressions whereof were taken by Andrew Bell, engraver in Edinburgh, who corrected many of the designs by the direction of John Adam Esq.' The meaning of this statement is not entirely clear and it may be misleading; Andrew Bell[88] was a pupil of Cooper's and three plates, among eighteen included in the book as ultimately published and added to the original series possibly by John Adam, were engraved by him. On the other hand there is little to suggest that 'many of the designs' were 'corrected', and in any case the original series appears to have existed as printed sheets long before 1766. It is possible that the existence of a few plates in variant forms may result partly from Bell's 'corrections', but this may not be the only explanation.

It would appear, though this cannot be certain, that the sheets already printed and possibly also the copper plates were handed over to Andrew Millar and stored by him in a warehouse, probably in London. On the other hand *The Book of Scotch Houses* appears in an inventory of John Adam's *Heritable Subjects and Effects* dated 31 December 1774, where it is valued at £1,144.19*s*.5*d*.,[89] so wherever it was stored it remained in John's possession. In 1767 Millar retired and was succeeded in business by Thomas Cadell,[90] his partner for the previous two years. Cadell retired in 1793, the year after John Adam's death, and was succeeded by his son, who on 18 June 1804 wrote to William Adam asking for 'instructions relative to the copies of the late Mr Adam's architectural plates' which had remained for some years in his late father's warehouse. It appears that Cadell had received notice to quit the warehouse and was having to move to new premises where he would not have room for the Adam material. Five days later he wrote again. 'I write to inform you that a person who is in the habit of purchasing large quantities of printed paper to cut up as waste . . . has this day offered to give £100 for the whole of the late Mr Adam's plates, an offer which I think it would be advisable for you to accept as the plates could not, I fear, be turned to any great advantage.' Adam evidently prevaricated, for two days later Cadell wrote again saying he could not possibly calculate the quantity accurately, declining to pay for the sheets to be counted and going on: 'this is to the detriment of the sale as the purchaser is in immediate want of paper'.[91]

The precise outcome is unclear, but it would appear that Adam arranged for the sheets to be removed from Cadell's premises, either immediately or some time later returned to Edinburgh, and from 1808 at the latest, stored in a garret wareroom in the Royal Infirmary arranged through a Mr Crawford. On 1 October 1808 Andrew Steele WS, Adam's Law Agent in Edinburgh, paid 6*s*. to a blacksmith for 'a new padlock in the garret in the Infirmary and making the door more easy to open' and on 10 November 1810 he paid £12 to Mr Crawford, 'the rent of the wareroom for holding the prints'. The postage entries in Steele's accounts[92] reveal correspondence with Mr Arnot of Arlary (probably on this subject) and with James Loch, Adam's nephew and agent at Blair Adam, in August 1809. In November Steele wrote again to Loch: 'Immediately on my coming to town from Blair Adam in September last I made application to Mr Constable to try to bring him to a final settlement about the prints and papers in the Infirmary called *The Book of Scotch Houses*; but I have not accomplished that object yet. Mr Constable says he had been very long detained in London and could not then attend to such an object which would require much time and investigation. I see it will be delayed till next spring, and if Mr Constable does not then come forward

I must apply to another'.[93] The matter was still unresolved in November 1810, when Steele was in correspondence with Miss Adam, possibly John Adam's youngest sister Peggy, and Constable was still apparently uncertain. Finally, however, on 19 November 1811 Steele received payment of £150.0s.0d. and on 1 May 1812 he wrote to William Adam at Bloomsbury Square, London, enclosing 'the balance of the price of *The Book of Scotch Houses*, prints and copper plates that were in the Infirmary, sold to Constable and Company'.[94]

As a somewhat reluctant purchaser, Constable seems to have driven a hard bargain; Adam received only £50 more than he would have got by selling the prints for scrap seven years previously and in the meantime a considerable amount had been spent on carriage, rent, postages and so on. For his part Constable seems almost immediately to have passed the material on to another publisher, Adam Black, who added a new title page and list of plans on paper watermarked 1809 and 1810 and bound the sheets into books, without bothering to resolve anomalies in the numbering associated with the additional plates and cutting up spare prints to form the guards on which the sheets were mounted. Black shared the publication with his London partner T. Underwood, and with J. and J. Robertson in Edinburgh and J. Taylor in London. There is no evidence that any new impressions were made, nor is there any record as to the fate of the copper plates, which may have been retained or destroyed by Constable. In any event there is no reason to doubt Black's statement in the preliminary matter that 'the following PLANS, drawn by the late William Adam Esq, Architect, were engraved at his Expense by the most eminent artists of the time, with a View to Publication. A few complete sets having come into the Publisher's hands, he now respectfully offers them to the Public.' It may be presumed that, allowing for some damage, the number of copies bound up was rather fewer than the 150 sets said to have been printed in John Adam's agreement with Andrew Millar of 1765.

It is almost certain that all the copies of *Vitruvius Scoticus* now in existence come from the edition released by Adam Black and his co-publishers, probably in 1812; it is possible, however, that a few sets and individual sheets emerged rather earlier. There are separate copies of the Inveraray plates at the castle, for example, and James Craig appears to have possessed a bound set on his death in 1795.[95] It has also been suggested that certain Irish and American houses were designed from plates in *Vitruvius Scoticus*, which would imply that copies were circulating in the 18th century, but the evidence so far presented seems unconvincing.[96] In the absence of firm evidence to the contrary, therefore, no individual sheets or bound sets should be presumed to have been in circulation before about 1812.

In view of its origins it is not surprising that there are minor variations between different copies of the book. It is inherently difficult to make detailed comparisons between known copies, most of which are in public collections, and no comprehensive list of differences has yet been made, but the following are cited as examples. Some of the Hopetoun plates (14, 15, 17 and possibly 19) exist in two versions, both by Cooper, the earlier of which show the pavilions as originally designed and the later the pavilions more or less as built. A bound volume in the National Monuments Record of Scotland, which contains *Vitruvius Scoticus* plates and other material all apparently from the collection of the London publisher J. Taylor includes the earlier versions of plates 14 and 15. The earlier version of plate 17 is reproduced by Fleming in *Robert Adam and his Circle* and, unusually, the Glasgow University Library copy, reproduced here, includes both versions of plate 15. A loose plate of the Royal Infirmary elevation (150) in the Edinburgh Public Library differs from the plate in the National Library copy.[97] The British Museum copy has the Tay Bridge (122) brought to life by the addition of soldiers and a coach and six! But despite these and other variations, the book is for the most part reasonably consistent.

The book normally contains 180 plates numbered from 1 to 160, so that twenty plates have duplicate numbers. The plates of the original series are all engraved by Richard Cooper and are identifiable from the fairly consistent style of the plate numbers; there are 155 of them (12, 45, 50, 63 and 71 missing). There are seven other plates by Cooper, which have been incorrectly numbered or renumbered (30, 50, 51, 107, 108, 139 and 140), and two plates (51 and 53) which are identical. Eighteen plates are by other engravers and were probably added in the 1760s, or at the time of publication; of these, six are by T. Smith[98] (31, 45, 63, 83, 121 and 135), four are by Peter Mazell[99] (5, 20, 94 and 123), three are by Andrew Bell (13, [71] and 74) one is by W. Proud[100] (21), one is by F. Patton[101] (136) and three are unsigned (19, 72 and 73). The additional plates show no real unity of purpose or style and are generally inferior to those of the original series.

Nearly all the plates are of straightforward architectural plans, elevations and sections. Only one of these, the Mavisbank elevation (47), shows any suggestion of planting. Much more topographical, however, is the view of Kinross House (62) engraved by Cooper from a drawing apparently of 1710/11 by J. G. Borlach.[102] The style and general character of this plate is close to those of Slezer's *Theatrum Scotiae*. The Kinross House plans (61) also differ in several respects from the other plates. All these are taken here to be part of the original series. Of the additional plates, the interior view of the Chapel Royal at Holyrood (5) engraved by Peter Mazell from a drawing presumably of 1688 by John Wyck[103] is out of character with the other plates.

The sequence of the plates in the original series may be of some significance. The first two designs in the book, for Holyrood Palace (1–5) and Hamilton House (6–8) are the most important executed works of William Adam's principal predecessors, Sir William Bruce and James Smith. After introducing himself with his project for extending Hamilton (9–13), William placed his own most important design, for Hopetoun House (14–21), in what was clearly intended to be the most important position in the book. He followed with Smith's Dalkeith (22–4) and Smith and McGill's Yester with his own additions (25–30), before coming to his second major design, for Newliston (32–6). The Drum (Somerville, 37–8), Arniston (39–44), Mavisbank (46–7) and Floors Castle (48–9) follow, so that practically all his own most important designs of the 1720s are illustrated in the first fifty plates. From then on the order is much more random, though there may be some relationship between sequence and chronology in the later parts of the book.[104]

Of the designs illustrated in the original series of plates, forty-eight are by William Adam and twenty-three are by others. The additional plates include two designs by William, eight by John Adam, or by the Adam office, and one by Roger Morris. In the original series an abbreviation for 'Gulhelmus Adam Invenit et Delineavit' is normally included at the bottom left hand corner of each plate, and for 'R. Cooper Sculpsit' at the bottom right hand corner; where the word 'invenit' is omitted, it is fairly certain that Adam was not the author of the design. In several cases, as with Gibbs' Balveny (90–1) and Bruce's Mertoun (Harden, 142) the name of the architect is given; in thirteen others no attribution is made. The authorship of five of these designs is known. The history of Heriot's Hospital[105] (105–6) is well documented, Leslie (66–8) and Panmure (129–31)[106] are known to be by John Mylne, and East Park (81–2)[107] can with reasonable confidence be attributed to James Smith; the 'Person of Quality' who designed the Royal Palace (109–10) is also identifiable as the Earl of Mar.[108] The other eight designs, however, remain anonymous; they probably all date from before 1720 and are of considerable interest. Longformacus (99) and Broomlands (118–19) are rather similar designs, as in different ways are Dryden (79–80) and Elphinstone (75–6), and Newbyth (137–8) and Rose Hall (132–4); Keith Hall (144–5) and the House of Gray (98) are not similar, and the name of Alexander McGill has been suggested, without supporting evidence, in connection with the latter. Of William Adam's designs, about thirty were built and about fifteen survive more or less intact; the book is, in fact, a good catalogue of his work, for very few of his significant buildings are excluded.[109] Neither of the designs for 'Persons of Quality' (96–7 and 124) have been identified, but it is possible that the patrons, if they existed, were attainted Jacobites.

The history of *Vitruvius Scoticus* is, then, a long and complicated one, and there is much about the book which is not yet, and may never be fully understood. The parallel with *Vitruvius Britannicus* in the minds of the author and his successors seems to be fairly clear, but that is not to say that William Adam necessarily wished to promote a particular architectural creed in the way that Campbell had promoted Palladianism. What then were his motives in the mid 1720s? Was the book to be simply a topographical record, or was it to promote his own designs among potential patrons? Was there an element of nationalism, arising from the fact that little of Scottish interest had been included in *Vitruvius Britannicus*,[110] or of rivalry with Campbell or Gibbs? In the absence of the intended text and – so far – of any manuscript draft or other relevant material, these questions cannot be adequately answered. It is likely, though, that the motives were mixed, and the purely topographical aspect should not be underestimated for 'views of seats' were much in demand in the 18th century and the portrait of a house in the more intellectual form of plans and elevations was often more highly valued than a mere prospect.[111] However, in any attempt at explanation, particularly in view of the evidence that William Adam was neither a literary nor a theoretically minded architect, it is difficult not to look for the influence of Sir John Clerk of Penicuik.

In 1726, while William was preparing his draughts for the engraver, Sir John was writing his poem on architecture and gardening, *The Country Seat*;[112] to what extent does the explanation of *Vitruvius Scoticus* lie in Clerk's verses and the associated notes? In the mid 1720s Clerk and Adam were probably at their closest; Mavisbank was building and, while the correspondence about the work reveals disagreements over details, it also suggests underlying friendship and mutual respect. William borrowed books and lent Sir John a drawing board, they met in Edinburgh, at Penicuik and at Kirkcaldy, and they went to London together; indeed it seems most probable that, as the two men travelled from Stamford to London in March 1727, they had with them both the drawings for *Vitruvius Scoticus* and the manuscript of *The Country Seat*![113] The correspondence between certain passages in the poem and the earlier part, at least, of *Vitruvius Scoticus* is marked; where Clerk describes a Royal Palace and 'three kinds of structure . . . a House of State; the second for Convenience and Use; the third a little villa . . .', Adam illustrates Holyrood, Hopetoun, Arniston and Mavisbank.[114]

In the poem Clerk is addressing would-be patrons; 'Palladio', he noted 'was . . . master to our admired Inigo Jones. . . . But whatsoever country has such Patrons of Arts and Sciences as his Grace the Duke of D——— and the right Honourable Earls of P——— and B——— will never want such great masters'.[115] His professed Palladianism is, however, tempered by much practical common sense; he warns for example against choosing an exposed site simply to emulate 'Palladio's manner in a warmer clime'. In London he most admired the work of James Gibbs, not the most obvious Palladian, and Gibbs' *Book of Architecture* tended to supersede *Vitruvius Britannicus* as Adam's favourite source book after its publication in 1728. As a strong advocate of the Union, Hanoverian Britain and the new Whig order, Clerk was promoting the patronage, not the Palladianism as such, but of the new British architecture, which he and Adam had discovered through *Vitruvius Britannicus*; for to Clerk, the classical origins themselves and the pedigree through Palladio and Inigo Jones were probably more important than the niceties of Palladian architectural theory as it is understood today.[116] Clerk may have seen Adam as the practitioner of the new architecture in Scotland, and *Vitruvius Scoticus* as a vehicle for its promotion. These things may have been important to Adam himself, but he must also have seen the book as a means of advancing his own reputation in Scotland, and perhaps also in the south; he can hardly have expected the project to be particularly profitable, at least compared with his other enterprises, but he may well have seen it as a route to new commissions.[117]

To John Adam in the 1760s, the topographical aspect may still have been relevant, but above all the printed sheets were an asset at a time when he badly needed cash. His son probably felt that it would be in some way disgraceful to sell the book as scrap paper and that by securing its publication he was honouring the memory of his father and grandfather. Today *Vitruvius Scoticus* is an invaluable record of Scottish architecture in the 18th century, principally the three decades from 1720 to 1750, an important period in which there was considerable activity and in which William Adam himself was pre-eminent. Because of its inherent difficulties, the book has often been misunderstood and treated with circumspection; it may now be better appreciated. If, as a result, the sheer quality of William Adam's buildings is more widely recognised, part at least of the original purpose will have been achieved; houses of the calibre of Mavisbank, Hopetoun, Duff, Arniston and Dun are rarely, if ever, outclassed.

No 28
Receiv'd the 17th day of Sepr 1727 of the Earle of Rothes Three Guineas — being the First Payment for Two Copys of My Designs for Buildings &c. in 150 Plates which will be deliver'd in Sheets to the Bearer hereof upon Payment of the like Sum
William Adam

FOOTNOTES

1 *Caledonian Mercury*, 30 June 1748. c.f. also *Edinburgh Evening Courant*, same day.

2 Blair Adam MSS, Pedigree 'certified by the Provost and Bailies of Forfar', quoted in Fleming, John, *Robert Adam and his Circle in Edinburgh and Rome* John Murray (London, 1962) p.323.

3 SRO, GD18/4736. Clerk of Penicuik MSS, letter from Adam dated 6 October 1741 mentioning having 'seen' the canal between Bruges and Ostend and the harbour at Dunkirk.

4 Ex. inf. Mr James L. Michie, Kirkcaldy.

5 Blair Adam MSS, Misc. Cor. and Papers 1830–9, MS of William Adam of Blair Adam, 'Account of a Scotch Family from 1688 to 1838' (hereafter – 'Account of a Scotch Family').
For Gladney House, see D. McGibbon and T. Ross, *Castellated and Domestic Architecture of Scotland* (1887–92), vol.5, pp.286–9. The house was demolished in 1930.

6 Kirkcaldy Museum, typescript, 'The Links of Kirkcaldy Pottery, 1714–1930'.

7 Parish Registers of Abbotshall, Kirkcaldy, quoted in Fleming, op. cit., p.323.

8 Darnaway Castle, Moray MSS, notes in NMRS, R6(P13).

9 SRO, GD18/4892. Clerk of Penicuik MSS, MS of John Clerk of Eldin, 'Mr Clerk's Life of R.A.', quoted in Fleming, op. cit., pp.3 and 323 (hereafter – 'Mr Clerk's Life of R.A.').

10 SRO, GD18/4736.

11 SRO, GD18. Clerk of Penicuik MSS, travel journal of Sir John Clerk quoted in Fleming, op. cit., p.7.

12 'Account of a Scotch Family'.

13 Parish Registers of Abbotshall, Kirkcaldy, quoted in Fleming, op. cit., p.323. See also Douglas, *Baronage of Scotland*, 1798, pp.253–7.

14 Blair Adam MSS, Library catalogue of 1883; see also Mowat, Ian, 'An 18th century Private Library: the Books of William and John Adam at Blair Adam', in *The Library Review*, vol.28, spring 1979, pp.8–13.
There is also an apparently earlier (? late 18th century) library list, but the implications of these documents have not yet been fully considered.

15 Hopetoun MSS, quoted in Fleming, op. cit., p.45.

16 Parish Registers of Abbotshall.

17 Floors Castle, Roxburghe MSS, Bundle 726; ex. inf. Mr Richard Emerson.

18 SRO, GD18/4719, Clerk of Penicuik MSS, letter from Adam dated 30 January 1723: 'there's just now among my hands a design of ane addition to Newliston House'.

19 SRO, GD18/1767, Clerk of Penicuik MSS, building accounts 1723–7; see also correspondence, etc.

20 *Clerk of Penicuik's Memoirs*, ed. J. M. Gray (1892): 'in May 1723 I not only finished my design for the House of Mavisbank, under the correction of one Mr. Adams, a skilful architect. . . .'

21 SRO, GD18/5005, Clerk of Penicuik MSS, correspondence of Clerk, Baxter and Lord Aberdeen.

22 'Mr. Clerk's Life of R.A.'

23 SRO, GD18, 2108 Clerk of Penicuik MSS, travel journal of Sir John Clerk, quoted in Fleming, op. cit., p.7.

24 SRO, GD18/4727, Clerk of Penicuik MSS, letter from Lord Annandale dated 23 January 1724.

25 'Account of a Scotch Family'.

26 Parish Registers of Abbotshall, quoted in Fleming, op. cit., p.323.

27 SRO, GD18/4729, Clerk of Penicuik MSS, letter from Adam, 'hopeful of making a bargain with Merchiston'.

28 Fleming, op. cit., pp.52 and 333.

29 Fleming, op. cit., p.51.

30 SRO, GD18/4722, Clerk of Penicuik MSS, letter from Lord Annandale, dated 28 March 1723.

31 SRO, GD18/4730, Clerk of Penicuik MSS, letter from Sir John Anstruther dated 20 December 1727.

32 'Mr. Clerk's Life of R.A.'.

33 Fleming, op. cit., pp.51, 52.

34 SRO, GD18/4729/2, Clerk of Penicuik MSS, letter from Adam dated 5 May 1726.

35 SRO, GD18/2107, Clerk of Penicuik MSS, travel journal.

36 SRO, GD18/4729/2, see note 34 above.

37 The portraits are in the collections of Mr Keith Adam at Blair Adam, and Sir John Clerk at Penicuik House.

38 NLS MS14551 Yester Papers, correspondence, accounts, etc, quoted in John Dunbar, 'Yester House' *Transactions of the East Lothian Antiquarian and Field Naturalists' Society*, vol.13, 1972.

39 Wigton Papers, in Maitland Club Miscellany, vol.2, p.480.

40 NMRS, notes on the Hamilton MSS at Lennoxlove. See also SRO, GD18/4782/2.

41 Garden plan in the muniment room at Blenheim, Oxon, ex. inf. Mr Howard Colvin.

42 A. A. Tait, 'William Adam at Chatelherault' THE *Burlington Magazine*, June 1962.

43 Braco Case Depositions, printed papers relating to the lawsuit in the possession of Mr Howard Colvin.

44 Records of Robert Gordon's College.

45 W. Hay, *Charters and Documents relating to the Burgh of Dundee*.

46 Glasgow University, Senate and Faculty Minutes.

47 NLS 7187, General Wade's Letter and Order Book.

48 SRO, GD95/vol.10/150.

49 James Grant, *Old and New Edinburgh*, Cassell (1882), pp.358–60.

50 James Grant, op. cit., pp.298–302.

51 'Account of a Scotch Family'. For Blair Adam see also NMRS, RCAHMS Record Sheet. For Maryburgh see Jean Munro 'William Adam's Village of Maryburgh' in Clan Donnaichaidh Annual (1978–9), pp.23–6.

52 Baptismal Registers of Edinburgh, quoted in Fleming, op. cit., p.323.

53 Douglas, *Baronage of Scotland* (1798), pp.253–7.
54 Fleming, op. cit., pp.5, 6.
55 SRO, GD112/9/45, etc, Breadalbane MSS, extracts in NMRS.
56 SRO, GD22/1/468, Graham MSS.
57 Fleming, op. cit., pp.63, 64.
58 Ian G. Lindsay and Mary Cosh, *Inveraray and the Dukes of Argyll*, Edinburgh (1973).
59 Public Record Office, London, Ordnance Board Declared Accounts, quoted in Fleming, op. cit., p.64. Also NLS MS10693.
60 Fleming, op. cit., pp.66 and 82.
61 *Scots Magazine*, 1748, p.354.
62 *Caledonian Mercury*, 30 June 1748.
63 'Account of a Scotch Family'.
64 Blair Adam MSS, Misc. Cor. and Papers 1820–29A, letter dated 19 February 1822, from William Adam of Blair Adam to his son about family financial affairs (hereafter – William Adam, letter to his son, 1822).
65 Soane Museum, Adam Collection; inscribed 'Robt. Adam archt. 1753'.
66 John Dunbar, 'Yester House', op. cit.
67 James Simpson, 'Lord Alemoor's Villa at Hawkhill', *Bulletin of the Scottish Georgian Society* (i), 1972.
68 NLS, Saltoun MSS; ex. inf. Miss Mary Cosh.
69 Ballochmyle Papers, ex. inf. Mr Boyd Alexander.
70 Fleming, op. cit.
71 SRO, GD18/4895, Clerk of Penicuik MSS.
72 William Adam, Letter to his son, 1882.
73 'Account of a Scotch Family'.
74 Her father was John Ramsay, of the Balmain family, possibly younger brother to Sir Alexander Ramsay of Balmain, William Adam's patron at Fasque.
75 *Dictionary of National Biography*.
76 William Adam, Letter to his son, 1822.
77 MS journal of a Tour to Scotland at Alscot Park, Warwicks. Quoted in Howard Colvin, *A Biographical Dictionary of British Architects*, John Murray (1978), p.56.
78 SRO, GD18/4729/2, Clerk of Penicuik MSS.
79 Bushnell, *Scottish Engravers*. Cooper is best known for his portraits. He built a house in St. John Street and is buried in Canongate Churchyard. His portrait by Jeremiah Davidson is in the Scottish National Portrait Gallery.
80 M. Wood, *The Lord Provosts of Edinburgh*.
81 A. H. Millar, *The Roll of Eminent Burgesses of Dundee*.
82 Kirkcaldy Museum, Rothes MSS.
83 Fleming, op. cit. p.48.
84 H. Gordon Slade, 'Craigston Castle' *Proceedings of the Society of Antiquaries of Scotland*, vol.108, 1976–7, p.265.
85 Ex. inf. Mr John Morris.
86 Blair Adam MSS, TD 77/63/4/226; ex. inf. Mr Ian Mowat.
87 Ex. inf. Mr Tim Connor.
88 Bell was a copper engraver in Edinburgh and part owner of the *Encyclopaedia Britannica*, for which he did the illustrations. He died in 1809. Ex. inf. Mr John Morris.
89 Blair Adam MSS, TD 77/63/4/185; ex. inf. Mr Ian Mowat.
90 Ex. inf. Mr Tim Connor.
91 Blair Adam MSS, Gen. Cor. 1804, C–F.
92 Blair Adam MSS, Gen. Cor. 1812, I–Z.
93 Blair Adam MSS, Gen. Cor. 1809, K–Z.
94 Blair Adam MSS, Gen. Cor. 1812, I–Z.
95 Craig's Executry and Testament dated 11 November 1795 lists: Adam – 'Plans of Public Buildings and Gentlemen's Seats in Scotland'. A. J. Youngson, *The Making of Classical Edinburgh*, (1966), p.295.
96 Desmond Fitzgerald, 'Nathaniel Clements and some 18th century Irish Houses', *Apollo*, October 1966. Also Desmond Guinness and Julius Thomsdale Sadler Jnr., *The Palladian Style in England, Ireland and America*, Thames and Hudson, (1976).
97 The loose plate is by Cooper and is lettered as follows: 'The North Front of the Royal Infirmary of Edinburgh as it is now Building Into which it is Proposed to Receive every Curable Patient who Offers from whatever place they come', ex. inf. Mr John Morris.
98 Possibly the T. Smith described as fl.1779 in Thieme Becker. Ex. inf. Mr John Morris.
99 Irish copper engraver and watercolour flower painter, fl.1761–97. Ex. inf. Mr John Morris.
100 Fl. *c.*1760. Ex. inf. Mr John Morris.
101 Copper engraver in London, 1745–64. Ex. inf. Mr John Morris.
102 John Borlach was left £400 under the will of James Gibbs, who describes him as 'for many years my draughtsman'. H. M. Colvin, *A Biographical Dictionary of English Architects*, John Murray, (1954), p.229.
103 Jan Wyck (*c.*1645–1700), was an Anglo-Dutch painter who frequently recorded interiors; many of his works were engraved. *Dictionary of National Biography*. He had a son of the same name.
104 Many of the later designs, the public buildings for example, are towards the end of the book, but they do not appear to be in consistent chronological sequence. In the absence of more firm dates the question must remain open.
105 George Heriot's Trust. Minute Books etc; by William Wallace *et al.* See note to plates 105,6.
106 R. S. Mylne, *Master Masons to the Crown of Scotland*, (1893).

107 SRO, GD244/625/1, Buccleuch MSS, Accounts, etc.

108 Howard Colvin, op. cit., p.296.

109 Of the designs listed by Colvin, op. cit., pp.57–9, the following: *Public Buildings, etc:* Aberdeen Town House, alterations (1729–30); Montrose Mausoleum, Aberuthven (1741–2); Haddington Town House (1742–5); Edinburgh, Royal Bank, Old Bank Close (plans 1744). *Domestic:* Mellerstain, wings (1725–6); Red Braes, Bonnington (*c.*1730); Edinburgh, Tweeddale Lodging, stables, etc (1737–8); Minto House, Roxburghshire (1738–43); Murdostoun, Lanarkshire (1735–40); Carnousie, Banffshire, additions (1740); Caroline Park, offices (1740–42); Castle Dounie, Inverness-shire (1745); Pollock House, Renfrewshire (1747–52); Makerstoun, Roxburghshire; and works at Airdrie, Barnton, Broxmouth and the Hirsel; possibly also Fife House, Potterrow and Ross House, both Edinburgh. Also possibly Marlefield, Roxburghshire, ex. inf. Mrs Audrey Mitchell, Kelso; Letter of 16 April 1721 from Gilbert Ramsay in Floors Castle MSS.

110 Is it possible that Adam had looked for inclusion in Campbell's third volume of 1725?

111 The suggestion of Mr Ian Gow.

112 Printed, without the original notes, in Hunt, J. D. and Willis, P., *The Genius of the Place*, (London, 1975).

113 GD18, 14404 Clerk of Penicuik MSS. A copy of the poem in the hand of Samuel Boyse is marked in Clerk's hand: 'I left this manuscript with Mr. Aikman at London in the year 1727. . . . it fell into the hands of Mr. Boyse the transcriber . . . I happened accidentally to make this discovery and at the expense of a little monie recovered it'.

114 c.f. A. A. Tait, 'Arniston and the Country Seat', *Burlington Magazine*, March 1969.

115 *The Country Seat*, note 7. Reference is to the Duke of Devonshire and Lords Pembroke and Burlington.

116 Fleming, op. cit., pp.41 and 42, implies that Clerk should have been dissatisfied with Mavisbank – a 'gawky provincial mansion' – on his return from London. With justification he was not.

117 c.f. Iain Brown, 'Sir John Clerk of Penicuik (1676–1755): Aspects of a virtuoso life': unpublished thesis. Cambridge 1980.

THE NOTES TO THE PLATES

It is the intention in these notes to supply in concise form the essential facts, insofar as they are known, about each design. These are presented in a systematic way, which may require some explanation. Against the title of each plate or series of plates are set down the designer/draughtsman/engraver combination and the plate numbers, as recorded on the plates, thus the Airth House plates (64–5), on which are 'Gul Adam Invenit et Delin'. and 'R. Cooper sculpt'. are noted 'Airth House – WA; WA; RC – 64–5'. On the second line the location of the building is marked by old county, parish and grid reference. Occasionally additional pieces of information are inserted after the location, as in the case of Somerville House, for example: 'usually known as The Drum'. The main body of information is set down in three sections, about the patron, the design and its author, and the building. Finally, significant sources are listed.

General works of reference and the following books which have been used consistently are not separately listed:

Sir James Balfour Paul, *The Scots Peerage* (Edinburgh 1904).

Colen Campbell, *Vitruvius Britannicus, or the British Architect* (3 vols. 1715, 1717 and 1725, continued by J. Woolfe and J. Gandon, vol.(iv), 1767, vol.(v), 1771).

Howard Colvin, *A Biographical Dictionary of British Architects 1600–1840* (London, 1978).

The Dictionary of National Biography (Oxford, from 1917).

John Fleming, *Robert Adam and his Circle in Edinburgh and Rome* (London, 1962).

Francis Groome, *The Ordnance Gazetteer of Scotland* (Edinburgh, 1882).

The New Statistical Account of Scotland (15 vols., 1845).

Margaret Stuart and Sir James Balfour Paul, *Scottish Family History* (Edinburgh, 1930).

Works quoted more than once in the notes are referred back to the following list:

J. G. Dunbar, *Sir William Bruce*, Exhibition Catalogue, Scottish Arts Council, 1970.

James Grant, *Old and New Edinburgh* (2 vols., Edinburgh, 1882).

Thomas Hannan, *Famous Scottish Houses* (London, 1928).

Thomas Hunter, *Woods, Forests and Estates of Perthshire* (Perth, 1883).

Ian G. Lindsay and Mary Cosh, *Inveraray and the Dukes of Argyll* (Edinburgh, 1973).

D. McGibbon and T. Ross, *The Castellated and Domestic Architecture of Scotland* (5 vols., Edinburgh, 1887–92).

P. H. M'Kerlie, *History of the Lands and their Owners in Galloway* (Paisley, 1906).

Colin McWilliam, *Lothian*, Buildings of Scotland, ed. Pevsner (Penguin, 1978).

John Macky, *A Journey through Scotland* Being the Third Volume which compleats Great Britain (London, 1723).

A. H. Millar, *Castles and Mansions of Ayrshire* (Edinburgh, 1885).

R. S. Mylne, *Master Masons to the Crown of Scotland* (1893).

James Paterson, *History of the Counties of Ayr and Wigtown* (Edinburgh, 1863).

John Small, *Castles and Mansions of the Lothians* (2 vols., Edinburgh, 1883).

A. and H. Taylor, *The Book of the Duffs* (1913).

Reference to 'Braco Case Depositions' is to the printed Depositions of witnesses in connection with the lawsuit of 1743 between William Adam and Lord Braco over his remuneration for designing and building Duff House. Copies of these papers are in the possession of Mr Howard Colvin.

The following abbreviations have been used:

BM	The British Museum
HMSO	Her Majesty's Stationery Office
OS	The Ordnance Survey
NLS	The National Library of Scotland, Edinburgh
NMR (England)	The National Momuments Record, London
NMRS	The National Monuments Record of Scotland
RCAHMS	Royal Commission on the Ancient and Historical monuments of Scotland
RIBA	The Royal Institute of British Architects
SRO	The Scottish Record Office, Register House, Edinburgh

AIRTH HOUSE WA; WA; RC 64, 65

Stirlingshire Airth Parish NS 900 868

James Graham (1676–1746); Advocate; m.(2) Mary Livingstone and purchased Airth in 1717; Judge Admiral of Scotland from 1739.

William Adam n.d.; possibly *c.*1720 and associated with garden plan of 1721.
Regularisation of existing house, partly of 1581; not executed; subsequent re-modelling by David Hamilton, 1807–9; now a hotel.

Sources NMRS: two garden plans, one by William Boutchart, 1721, plans for additions by David Hamilton, 1806.
McGibbon & Ross, op. cit., vol.2, pp.403–4.
RCAHMS, *Inventory of Stirlingshire*, 1963, vol.1, pp.230–7.

ARNISTON HOUSE WA; WA; RC 39–44

Midlothian Borthwick and Temple Parish NT 325 595

Robert Dundas (1685–1753); Advocate; Solicitor General 1717–20; Lord Advocate 1720–25; succeeded to Arniston in 1726; Lord of Session 1737–47; Lord President 1747–53.

William Adam 1726.
New house incorporating parts of existing courtyard mansion; largely built 1726–32; completed with modifications, John Adam, 1753–5; garden front pediment, etc., *c.*1800; new library 1868; communications raised, north and south porches, servants' wing, etc., Wardrop & Reid, *c.*1876–8: private house.

Sources Arniston House MSS: Plan of Arniston, 1690.
Plan of layout proposed, 1726.
Half elevation of North Front – William Adam? – n.d.
West elevation – John Adam, 1753.
Plans for North Porch, etc – Wardrop & Reid, 1876.
Arniston Journals and Letters, 4 vols.,
George Omond, *Arniston Memoirs*, Edinburgh, 1887.
John Small, op. cit.
Country Life, 15–22 August 1925.
Sheila Forman, 'The Dundases of Arniston', Scottish Field, June 1953.
A.A. Tait, 'Arniston and the Country Seat', *Burlington Magazine*, March 1969.

BALGREGGAN HOUSE WA; WA; RC 127, 128

Wigtownshire Stoneykirk Parish NX 087 503

John McDowall of Freugh; m. Lady Elizabeth Crichton Dalrymple, niece of Field Marshall Stair, in 1725; succeeded to Freugh in 1733.

William Adam n.d.; probably after 1725 and before 1730.
Re-modelling of existing house, partly of 1672; probably completed 1730; slated third storey added early 20th century; demolished 1966.

Sources Wigtown Museum, carved stones, 1672 and 1730.
NMRS, photograph by George Washington Wilson.
James Paterson, op. cit.
NMR (England), Estates Exchange, London, No.1534, Sales Brochure, 1902.
P. H. M'Kerlie, op. cit., vol.1, p.63.

BALLOCHMYLE HOUSE WA; WA; RC 63

Ayrshire Mauchline Parish NS 518 267

Plate engraved by T. Smith and added to the original series.

Allan Whiteford (–1767), purchased Ballochmyle in the 1750s.

John Adam n.d.; probably late 1750s.

New house built *c.*1760; nursery wing added in 1791; extensive re-modelling by H. M. Wardrop, 1887/8; hospital 1945–69; future uncertain.

Sources Ballochmyle Papers: extracts by Boyd Alexander, Upton, Didcot (copy in NMRS).
Sketch plans for addition, after D. Hamilton, 1813 (copy in NMRS).
University of Edinburgh, Rowand Anderson Collection, survey drawings, Wardrop & Reid, January 1880 and drawings for alterations and additions, Wardrop & Anderson, 1886.
Ayr Public Library, photographs by Valentine of Dundee, before 1886 (copies in NMRS).
Colin McWilliam, 'Ballochmyle', *Notes for the Scottish Georgian Society*, 1970 (copy in NMRS).
James Paterson, op. cit., vol.1, pp.551–5.
A. H. Millar, op. cit.

BALVENY HOUSE Gibbs/RC 90, 91

Banffshire Mortlach Parish NJ 321 424

William Duff of Braco (1697–1763), succeeded to extensive estates, 1722; m. (2) Jean Grant 1723; M.P. for Banffshire, 1727; began building Duff House, 1735; created Lord Braco, 1735, Earl of Fife, 1759.

James Gibbs *c.*1723.

New house; built 1724–5; repaired by William Adam, 1739; last occupied, 1878; largely demolished 1929; lower parts survive within Balveny Distillery.

Sources Aberdeen University Library; Fife MSS.
NMRS; copy of photograph before demolition.
Alistair & Henrietta Tayler, op. cit.

BARHOLM HOUSE Adams/Mazell 94

Kirkcudbrightshire Kirkmabreck Parish MX 471 592

Plates engraved by R. Mazell and added to the original series.

John McCulloch n.d.; probably mid 1750s.

John Adam Succeeded to Barholm, 1753.

New house, not built; updated design of 1788 by Robert Adam, executed *c.*1790; demolished *c.*1960.

Sources Soane Museum Adam Collection, 'Design of a House at Balhazy Galloway', 1788, vol.30, nos.112–18 (copies in NMRS).
NMRS; Incomplete client's plans and Adam Office Working Drawings.
Copy of photograph, Valentine & Sons.
P. H. M'Kerlie, op. cit., vol.vi, pp.259–70.

BELHAVEN HOUSE WA; WA; RC 154

East Lothian Dunbar Parish NT 663 787

John Hamilton, 4th Lord Belhaven (–1764), succeeded 1721.

William Adam n.d.; on stylistic grounds, possibly late 1730s.

New house; probably not built; site uncertain, possibly that of the present Belhaven House of *c.*1825, where fragments of 18th century date survive; possibly that of Belhaven Hill, a later 18th century house formerly with pavilions, removed with other alterations and additions early 19th century, a school.

Sources Colin McWilliam, op. cit. p.99.

BELVIDERE WA; WA; RC 72

Midlothian Ratho Parish NT 145 687

Elevation only; the plan, presumably plate 71 of the original series, is missing. The old name of Dalmahoy House was retained.

George Dalrymple (*c.*1680–1745), Advocate; Baron of Exchequer, 1709; m. Euphame Myreton and purchased Dalmahoy 1720.

William Adam 1720 or after and before 1728.
New house, built 1725–8; dated 1725; alterations and additions by Alexander Laing, 1786/7, by William Burn, 1830, by Brown & Wardrop, 1851, and unattributed, early 20th century; now a golf and country club.

Sources University of Edinburgh; Rowand Anderson Drawings Collection, plans for additions by William Burn, 1830, and Brown and Wardrop, 1851.
John Small, op. cit.
Thomas Hannan, op. cit.
Colin McWilliam, op. cit., p.166.

BLAIR DRUMMOND HOUSE McGill; WA; RC 83–85
Perthshire Kincardine Parish NS 731 989
George Drummond Purchased the estate in 1684; enlarged it to include the site in 1714; succeeded by his son James Drummond (–1739).
Alexander McGill *c.*1714; possible involvement of the Earl of Mar, c.f. H. M. Colvin, op. cit., p.296.
New house, built 1715–17; unexecuted design for new house by Robert Adam, 1780s; attached south wing added, n.d.; demolished, 1870; new house by James Walker on adjacent site, 1871; fragment of McGill house remains.

Sources Blair Drummond Drawings, Survey Plans and Elevations, James Walker, 1868, includes engraved view by T. M. McQueen (copies in NMRS).
SRO: RHP 4071 Plan and Elevation by Robert Adam (Ex GD/1/869).
SRO: GD24/5/4/18, Account for mason work, 1714, and GD24/5/4/41, Account for work, 1720.
Lord Woodhouslee, *Life of Lord Kames*, vol.ii, p.27.
Drummond, *Genealogy of the House of Drummond* (1831), p.111.
Thomas Hunter, op. cit., p.244.

BROOMLANDS HOUSE WA; RC 118, 119
Roxburghshire Kelso Parish NT 734 348
John Don of Attonburn Probably a son of Patrick Don of Auldtonburn and Anne Wauchope, heiress of Edmondstone.
Unattributed Design related to that of Longformacus House, plate 99; n.d., before 1719.
New house, possibly incorporating earlier building; dated 1719, third course above ground, south quoin; pavilions probably not built; substantially altered and extended, 19th century; presently unoccupied, future uncertain.

Sources NMRS: Photograph.
James Haig, *Topographical and Historical Account of the Town of Kelso* (Edinburgh, 1825), p.146.
G. Tancred, *Annals of a Border Club* (Jedburgh, 1889), p.107.
Proceedings of the Berwickshire Naturalists' Club, vol.xiv, p.219 et seq.
RCHAMS: *Inventory of Roxburghshire*, vol.i, p.251.

BUCHANAN HOUSE WA; WA; RC 135, 136
Stirlingshire Buchanan Parish NS 457 888
James Graham, 1st Duke of Montrose (1682–1742); succeeded 1685; created Duke 1707; Secretary of State 1714; lived mainly in Glasgow; William Graham, 2nd Duke (1712–90); sold Glasgow house, 1751, to concentrate estates in Stirlingshire.
William Adam n.d., possibly *c.*1725, but probably 'the plan and estimate of the intended buildings at Buchanan A° 1741', for which Adam was paid £315.
New house, probably not built; old house taken down, 1724; substantial work by John Adam, 1750s; alterations by James Playfair, 1789; unexecuted schemes by Robert Adam, n.d. and Charles Barry, 1837; burnt 1850; new house on a different site by William Burn, 1853; Burn's house gutted 1954; fragments of the old house survive, now a golf club.

Sources SRO: GD220 6, Montrose MSS; RHP 6150, plan by William Adam.
Soane Museum Drawings, Adam Collection, 'Plans and elevations, design for a new house', Robert Adam (vol.43, nos.16–20).
Montrose Estate Office, Drawings by Charles Barry, 1836.
Walter Macfarlane, *Geographical Collections*, ed. Mitchell (Scottish History Society, 1906), vol.(i), pp.344.

CALLY HOUSE WA; WA; RC 111, 113

Kirkcudbrightshire Girthon Parish NX 599 554

Alexander Murray of Broughton; m. Lady Euphemia Stewart, daughter of the 5th Earl of Galloway, 1726; succeeded to Cally, probably in the 1730s.

William Adam n.d., possibly *c.*1740.

New house; not built except two pavilions by 1742, subsequently removed; various schemes, including one 'with gables', *c.*1742; designs by other architects, Robert Mylne's executed 1763–5; alterations by Thomas Boyd, 1794; additions by J. B. Papworth, 1833–7; now a hotel.

Sources SRO: GD10/1421/212, 287, 288A and 411.

Broughton and Cally MSS, correspondence, 1742. Design and description, Robert Mylne, *c.*1762.

SRO: RHP 8822, design by Stephen Price.

Issac Ware, *Complete Body of Architecture*, (1756), design.

RIBA: Drawings Collection, Cat. B. p.99 and Papworth, p.110.

M'Kerlie, op. cit., vol.iii, pp.495–7.

Scotland's Magazine, October 1954.

CAMMO HOUSE WA; WA; RC 141

Edinburgh Cramond Parish NT 174 747

John Hog of Ladykirk Purchased Cammo from Sir John Clerk of Penicuik in 1724; sold to James Watson of Saughton, 1741.

William Adam n.d.; if patron was Hog, not Clerk, probably *c.*1724.

Addition of perron, frontispiece and pavilions to existing house of 1693, built for John Menzies, possibly by Robert Mylne; not executed; pavilion, stair and terrace subsequently added, James Salisbury, 1787–91; gables removed, crenellated parapet added, probably early 19th century; addition, John Watherston and son c.1900; burnt 1977, reduced to a low ruin, 1979.

Sources SRO: Clerk of Penicuik MSS, GD18/1855; garden plan and memorandum of improvements, Clerk, *c.*1723.

SRO: GD150/3199 and 3326, Accounts, etc, 1787–91.

NMRS: Drawings for additions, John Watherston and Son, *c.*1900. Basement plan, unsigned. Also RCAHMS Record Sheet.

J. P. Wood, *Parish of Cramond*, (1794), engraved view, p.63.

Clerk of Penicuik's Memoirs, ed. Gray, (1892).

John Small, op. cit.

CASTLE KENNEDY WA; WA; RC 120, 121

Wigtownshire Inch Parish NX 111 609

John Dalrymple, 2nd Earl of Stair (1673–1747) succeeded 1707; Ambassador in Paris; returned to Scotland, 1720; Newliston and Castle Kennedy landscapes; promoted Field Marshall, Dettingen, 1742; important patron of William Adam.

William Adam n.d., probably early/mid 1720s.

Temple at the end of the Bowling Green; probably not built, but if built probably removed before 1798, certainly before 1849.

Sources SRO: GD135/144, 139/1, Stair MSS.

BM: General Roy's Military Map, c. 1747 (copy in NMRS).

OS: 6 in. map, sheet 16, 1849.

Samuel Boyse.

H. H. Dalrymple, *A Description of Castle Kennedy* (Edinburgh, 1908), p.14. Account, 1798, for Logie Class, University of Glasgow.

CHATELHERAULT See Hamilton 'Dog Kennel'.

CRAIGDARROCH WA; WA; RC 77, 78

Dumfriesshire Glencairn Parish NX 742 909

Alexander Fergusson (1685–after 1740), succeeded 1689; m. Annie Laurie, 1710.

William Adam *c.*1726.

Re-modelling of existing house; carried out with differences; building estimate dated 1726, doorpieces dated 1729; pavilions probably not built; alterations to interior and frontispiece, probably early/mid 1830s; Chapel and other alterations, John Starforth, 1889; Rear loggia, 1912; private house.

Sources — SRO: Fergusson of Craigdarroch MSS GD77/204/1, estimate for building 1726.
NMRS: MS notes by John Gladstone.
John Corrie, *Annals of Glencairn* (Dumfries, 1910).
Fergusson, *Records of the Clan Fergusson or Ferguson.*
C. L. Johnston, *Historic Families of Dumfriesshire* (Dumfries).
Sheila Forman, *Scottish Field*, August 1950.

CRAIGIEHALL — WA; WA; RC — 86, 87

West Lothian — Dalmeny Parish — NT 166 755

Charles Hope — (1710–91) succeeded to Craigiehall, 1730; m. (1) Catherine Vere, heiress of Blackwood, 1733; m. (2) Anne Vane, 1745–6; m. (3) Helen Dunbar, 1766.

William Adam — n.d., possibly early 1730s.
Additions of pavilions, rearrangement of rooms and addition of main doorway and steps to existing house dated 1699, built for William Johnstone, 2nd Earl of Annandale; one pavilion built, doorway and steps not executed; scheme for alterations by Thomas Brown, 1818, not executed; alterations and additions by William Burn, 1828, David Bryce, 1852 and Sir Robert Lorimer, 1926–7.

Sources — Rosebery MSS at Dalmeny: drawings by Brown, Burn and Bryce, etc.
John Small, op. cit.
J. G. Dunbar, op. cit.

CUMBERNAULD HOUSE — WA; WA; RC — 125, 126

Dunbartonshire — Cumbernauld House — NS 772 759

John Fleming, 6th Earl of Wigton (*c.*1673–1744); succeeded 1681; m. (1) Margaret Lindsay, 1689; m. (2) Mary Keith, 1711; m. (3) Euphame Lockhart, after 1721.

William Adam — n.d., probably late 1720s.
New house; built, possibly without stable pavilions; dated 1731; burnt 1877; reinstated by John Burnet Sen.; now offices.

Sources — Wigton Papers in *Maitland Club Miscellany*, vol.ii, p.480.
Joseph Irving, *History of Dunbartonshire* (1860), p.494.
Joseph Irving, *The Book of Dunbartonshire* (W. and A. K. Johnston, 1879), vol.2, p.396.

DALKEITH HOME FARM See East Park.

DALKEITH HOUSE — Smith/WA; RC — 22–24

Midlothian — Dalkeith Parish — NT 333 679

Anne Scott, Duchess of Buccleuch (1651–1752); Countess in her own right, 1661; m. James Crofts, Duke of Monmouth, 1663; Monmouth executed 1685; returned to Scotland, 1693; remodelled East Park, 1710/11, see plates 81 and 82.

James Smith — 1701, various schemes exist.
Remodelling of mediaeval and later castle; carried out 1702–11; stables and coach house by William Adam 1741–2; house repaired by John Adam 1751–2 and 1762–3; unexecuted scheme for wings by James Craig, 1777; minor alterations by James Playfair 1789; unexecuted scheme and minor alterations by William Burn, 1830–1; minor alterations by Schomberg Scott, 1973; now administrative offices.

Sources — SRO: GD26/5/489, 492. Leven and Melville MSS.
SRO: GD224/379, 625/1. Buccleuch MSS; building accounts.
Drawings by James Smith, RIBA drawings collection. Copies in NMRS.
John Small, op. cit.
McGibbon and Ross, op. cit., vol. (iv), p.390.
RCAHMS: *Inventory of Midlothian*, (1929), p.61.
Colin McWilliam, op. cit., p.158.

DALMAHOY HOUSE See Belvidere.

DONIBRISTLE HOUSE — McGill/WA; RC — 92–94

Fife — Dalgety Parish — NT 160 829

Charles Stewart, 6th Earl of Moray (1658–1734); succeeded 1700.

Alexander McGill 1719.

New house with extensive forecourt and offices; built 1719–23; William Adam supplied iron and bricks; chapel, McGill, 1729; proposed alterations, J. Gillespie Graham, early 19th century, not executed; house burnt, 1858; wings and screen survive; now offices.

Sources Darnaway Castle, Moray Muniments, plans and elevations as existing and as proposed, J. Gillespie Graham, early 19th century.
SRO: RHP 14331 Plan of improvement, 1772.
NMRS: MS notes on the Moray Muniments (R6, P13), and measured drawings of ironwork by J. Scott Lawson.
RCAHMS: *Inventory of Fife* (1933), p.98.
Bailie Murphy, *English and Scottish Wrought Ironwork*, plates 77–80 (London, 1904).

DOUGLAS CASTLE Adams/Smith and Patton 135, 136

Lanarkshire Douglas Parish NS 843 318

The first plate engraved by T. Smith, the second by T. Patton; added to the original series with the same numbers as the Buchanan House plates.

Archibald Douglas, Duke of Douglas (1694–1761); succeeded 1700; created Duke 1703; m. Margaret Douglas, 1758.

John Adam Probably with James Adam, 1757; (c.f. Inveraray Castle, plates 71–3).
New Castle, partly built 1757–61; old castle burnt, 1758; unexecuted proposals for completion by James Playfair, 1791 and by James Gillespie Graham, 1826; Chapel by George Henderson, 1888; unroofed 1939 and subsequently demolished.

Sources Douglas Home MSS at the Hirsel:
Plans and elevations, Adam office, *c.*1757.
Designs for additions, James Playfair, 1791.
Designs for additions, James Gillespie Graham, 1826.
Photographs, etc. (Copies in NMRS).
Building accounts.
Ian G. Lindsay and Mary Cosh, op. cit., pp.327–9, 402.
T. Hannan, op. cit.
Wilson, *History of Lanarkshire*, 2 vols., (Glasgow, 1936–7).
George Vere Irving and A. Murray, *Upper Ward of Lanarkshire*, 2 vols., (Glasgow, 1864), p.165.
George Crosbie, *Scottish Field*, October 1965.

THE DRUM See Somerville House.

DRYDEN –; WA; RC 79, 80

Midlothian Lasswade Parish NT 274 644

George Lockhart of Carnwath (1673–1731); succeeded 1689; prominent Jacobite; M.P. 1702–7, 1707–15; active in 1715; Jacobite agent 1718–27; in France 1727–8.

Unattributed Design related to that of Elphinstone, plates 75 and 76; probably before 1715.
New house, probably not incorporating earlier work; built, n.d.; probably abandoned after mining subsidence, *c.*1865; demolished *c.*1900.

Sources NMRS: photograph.
NMRS: MS notes by Gavin Goodfellow.
OS: 25 in. map, Edinburgh, Sheet VII, 16, 1894.

DUFF HOUSE WA; WA; RC 146–148

Banffshire Banff Parish NJ 691 634

These plates refer to the Earl of Fife and so must have been engraved or altered after 1759.

William Duff, Earl of Fife (1697–1763); succeeded to extensive estates, 1722; built Balveny House, plates 90 and 91, 1724/5; created Lord Braco 1735; Earl of Fife 1759.

William Adam 1735.
vol.(v), 1771; dispute with Duff settled in Adam's favour before his death; occupied by 2nd Earl in father's lifetime; interior completed *c.*1780; wings by David Bryce Jnr., *c.*1870, demolished *c.*1950; now an Ancient Monument in Guardianship.

Sources Aberdeen University Library, Fife MSS.
Braco Case Depositions, printed papers relating to the lawsuit in the possession of Mr Howard Colvin.
NMRS: Design for wings, David Bryce Jnr., 1870.

Wolfe and Gandon, *Vitruvius Britannicus*, vol.5, 1771, plates 58–60.
Thomas Newton, *A Tour in England and Scotland*, 1791, p.167.
A. and H. Tayler, op. cit., also *Lord Fife and his Factor*, 1926.
James Imlach, *History of Banff*, 1868.
William Cramond, *Annals of Banff*, 1891.
James Simpson, 'The Building of Duff House', *Archaeological Journal*, vol.130, 1973, p.22.

DUMFRIES HOUSE Adams/Mazell 19–21

Ayrshire Cummock Parish NS 542 204

William Crichton-Dalrymple, 4th Earl of Dumfries (*c*.1700–1768); m. (1) Anne Gordon, daughter of 2nd Earl of Aberdeen, 1731; a.d.c. to his uncle, Field Marshall Stair at Dettingen, 1743; succeeded as Earl of Dumfries, 1744; m. (2) Anne Duff, after 1755; succeeded as Earl of Stair, 1760.

*John Robert, and James Adam; c.*1754; design first commissioned from William Adam, 1748.
New house built, 1754–9; additions and alterations, R. Weir Schultz, 1905; minor alterations to attic, A. Stevenson, 1913–14; private house.

Sources Dumfries House, Bute MSS: Building accounts and drawings.
NMRS: Drawings and Extracts from office papers of R. Weir Schultz.
W. Aiton Ayrshire Agricultural Report (1811), p.110.
A. H. Millar, op. cit.

DUN HOUSE WA; WA; RC 57, 58, 69 and 70

Angus Dun Parish NO 670 598

David Erskine, Lord Dun (1670–1758); advocate; Lord of Session, 1710; m. Magdalene Riddell.
Plates 69 and 70 show an updated version of the scheme in plates 57 and 58 and is described 'as its now executing, differing somewhat from the former'; the plan is almost unchanged, the pediment on the garden front is replaced by a balustrade, parapets replace the shedding eaves on the main elevations and a new frontispiece is added to the north front based on the triumphal arch motif of the Earl of Mar's unexecuted scheme of 1723.

William Adam First scheme probably mid 1720s, c.f. Craigdarroch, plates 77 and 78; second scheme probably *c.*1728; previous scheme by the Earl of Mar, Paris, 1723.
New house; occupied and dated 1730; south front refaced probably after 1900, otherwise little altered; a hotel.

Sources SRO: RHP 13288, design by the Earl of Mar.
NMRS: pamphlet, Victoria Gaul, *The House of Dun*, photograph, *c.*1900.
RCAHMS: Record Sheet No.ANR/16/1, November 1971.

DUNDEE TOWN HOUSE WA; WA; RC 104

Dundee High Street NO 380 320

Lord Provost and Magistrates of Dundee; Alexander Robertson was Lord Provost in 1731–2.

William Adam 1731; (c.f. James Gibbs, St. Martin's in the Fields, *Book of Architecture*, 1728).
Replacement for the old Tolbooth; Adam advised dismantling the old building June 1730; new design approved November 1731; built 1732–5; demolished 1932 to form City Square.

Sources NMRS: photographs.
Charles Mackie, *History of Dundee*, (Glasgow, 1836).
W. Hay, *Charters and Documents relating to the Burgh of Dundee.*
James Maclaren, *History of Dundee*, (Dundee, 1874).
William Kidd, *Dundee Market Crosses and Tolbooths*, (Dundee, 1901).

EAST PARK –; WA; RC 81, 82

Midlothian Inveresk Parish NT 348 698

The first plate refers to the Duchess of Buccleuch, the second to her grandson, the second Duke; probably engraved at about the time of the Duchess' death in February 1732. Formerly Smeaton House, now known as Dalkeith Home Farm.

Anne Scott, Duchess of Bucclench (1651–1732); Countess in her own right, 1661; m. James Crofts, Duke of Monmouth, 1663; Monmouth executed, 1685; returned to Scotland, 1693; remodelled Dalkeith House, 1702–11.

Attributed to

James Smith c.1710.
Remodelling of Smeaton House, 16th century courtyard mansion with round angle towers; purchased 1707 and renamed 'East Park'; carried out 1710–11; subsequently became ruinous, partly repaired; private house.

Sources SRO: GD244/625/1 Buccleuch MSS; building accounts.
Richard Pococke, 'Tours in Scotland', 1747, *Scottish History Society*, 1887, p.312.
James Paterson, *History of the Regality of Musselburgh*, (1857), pp.169–70.

EGLINTON WA; WA; RC 123
Ayrshire Kilwinning Parish NS 323 422

Susanna Montgomerie, Dowager Countess of Eglinton (1690–1780); managed following the 9th Earl's death in 1729, during the minority of the 10th Earl, b.1723.

William Adam After 1729, possibly c.1738. (c.f. James Gibbs' almost identical design for a temple at Hackwood; *Book of Architecture*, 1728, plate 72.)
Temple for the centre of a belvidere; possibly built c.1738 when statues were being put up in the wilderness; if so removed c.1790; Adam also rebuilt the east side, kitchen and back court of Eglinton Castle for the 9th Earl, before 1729.

Sources BM: General Roy's Military Map, c. 1747 (copy in NMRS).
SRO: RH2027 Part of Eglinton Policy, Map 1807.
OS: 6 in. Map, Sheet 17, first edition, 1856.
J. C. Nattes, *Scotia Depicta*, 1804, plate 22 and text.

ELIE HOUSE WA; WA; RC 88, 89
Fife Elie Parish NO 495 008

Sir John Anstruther (1673–1753), m. Lady Margaret Carmichael, 1717; she d. c.1728; Master of Works in Scotland.

William Adam n.d., possibly c.1740.
Remodelling of existing house, retaining earlier south front; not executed, but pediment carved, c.1740; later scheme by Sir James Clerk, not executed; remodelling carried out incorporating earlier pediment in new west front, possibly by John Adam, probably after 1753; further alterations and additions, 19th century; a convent, future uncertain.

Sources SRO: GD18 Clerk of Penicuik MSS, two plans and two elevations, Sir James Clerk (copies in NMRS).
NMRS: Copy of watercolour in possession of J. G. Dunbar.
Braco case depositions.
Rev. W. Wood, *East Neuk of Fife*, Edinburgh, 1887, pp.225–232.
M. F. Conolly, *Eminent Men of Fife*.
H. Fenwick, 'Who Built Elie House?', *Edinburgh Tatler*, December 1968.

ELPHINSTONE HOUSE –; WA; RC 75–76
Stirlingshire Airth Parish NT 390 698

Charles, 9th Lord Elphinstone; (1682–1757); m. Elizabeth Primrose, 1702; succeeded 1717/18.

Unattributed n.d., possibly c.1718; (design related to that of Dryden, plates 79 and 80).
New house incorporating 16th century tower with south and west wings; not executed; house replaced on another site, Dunmore Park by William Wilkins, 1820–22; wings demolished, tower adapted as Dunmore Burial Vault, 1830; embellished probably c.1850; presently derelict, future uncertain.

Sources RCAHMS: *Inventory of Stirlingshire* (1963).
NMRS: Designs for Dunmore Park by William Wilkins, 1820–22.

FALA HOUSE See Hamilton Hall House.

FASQUE HOUSE WA; WA; RC 100
Kincardinshire Fettercairn Parish NO 648 756

Sir Alexander Ramsay of Balmain; (–1754); succeeded 1710; unmarried.

William Adam n.d.
Regularisation of existing 'L' plan house; possibly not executed; south avenue of beeches planted c.1730s; new house, possibly incorporating earlier work, c.1809, attributed to John Paterson.

Sources J. S. Paterson, *Sketches of Scenery in Angus and Mearns*, 1824. Lithographic view.
Archibald Cameron, *History of Fettercairn*, 1889, pp.107–17.
Marcus Binney, *Country Life*, 9 and 16 August 1979.

FLOORS CASTLE WA; WA; RC 48, 49

Roxburghshire Kelso Parish NT 712 347

John Ker, 1st Duke of Roxburghe (–1741); succeeded 1694; created Duke 1707; m. Mary Finch, 1708, she died 1718; Secretary of State 1716–25.

William Adam *c.*1721; (c.f. Inigo Jones, Wilton garden front in *Vitruvius Britannicus*, plates 61 and 62).
New house incorporating earlier work; built 1721–6; various unexecuted schemes by Robert Adam, 1772–7; scheme for castellation, possibly by Archibald Elliot, early 19th century; remodelled by W. H. Playfair, 1837–45; private house.

Sources Floors Castle, Roxburghe MSS, Bundle 726, reference to laying foundation stone, 18 May 1721; also building accounts and elevation by Playfair, as existing in 1837 (castellated).
Soane Museum, Adam Collection, vol.37 (12–20), elevations and plans for alterations.
Edinburgh University Library, Playfair drawings.
RCAHMS, *Inventory of Roxburghshire*, (1956).
Sheila Forman, *Scottish Field*, August 1960.
Marcus Binney, *Country Life*, 11 and 18 May 1978.
Floors Castle Guidebook, introductory note by H. M. Colvin, 1965, and subsequent editions.

GARTMORE HOUSE WA; WA; Smith 83

Perthshire Port of Menteith Parish NS 530 978
Plate engraved by T. Smith and added to the original series with the same number as the first Blair Drummond plate.

Nicol Graham (*c.*1700–); m. Lady Margaret Cunningham, 1732.

William Adam n.d., possibly *c.*1740.
New house, built to a slightly different design, *c.*1740–45; alterations by John Baxter, 1779–80; remodelled by David Barclay, 1901–2; now a school.

Sources SRO: GD22/1/468. Graham MSS,
J. F. Hendry, *Scottish Field*, November 1958, p.40.
NMRS: Copy of a photograph in possession of Sir James Cayzer.

GLASGOW COLLEGE LIBRARY WA; WA; RC 155–157

Glasgow High Street NS 591 652

University of Glasgow; with the aid of an endowment of £500 made by the Duke of Chandos in 1720.

William Adam 1732; the design was preferred to another by John Craig and Allan Dreghorn 1732. (c.f. James Gibbs, e.g. King's College, Cambridge, *Book of Architecture*, 1728, plate 34.)
Library built 1732–45 to a simplified design; extended 1782; demolished *c.*1887.

Sources SRO: GD220/5/1214/1–4, Letters from Charles Northland, Professor of Oriental languages to Mungo Graham of Gortly, 1732.
Glasgow University Archives; Senate and Faculty Minutes; Adam's designs, also drawings of stair.
T. Pennant, *Tour in Scotland*, 1769.
J. Coutts, *History of the University of Glasgow*, Glasgow, 1909.
J. D. Mackie, *University of Glasgow*, Glasgow, 1954.
C. H. C. and M. I. Baker, *The Life and Circumstances of James Brydges, 1st Duke of Chandos.*
London University, Courtauld Institute of Art, Conway Library, photograph before demolition (copy in NMRS).

GORDON'S HOSPITAL WA; WA; RC 107–108

Aberdeen St. Andrew's Street NK 930 072

Aberdeen Town Council, Trustees for Gordon's Hospital; Robert Gordon died in 1730.

William Adam 1730–31; (c.f. James Gibbs, e.g. *Book of Architecture*, 1728, plate 31).
Hospital built with differences 1731–2; pediment and steeple omitted, outer sections advanced with shaped gables, unfinished and unoccupied, except by troops in 1746, until 1750; statue of founder by John Cheere, 1753; unexecuted proposals by William Burn, 1820s; alterations and additions by John Smith, 1830–34; now Robert Gordon's College.

Sources Robert Gordon's Institute of Technology, Records of Robert Gordon's College.
NMRS: Copies of various drawings including one showing the hospital as built and measured drawings by S. J. Watts, 1928.
Country Life, 12 May 1955 and 19 August 1965.
David Murray, 'Robert Gordon's Hospital and William Adam's other Public Buildings' unpublished thesis, Scott Sutherland School of Architecture, 1975 (copy in NMRS).
R. Anderson, *History of Robert Gordon's Hospital*, 1883.
A. Walker, *Robert Gordon, his Hospital and his College.*

GRAY HOUSE –; WA; RC 98

Angus | Liff and Benvie Parish | NO 338 321

John, 10th Lord Gray (1683–1724); purchased Benvie, 1713; 11th Lord Gray, d.1738; 12th Lord Gray, m. Margaret Blair, heiress of Kinfauns, 1741.

Unattributed 1714; possibly Alexander McGill (c.f. Nairne, Mount Stuart and Yester; c.f. also, later design by James Gibbs, *Book of Architecture*, 1728, plate 56).
New House Built 1714–16; unfinished, according to Macky, 1723; minor alterations *c.*1740 and *c.*1830; undergoing restoration, to be private houses.

Sources Darnaway Castle, Moray Muniments, Gray of Kinfauns MSS.
John Macky, op. cit.
Forfarshire Illustrated, (Gersham Cunningham, 1848).
A. J. Warden, *Angus and Forfarshire*, 1880, vol.(ii), p.28.
Peter Gray, *Descent and Kinship of the Master of Gray*, 1903, p.15.

HADDO HOUSE WA; WA; RC 54–56

Aberdeenshire | Methlick Parish | NJ 868 348

William Gordon, 2nd Earl of Aberdeen; (1679–1745; m. (1) Lady Mary Leslie, 1708; m. (2) Lady Anne Murray, 1716; succeeded 1720; m. (3) Lady Anne Gordon, after 1725.

William Adam n.d., first design 1724, second 1728, possibly revised again before building; (influenced by Sir John Clerk).
New house, possibly incorporating parts of the old house of Kellie; built 1732–5; additions by Archibald Simpson, 1820s; alterations and additions, including parapets and terrace by Wardrop and Reid, 1879–81; Library, etc, Wright and Mansfield 1880s; Chapel by G. E. Street, 1882; now in the care of the National Trust for Scotland.

Sources Drawings by William Adam, presently lost, existed in 1925.
SRO: GD18/5005, Clerk of Penicuik MSS, correspondence of Lord Aberdeen and John Baxter, mason, with Baron Clerk.
Haddo Estate Offices: Plans for additions, Archibald Simpson, *c.*1828.
Plans for alterations and additions, Wardrop and Reid, 1879–81.
Plans for interior work, Wright and Mansfield, 1880–*c.*1890 (copies in NMRS).
Christopher Hussey, *Country Life*, 18 and 25 August 1966.

HAMILTON CHURCH WA; WA; RC and Bell 12, 13

Lanarkshire | Hamilton Parish | NS 737 539

The second plate engraved by Andrew Bell, with the same number as the last of the Hamilton Palace plates; possibly a re-engraving of a missing original plate; both plates out of place in the original series.

William Adam *c.*1729; Adam refers to a visit to the work in a letter to Sir John Clerk in 1729.
Church built *c.*1729–32; interior remodelled 1926, part of the pulpit and other details survive; church in use.

Sources SRO: GD31/554, Fea of Clestrain MSS.
SRO: GD18/4782/2, Clerk of Penicuik MSS.
George Hay, *The Architecture of Scottish Post Reformation Churches 1560–1843*, (OUP, 1957).

HAMILTON DOG KENNEL WA; WA; RC 160

Lanarkshire | Hamilton Parish | NS 737 539

Usually known as 'Chatelherault'.

James, 5th Duke of Hamilton; (1702/3–1743); succeeded 1712.

William Adam 1731.
Eyecatcher, hunting lodge and offices; built 1732–43, decoration of the banqueting and upper rooms continued until *c.*1746; presently derelict, to be restored.

Sources SRO: GD31/554, Fea of Clestrain MSS.
Lennoxlove, Hamilton MSS – notes in NMRS.
A. A. Tait, 'William Adam at Chatelherault', *Burlington Magazine*, June 1962.
D. M. Walker, 'Threat to a Ducal Dog Kennel', *Country Life*, 17 December 1964.
James Macaulay, 'Chatelherault', *Edinburgh Tatler*, May 1967.

HAMILTON HALL HOUSE WA; WA; Smith 121

Midlothian | Fala and Soutra Parish | NT 441 608

Plate engraved by T. Smith with the same number as the last Castle Kennedy plate; added to the original series. Usually known as Fala House.

Thomas Hamilton of Fala; (1707–79); succeeded 1713; m. Elizabeth Dalrymple, 1735.

William Adam — c.1735; (c.f. James Gibbs' very similar design for a villa at Whitton, *Book of Architecture*, 1728, plate 61). New house built c.1735; unoccupied 1779–86; struck by lightning, 1826, demolished shortly afterwards.

Sources — Oxenfoord Castle, Stair MSS.
Braco case depositions.
Thomson's Atlas, (Edinburgh, 1821).
Sir H. H. Dalrymple, *A Short Account of the Hamiltons of Fala, and of Fala House*, 1907.

HAMILTON PALACE — Smith and WA; WA; RC — 6–13

Lanarkshire — Hamilton Parish — NS 728 557

Plates 6–8 refer to Hamilton House and show the house as it existed at the time of engraving, probably c.1728; plates 9–11 and 13 refer to Hamilton Palace and show a scheme for enlargement. Plate 12 of the original series appears to be missing.

Anne, Duchess of Hamilton; (c.1636–1716); created Duchess in her own right, 1643; m. William Douglas, 1656; created Duke, 1660; he died 1694; Smith's patrons.

James, 5th Duke of Hamilton; (1702/3–1743); grandson of the above; succeeded 1712; m. (1) Anne Cochrane, 1723; m. (2) Elizabeth Strangeways, 1727; m. (3) Anne Spenser, 1737; Adam's patron.

James Smith — c.1691; first consulted 1682, again 1691; Sir William Bruce and Tobias Bauchop consulted 1692; contract with 'Mr. James Smith and James Smith', 1693.

William Adam — n.d., probably 1727 or after.
Remodelling of existing house carried out by James Smith, 1693–1701; William Adam's scheme not executed, minor works only, 1727–42; extensive remodelling by David Hamilton, 1822–38; library by H. E. Goodridge; various unexecuted schemes; demolished c.1929.

Sources — Lennoxlove, Hamilton MSS: Drawings attributed to James Smith.
Drawings by David Hamilton, 1822–38 (copies in NMRS).
SRO: GD31/554, Fea of Clestrain MSS.
Country Life, 7, 14 and 21 June 1919.
F. Wordsall, *Scottish Field*, May 1964, p.52.
Rosalind K. Marshall, *The Days of Duchess Anne*, 1973.

HARDEN HOUSE — Bruce; WA; RC — 142

Berwickshire — Mertoun Parish — NT 617 318

Usually known as Mertoun House.

Sir William Scott of Harden; (–1707): M.P. for Selkirk, 1689–93; m. (1) Jean Nisbet, 1673; m. (2) Magdalene Scott, 1700.

Sir William Bruce — 1702–3.
New house, begun 1703; possibly still incomplete in 1707; alterations and additions by William Burn, 1843; further extended, 1913; reduced and restored by Ian Lindsay, 1953–5; private house.

Sources — NMR (England): Estates Exchange, No.492, Sale Brochure, London, 1912.
Sheila Forman, *Scottish Field*, November 1957.
John Cornforth, 'Mertoun', *Country Life*, 2 and 9 June 1966.
J. G. Dunbar, op. cit.

HAWKHILL VILLA — John Adam/ – /Mazell — 123

Edinburgh — Lochend Road — NT 275 752

Plate engraved after 1759 by P. Mazell with the same number as the plate of the Eglinton Temple, and added to the original series.

Andrew Pringle — (–1776); Solicitor General, 1755; Session Court Judge, Lord Alemoor, 1759; a bachelor.

John Adam — c.1757; (c.f. Plan of Broomlands, plate 118).
New house, built 1757; demolished 1971.

Sources — George Brunton and David Haig, *Senators of the College of Justice*, (1832, p.523).
Dr Alexander Carlyle, *Autobiography*, 1722–1805, (Edinburgh, 1860).
Dr Thomas Somerville, *Own Life and Times*, (Edinburgh, 1861).
T. Craig-Brown, *History of Selkirkshire*, two vols., (Edinburgh, 1886), vol.(ii), pp.309–10.
James Simpson, 'Lord Alemoor's Villa at Hawkhill', *Bulletin of Scottish Georgian Society*, (i), 1972.
Ian Gow, 'The Edinburgh Villa', 1975, unpublished thesis, Cambridge University (copy in NMRS).

HERIOT'S HOSPITAL –; WA; RC 105, 106

Edinburgh Lauriston Place NT 255 733

George Heriot's Trustees; George Heriot died in 1624, leaving 23,625 English pounds to endow the hospital.

William Wallace Plan derived from Serlio in 1627 by Walter Balcanquall, Dean of Rochester, with Walter Alexander 'overseer and supervisor' of Heriot's will; design by Wallace, Master Mason to the Crown, succeeded by William Ayton, John Mylne and Robert Mylne; often incorrectly attributed, in the 18th century to Inigo Jones.

Hospital founded 1628; work interrupted 1639–42; completed late 1640s; alterations including domed steeple by Robert Mylne, *c.*1690–95; alterations by John Adam, 1762; alterations and additions including lodge, terraces and refacing by William Playfair, 1829–32; chapel refitted by James Gillespie Graham, 1837; now a school.

Sources George Heriot's Trust, Drawings for additions and alterations (copies in NMRS).
Minute Books, etc (typed extracts in NMRS).
Alistair Rowan, *Country Life*, 6 and 13 March 1975.
RCAHMS, *Inventory of Edinburgh*, (1951), pp.110–14.
Alan J. Scott, 'History of Heriots Hospital', 1978, unpublished thesis, Scott Sutherland School of Architecture, Aberdeen (copy in NMRS).

HOLYROOD HOUSE, CHAPEL ROYAL – /Wyck/Mazell 5

Edinburgh Canongate NT 269 739

This plate was engraved by P. Mazell from a painting by John Wyck (1652–1700) and added to the original series with the same number as the last of the palace plates.

King James VII and II; (1633–1701); succeeded 1685; instructed the Privy Council in December 1687 to fit out the Abbey Church as a Catholic Chapel Royal and as a Chapel for the Order of the Thistle.

Attributed to James Smith, overseer of the Royal Works in Scotland, 1688; see also plates 4 and 5 for elevations apparently executed and possibly associated with this scheme.

Fitting out and furnishing of the existing Abbey Church nave, carried out during 1688; woodwork, etc., apparently executed in London; destroyed by the mob, December 1688; roof fell in, 1768; Ancient Monument in Guardianship.

Sources SRO: E26/12/3, E28/369/54, E28/477/2, SP57/13, Accounts.
NLS: Inv. No.237 and 238, Fettercairn Drawings, sketches of the west front of the abbey.
C. Rodgers, *History of the Chapel Royal of Scotland.*
HMSO: *Official Guide.*
David McRoberts and Charles Oman, *Antiquaries Journal*, 1968, vol.48, part 2, 'Plate . . . for the Chapel Royal . . . 1686'.

HOLYROOD HOUSE, ROYAL PALACE Bruce/WA; RC 1–5

Edinburgh Canongate NT 269 739

These plates, probably engraved *c.*1728, show the Palace with its ancillary wings serving the various suites of apartments, which were subsequently removed. The kitchen block, contrived to balance the Abbey Church did not exist in the form shown, but it is not clear whether this was a contemporary or an earlier proposal. For the church see also the 'Chapel Royal', duplicate plate 5.

King Charles II Principally through the agency of John Maitland, 2nd Earl of Lauderdale (1616–82), virtual ruler of Scotland, 1663–79; Lauderdale created Duke, 1672; remodelled Hamilton House, 1673–5; Thirlestane Castle, 1670–77, Brunstane House, 1672–5, etc; principal patron of Sir William Bruce.

Sir William Bruce Surveyor General and Overseer of the King's Buildings in Scotland; *c.*1671.

Remodelling and repair of existing palace, including James V's tower of 1528–32; carried out 1671–9; repairs and other work by James Smith; repairs, 1733–4, Hamilton apartment, 1740–42 and other work by William Adam and later by John Adam; subsequent repairs and alterations, esp. redecoration of State apartments by Robert Reid for George IV, 1824–35 and by H. M. Office of Works for Victoria and for George V.

Sources BM: Egerton MSS 2870–1, drawings and contracts.
Lennoxlove, Hamilton MSS.
SRO: Masters of Works Accounts, various volumes.
SRO: GD31/554, Fea of Clestrain MSS.
SRO: GD18/4729, 4783 and 5004, Clerk of Penicuik MSS.
National Trust, Dyrham Park; view from the N.W.
HMSO: *History of the King's Works*, vol.6, p.251.
RCAHMS: *Inventory of Edinburgh*, (1951), pp.144–53.
R. S. Mylne, *Master Masons to the Crown of Scotland*, (1893).
J. G. Dunbar, op. cit.
HMSO, *Official Guide*

HOPETOUN HOUSE WA; WA; RC 14–21

West Lothian Abercorn Parish NT 089 790

Plates 14, 15, 17 and 19 exist in two versions; they were re-engraved following updating of the design of the pavilions. The Glasgow University Library copy, reproduced here, has the later versions of plates 14 and 17, and, unusually contains both versions of plate 15.

Charles Hope, 1st Earl of Hopetoun; (1681–1742); succeeded 1682; m. Henrietta Johnstone, 1699; created Earl 1703; John Hope, 2nd Earl (1704–81).

William Adam *c.*1723; revised pavilion design attributed to John and Robert Adam, *c.*1750.
Remodelling and enlargement of existing house by Sir William Bruce of 1699–1703; first contract, 1721; carried out *c.*1723–48, portico and perron not built, interior and pavilions not finished; frontispiece, steps, interiors and pavilions completed by John and Robert Adam, 1750–56; subsequent minor alterations and additions; private house.

Sources Hopetoun House MSS.
R. Sibbald, *History of the Sheriffdoms of Linlithgow and Stirling* (1707).
John Macky, op. cit., vol.3, p.205.
John Dunbar, op. cit.
John Fleming, *Country Life*, 5 and 12 January 1956.

BRIDGES AT INVERARAY Morris, James and John Adam/Bell 74

Argyllshire Inveraray Parish

Plate engraved by A. Bell and added to the original series with the same number as the second Newhall plate.

Garron Bridge (NM 115 101); Roger Morris, *c.*1747 for Archibald Campbell, 3rd Duke of Argyll and Major Caulfield, Inspector of Roads and Bridges in North Britain; built 1748/9; supervised by John Adam; still in use, carrying the main road.

Garden Bridge (NM 095 096), or Frew's Bridge; John Adam, possibly with James Adam, 1758, for the 3rd Duke of Argyll; built 1759–61; still in use, carrying an estate road.

Aray Bridge (NM 098 091), or Sea Bridge; John Adam, 1757 for the 3rd Duke of Argyll and Major Caulfield; built 1758/9; swept away, 1772; new bridge by Robert Mylne, 1773; built 1775/6; still in use, carrying the main road.

Sources NMRS: Copies of drawings by J. Adam and R. Mylne, in possession of Duke of Argyll.
Blair Adam MSS: drawings by John Adam.
Ian G. Lindsay and Mary Cosh, op. cit., pp.125–6, 135–40.

INVERARAY CASTLE Morris/Bell 71–73

Argyllshire Inveraray Parish NN 095 093

These plates, the first engraved by Andrew Bell, were added to the original series, with the same numbers as the Belvidere and the first of the Newhall plates. There are loose sheet copies at Inveraray.

Archibald Campbell, 3rd Duke of Argyll; (1682–1761); lawyer, soldier and politician; Commissioner for the Union; created Earl of Islay, 1706; representative peer, Extraordinary Lord of Session, etc; Walpole's Scottish 'manager'; succeeded as Duke, 1743.

Roger Morris 1744; for discussion of the design, see Lindsay and Cosh, op. cit.
New castle; built 1745–58, supervised by William and John Adam; decoration and minor alterations by Robert Mylne, 1772–88; burnt 1877; repairs and alterations by Anthony Salvin, 1877–9; burnt 1975, restored by Ian G. Lindsay and Partners, 1975–8.

Sources Inveraray Castle, Argyll MSS.
NLS: Saltoun MSS.
NMRS: R.6(P), inventory of plans; copies of photographs before 1877.
Ian G. Lindsay and Mary Cosh, op. cit.; includes comprehensive source list.
Country Life, 30 July 1927; 28 June 1953; 13 and 20 July 1972.

KEITH HALL – ; WA; RC 144, 145

Aberdeenshire Keith Hall Parish NK 788 212

John Keith, 3rd Earl of Kintore; (1699–1758); succeeded 1718; m. Mary Erskine, niece of John, Earl of Mar, 1729; Knight Marshall, 1733.

Unattributed n.d., a marked altar indicates that the north room on the principal floor was a chapel, presumably Catholic.
Remodelling of existing house, late 16th century tower of Caskieben already altered and regularised, 1697–9; no external work done; insertion of stairs into central courtyard probably not done at this time; some redecoration, possibly *c.*1730; alterations and additions, probably including stairs by John Smith, before 1811; addition by David Bryce, 1851; further alterations, *c.*1900; private house.

Sources NMRS: Copies of survey drawings, Geo. Bennet Mitchell, 1938.
McGibbon and Ross, op. cit., vol.(iv), p.61.
NMR (England): Estates Exchange, London, No.1472, sale brochure, 1914.

KENMURE CASTLE WA; WA; RC 51–53
Stewartry of Kirkcudbright; Kells Parish NX 635 764

Despite interleaving with the plates of Taymouth Castle, near the Perthshire village of Kenmore, the pediments bear Gordon arms, suggesting that the design was for Kenmure Castle, at the head of Loch Ken in Galloway. Plate 53 appears to be plate 51 renumbered.

Robert Gordon, but for attainder, 7th Viscount Kenmure; (*c.*1712–43); 6th Viscount executed, 1716; estates managed by Lady Kenmure until Robert Gordon came into full possession, 1736; built new house of Greenlaw; succeeded by his brother, John Gordon (*c.*1713–69); according to M'Kerlie he set about repairing Kenmure Castle.

William Adam n.d., possibly 1736, probably *c.*1744.
New house, possibly incorporating earlier work; not built; Kenmure Castle remained derelict until remodelling, early 20th century; again derelict.

Sources Francis Grose, *Antiquities of Scotland,* (London, 1789–91); vol.2, p.184.
McGibbon and Ross, op. cit., vol.4, p.256.
M'Kerlie, op. cit., vol.4, pp.65 and 66.
RCAHMS: *Inventory of Kirkcudbrightshire,* (1914), p.94.

KINROSS HOUSE Bruce/Borlach/RC 61, 62
Kinross-shire Kinross Parish NO 127 021

Plate 62 was engraved by Richard Cooper from a drawing now at Kinross House by John Borlach, known to have been James Gibbs' draughtsman; it is the only perspective view in the book. The style of plate 61 also differs from that of the other plates. They may have formed part of the original series although they may have been originally intended for another purpose, possibly for Slezer's 'Theatrum Scotiae'; the plans and front of Kinross are included in Slezer's list of intended plates.

Sir William Bruce (*c.*1630–1710); Surveyor-General and Overseer of the King's Buildings in Scotland, 1671–8; purchased Kinross estate, 1675; Sir John Bruce succeeded 1710 and died 1711; private house.

Sir William Bruce 1679; drawings by Alexander Edward.
New house; garden work and site preparation began 1679; the house built 1686–93; private house.

Sources SRO: GD29/263, Bruce of Kinross MSS.
SRO: GD1/51/62, Mylne Papers.
Edinburgh College of Art: Plans, elevations and garden layout by Alexander Edward, *c.*1685. Copies in NMRS.
Mark Girouard, *Country Life,* 25 March, 1 April 1965.
J. G. Dunbar, 'Kinross House' in *The Country Seat,* ed. Colvin and Harris, (1970), p.64.
J. G. Dunbar, op. cit.

LAWERS HOUSE WA; WA; RC 158, 159
Perthshire Monzievaird and Strowan Parish NN 799 231

James Campbell (1667–1745); military career linked with that of Lord Stair; returned to Scotland 1722; M.P. 1734–41; Brigadier General, 1735; Major-General, 1739; Lieutenant General, knighted after Dettingen, 1742; killed at Fontenoy, 1745.

William Adam *c.*1737.
Remodelling of existing house; carried out in two phases, 1724/5 and 1737–44; alterations and additions by Richard Crichton, 1814–17; further alterations, *c.*1850 and by William Black, *c.*1919/20; interior partially removed and sold, 1950s; private house.

Sources SRO: GD237/99, Earl of Glasgow's MSS, per Tods, Murray and Jamieson, W.S.; building accounts.
Country Life, 10 October 1925.

LESLIE HOUSE – ; WA; RC 66–68
Fife Leslie Parish NO 260 018

John Leslie, 7th Earl of Rothes; (*c.*1630–81); succeeded 1641; Royalist; m. Anne Lindsay, 1648; President of the Council, 1660; Lord High Treasurer, 1663; Lord High Chancellor, 1667, etc; created Duke, 1680.

John and Robert Mylne; *c.*1666 (advice from Sir William Bruce).
Remodelling of existing house; carried out 1667–72; repairs, etc., William Adam, 1730s; burnt 1763; repaired 1765; alterations by Sir Robert Lorimer, 1906; now a Church of Scotland home.

Sources Kirkcaldy Museum: Rothes MSS.
R. S. Mylne, op. cit.
J. G. Dunbar, op. cit.

LONGFORMACUS HOUSE – ; WA; RC 99
Berwickshire Longformacus Parish NT 696 573
Sir Robert Sinclair (–1727); 3rd Baronet; succeeded 1698; m. Christian Cockburn.
Unattributed *c.*1714; (c.f. Broomlands House, plates 118 and 119).
New house; built *c.*1715; according to the late Miss Brown, the prepared roof timbers burnt by Jacobites; datestone seen during later alterations and additions, *c.*1870; private house.
Sources *Proceedings of the Berwickshire Naturalists' Club*, 1882–4, vol.(10), p.25.

LONMAY HOUSE WA; WA; RC 95
Aberdeenshire Lonmay Parish NK 046 608
James Fraser (–1729); purchased Lonmay 1718; m. Eleanor Lindsay; Lonmay sold by her to William Moir of Whitehills, 1731.
William Adam n.d., possibly *c.*1720.
New house; pavilions only built; one survives; private house.
Sources J. B. Pratt, *Buchan*, (Aberdeen, 1901), p.225.
OS: 25 in. map, Aberdeenshire, Sheet VIII, 3, 1870.

MAVISBANK WA; WA; RC 46, 47
Midlothian Lasswade Parish NT 288 652
The planting shown on plate 47 through the communicating arcades is the only indication of landscape in the book, excepting the view of Kinross House, plate 62.
Sir John Clerk of Penicuik; (1676–1755); advocate; M.P. 1702–7; Commissioner for the Union; Baron of Exchequer 1708; owned Cammo 1710–24, see plate 141; succeeded to Penicuik 1722; noted antiquarian, musician, collector, amateur architect, writer on architectural and landscape matters, etc; important patron of William Adam.
William Adam and Sir John Clerk jointly; 1722/3; (elements probably drawn from *Vitruvius Britannicus*, e.g. for convex roof see vol.[1], plate 20).
New house; begun 1723, first occupied 1727, completed *c.*1728; chimney-pieces, etc, *c.*1735; alterations and additions, mid 19th century removed 1954; burnt 1973; future uncertain.
Sources Penicuik House MSS, plans, etc (copies in NMRS).
SRO: GD18/1765–74, Clerk of Penicuik MSS: Accounts, correspondence between Clerk, Adam and John Baxter, mason, etc.
NMRS, RCAHMS: measured drawings and Record Sheet No.MCR/7/1, 1973.
Sir John Clerk, *The Country Seat*, unpublished MS poem in SRO, printed without original notes in J. D. Hunt and P. Willis, *The Genius of the Place*, (London, 1975).
Clerk of Penicuik's Memoirs, ed. J. M. Gray, (1892).
Stuart Piggott, 'Sir John Clerk and the Country Seat', essay in H. Colvin and J. Harris, *The Country Seat*, (London, 1970), p.110.

MERTOUN HOUSE See Harden House.

LORD MILTON'S HOUSE Adams/Smith 45
Edinburgh Canongate NT 267 738
Andrew Fletcher, Lord Milton; (1692–1766); Lord of Session 1724; Lord Justice Clerk, 1735–48; close political associate of 3rd Duke of Argyll.
John Adam n.d., probably *c.*1754.
New town house, built c.1755–58; decoration by William Delacour, 1758; demolished *c.*1887.
Sources NLS: Saltoun MSS, SB44, 78, 86(a), 89, 93, 100, 329 and 419(1).
National Gallery of Scotland, Samuel Buck, 'View of Edinburgh from Salisbury Crags' (shows rear elevation).
SRO: GD18; Clerk of Penicuik MSS, letter from Robert Adam to his sister Nell, 23 October 1756.
Edinburgh Public Library, Boog Watson MSS, vol.2, p.92, etc.
Mary Cosh – typed notes (copy in NMRS).
Ian G. Lindsay and Mary Cosh, op. cit., p.8.

MINTO HOUSE WA; WA; RC 59, 60

Edinburgh Chambers Street (now) NT 257 734

Sir Gilbert Elliot, Lord Minto; (1693–1766); succeeded 1718; Lord of Session, 1726.

William Adam Probably *c.*1738, but ref. to 'estimate of a house of 42 foot long and 38 broad and 3 stories high . . . 15 December 1726' (Minto MSS, Box 2).
New town house, built 1738–43; surgical hospital, 1829; demolished 1840s.

Sources NLS: Minto MSS 13233; Plan, drawings, accounts, etc.
Bodleian Library, Oxford: Gough maps 39 f.28; plan and elevation, 1766.
Edinburgh Public Library: Boog Watson MSS.
James Grant, op. cit., vol.2, pp.251, 274–6.
George Tancred, *Annals of a Border Club*, (Edinburgh, 1899), p.179.

MOUNT STUART HOUSE – /Smith 31

Bute Kingarth Parish NS 108 595

This plate engraved by T. Smith and added to the original series.

John Stuart, 3rd Earl of Bute; (1713–92); m. Mary Montague, 1736; representative peer from 1737; principal minister to George III, 1760–63.

*Attributed to William Adam; c.*1740; main block only.
New main block apparently built *c.*1740, retaining pavilions of existing house by Alexander McGill, 1718–22; unexecuted scheme for remodelling by James Craig, 1768–9; burnt 1877; rebuilt by Sir Robert Rowand Anderson, 1879; McGill pavilions survive; private house.

Sources Mount Stuart, Bute MSS; drawings by McGill, 1716, drawings by James Craig, 1769, etc.
James K. Hewison, *The Isle of Bute in the Olden Time*, (1895), vol.2 – photograph of painting of 18th century house.
William Daniell, *Voyage round Great Britain 1814–25*, incl. engraved view, 1819, vol.3, p.20.

NEWBYTH HOUSE – ; WA; RC 137, 138

East Lothian Whitekirk Parish NT 588 801

Sir William Baird (1654–1737); Baronet 1680; m. Catherine Binning, 1697.

Unattributed n.d.; (c.f. Rosehall, plates 132–4).
New house; apparently built; burnt 1813, stables survive; rebuilt by Archibald Elliot, 1817–19; now subdivided into flats.

Sources NMRS: Alistair Rowan, MS notes.
John Small, op. cit.
William Baird, *Account of the Surname of Baird*, ed. W. N. Fraser, (1870).
Gentleman's Magazine, 1813(i), p.479.

NEWHALL HOUSE WA; WA; RC 73, 74

East Lothian Yester Parish NT 511 671

Lord William Hay (1670–1723); soldier; m. Margaret Hay, heiress of Linplum; succeeded by John Hay, advocate.

William Adam Before 1723; c.f. Makerstoun House, Roxburghshire.
New house; built with advanced pedimented frontispiece, bonded quoins and probably without pavilions; north-west wing and porch added; demolished, 1909.

Sources OS: 25 in. map, Haddingtonshire, Sheet XV 6, 1894.
NMRS: Photograph.
NMRS: Gavin Goodfellow, MS note.
Braco case depositions, 1743.

NEWLISTON HOUSE WA; WA; RC 32–36

West Lothian Kirkliston Parish NT 111 736

John Dalrymple, 2nd Earl of Stair; (1673–1747); succeeded 1707; Ambassador in Paris; returned to Scotland, 1720; Newliston and Castle Kennedy landscapes; promoted Field Marshall, Dettingen, 1742; important patron of William Adam.

William Adam n.d., 1725–35.
New house; not executed; other work by Adam, 1725–35, included a design for an addition to the old house, 1723, the landscape 1731, and stables; new house built by Robert Adam, 1792; wings and forecourt by David Bryce, 1845; private house.

Sources SRO: GD18/4719; Clerk of Penicuik MSS.
Blenheim Palace Muniments; garden plan by William Adam, later copy at Newliston.
Braco case depositions.
J. M. Graham, *The Stair Annals,* (1875).
Colin McWilliam, op. cit., p.355.
Scottish Field, March 1965, p.58.

NIDDRIE HOUSE WA; WA; RC 114, 115

Edinburgh Niddrie NT 302 718

Andrew Wauchope Succeeded 1725; m. Helen Home, 1735.

William Adam *c.*1735; triumphal arch motif probably derived from the Earl of Mar, through Dun House, c.f. plate 70. Regularisation of existing tower and south wing of 1636; work to main house not executed, but one pavilion with communication built *c.*1735; mausoleum and forecourt also built by William Adam; extensive additions by William Burn, 1823; burnt New Year's Eve, 1959, subsequently demolished.

Sources Braco case depositions, 1743.
MacGibbon and Ross, op. cit., vol.(ii), pp.62–6.
John Small, op. cit.
Thomas Hannan, op. cit.

THE ORPHANS' HOSPITAL WA; WA; RC 139, 140

Edinburgh Waverley Station (now) NT 259 739

Plate 139 is inscribed 'Begun in the Year 1734'; this is the only plate dated in this way.
Founded by public subscription from a proposal by Andrew Gardner in March 1733. By 1734 the original accommodation in Bailie Fyffe's Close was inadequate and a site adjacent to Trinity College was acquired for a new building.

William Adam 1734; the first of Adam's hospital designs; the same barrack formula with square domed centrepiece subsequently applied to the others; c.f. Watson's Hospital, plate 151 and the Royal Infirmary, plates 149 and 150.
New hospital; west section built June 1734 – March 1735; occupied April 1735; centre section built 1736; east section built 1791; superseded by Thomas Hamilton's Dean Orphanage, 1833; demolished 1845.

Sources SRO: GD95/vol.10/150, Description of Work so far accomplished, 1740.
William Maitland, *History of Edinburgh,* (Edinburgh, 1753, p.364).
James Grant, op. cit., p.359.

PANMURE HOUSE – ; WA; RC 129–131

Angus Panbride Parish NO 534 387

George Maule, 2nd Earl of Panmure; (–1671); m. Jean Campbell 1645; succeeded 1661; James Maule, 3rd Earl of Panmure.

John Mylne 1666, contract dated 28 February.
New house, built 1666–73; Mylne d.1667, work supervised by Alexander Nisbet from 1668; additions to offices, etc. by Tobias Bauchop, 1694–9; unexecuted scheme for stables and alterations to the west front, by Robert Adam, *c.*1760; remodelled by David Bryce, 1852–5; demolished 1955.

Sources SRO: GD45/18, 26 and 27, Panmure MSS (extracts in NMRS).
Soane Museum Drawings, Adam Collection, vol.22, No.71, vol.41, Nos.32–4 (copies in NMRS).
Registrum de Panmure, ed. John Stuart, (Edinburgh, 1876).
R. S. Mylne, op. cit., pp.153–8.

PRESTONHALL HOUSE WA; WA; RC 107, 108

Midlothian Cranston Parish NT 395 658

Henrietta, Duchess of Gordon; (–1760); widow of Alexander, 2nd Duke of Gordon who d.1728; purchased Prestonhall, 1738; in her portrait, attr. to Phillipe Mercier *c.*1750, she is holding a drawing similar to the original of plate 108, the pavilion shown without a pedimented frontispiece.

William Adam n.d., probably *c.*1738.
Alterations and addition of pavilions to existing house, probably built *c.*1700 for Roderick Mackenzie from 1703 Lord Prestonhall; probably executed without pavilion frontispieces; largely demolished 1790, new house built by Robert Mitchell for Alexander and John Callander, 1791–*c.*1800, probably incorporating Adam's east pavilion; private house.

Sources Robert Mitchell, *Plans, etc, of Buildings erected in England and Scotland . . .,* (1801), plates 9–13.
Rosalind K. Marshall, *Women in Scotland, 1660–1780'* (Edinburgh, 1979), pp.445, including portrait, drawing, etc.
Colin McWilliam, op. cit., pp.395–8.

DESIGN FOR A PERSON OF QUALITY (1) WA; WA; RC 96, 97

Unidentified, but c.f. Tullibardine, plates 101–3; n.d., on stylistic grounds probably *c.*1740 or later. Apparently a new house for a peer, possibly under attainder. (Perhaps Castle Dounie for Lord Lovat, c.f. Fleming, op. cit., pp.64–5.)

DESIGN FOR A PERSON OF QUALITY (2) WA; WA; RC 124

Unidentified, but c.f. Belhaven House, plate 134 and Tinwald, plate 153; n.d., on stylistic grounds possibly late 1730s. Perhaps also for an attainted patron. From the plan, existing work may be incorporated.

ROYAL PALACE INVENTED BY A PERSON OF QUALITY – ; WA; RC 109, 110

Attributed to John Erskine, 11h Earl of Mar (1675–1732); design based, as pointed out by Mr Howard Colvin, on Mansart's Marly; n.d., possibly late 1720s.

Sources SRO: RHP 13256, Mar and Kelly MSS, 'Lord Mar's Plans, 1700, etc'.
Howard Colvin, op. cit., pp.295–7.

ROSEHALL HOUSE – ; WA; RC 132–134

Lanarkshire NS 723 622

Sir James Hamilton (1682–1750); m. Frances Stuart, 1707; succeeded before 1710; M.P. from 1735.

Unattributed n.d., c.f. Newbyth, plates 137 and 138.

Extensive remodelling and enlargement of existing house; at least one pavilion executed; renamed 'Douglas Support'; additions, 1794; further extensive alterations and additions; demolished 1933.

Sources NLS: *Glasgow and Lanarkshire Illustrated*, (1910).
NMRS: Demolition sale catalogue, 1933.
OS: 25 in. map, first edition, 1860; Sheet XI/4.

ROYAL INFIRMARY WA; WA; RC 149, 150

Edinburgh Infirmary Street NT 261 735

The prints and copper plates of *Vitruvius Scoticus* were stored in a garret in the infirmary leased by Commissioner William Adam from *c.*1804 to *c.*1810 (Blair Adam MSS).

Edinburgh Infirmary Trustees; first infirmary in Robertson's Close; Royal Charter, 1736.

William Adam 1736/7; barrack design, central teaching block with square dome and grand frontispiece (c.f. the Orphans' Hospital, plates 139 and 140, and Watson's Hospital, plate 151).

New hospital; foundation stone laid 2 August 1738; first patients December 1741; completed *c.*1748; vacated for the new infirmary in Lauriston Place 1879; demolished 1884; fragments of the frontispiece survive on a lodge at Redford, gates in Drummond Street.

Sources NMRS: Photographs.
Maitland, *History of Edinburgh*, (1753), p.450.
James Grant, op. cit., vol.2, pp.298–302.
Hamish Mackinven, *Scottish Field*, January 1966.

SAUGHTON HOUSE WA; WA; RC 116, 117

Edinburgh Corstorphine Parish NT 205 713

James Watson (–1781); succeeded 1716; purchased Cammo 1741.

William Adam n.d., probably late 1730s.

Regularisation of existing 'L' plan house; not executed, burnt *c.*1920; subsequently demolished.

Sources McGibbon and Ross, op. cit., vol.5, pp.337–41.
G. Upton Selway, *A Midlothian Village*, (1890), pp.38–42.

SMEATON HOUSE See East Park.

SOMERVILLE HOUSE WA; WA; RC 37, 38

Edinburgh Liberton Parish NT 301 680

Usually known as The Drum.

James, 12th Lord Somerville; (1698–1765); succeeded 1715; m. (1) Anne Bayntun, 1724; returned to Scotland, 1726; m. (2) Frances Rotherham, 1736.

William Adam — *c.*1724.
New house; built 1725/6, decoration followed; existing house altered to form north pavilion, south pavilion not executed, upper floor redecorated, plaster by Thomas Clayton, 1740; private house.

Sources — SRO: GD18/4728, 9, etc, Clerk of Penicuik MSS.
McGibbon and Ross, op. cit., vol.2, p.557.
Country Life, 9 October 1915.
John Small, op. cit.

BRIDGE OF TAY — WA; WA; RC — 122

Perthshire, Aberfeldy; Parish of Weem and Dull — NN 851 493

There is a variant of this plate with figures, e.g. in the British Museum copy.

General Wade — Commander-in-Chief, North Britain, 1724–40.

William Adam — From 1730 mason to the Board of Ordnance; 1732.
New bridge; built 1733; 'Free Stone Bridge of 5 Arches over the River Tay 400 feet in length the middle arch 60 foot wide, the Starlings of Oak and the Piers and Land Breasts founded on 1200 piles shed with Iron'; still in use, carrying the main road.

Sources — NLS: MS 7187, General Wade's Letter and Order Book.
J. B. Salmond, *Wade in Scotland.*
William Taylor, *The Military Roads in Scotland,* (1976), p.56.
N. D. Mackay, *Aberfeldy,* (1954), p.62.

TAYMOUTH CASTLE — WA; WA; RC — 50, 51

Perthshire — Kenmore Parish — NN 784 467

John Campbell, 2nd Earl of Breadalbane (1662–1752); m. (1) Frances Cavendish; m. (2) Henrietta Villiers, 1695; representative peer 1736–52; 3rd Earl d.1782.

William Adam — ? 1720.
Regularisation of old castle and addition of hall, stair and pavilions; carried out 1737–42; various schemes proposed and work carried out for the 3rd Earl involving John Douglas, 1743–50, Roger Morris, 1747, and John Paterson, 1770; unexecuted proposals by Robert Mylne, 1789; scheme for remodelling by John Paterson, 1797, begun 1801, demolished 1805; now castle by Archibald and James Elliott, 1806–13; east wing by William Atkinson, 1818/19; Adam's west pavilion remodelled by James Gillespie Graham, 1838; now a school.

Sources — SRO: GD112/9/45, etc, Breadalbane MSS (extracts in NMRS).
Nat. Gal. of Scotland: Estate plan of 1720.
NMRS: Various drawings, views and other references.
NMRS: Alistair Rowan, typed notes on Taymouth Castle.
Alistair Rowan, *Country Life*, 8 and 15 October 1964.
Braco case depositions.

TINWALD HOUSE — WA; WA; RC — 152, 153

Dumfries-shire — Tinwald Parish — NY 017 803

Charles Erskine — (–); Lord of Session 1744; sold Tinwald to 3rd Duke of Queensberry 1759.

William Adam — 1737/8; advice from Sir John Clerk.
New house; built 1738–40; rainwater heads dated 1740; interior burnt 1948.

Sources — NLS: 5074/f.153 and 195, Erskine Murray MSS.
SRO: GD18/5008, Clerk of Penicuik MSS.
Scottish Georgian Society: Notes by John Gladstone, 1967.

TORRANCE HOUSE — WA; WA; RC — 139, 140

Lanarkshire — East Kilbride Parish — NS 655 526

This plate appears to have been engraved in Col Stewart's time, 1733–43.

Alexander Stuart — (–1733); m. Isabel Nisbet; succeeded by his son, Col. James Stuart (–1743).

William Adam — *c.*1740.
Regularisation of existing house of *c.*1605; pavilions apparently built *c.*1723, possibly not by Adam; not executed but alterations to existing house carried out *c.*1740; further alterations including baronial casing of pavilions, 1879; now offices.

Sources NLS: MS 8222/2; drawings, including set by Adam dated 1740.
David Ure, *History of Kilbride and Rutherglen*, (1793), p.150, ref. to removal of slates from Mains Castle, 'about 70 years ago' for 'some office houses at Torrance'. Also engraving showing wings with the old house.
McGibbon and Ross, op. cit., col.3, pp.231 and 232.

TULLIBARDINE WA; WA; RC 101–103

Perthshire Blackford Parish NN 910 139 (approx.)

James Murray (1690–1764); M.P. 1715–24; succeeded 1724; m. (1) Jane Frederick, 1726; Lord Privy Seal, 1733; K.T. 1734; m. (2) Jean Drummond, 1749.

William Adam n.d.; described as 'a new design'; (c.f. Design for a Person of Quality, plates 96 and 97).
New house, probably incorporating parts of the old castle; not executed; castle abandoned after 1745, finally demolished *c.*1830.

Sources BM: General Roy's Military Map, c. 1747 (copy in NMRS).
Thomas Hunter, op. cit., p.324.

WATSON'S HOSPITAL WA; WA; RC 151

Edinburgh Royal Infirmary, Lauriston Place (now) NT 255 730

George Watson, d.1723; left £12,000 to endow a hospital for sons and grandsons of merchants.

William Adam 1738.
New hospital; built 1738–41; twelve boys admitted 1741, over 60 by 1780; sold 1870 as site for new Royal Infirmary; parts of the Adam building incorporated and survive.

Sources James Grant, op. cit., pp.358–60.

YESTER HOUSE Smith, McGill and WA; WA; RC 25–30

East Lothian Yester Parish NT 544 672

John Hay, 2nd Marquess of Tweeddale (1645–1712); succeeded 1697; Charles Hay, 3rd Marquess (*c.*1665–1715); John Hay, 4th Marquess (–1762).

*James Smith and Alexander McGill; c.*1699, possibly with advice from Sir William Bruce.
New house; built; pavilions, etc, 1699–1710, main house *c.*1710–15, fitting out and decoration *c.*1720–*c.*1728, by Smith and McGill; platform roof, gabled attics and frontispiece, 1729–*c.*1730, decoration, etc, *c.*1734–*c.*1746, by William Adam; saloon, 1761, new frontispiece and carriage ramp, 1788–90 by Robert Adam; west pavilion removed, replanning and new porte-cochere, 1830 and 1838/9, by Robert Brown.

Sources NLS: 14551, Yester Papers: correspondence, accounts, etc.
Soane Museum, Adam drawings, vol.41, Nos.5–9, Robert Adam, 1789.
NMRS: Design by Robert Adam for new frontispiece.
John Dunbar, 'Yester House', in the *Transactions of the East Lothian Antiquarian and Field Naturalists' Society*, vol.13, 1972.
Alistair Rowan, *Country Life*, 9, 16 and 23 August 1873.

LIST of the PLANS, &c.

Plate 67. The West Front of Leslie House toward the Court.
68. The East Front of Leslie toward the Court.
69. The Plans of the First and Second Floors of Dun House.
70. The North Front of Dun House towards the Court. The South Front towards the Garden.
71. Ground Story of Inverary Castle, with the Fosse and Casements. Elevation of one of the Bridges across the Fosse.
72. Principal Floor of Inverary Castle. Plan of the Attic Story.
72. General Front of Belvidere towards the West.
73. Plan of the Principal Floor of Newhall House. Plan of the Lodging Story.
73. South Front of Inverary Castle.
74. East Front of Newhall House towards the Court.
74. Bridges at Inverary.
75. Plan of the First Floor and Lodging Story of Elphingston House.
76. Front of Elphingston House towards the East.
77. Plan of the Vestibule Floor of Craigdarroch. Plan of the Principal Floor.
78. The East Front of Craigdarroch towards the Court.
79. Plan of the Principal Floor and Lodging Story of Dryden House.
80. West Front of Dryden House towards the Court.
81. A Plan of the First Floor of Eastpark.
82. Front of Eastpark House towards the Court. West Front towards the Garden.
83. General Plan of the Ground Story of the House, Offices, &c. Courts of Blair Drummond, with the General Front.
83. Elevation of Gartmore House. Plan of the Principal Story.
84. Plan of the First, and of the Second Floor of Blair Drummond House.
85. Court Front of the Body of the House towards the East. Plan of the Lodging Story.
86. General Plan of the First, and of the Second Ground Floors of Craigiehall.
87. The General Front of Craigiehall House towards the East.
88. General Plan of the Ground Story, and of the Principal Floor of Ely House.
89. The West Front of Ely House towards the Coast.
90. Plan of the Principal Floor of Balveny House. Plan of the Lodging Story.
91. Plan of the Ground Story of Balveny House, with the Front towards the Court.
92. Plan of the First Story of Dunibirsle House. Plan of the Principal Floor up one pair of stairs.
93. South Front of Dunibirsle House. Plan of the Third Story.
94. General Front of Dunibirsle House towards the South. Plans of the Ground Floors of the Offices under the level of the Court.
94. Design of a House for John M'Culloch, Esq. of Barholm, in Galloway. Plan of the Attic Story. Principal Floor. Ground Story.
95. South Front of Lowmay (Aberdeen). Plan of the Lodging Story, of the Principal Floor, and of the Ground Story.
96. Plan of the Principal Floor, designed for a person of Quality. Plan of Mezzanine Story.
97. South Front of a Design, for a Person of Quality in Scotland, not yet built.
98. The South Front of Gray House towards the Court. General Plan of the First Floor.
99. The Elevation of Longfamacus House. Plan of the Principal Floor.

Plate 100. South Prospect of Taskie House towards the Court. Plan of the Lodging Floor. Plan of the Principal Floor.
101. The General Plan of the Ground Floor and Offices of Tulliebardin.
102. Plan of the Vestibule Floor, and of the Principal Floor of Tulliebardin.
103. The General Plan of a New Design, for His Grace the Duke of Athol, intended at Tulliebardin.
104. Plan of the Principal Floor, and Elevation of the Town-House of Dundee.
105. Ground Plan of Heriot's Hospital. Plan of the First Floor.
106. Elevation of the North Front of Heriot's Hospital.
107. Plan of the Ground Story, of the Second Story, and of the Third Story, of Gordon's Hospital, at Aberdeen.
107. Plan of the Principal Floor of Prestonhall House. Plan of the Ground Story. Plan of the Attic Story.
108. South Front of Gordon's Hospital, Aberdeen.
108. The General Front of Prestonhall House towards the South.
109. Plan of the First and Second Floor of a Royal Palace, invented by a Person of Quality.
110. One of the Fronts of the Royal Palace, designed for the preceeding Plans.
111. A General Plan of the Ground Floor of Callie House and Offices, as designed for Alex. Murray, Esq.
112. General Plan of the First Floor of Callie House and Offices.
113. The General Front of a New Design, made for Alex. Murray, Esq. at Callie
114. General Plan of the Ground Floor of Niddrie House. Plan of the Principal Story.
115. The General Front of Niddrie towards the Court. Plan of the Mezzanine Story. Plan of the Attic Story.
116. General Plan of the Ground Floor of Saughton House. Plan of the First Floor. Plan of the Attic Story.
117. East Front of Saughton House towards the Court.
118. Plan of the Principal Floor above the Vaults of Broomland House. Plan of the Lodging Story.
119. The East Front of Broomland House.
120. Plan and Front of a Temple designed at the End of the Bowling-Green of Castle Kennedy.
121. Elevation of Hamilton-Hall House. Attic Story. Principal Floor. Ground Story.
121. Section of the Temple at Castle Kennedy.
122. The South Prospect. Plan of the Piers and Causeway of the Bridge of Tay, in the Highlands of Scotland.
123. Plan and Elevation of a Temple, designed for the Right Honourable the Countess of Eglinton, to be built in the centre of a Belvidere, at Eglinton.
123. Lord Alemore's Villa at Hawkhill, near Edinburgh. East Front. West Front. Principal Floor. Ground Floor.
124. General Front of a House intended for a Person of Quality. Plan of the Attic Story. Plan of the Principal Floor. Plan of the Ground Floor.
125. General Front of Cumbernauld House towards the Court. The General Plan of the Ground Story. Of the House and Offices.
126. Plan of the First Floor of Cumbernauld House. Plan of the Second Floor.
127. Plan of the Principal Floor of Balgregan. Plan of the Ground Floor.
128. The Front of Balgregan House towards the Court. Plan of the Lodging Story.
129. General Plan of the House and Offices of Panmure.
130. Plan of the First Floor of Panmure House. Plan of the Principal Floor. Plan of the Roof Story.

Plate 131. General Front of Panmure House towards the West.
132. General Front of Rose-Hall House towards the North. General Plan of the First Floor of the House, and Offices.
133. Plan of the Second Story of the House, and of the Lodging Pavilion of Rose-Hall. Plan of the Library above the Roof.
134. Section of Rose-Hall, with the Front of the two Pavilions towards the Country.
135. Principal Floor of Douglas Castle. Plan of the One Pair of Stairs Story.
135. General Front, and Plan of a House and Offices, as designed for His Grace the Duke of Montrose.
136. West Front of Douglas Castle. Elevation of the End. East Front.
136. Plan of the First Floor of the House, designed for His Grace the Duke of Montrose. Plan of the Lodging Story.
137. General Front of Newbaith House and Offices. Plan of the Principal Floor.
138. North Front of Newbaith House towards the Court.
139. A General Plan of the Orphan's Hospital, Edinburgh. Plan of the Mezzanine, or Half Story.
139. General Plan of the Principal Floor of Torrance House. General Plan of the Ground Story. Plan of the Lodging Story.
140. The General Front, designed for an Orphan's Hospital at Edinburgh.
140. The North Front of Torrance House towards the Court.
141. The South Front of Cammo House towards thè Court. Plan of the Attic Story. General Plan of the First Floor.
142. The Court Front of Harden House. Plan of the Attic Story. Plan of the First Floor. Plan of the Cellar Story.
143. General Plan of the Ground Floor of Keith-Hall House.

Plate 144. General Plan of the Principal Floor of Keith-Hall House.
145. The South Front of Keith-Hall House towards the Court.
146. General Plan of the Ground Floor of Duff House.
147. General Plan of the First Floor of Duff House.
148. The General Front of Duff House towards the Court. Plan of the Principal Floor. Plan of the Attic Story.
149. Plan of the Ground Floor, of the Second Story, of the Third Story, and of the Attic Story, of the Royal Infirmary of Edinburgh.
150. The North Front of the Royal Infirmary, facing the City of Edinburgh.
151. The North Front of Watson's Hospital. Plan of the Lodging Story. Of the Principal Floor. Of the Ground Story.
152. General Plan of the Ground Story, and of the First Floor of Tindwall House.
153. The West Front of Tindwall House towards the Court. Plan of the Attic Story.
154. The North Front of Belhaven House towards the Court. Plans of the Lodging Story, of the Principal Floor, and of the Attic Story.
155. A Plan of the New Library built for the University of Glasgow. Plan of the Gallery Story.
156. The North Front of the Principal Entrance of the College Library of Glasgow. East Front towards the Garden.
157. Section of the College Library of Glasgow.
158. The South Front of Lawers House towards the Court. Plan of the Principal Floor. Plan of the Grouud Story.
159. Section of the Saloon of Lawers House.
160. General Front toward the North of the Dogs Kennel at Hamilton, situated at the head of the South Avenue, a Mile distant from, and facing the Palace.

The following PLANS, drawn by the late William Adam, Esq. *Architect,* were engraved at his Expence by the most eminent Artists of the time, with a View to Publication. A few complete Sets having come into the Publisher's hands, he now respectfully offers them to the Public.

No 57, South Bridge, Edinburgh.

VITRUVIUS SCOTICUS

[NOTE: Blank pages have been inserted throughout in order to present double-page spreads on facing pages.]

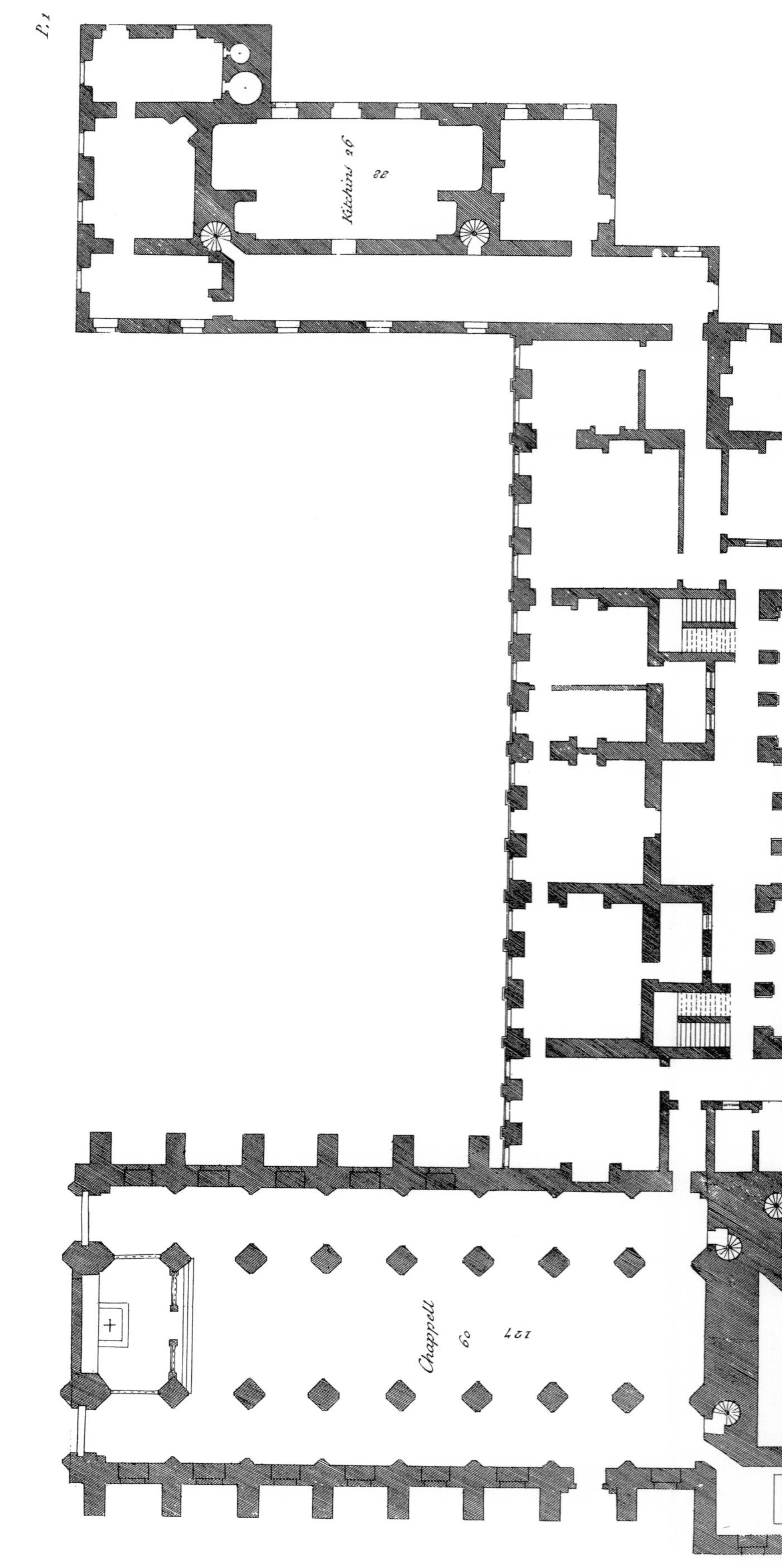
Kitchins 26
88
Chappell
60
124

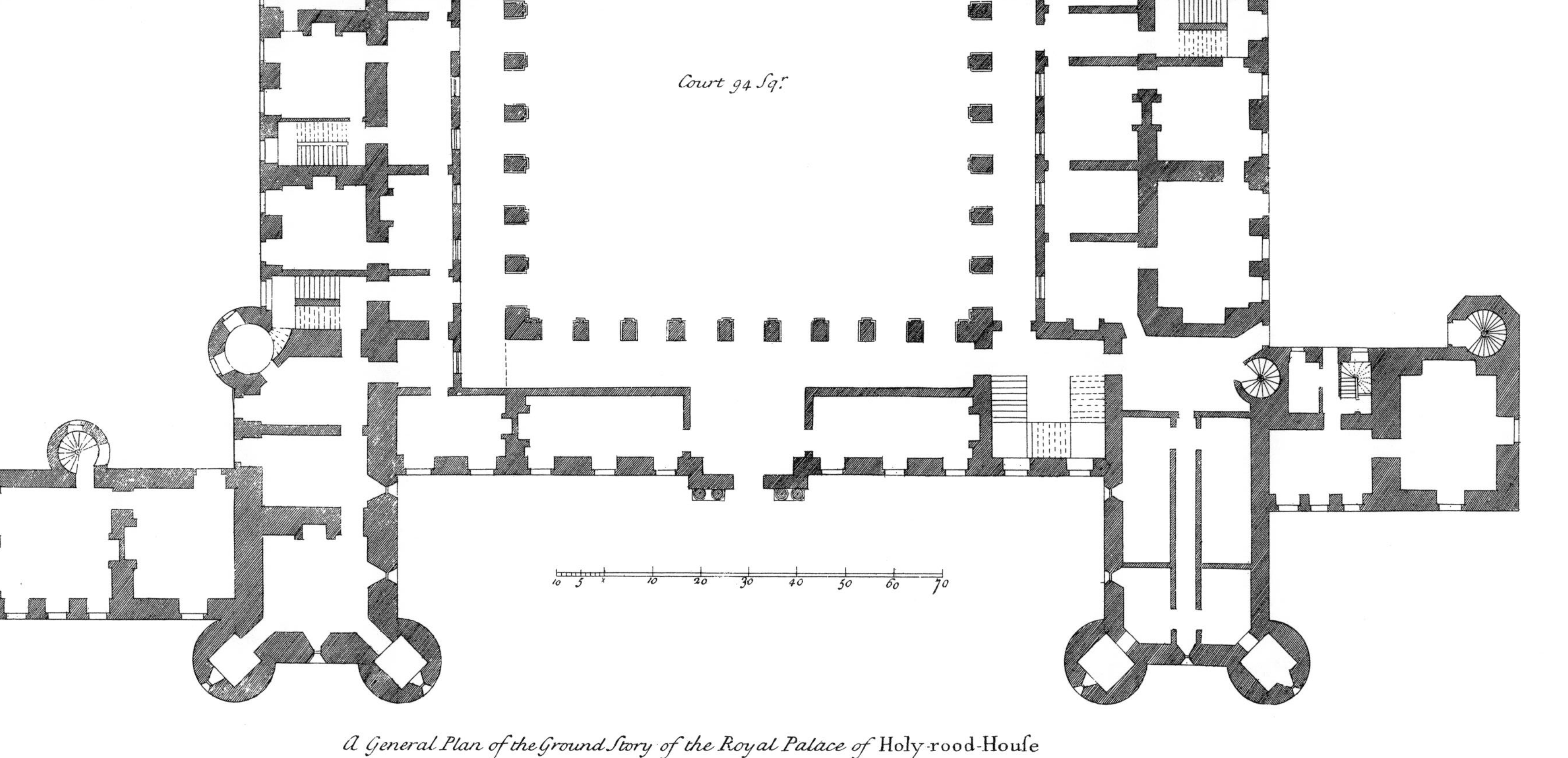

A General Plan of the Ground Story of the Royal Palace of Holy-rood-House
Design'd by S.r Will.m Bruce.

Gul. Adam delin.

R. Cooper sculp.

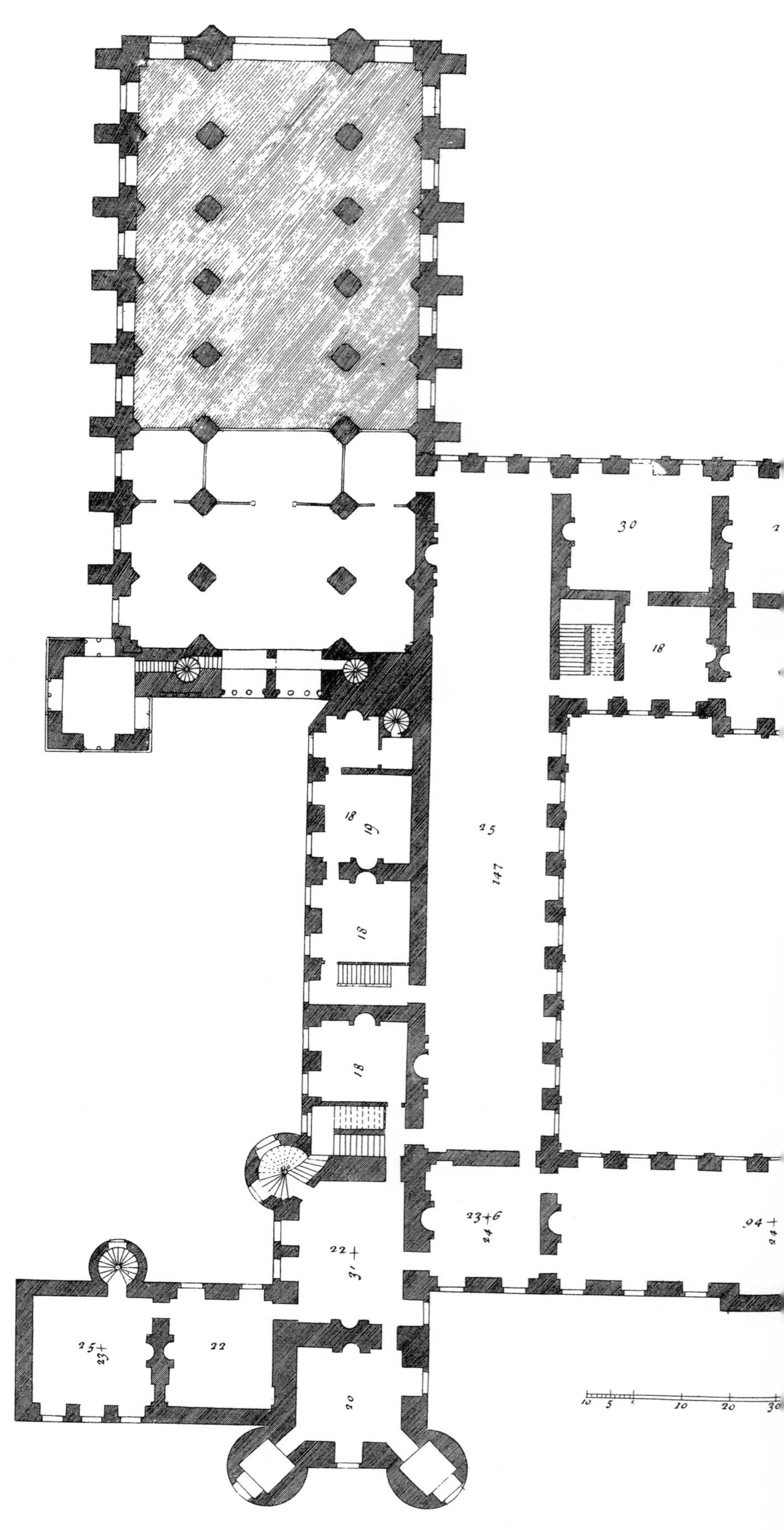

Gul: Adam delin.

A General Plan of the Principal Story of the Roy
Design'd by Sr. Will

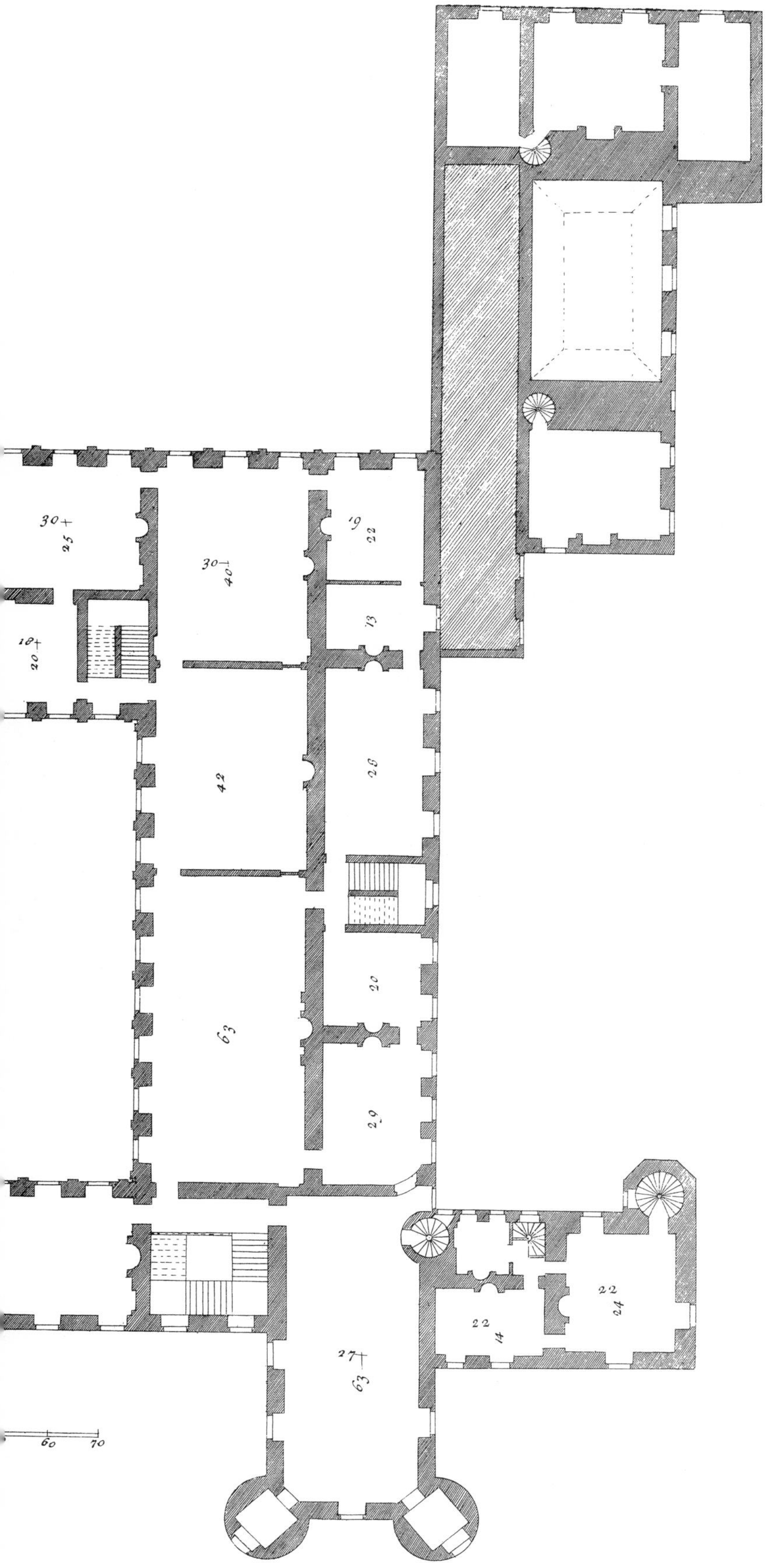

of Holy-rood-House

R. Cooper Sculp.

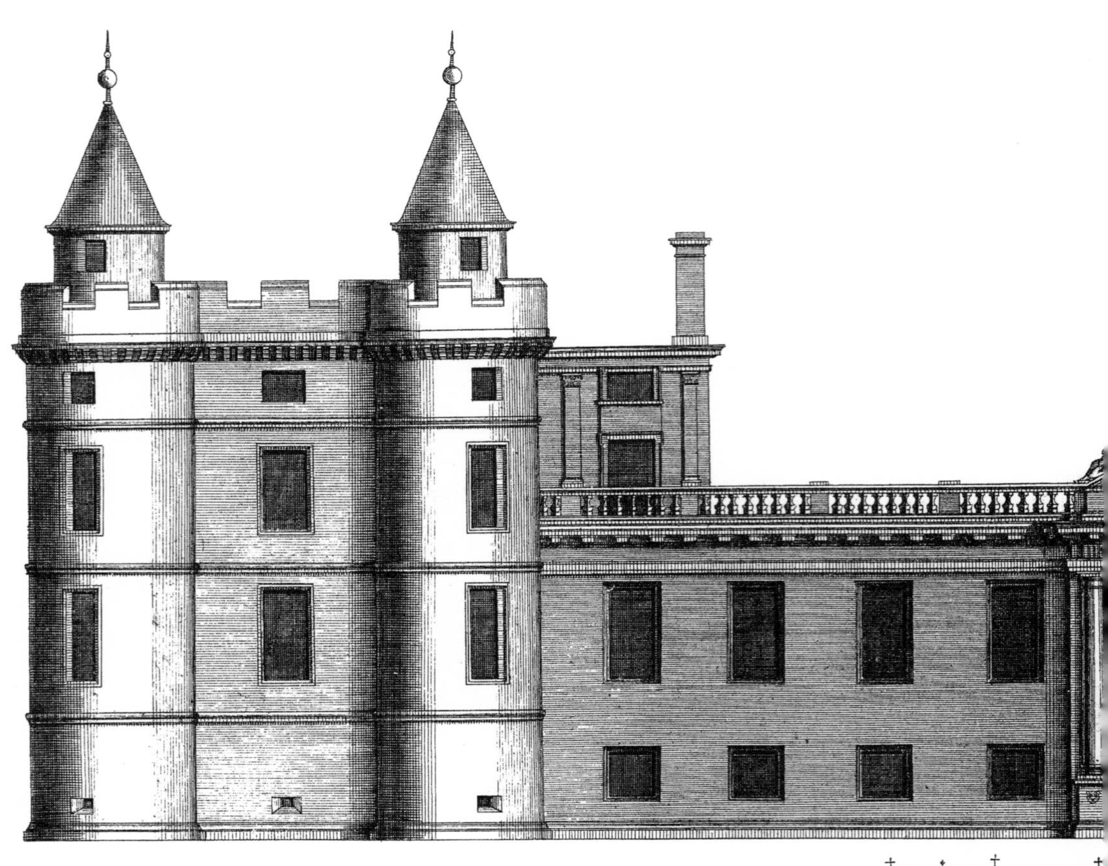

The West Front of the Royal Palace of Holy-rood House toward the great Court, with the Pla
Prince of Wales Duke of Cornwal, Earl of Chester, High Steward of

S.r W.m Bruce Arch.t
Gul: Adam delin

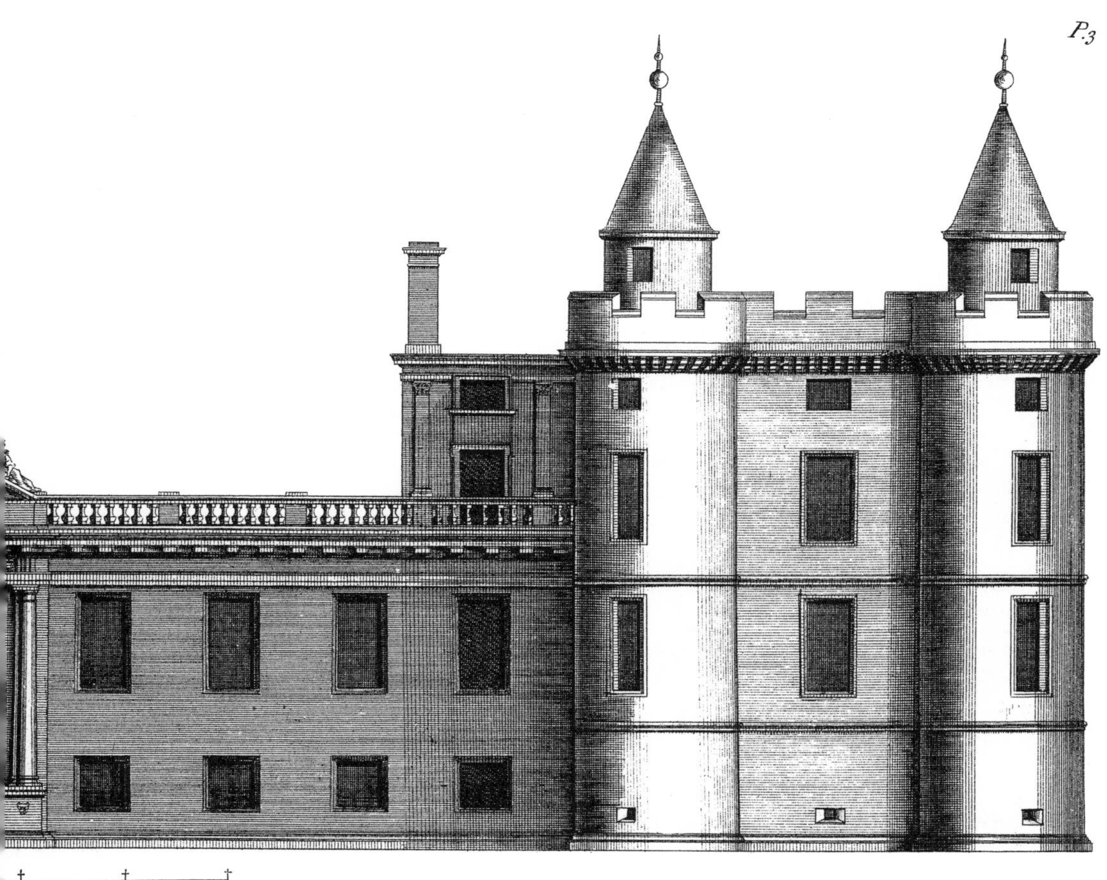

...ronts of this Royal Palace, Is most humbly Inscrib'd To His Royal Highness FREDERICK
...of Edinburgh & Knight of the most Noble Order of the Garter &c.

R: Cooper Sculp.

The East Front of the Royal Palace of Holy-rood-House *toward the Pa*

Gul. Adam delin.

Forth As design'd & directed by Sr. Willm. Bruce.

R. Cooper sculp.

Wyck Delin!

Inside of the CHAP

p. 5

...AL of Holyroodhouse

P. Mazell Sculp.

Section of the Royal Palace of Holy-rood-House *from Nor*

Gul. Adam delin.

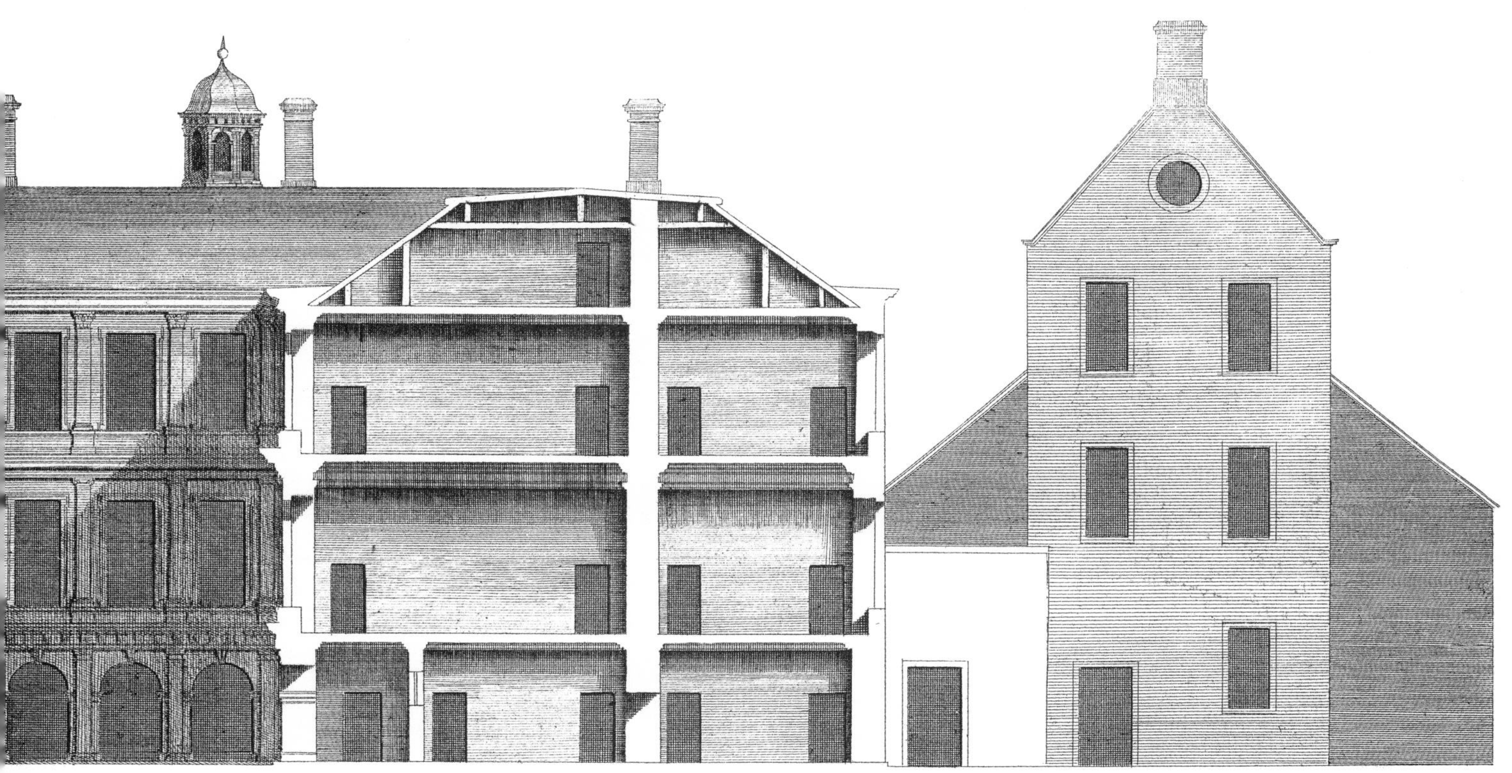

design'd & directed by S.r William Bruce.

R. Cooper sculp.

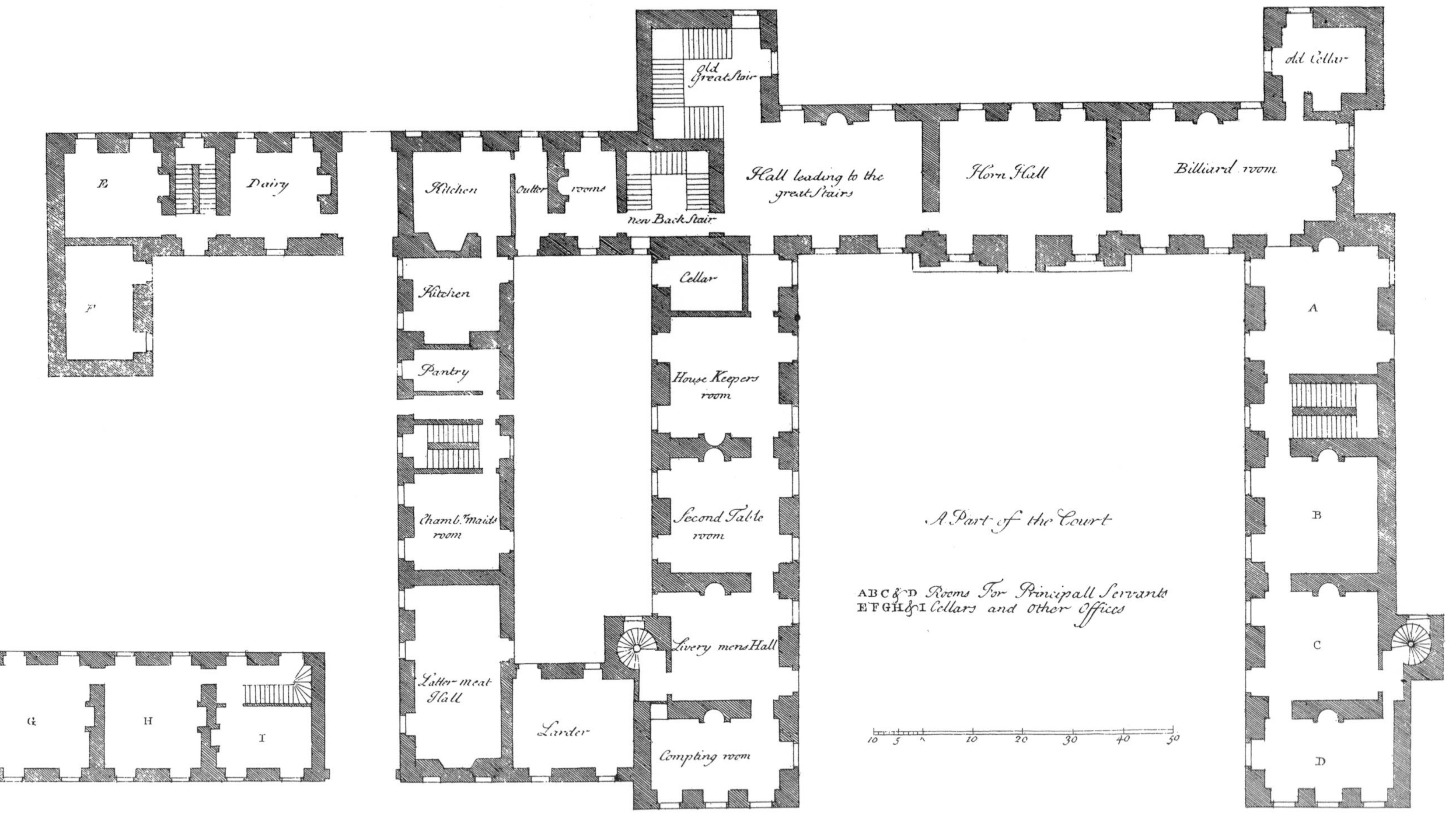

The ground Plan of Hamilton House and Offices as they now are

Gal Adair Delin

R. Cooper Sculp

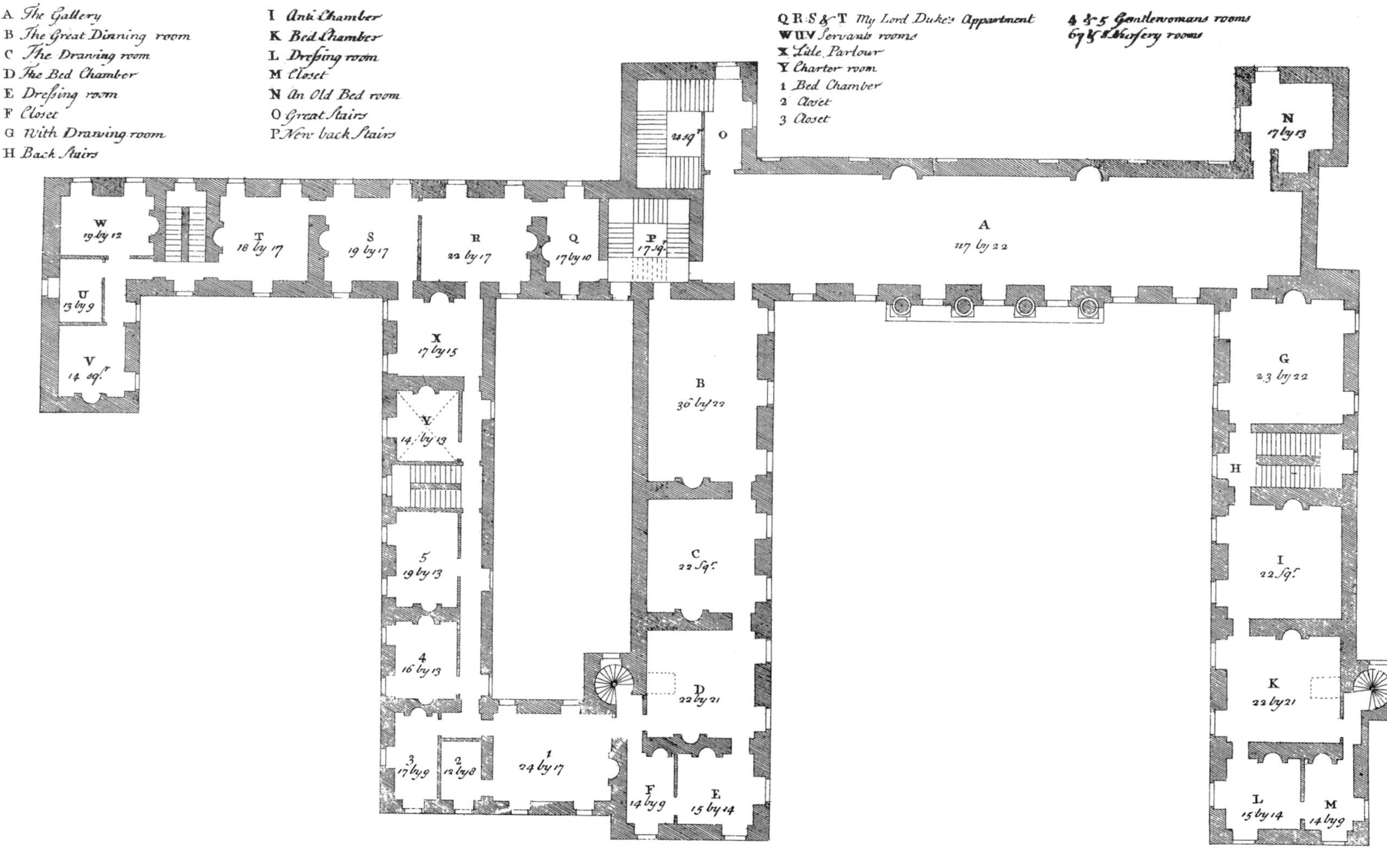

Plan of the Principall Floor of Hamilton House up one pair of Stairs
The Seat of his Grace The Duke of Hamilton Brandon &c.

Gul. Adam Delin R: Cooper Sculp

The Court Front of Hamilton The Seat of his Grace the Duke of Hamilton & Brandon &c. in the County of Clydsdale

Ja. Smith Arch.t
Gul. Adam delin.

R. Cooper sculp.

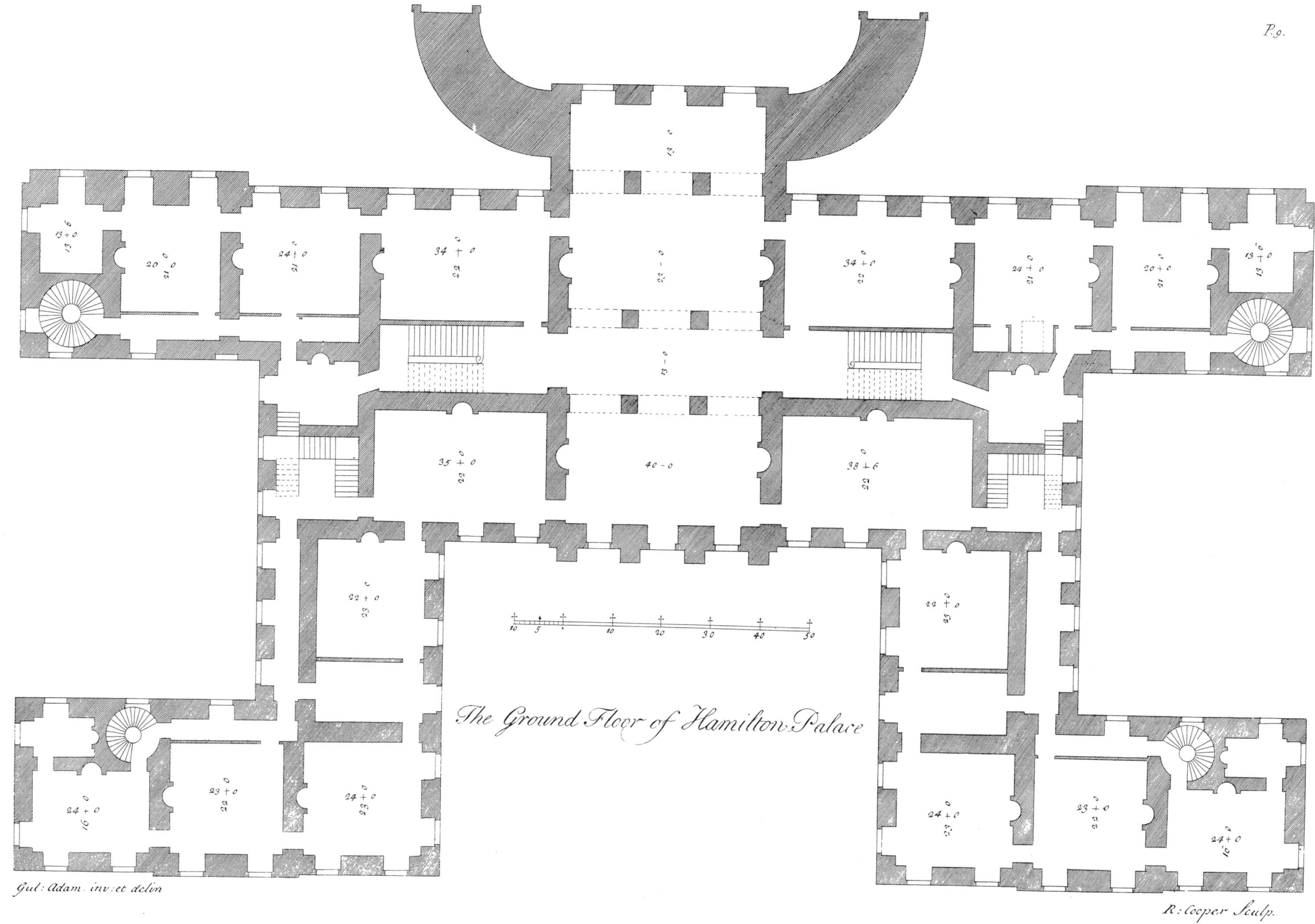
The Ground Floor of Hamilton Palace
10 5 10 20 30 40 50
Gul: Adam. inv: et delin
R: Cooper Sculp.

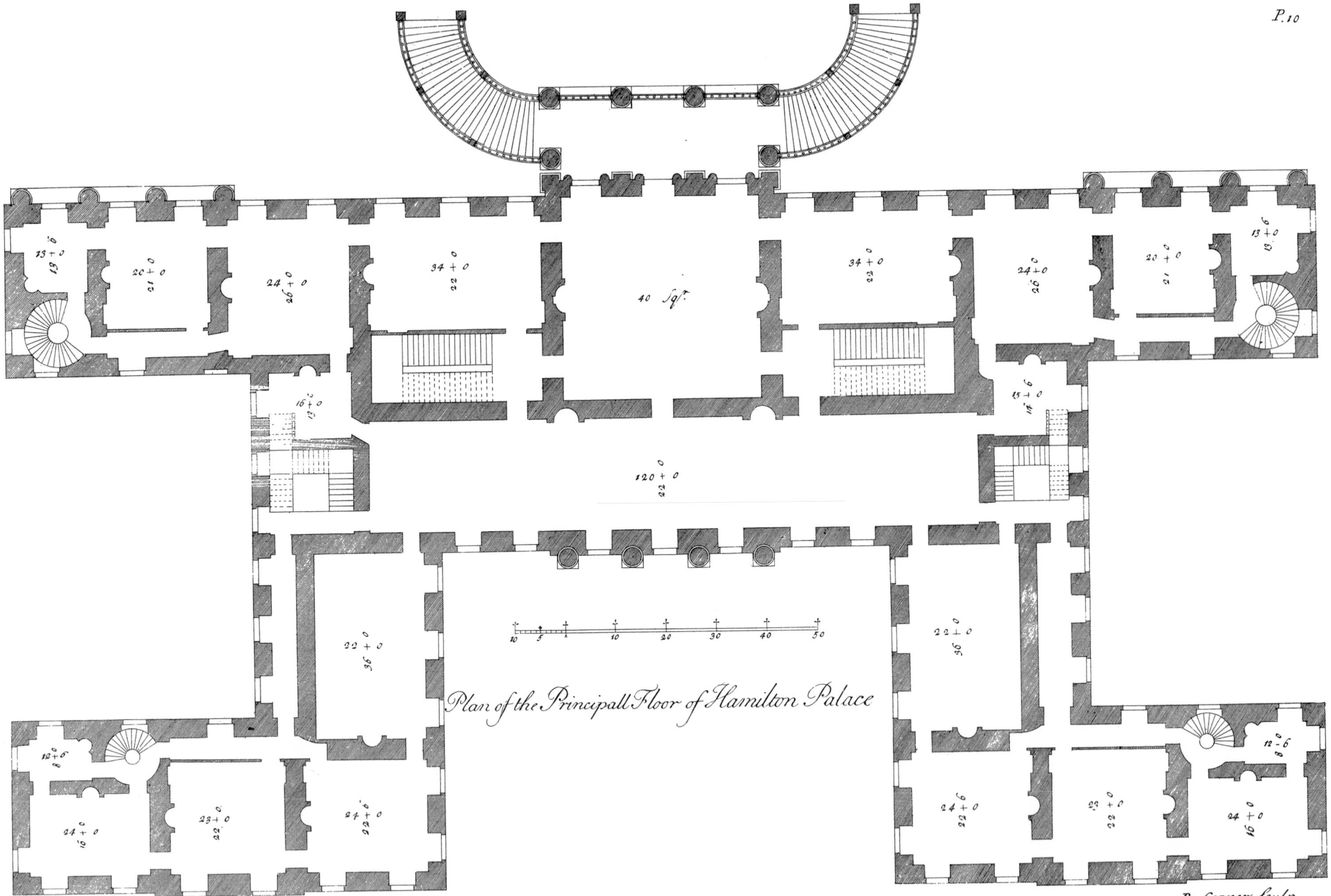

Plan of the Principall Floor of Hamilton Palace

10 5 0 10 20 30 40 50

Gul: Adam inv: et delin

R: Cooper Sculp.

The North Front of

The South Front of Hamiltone House
Brandon in

Gul: Adam inv: et. delin

n House toward the Gardens

urt the Seat of his Grace the Duke of Hamilton &
f Clydsdale Extends 260 feet

R: Cooper Sculp.

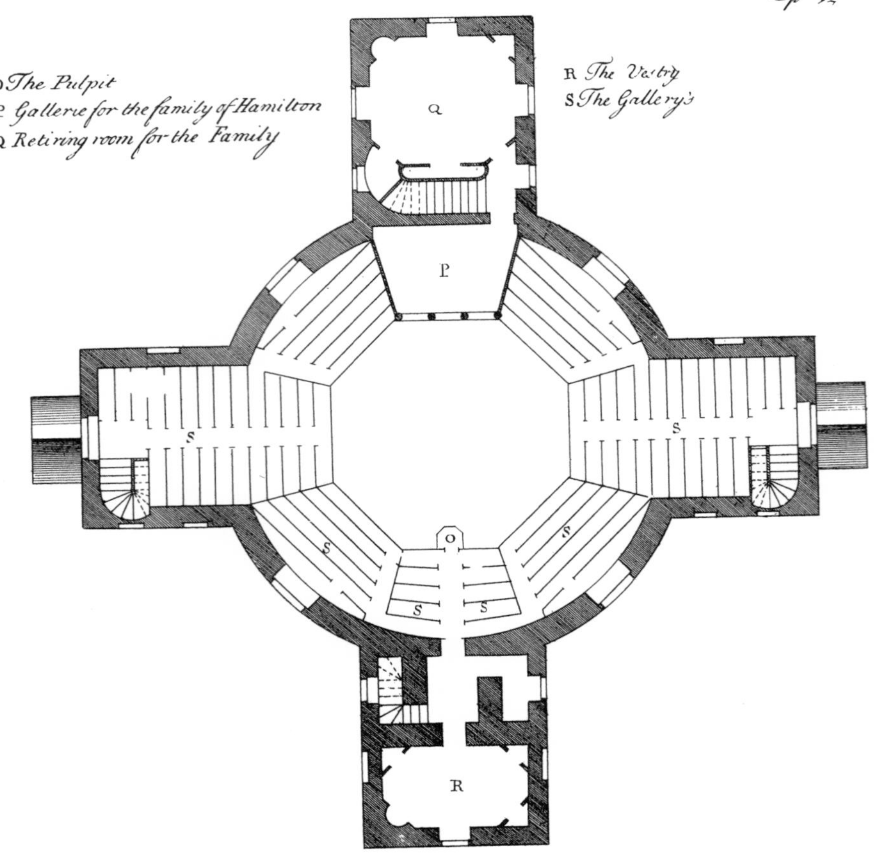

Plan of the Gallery Story

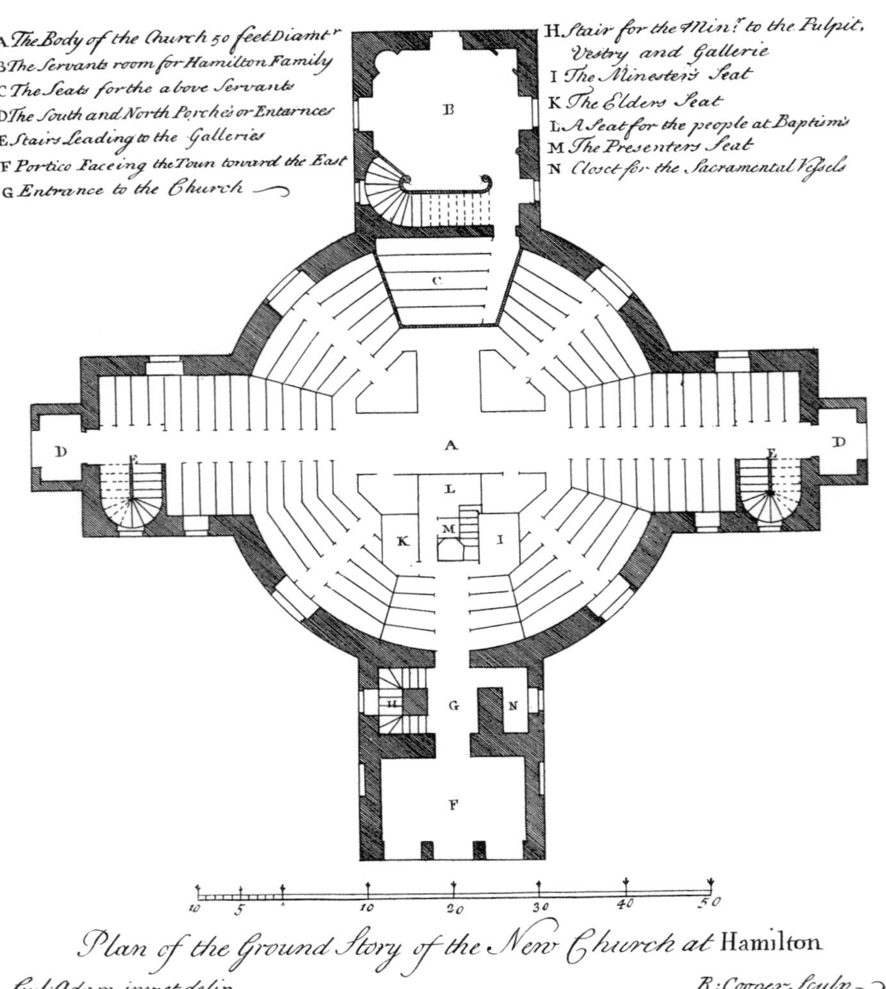

Plan of the Ground Story of the New Church at Hamilton

Gul: Adam inv: et delin

R: Cooper Sculp

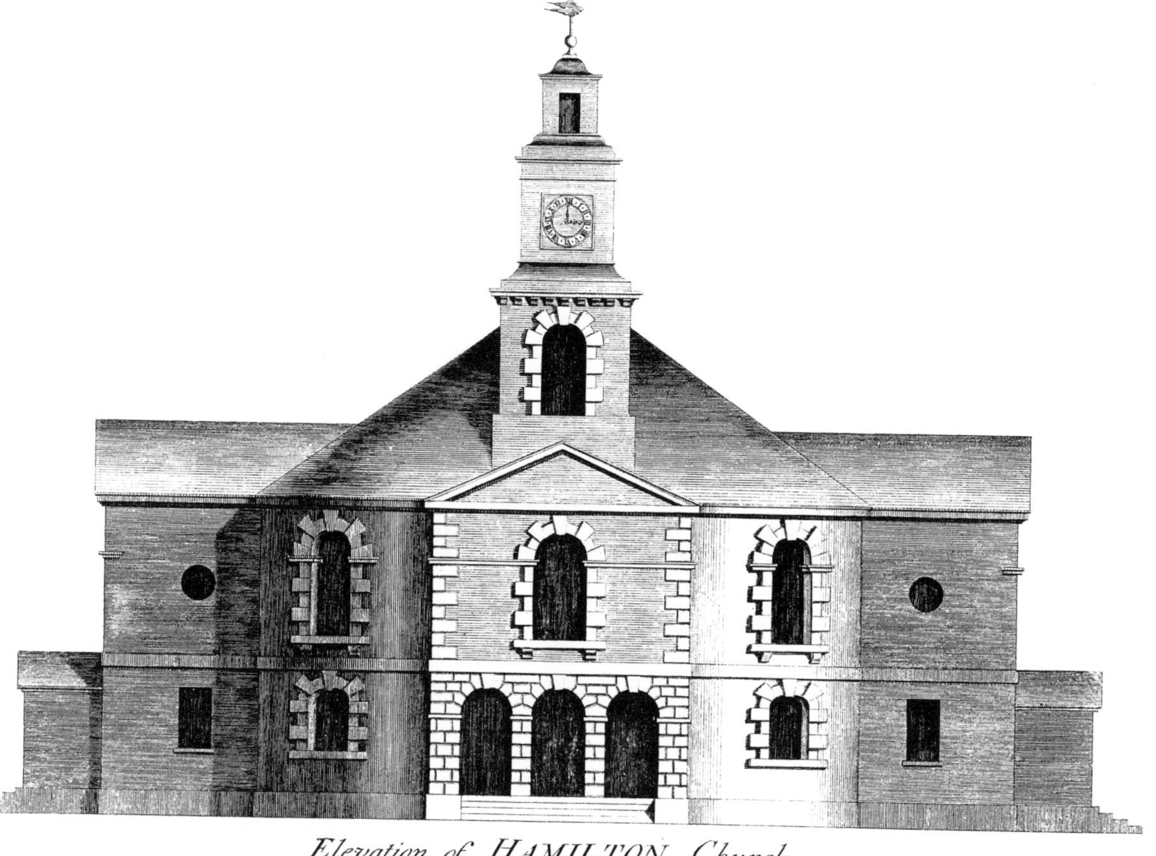

Elevation of HAMILTON Church

Gul. Adam Inv.t & Delin.t

A. Bell Sculp.t

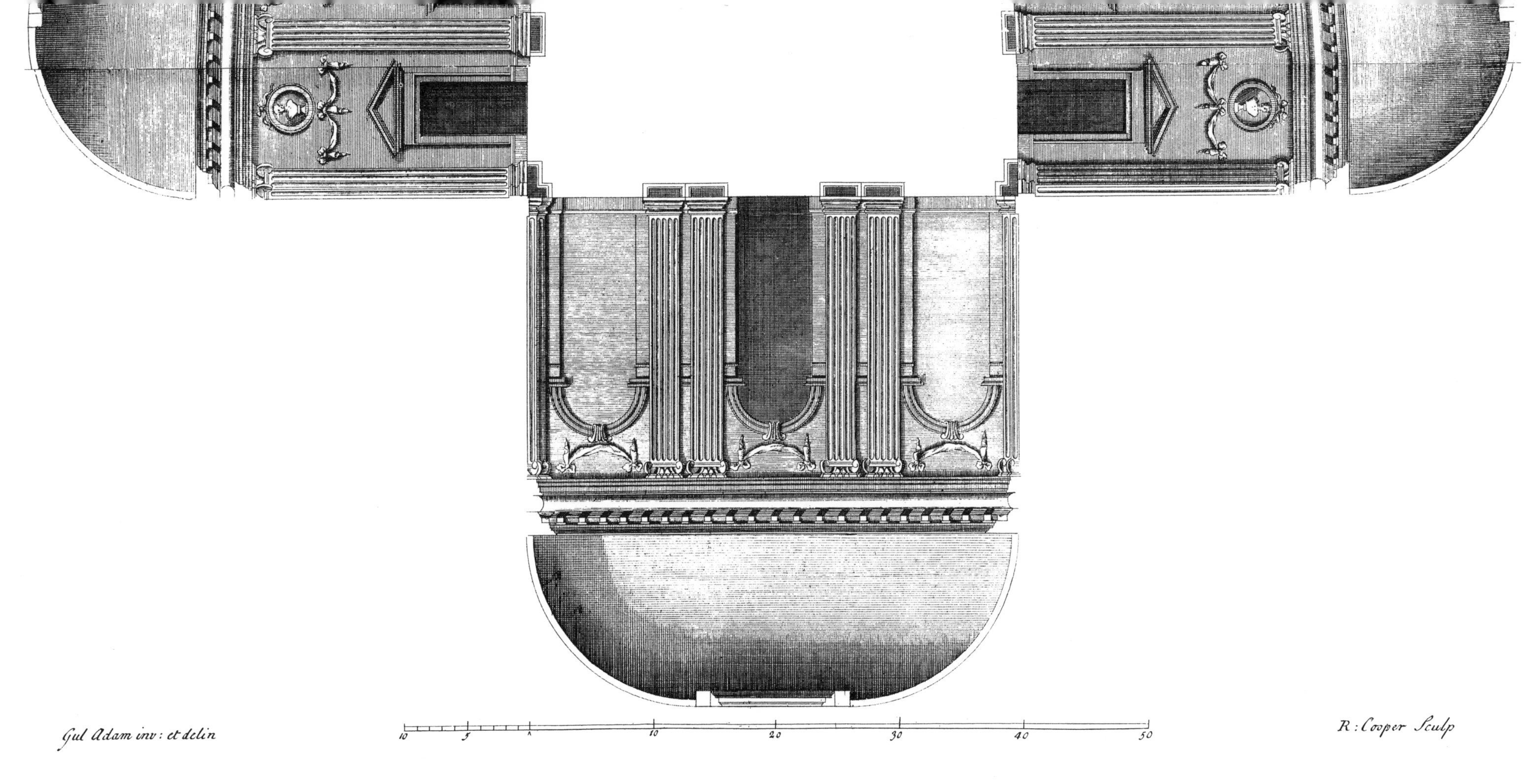

Gul Adam inv: et delin

R: Cooper Sculp

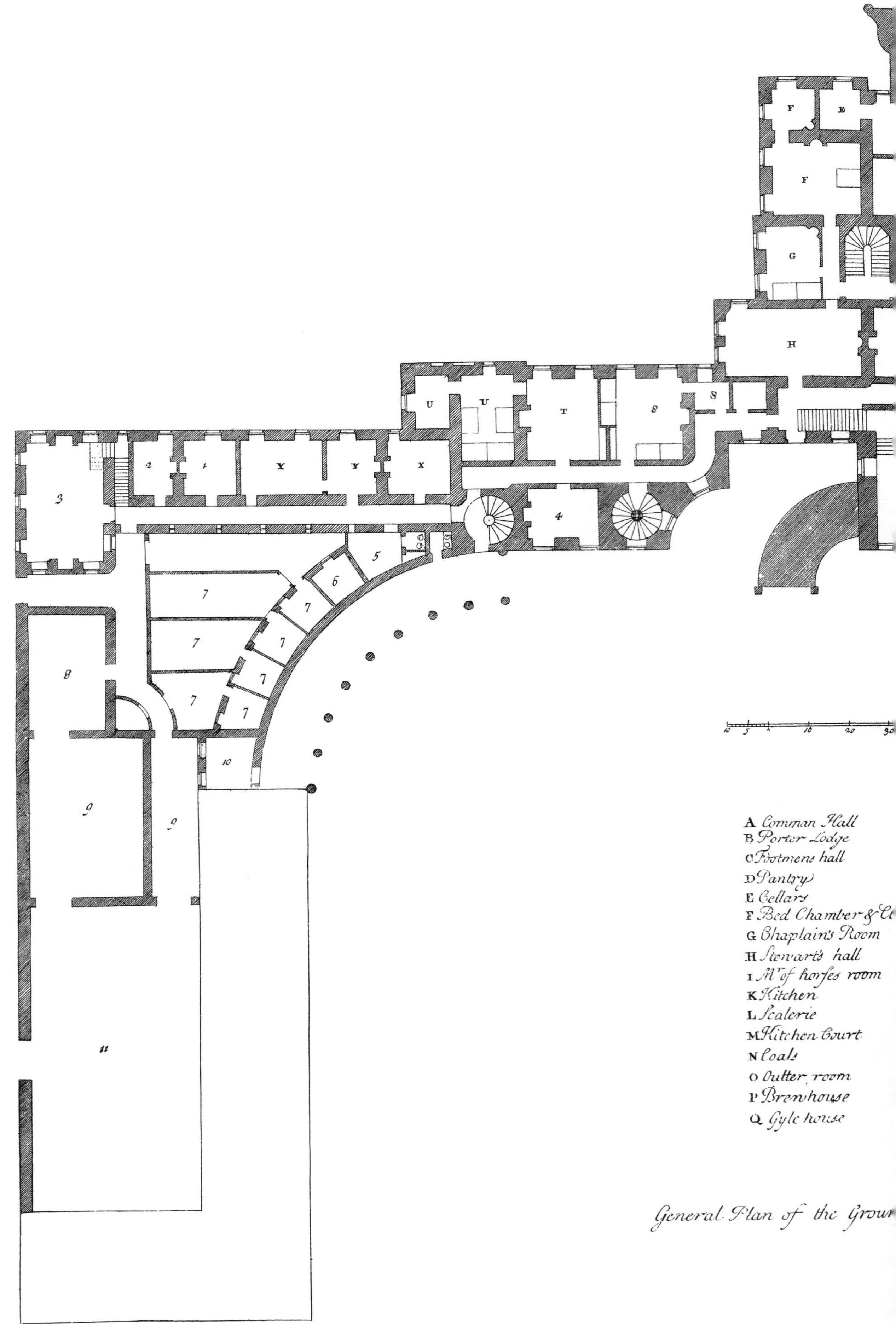

Gul: Adam inv: Delin

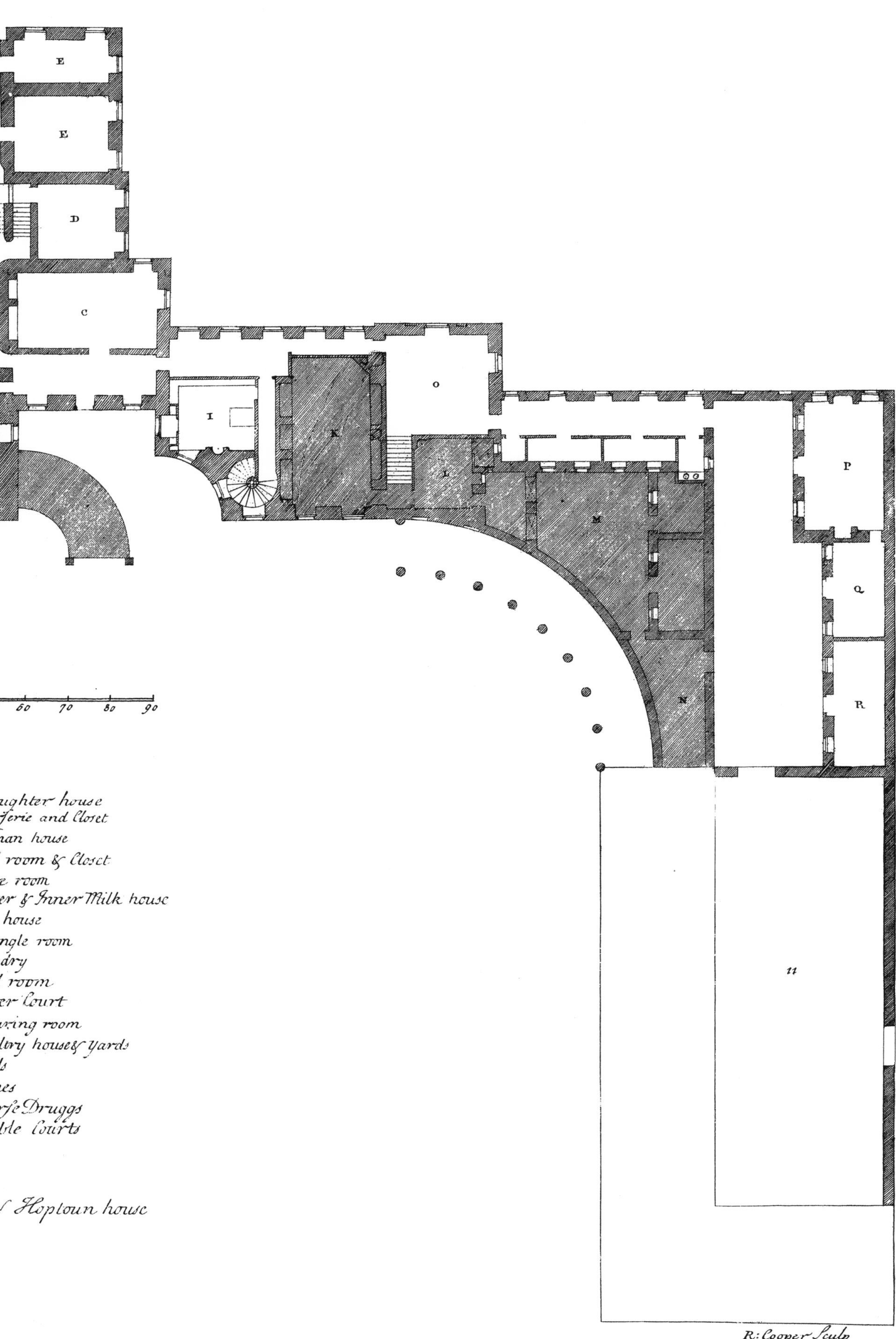

R: Cooper Sculp

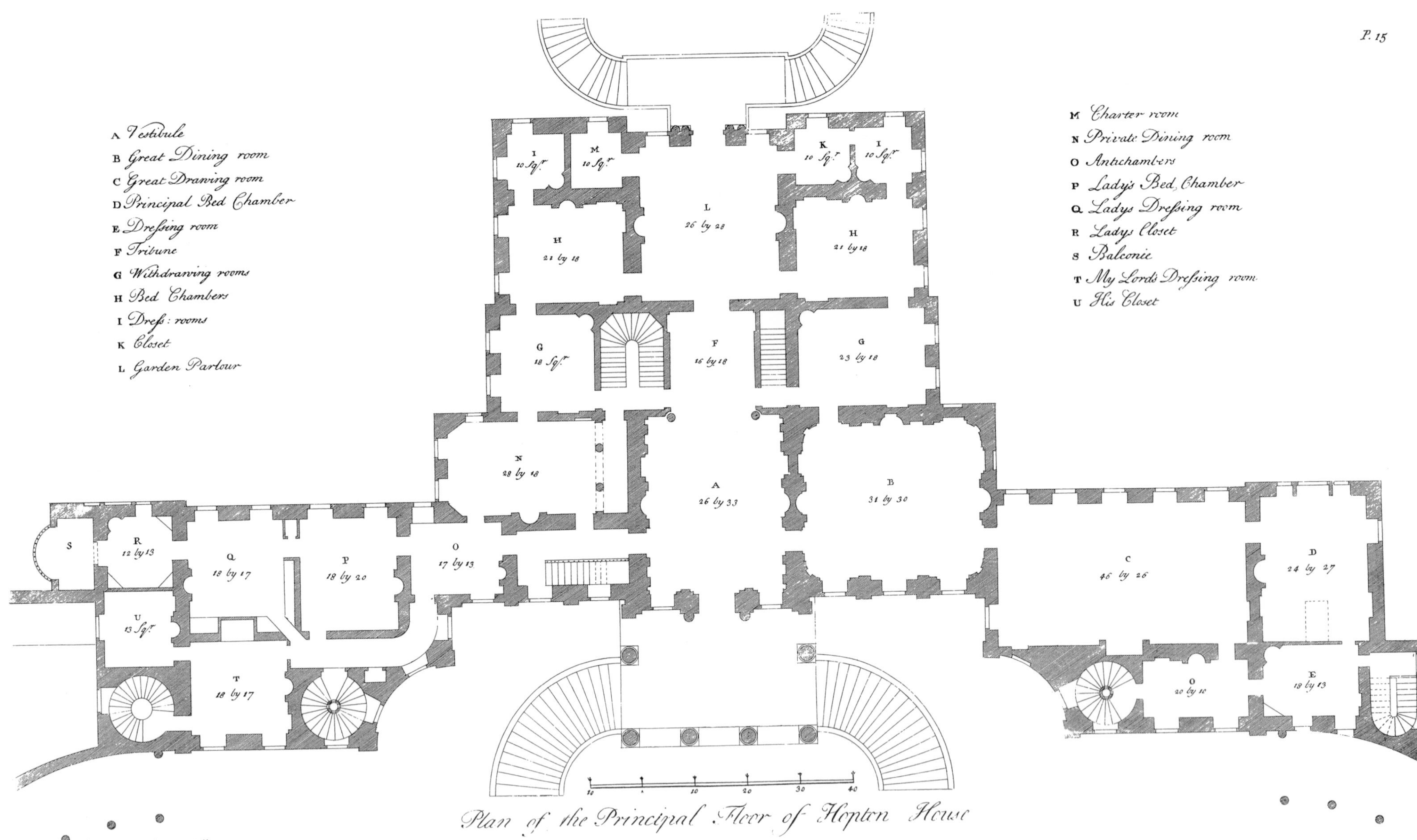

Plan of the Principal Floor of Hopton House

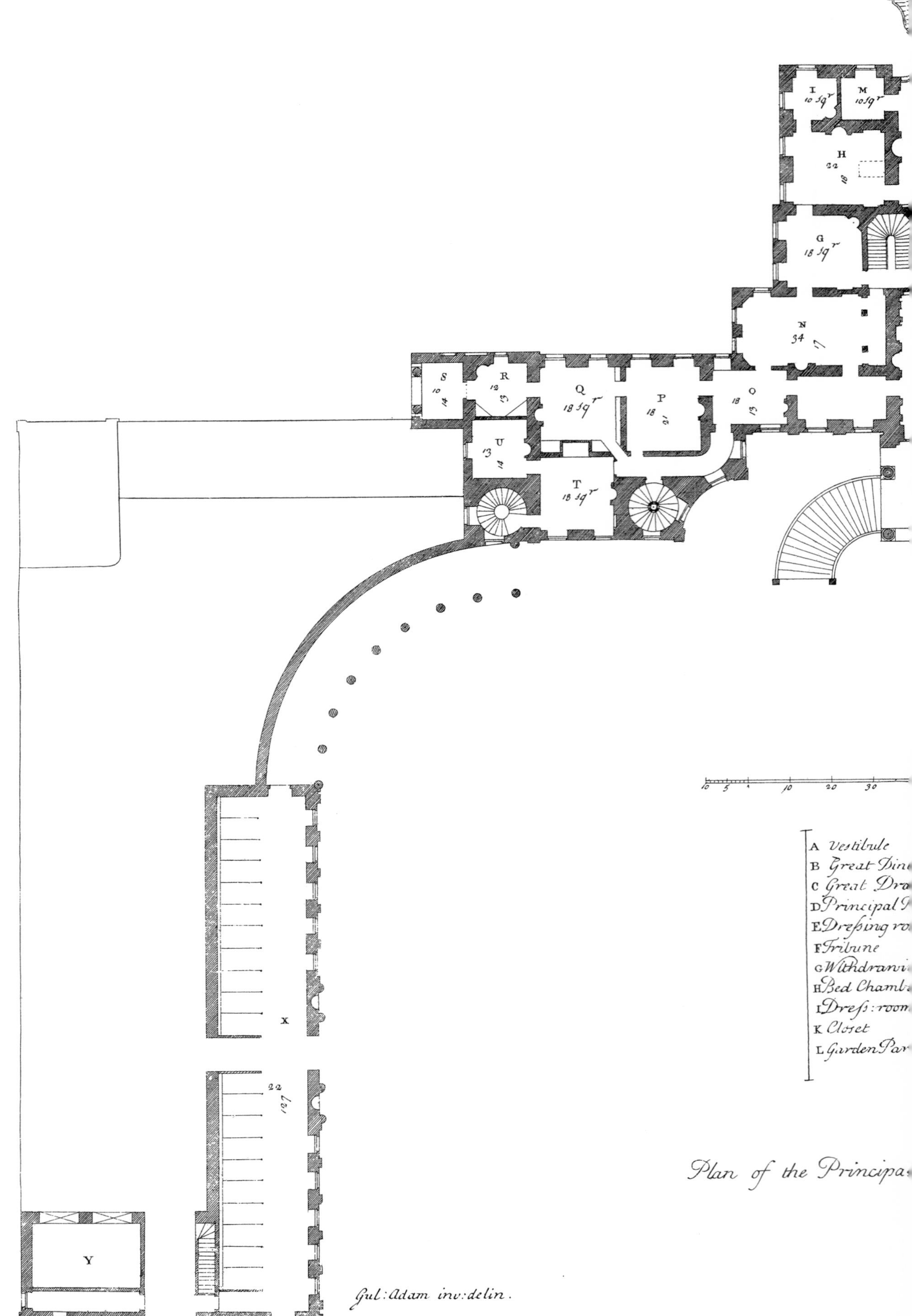
I
10 Sq^r
M
10 Sq^r
H
22
18
G
18 Sq^r
N
34
17
S
10
14
R
12
13
Q
18 Sq^r
P
18
21
O
18
13
U
13
14
T
18 Sq^r
X
22
127
Y
10 5 10 20 30
A Vestibule
B Great Din
C Great Dra
D Principal
E Dressing ro
F Tribune
G Withdrawi
H Bed Chamb
I Dress: room
K Closet
L Garden Par
Plan of the Principa
Gul: Adam inv: delin.

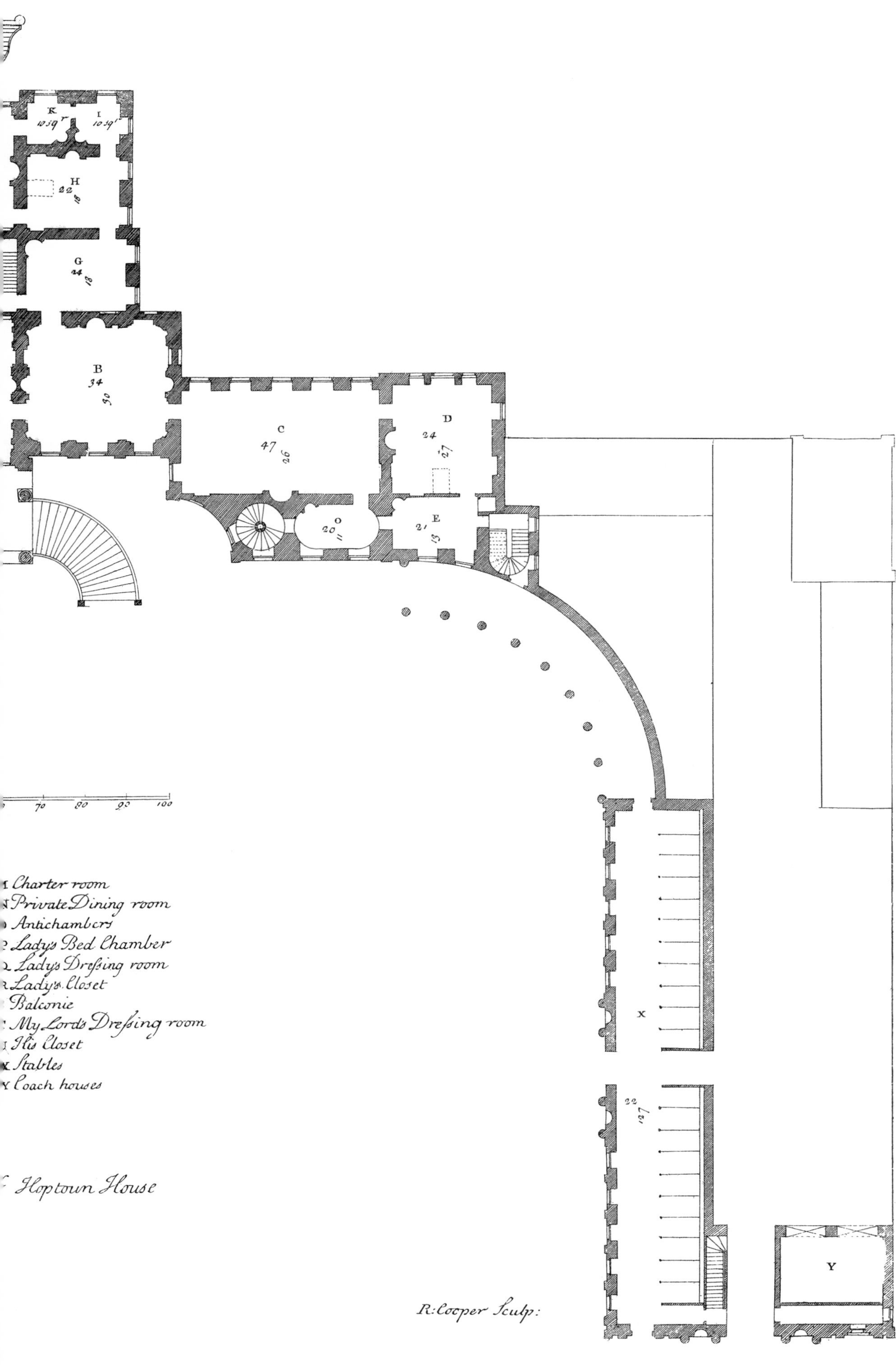

K
I
H
G
B
C
D
O
E
X
Y
Charter room
Private Dining room
Antichambers
Lady's Bed Chamber
Lady's Drefsing room
Lady's Closet
Balconie
My Lord's Drefsing room
His Closet
X Stables
Y Coach houses
Hoptoun House
R:Cooper Sculp:

The East Front of Hopton

Gull: Adam inv: et delin.

-rd the Court

R. Cooper sculp

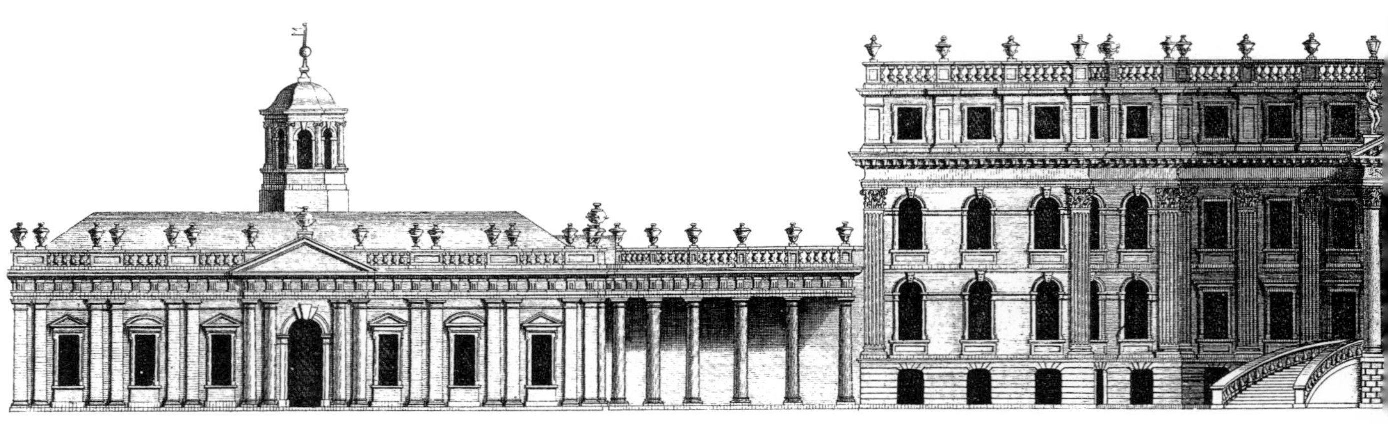

The Generall Front of Hopton House *toward the* Court *The Sea*

Gul.: Adam inv: et delin

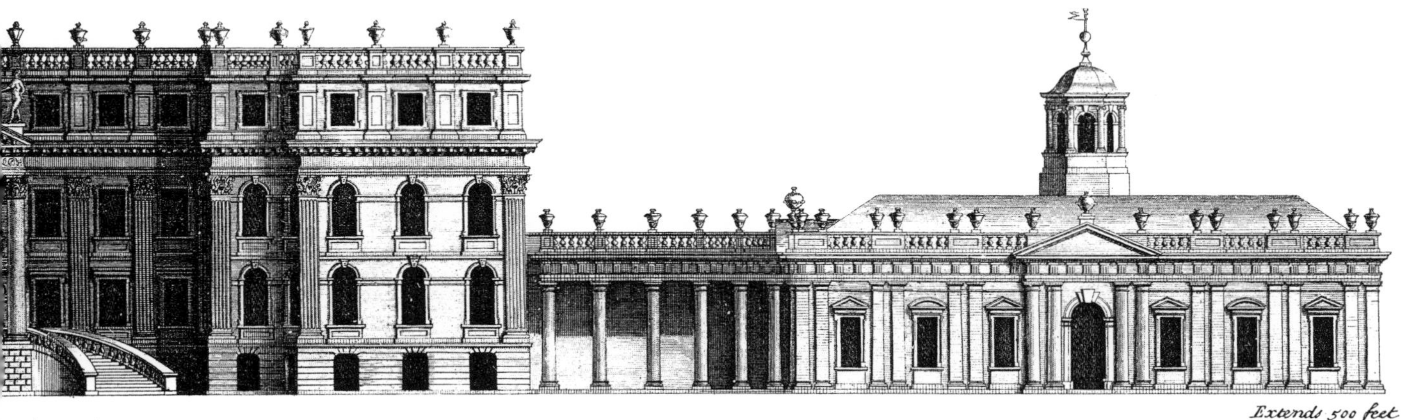

ht Honourable the Earl of Hopton *in the County of* LINLITHGOW

R: Cooper Sculp

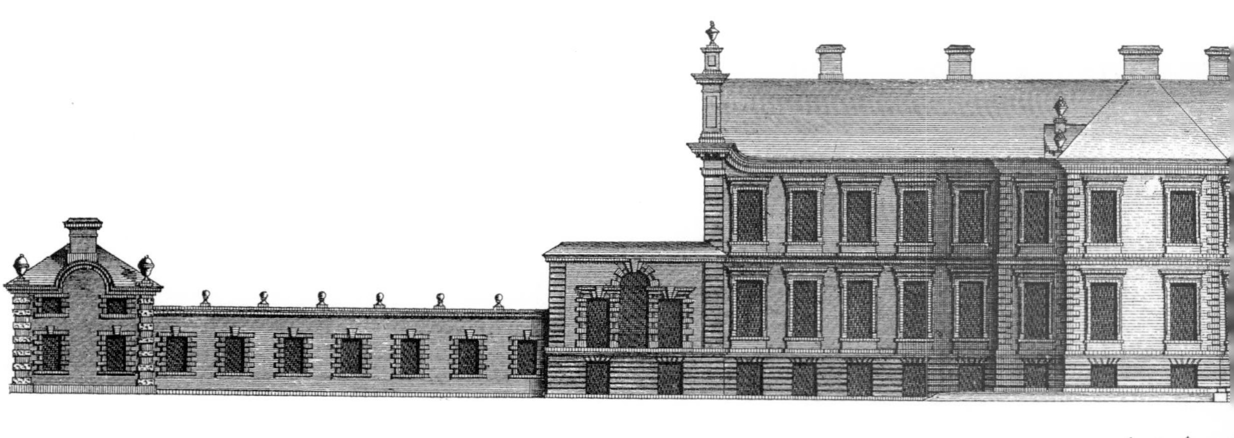

The General Front of

Gul: Adam inv: et delin

-use toward the Gardens

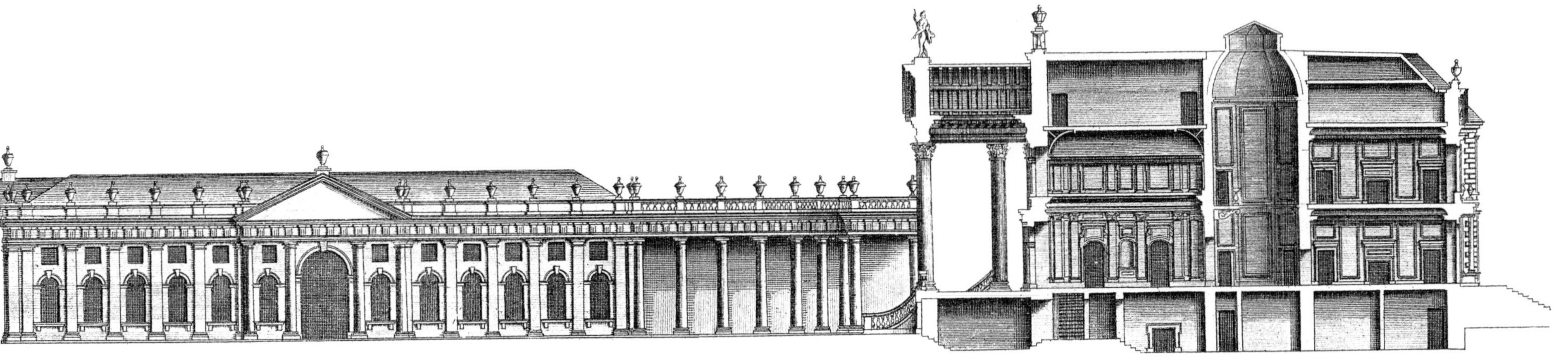

Front of one of the Large Pavillions towards the Court

A Section of Hopton House in the midle from East to West

Gull. Adam inv. et delin.

R. Cooper Sculp.

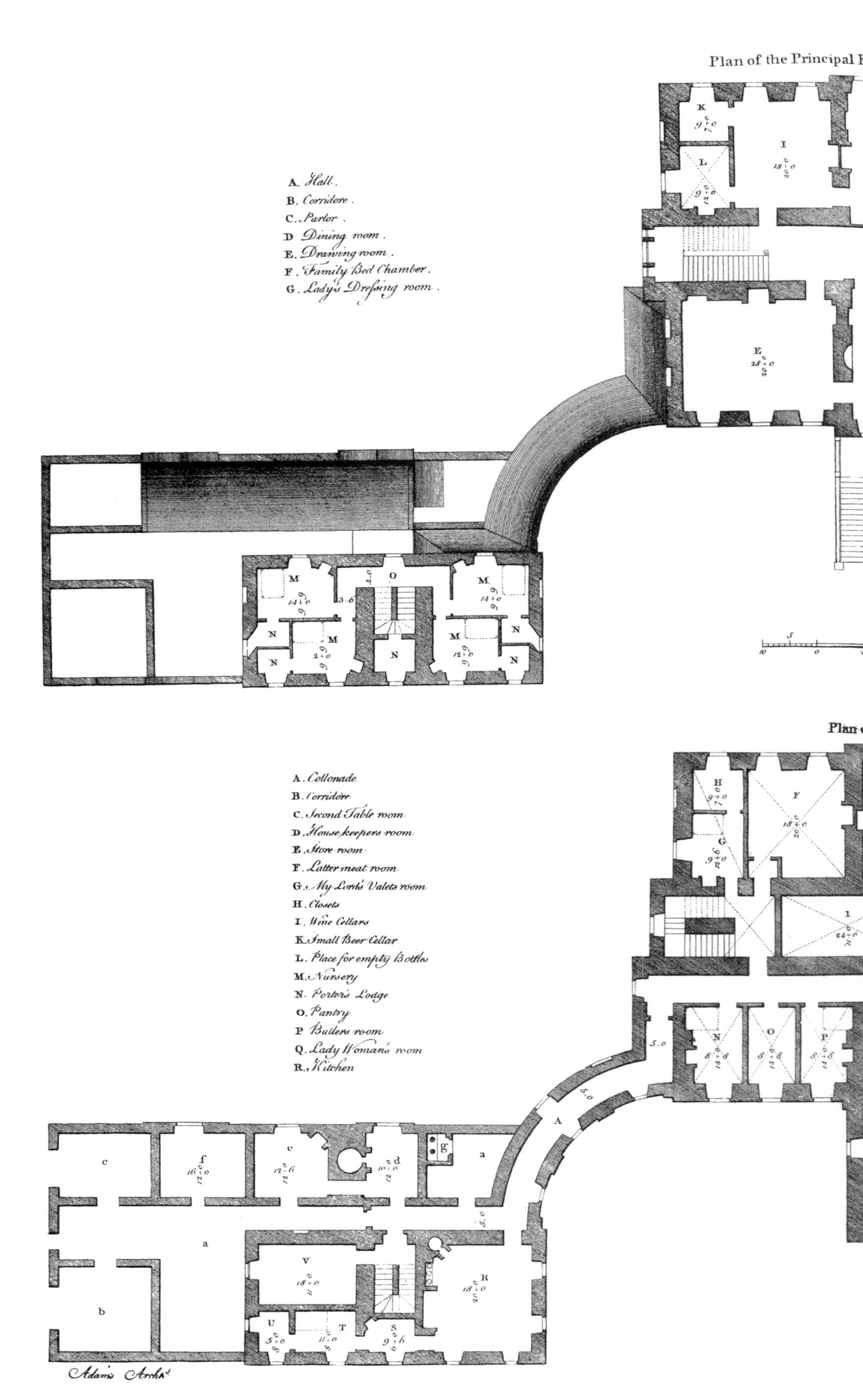
Plan of the Principal Flo
A. Hall.
B. Corridore.
C. Parlor.
D Dining room.
E. Drawing room.
F. Family Bed Chamber.
G. Lady's Dressing room.
Plan of t
A. Collonade
B. Corridore
C. Second Table room
D. House keepers room
E. Store room
F. Latter meat room
G. My Lord's Valets room
H. Closets
I. Wine Cellars
K. Small Beer Cellar
L. Place for empty Bottles
M. Nursery
N. Porter's Lodge
O. Pantry
P Butlers room
Q. Lady Woman's room
R. Kitchen
Adams Archt.

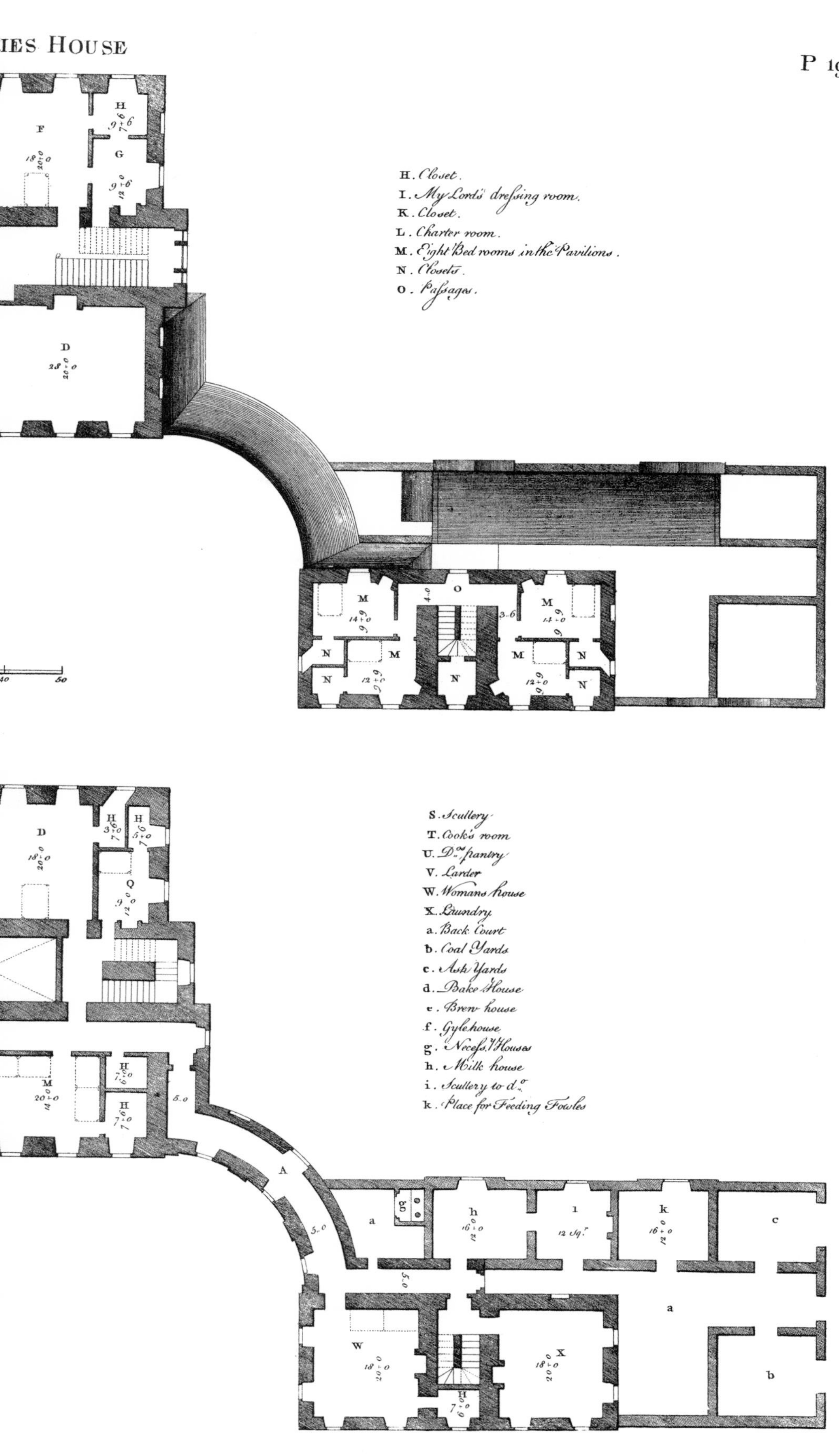
H. Closet.
I. My Lords dressing room.
K. Closet.
L. Charter room.
M. Eight Bed rooms in the Pavilions.
N. Closets.
O. Passages.
S. Scullery.
T. Cook's room
U. D.º pantry
V. Larder
W. Womans house
X. Laundry
a. Back Court
b. Coal Yards
c. Ash Yards
d. Bake House
e. Brew house
f. Gylehouse
g. Necess.y Houses
h. Milk house
i. Scullery to d.º
k. Place for Feeding Fowles

South Front of DUMFRIES HOUSE The Seat of The EARL of DUMFRIES & STAIR

North Front

Adams Archt. P. Mazell Sculpt.

P. 20

A Section of the Hall of Hopton House

Gul Adam inv. et. delin

R. Cooper Sculp.

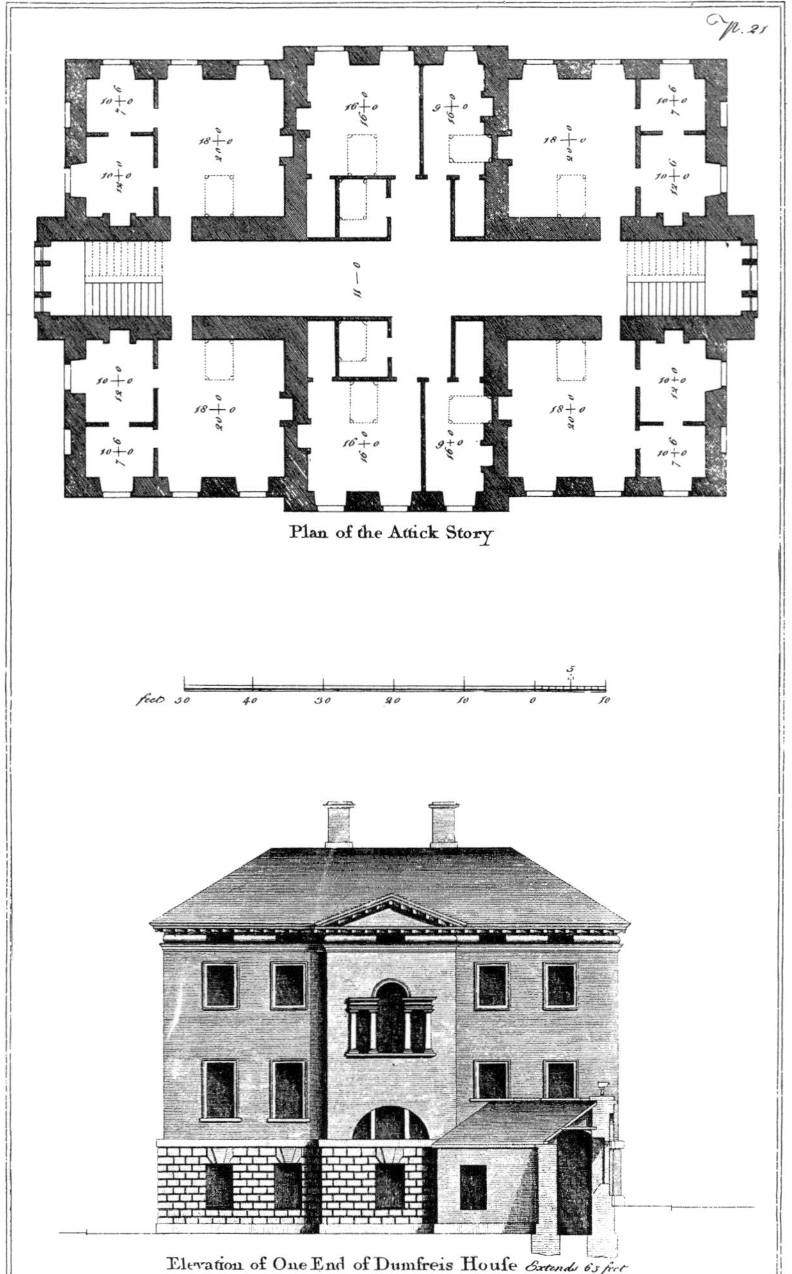
Pl. 21
Plan of the Attick Story
feet 50 40 30 20 10 0 10
Elevation of One End of Dumfreis House Extends 63 feet
W. Fraser Sculp.

P. 21

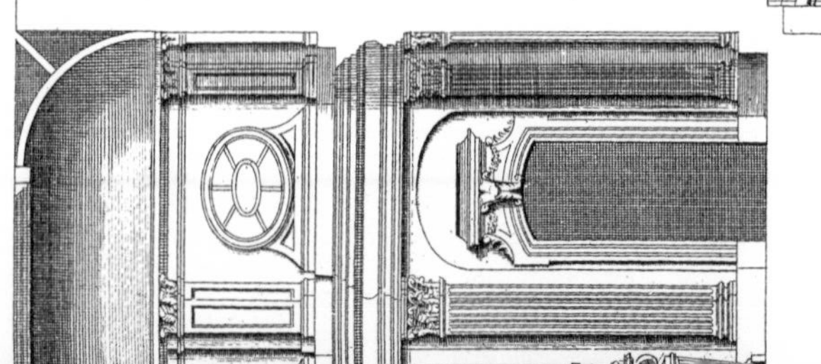

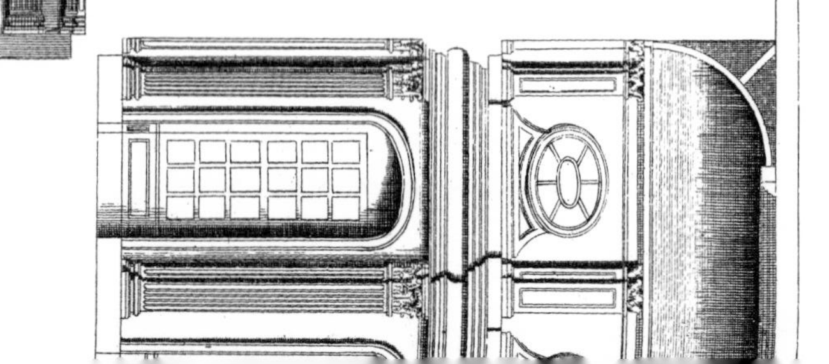

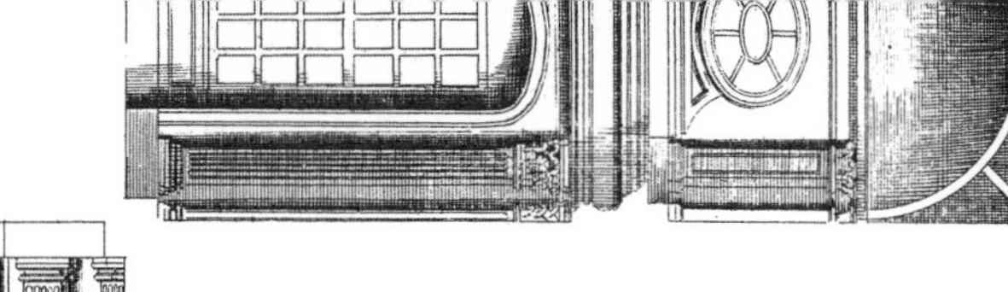

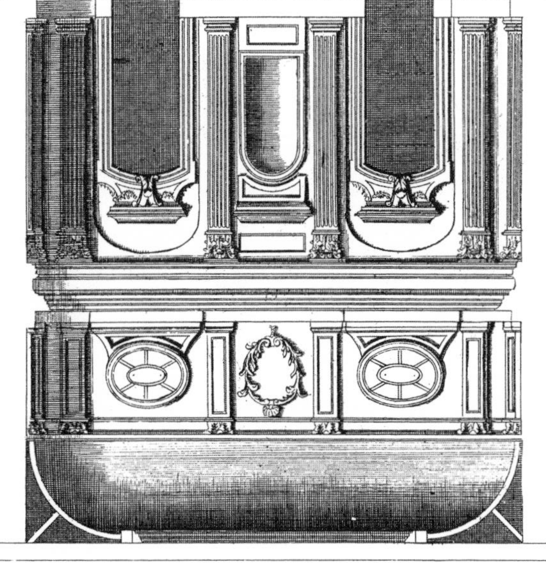

A Section of the Sallon of Hopton House

Gul. Adam inv. et delin.

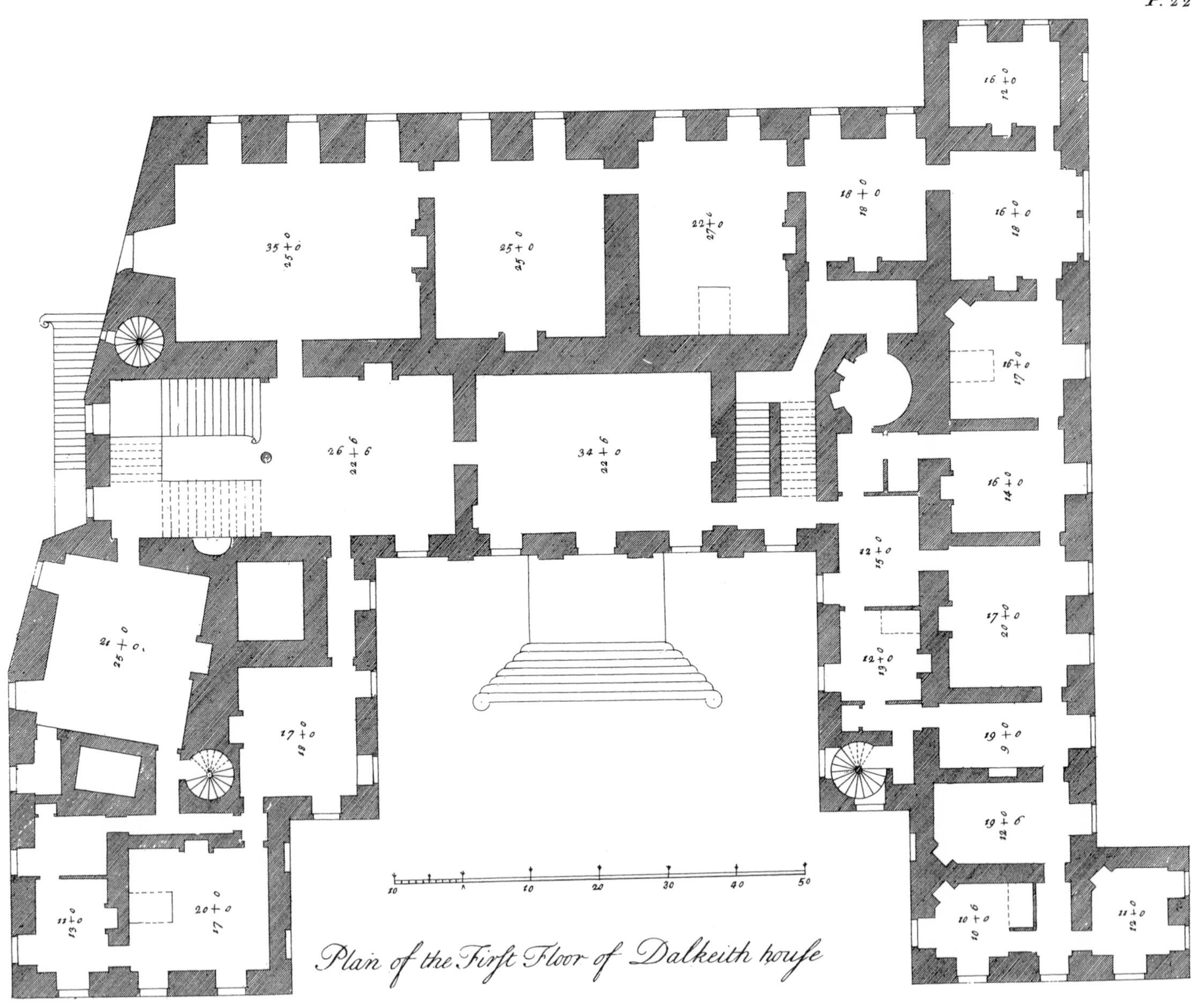

Plain of the First Floor of Dalkeith house

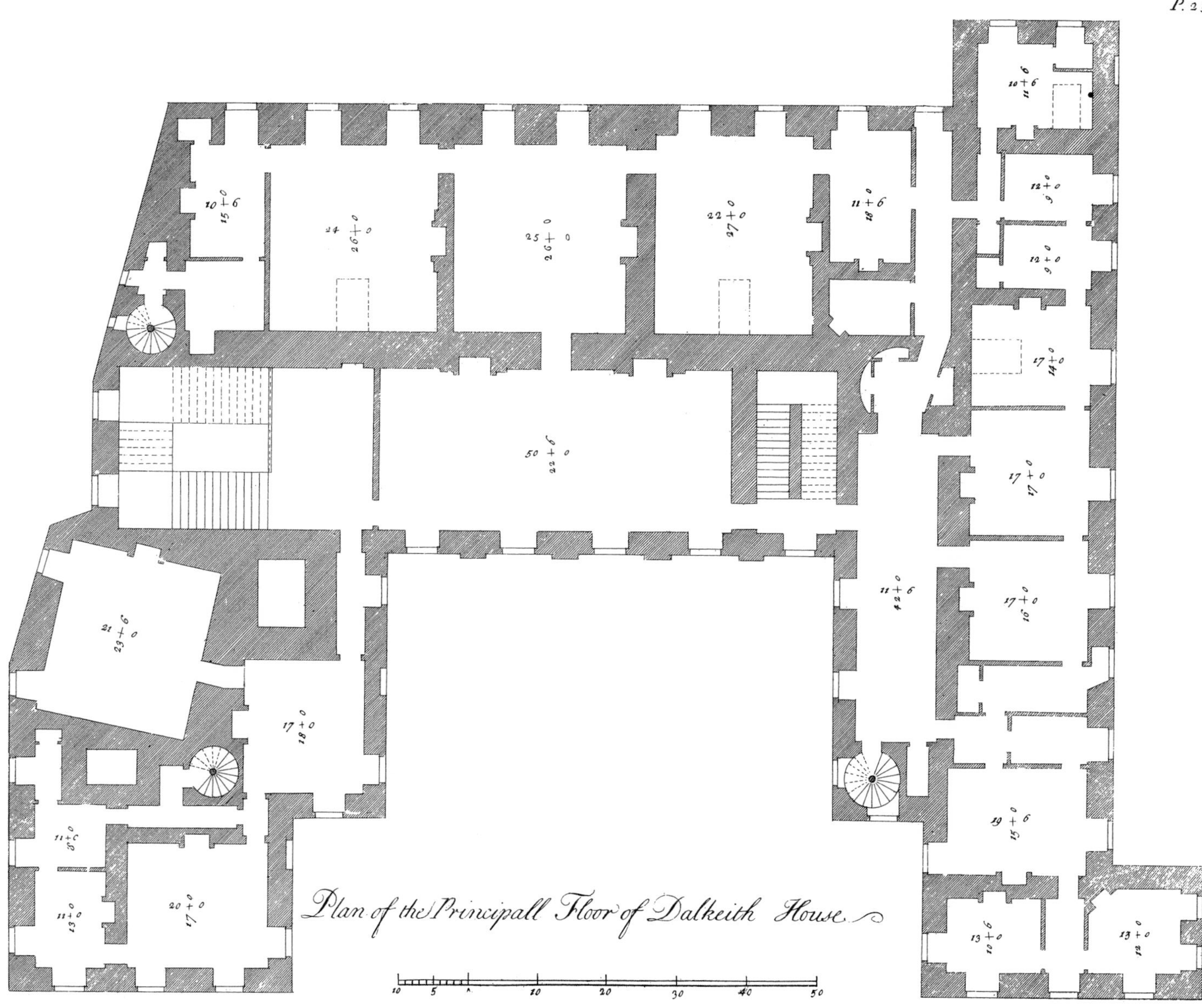
Plan of the Principall Floor of Dalkeith House
10
5
10
20
30
40
50

40 13 64 15 40 Extends 170

10 5 10 20 30 40 50 60 70

The South Front of Dalkeith House toward the Court, the Seat of her Grace the Dutchess of Bucleugh in the County of Mid-Lothian

Ja: Smith Architect
Gul: Adam del.

R. Cooper sculp.

A The Portico
A Common Hall
B Ale Cellars
C Wine Cellars
D Servants Waiting Room
E Servants Bed room
F Wett and Dry Larders
G Pantry
H Porter Lodge
I Footmens Hall
K Stewar's Hall or 2d Table room
L House keepers room with Closet for Linning
M Outter Room to Bagnio
N Bagnio
O Latter Meal Room
P Lumber Room
Q Butler's Room
R Room for Plate
S Corridor
T Milk house

W Outter Milk house
X Store Room
Y Women's Work house
Z Wash house
& Stell house
a Kitchen
b Scalerie
c Room for the Cook's Servants
d Cook's Room
e Valie's Room
f Bathing house
g Brewing house
h Gyle House
i Malt Miln
k Coal Yard
l Faggot or Wood yard
m Slaughter house
n Ash Court
o Pav'd Court

10 5 10 20 30 40 50

General Plan of the Ground Floor of Yester house

R: Cooper Sculp.

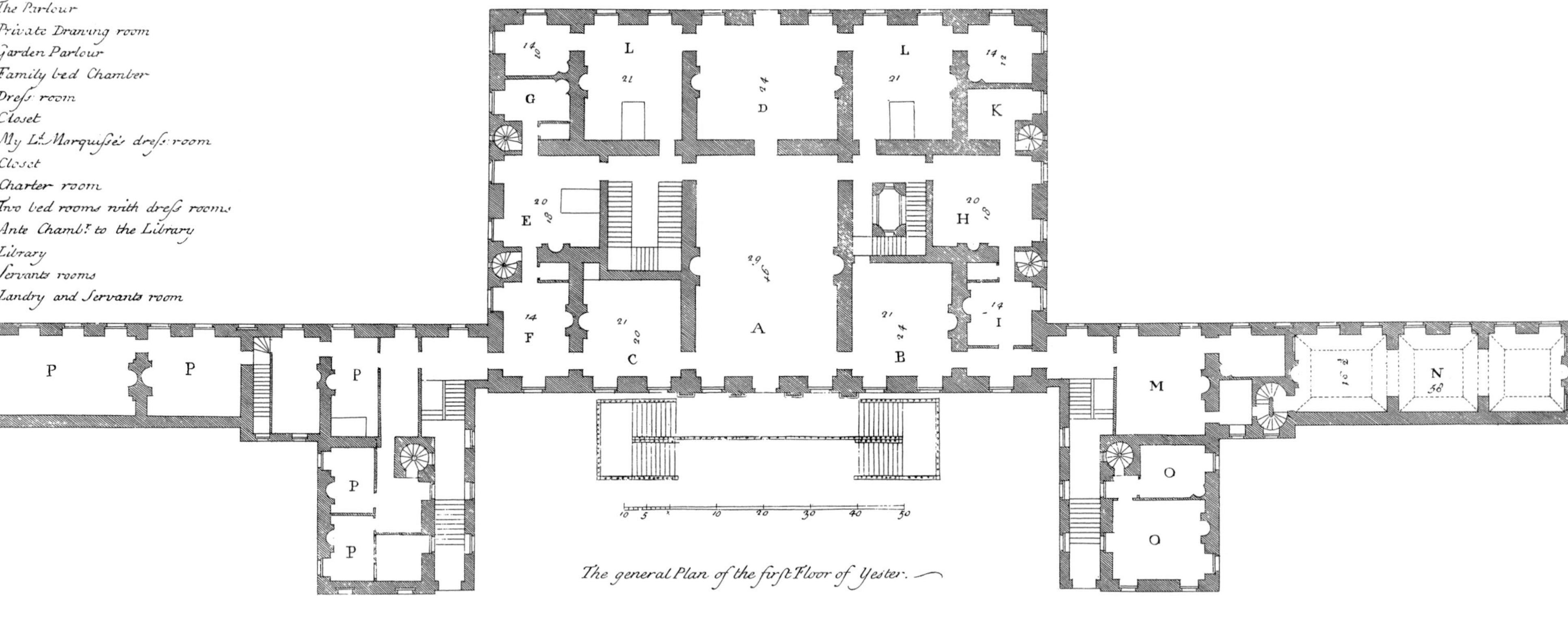

The general Plan of the first Floor of Yester.

Gul: Adam delin

R. Cooper Sculp.

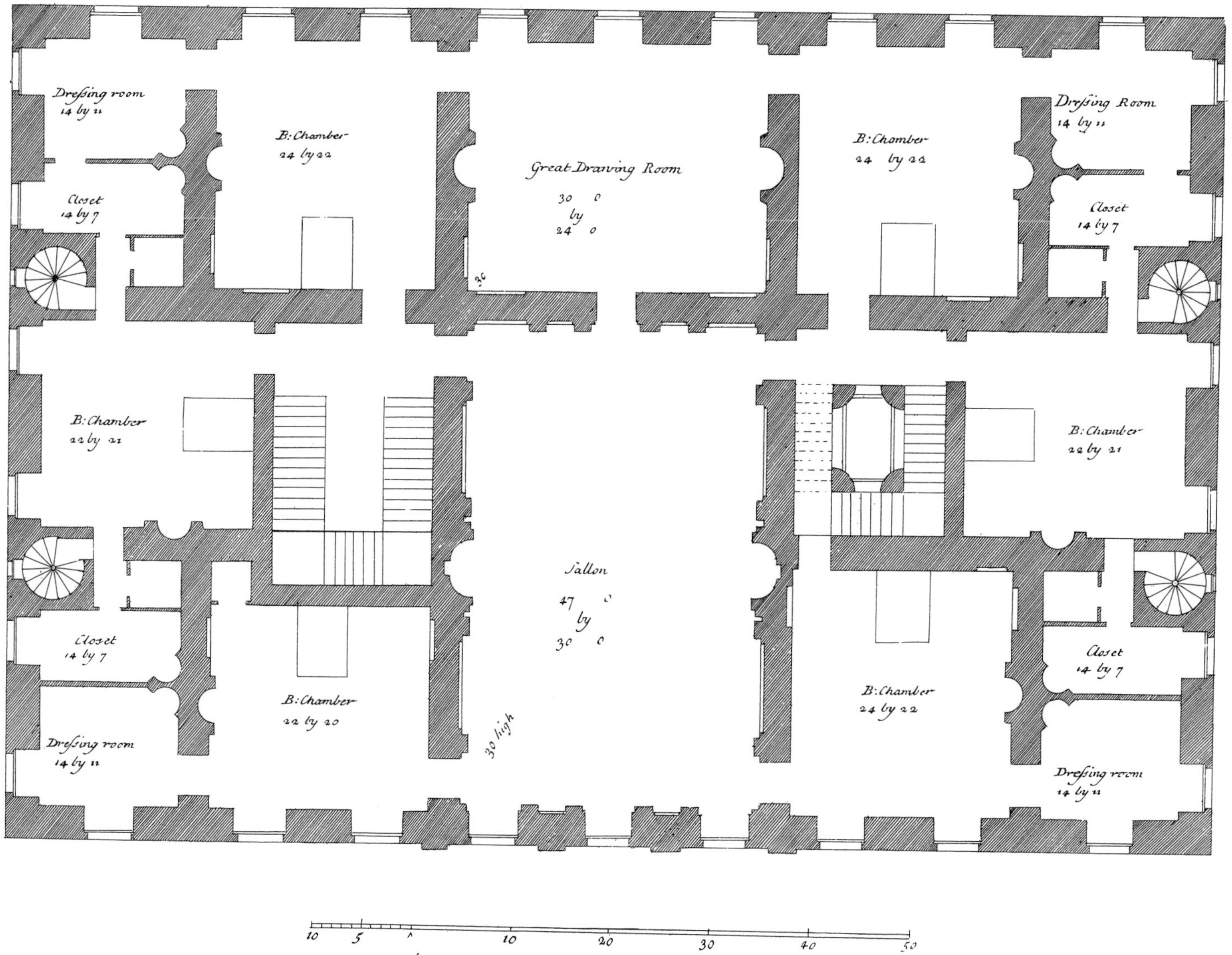

The Plan of the State Floor of YESTER HOUSE

Gul. Adam inv: et delin.

R: Cooper Sculp.

The North Front of Yester House toward the Court The Seat of the most Honourable the Marquis of Tweddale in the County of East-Lothian

Ja: Smith & Alex.r Mc Gill } Architects

R. Cooper sculp.

The Outward Stair & Pilasters with the Attick were added by Will: Adams

The Generall Front of Yester House toward the Gardens Extends over all 344.

Gul. Adam Delin.

R. Cooper Sculp.

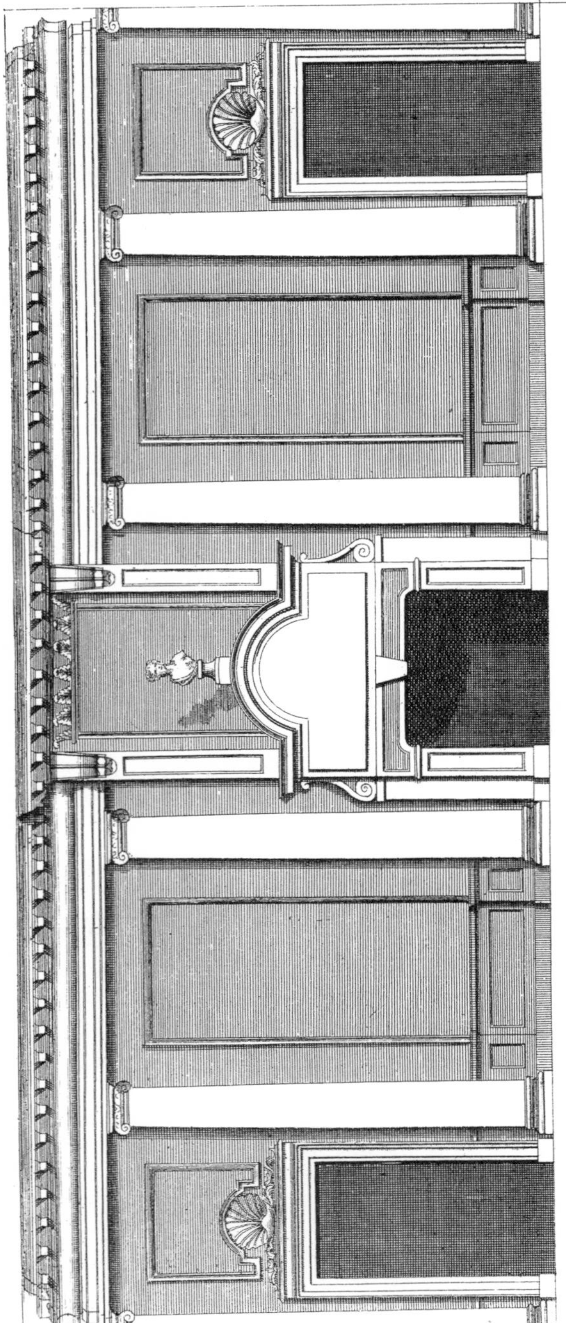

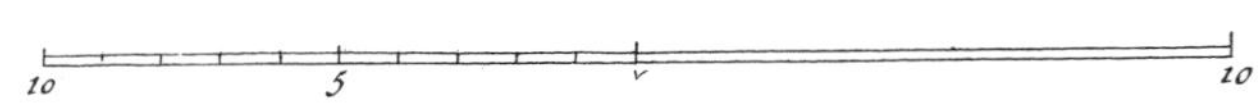

Section of one Side & one end of the Hall att Yester

45 by 30 foots

Gul. Adam del.

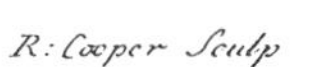

Section of the Sallon at Yester

46 by 30 & 30 high

Gul: Adam inv: et delin

R: Cooper Sculp

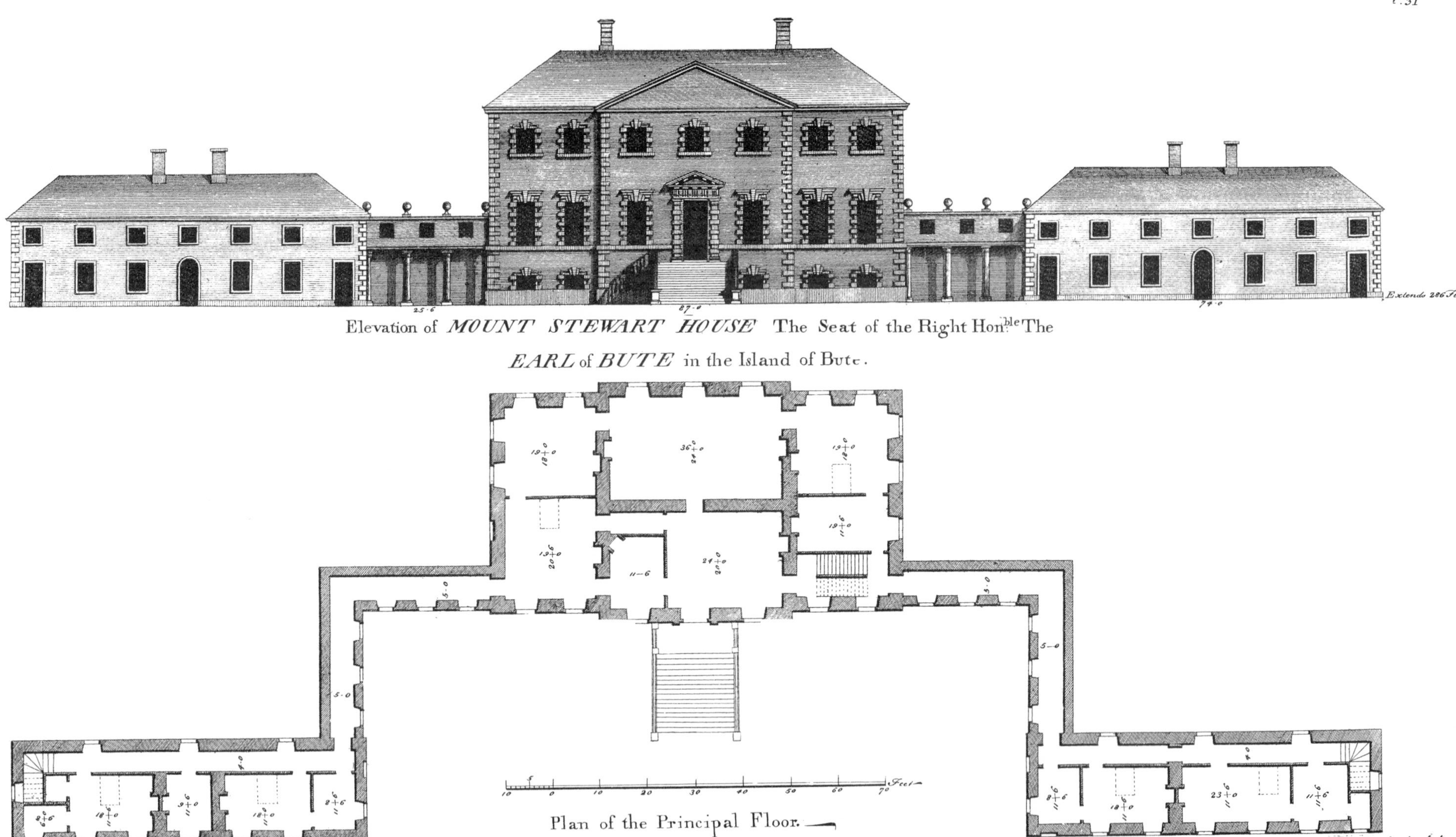

Elevation of *MOUNT STEWART HOUSE* The Seat of the Right Hon.ble The *EARL* of *BUTE* in the Island of Bute.

Plan of the Principal Floor.

The General Plan of the Ground Floor of Newliston

Gul. Adam inv. et delin | *R: Cooper Sculp*

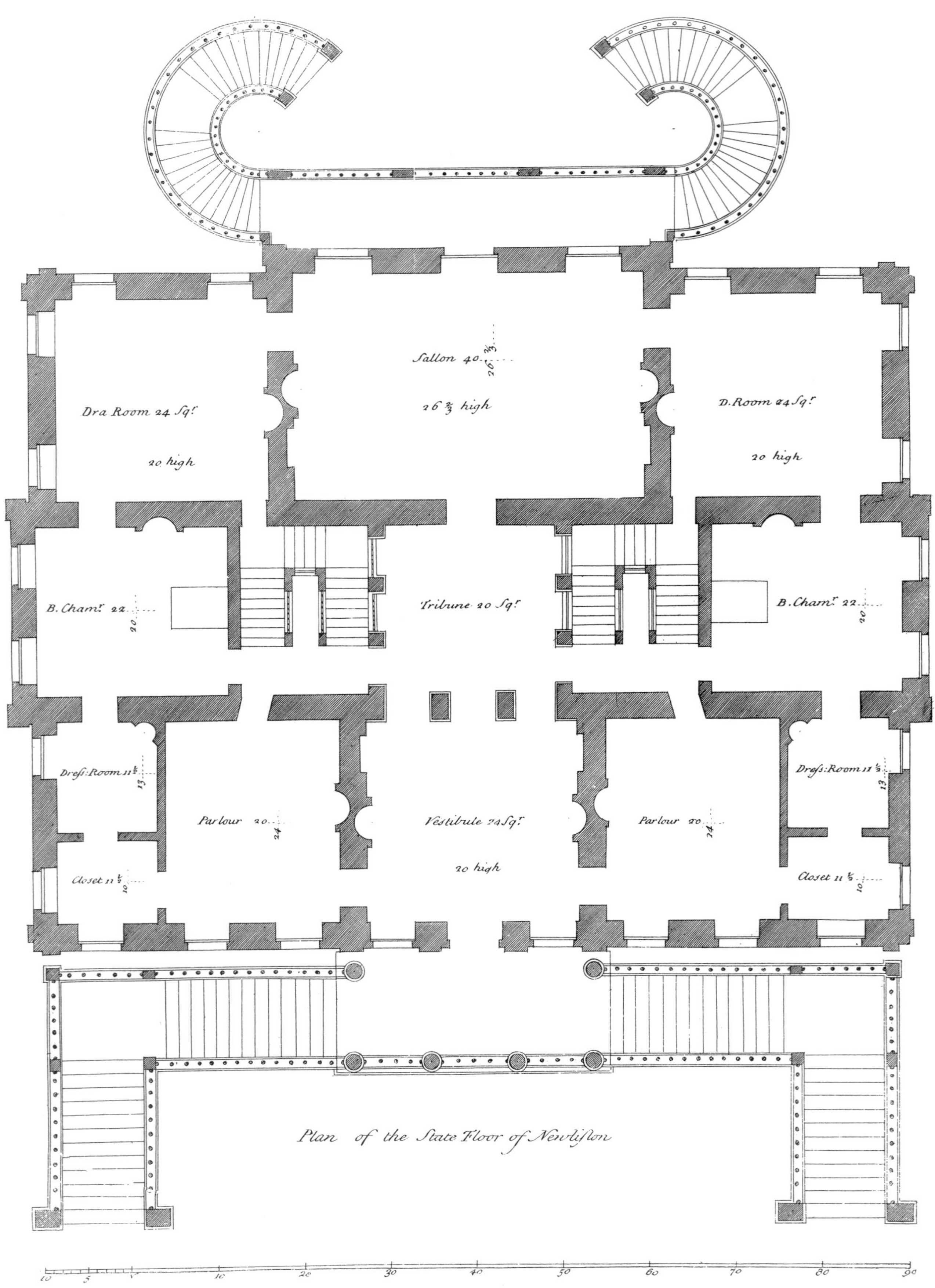

Gul: Adam inv: & del:

R. Cooper sculp:

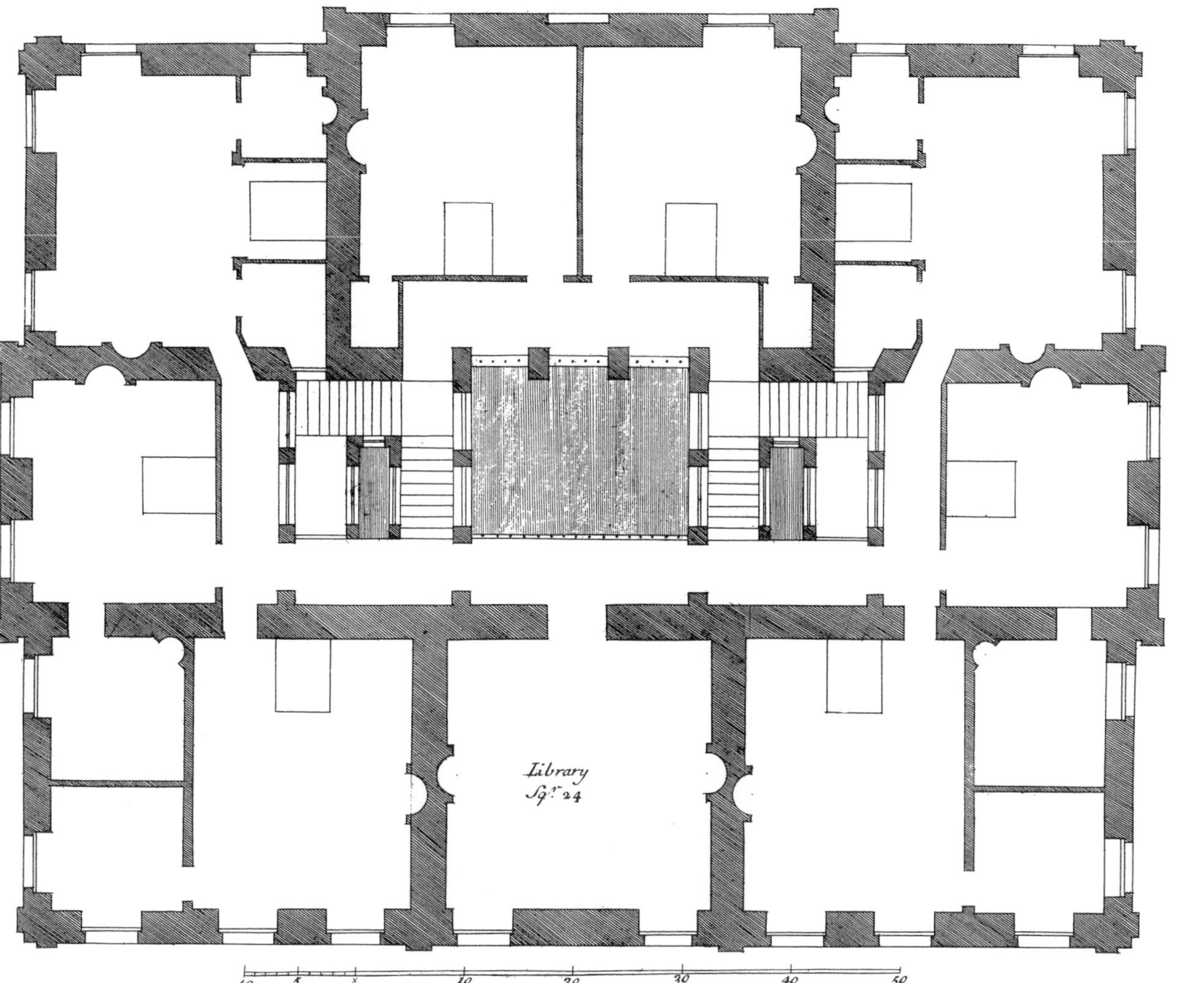

A Plan of the Lodging Storie of Newliston

Gul. Adam Inv. et. delin.

R. Cooper Sculp.

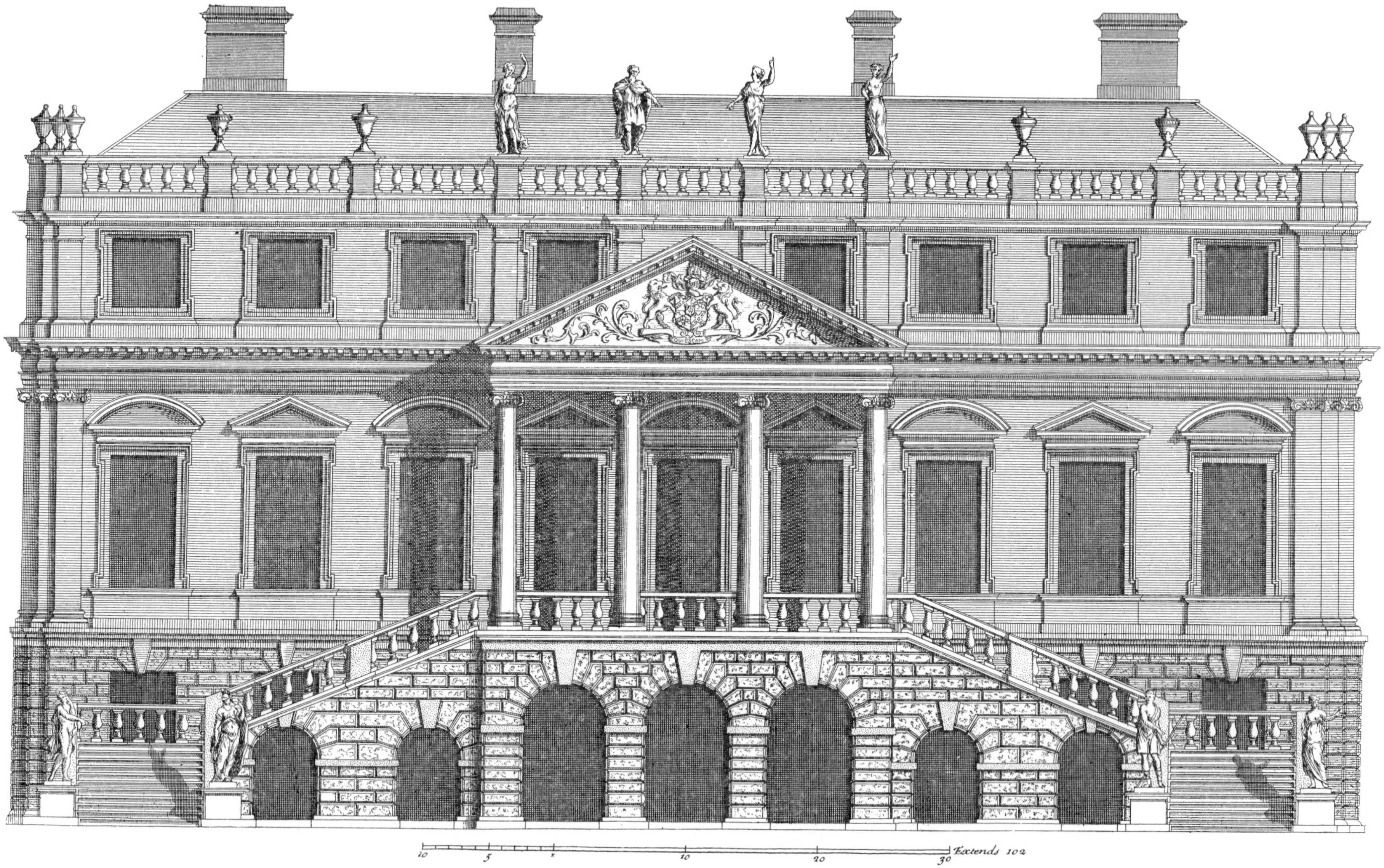

10 5 0 10 20 30 Extends 102

The South Front of Newliston toward the Court

Gul. Adam inv. et delin.

R. Cooper sculp.

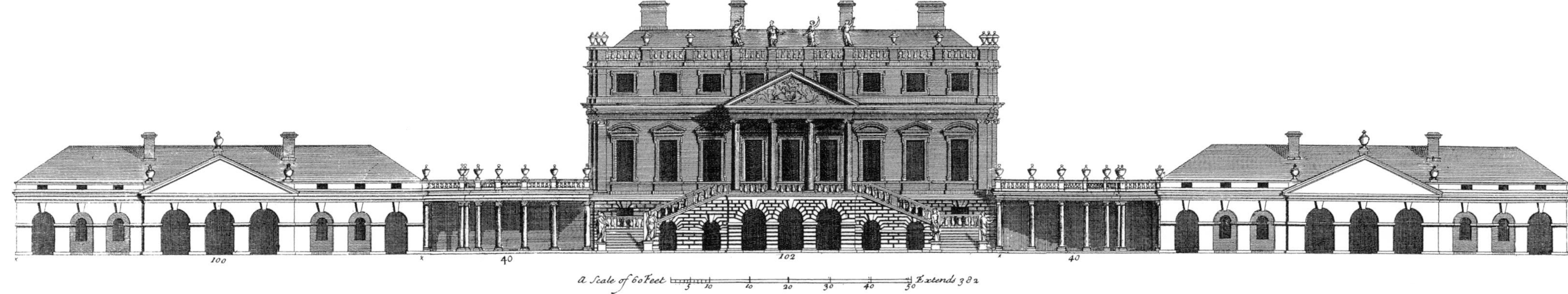

The General Front of a new design for the Rt. Hon.ble The Earl of Stair intended at Newliston being one of the Seats of his Lordship in the County of West-Lothian

Gul. Adam Inv. et delin.

R. Cooper Sculp.

36
18
18
24
18
22

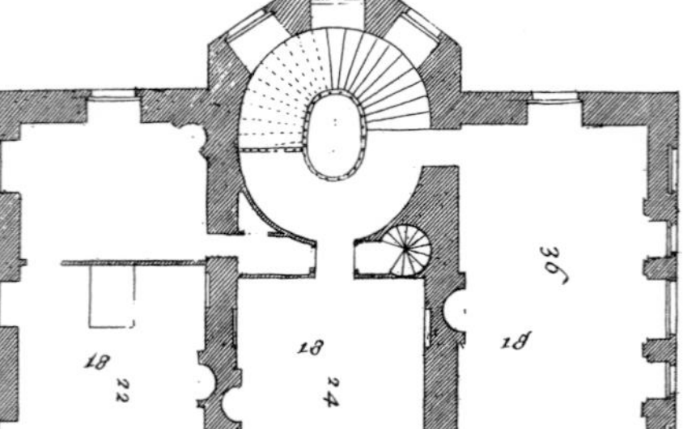

The Plan of the State Floor

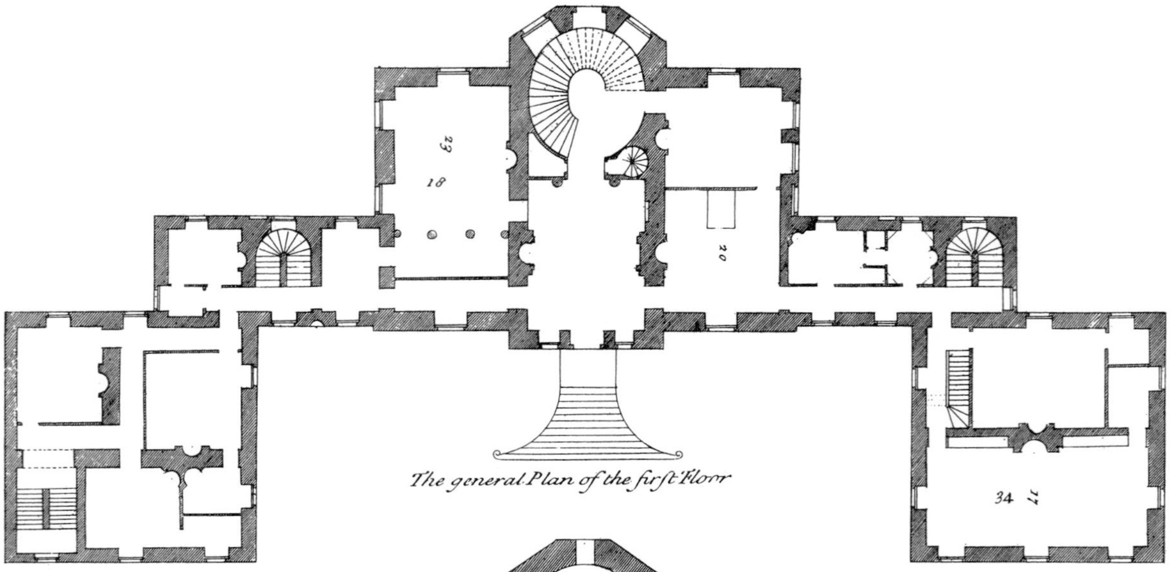

23
18
20
34
17

The general Plan of the first Floor

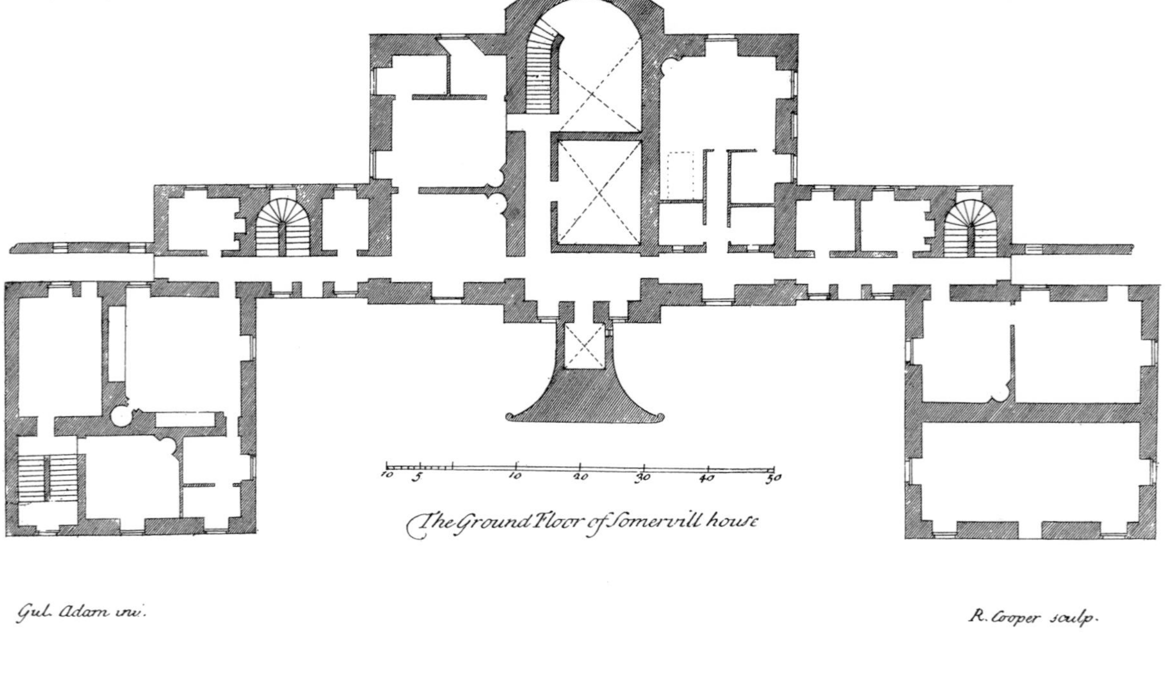

10 5 10 20 30 40 50

The Ground Floor of Somervill house

Gul. Adam inv. *R. Cooper sculp.*

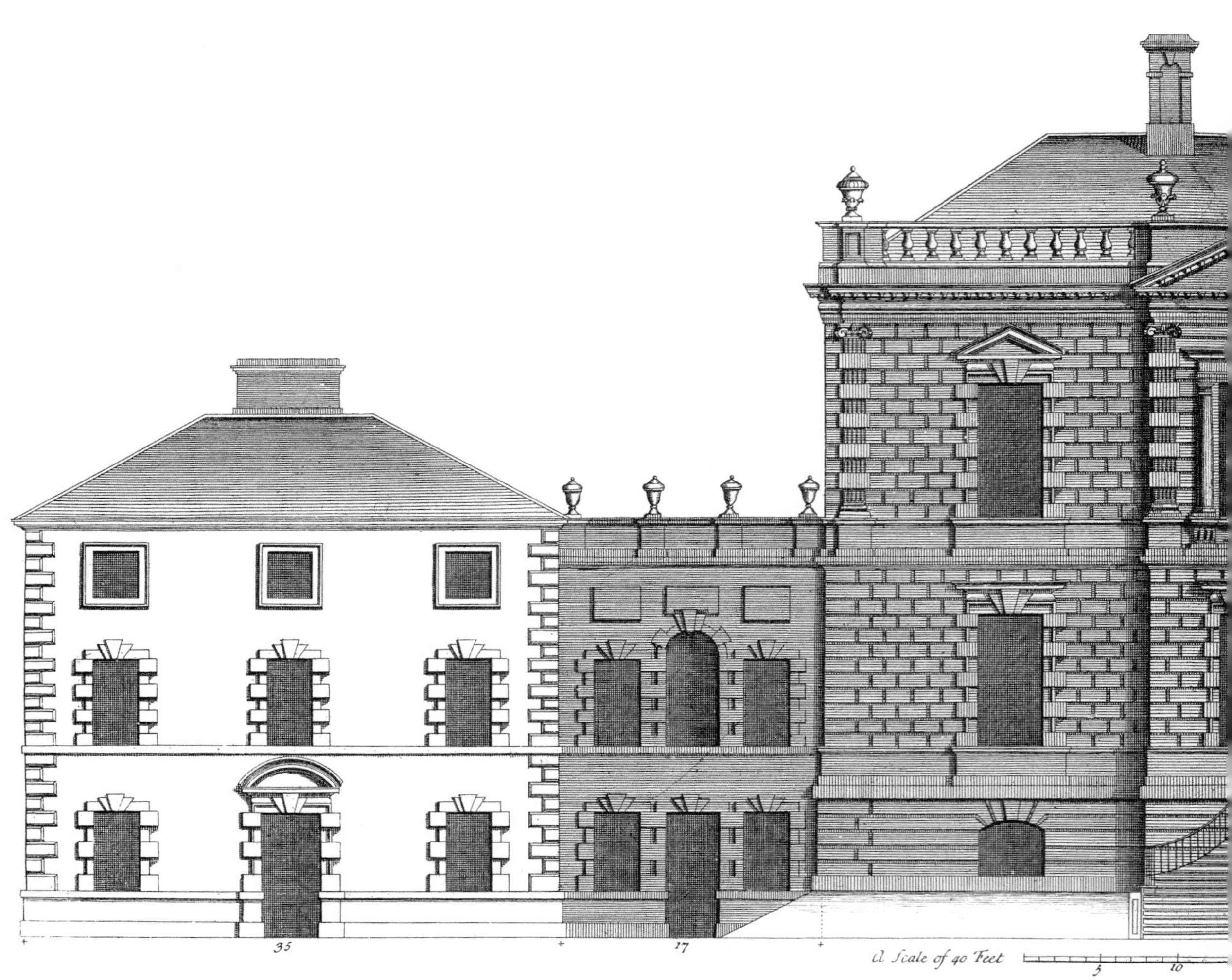

The General Front of Sommervel House the Seat of the Right

Gul: Adam Architectus

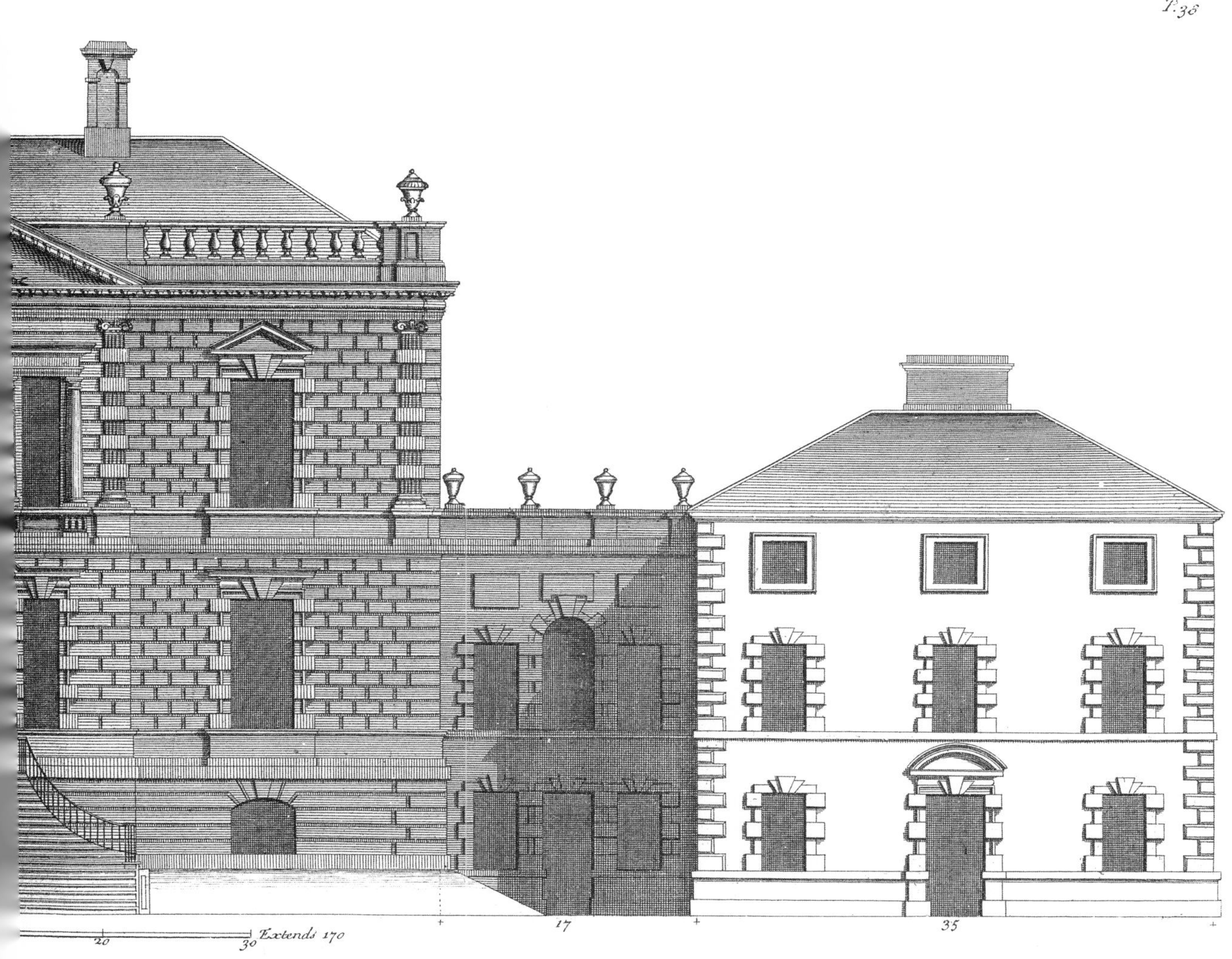

ames Lord Sommervel in the County of Midd-Lothian

R. Cooper Sculp.

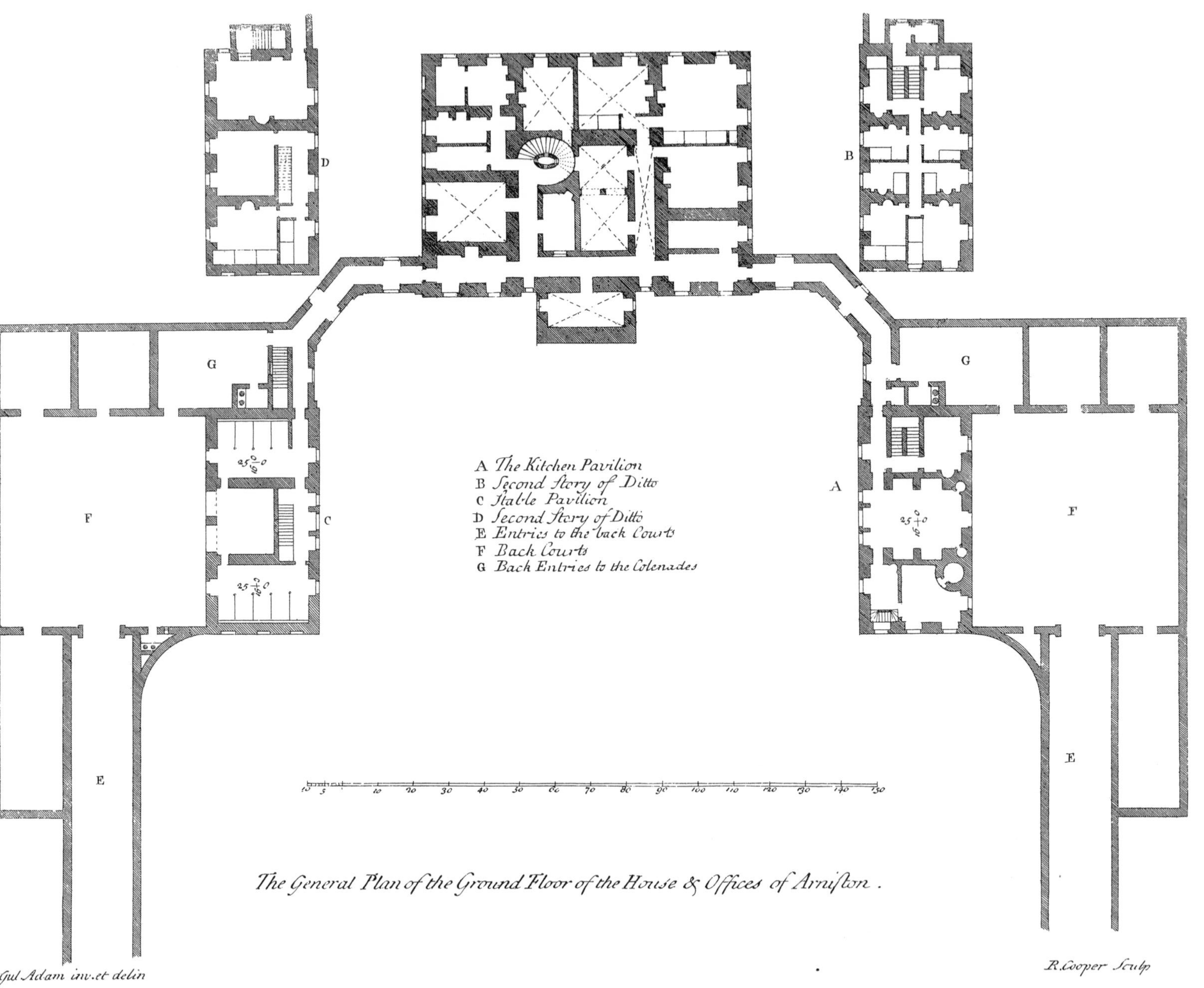

The General Plan of the Ground Floor of the House & Offices of Arniston.

Gul Adam inv. et delin

R. Cooper Sculp

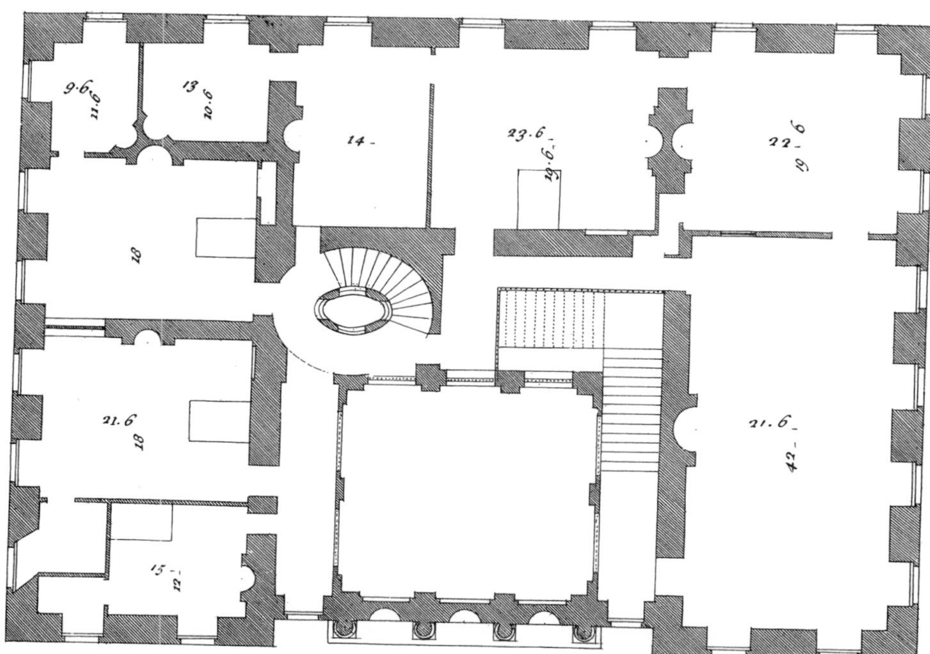

The Plan of the 2d Floor of Arniston.

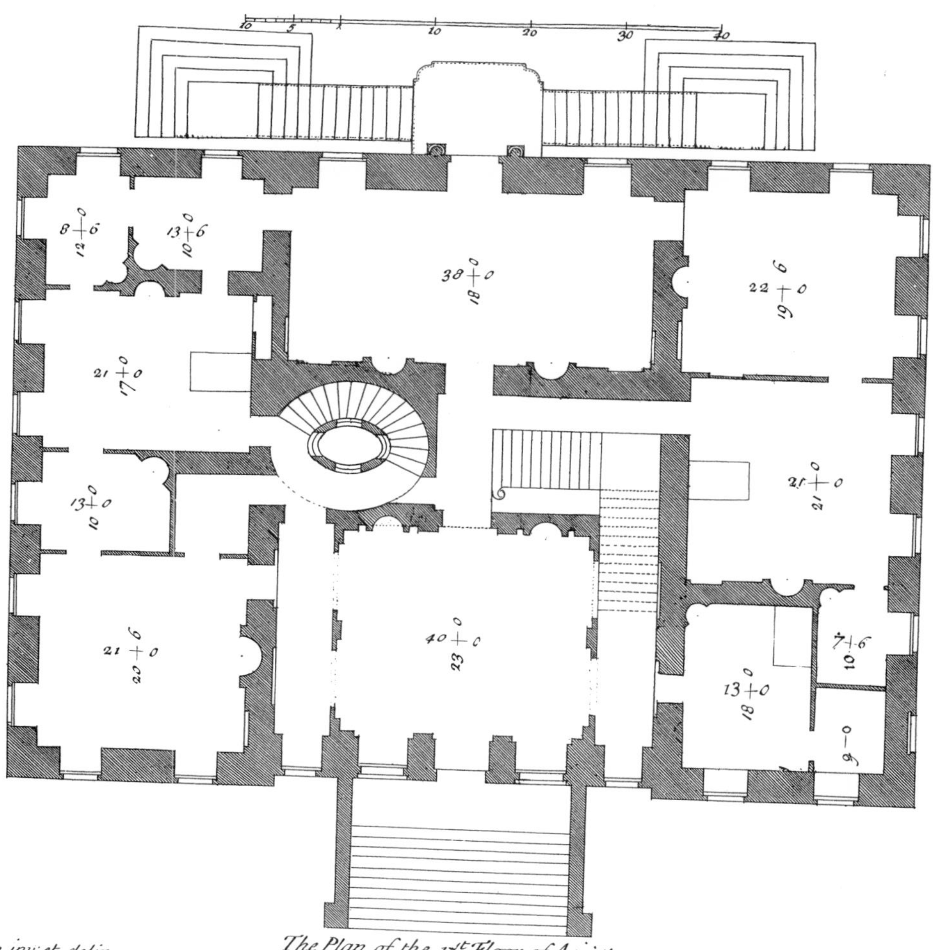

Gul Adam inv: et delin

The Plan of the 1st Floor of Arniston

R Cooper Sculp

10 5 10 20 30

Section of the Library at Arnistone

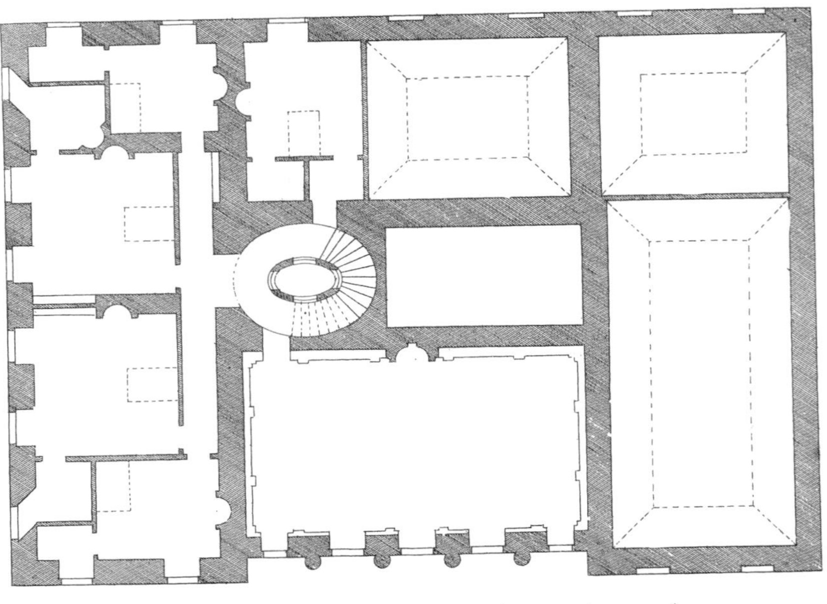

10 5 10 20 30 40 50

Plan of the Attick Story

Gul. Adam Archit. *The General Front of Arniston toward the Court The Seat of the Honourable Mr. Robert Dundass of Arniston.* R. Cooper sculp.

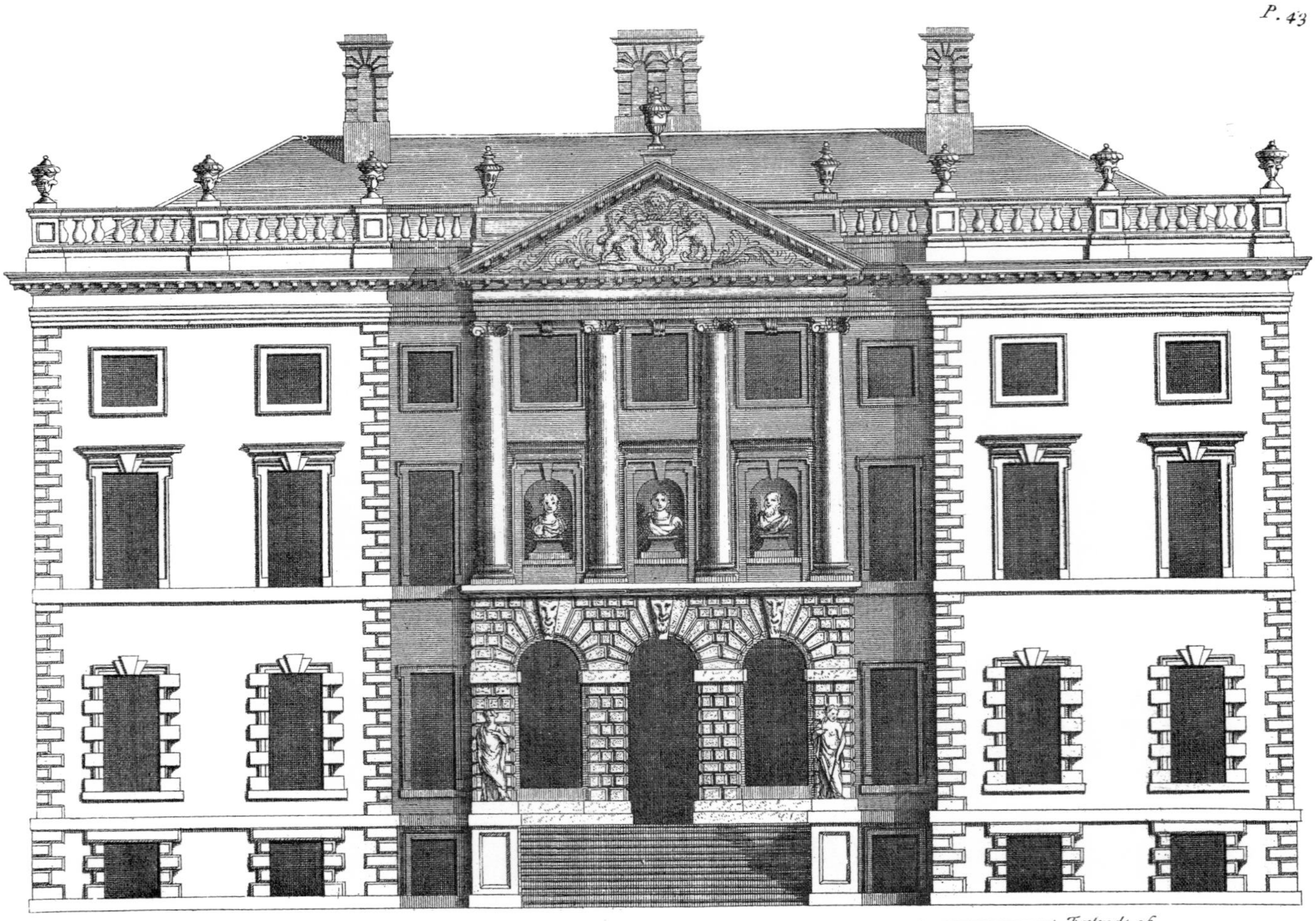

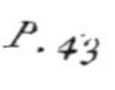

a Scale of 60 feet 10 5 10 20 30 40 50 Extends 96

The North Front of Arnistone House *towards the* Court *on A Large Scale.*

Gul: Adam Invent. et Delin. *R. Cooper Sculp.*

Prospect of the End Front of Arnistone House *toward the* West

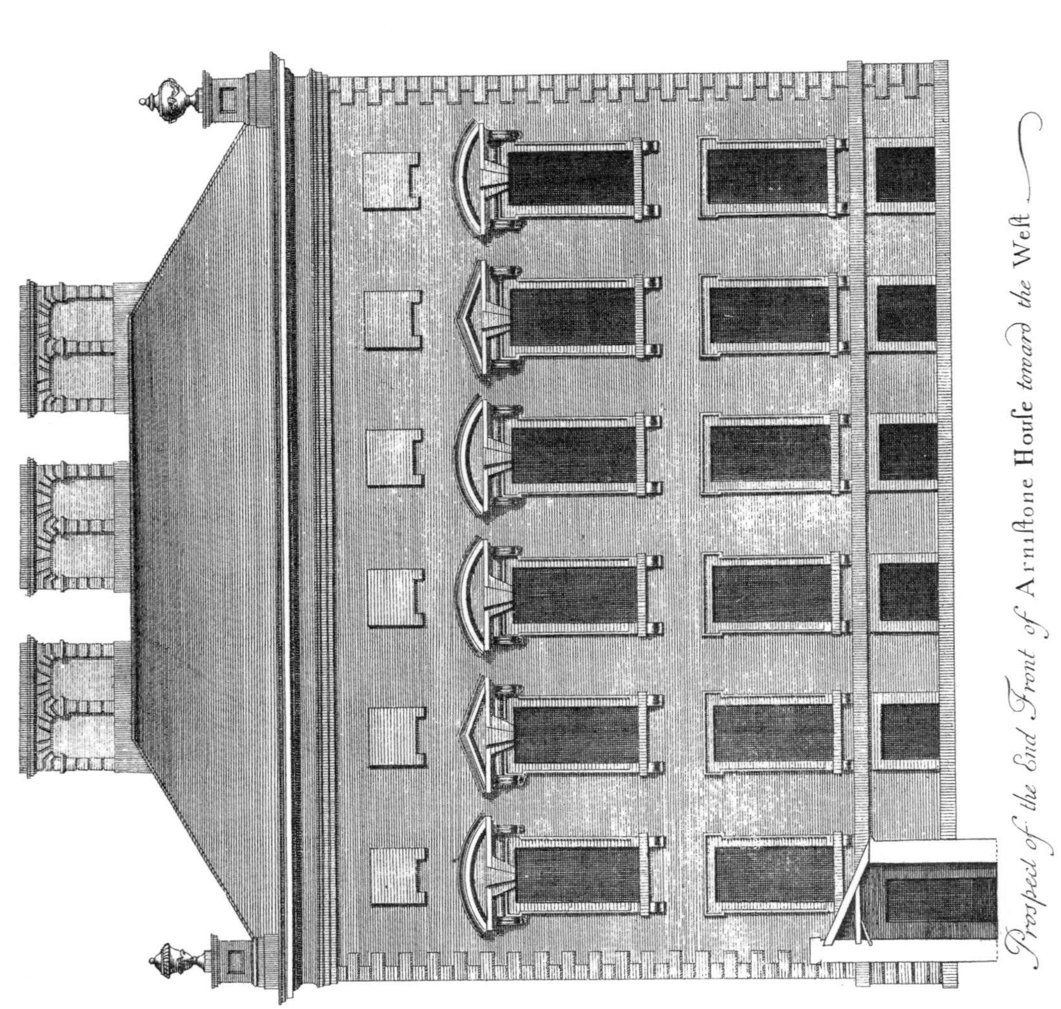

The Garden Front of Arniston House towards the South

Gul: Adam Inv: et del:

R: Cooper sculp:

North Front of The Right Hon.ble LORD MILTON'S HOUSE in EDINBURGH.

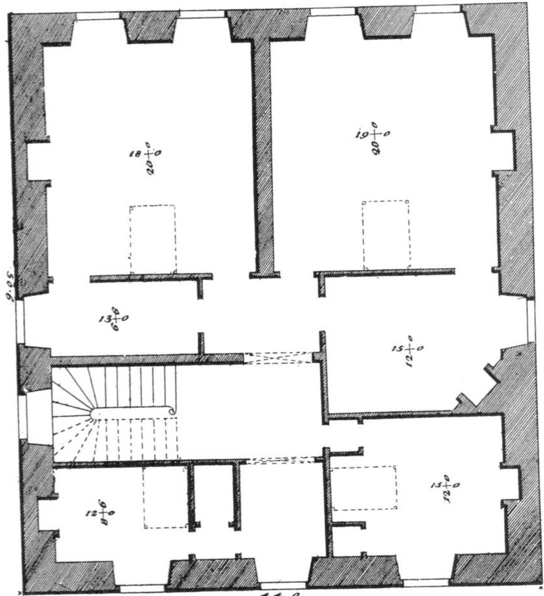

Bed Chamber Story.

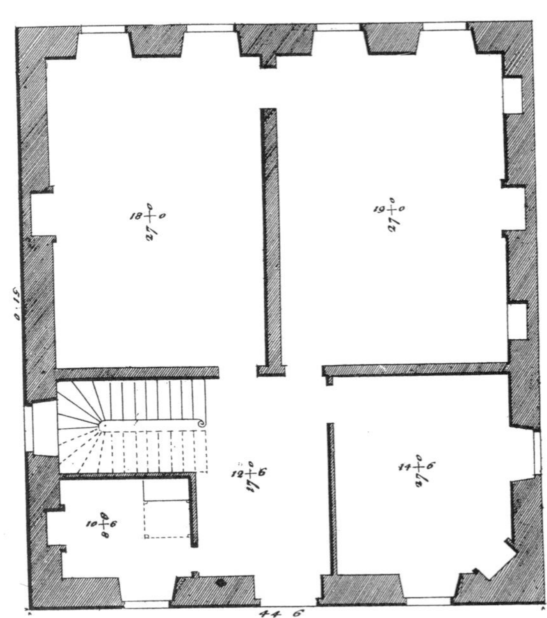

Principal Floor.

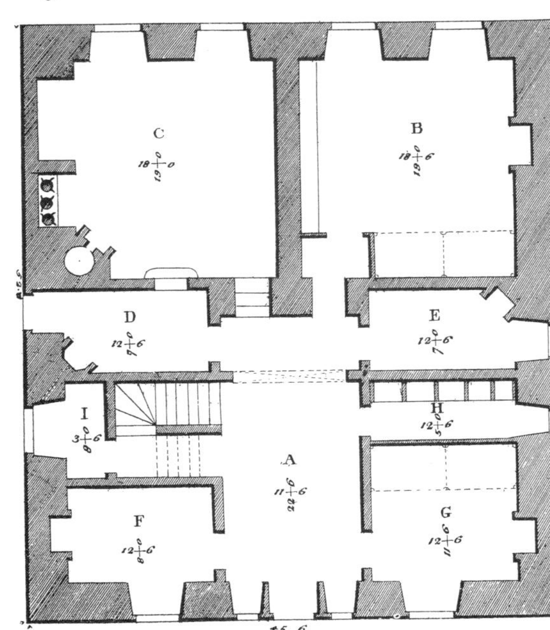

A Footman's Hall.
B House keepers room.
C Kitchen.
D Scullery.
E Pantry.
F. Second Table room.
G. Latter meat room.
H. Wine Celler.
I. Celler.

Ground Story.

Adam's Arch.ts

T. Smith Sculp.

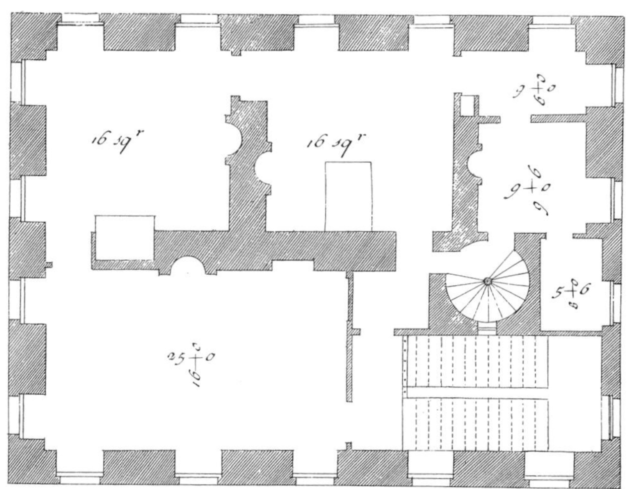

Plan of the Second Story or principal floor

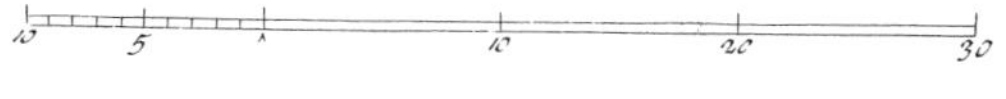

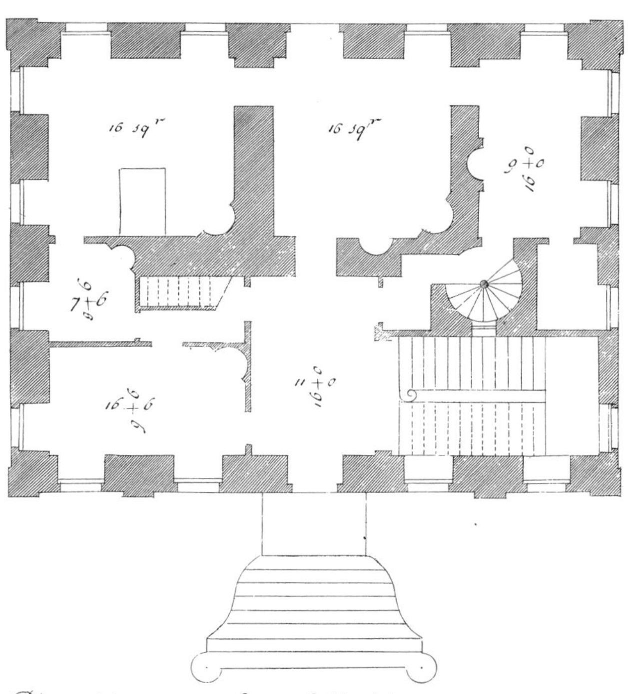

Plan of the Vestible floor of Mavisbank House

Gul. Adam inv: et delin

R: Cooper Sculp.

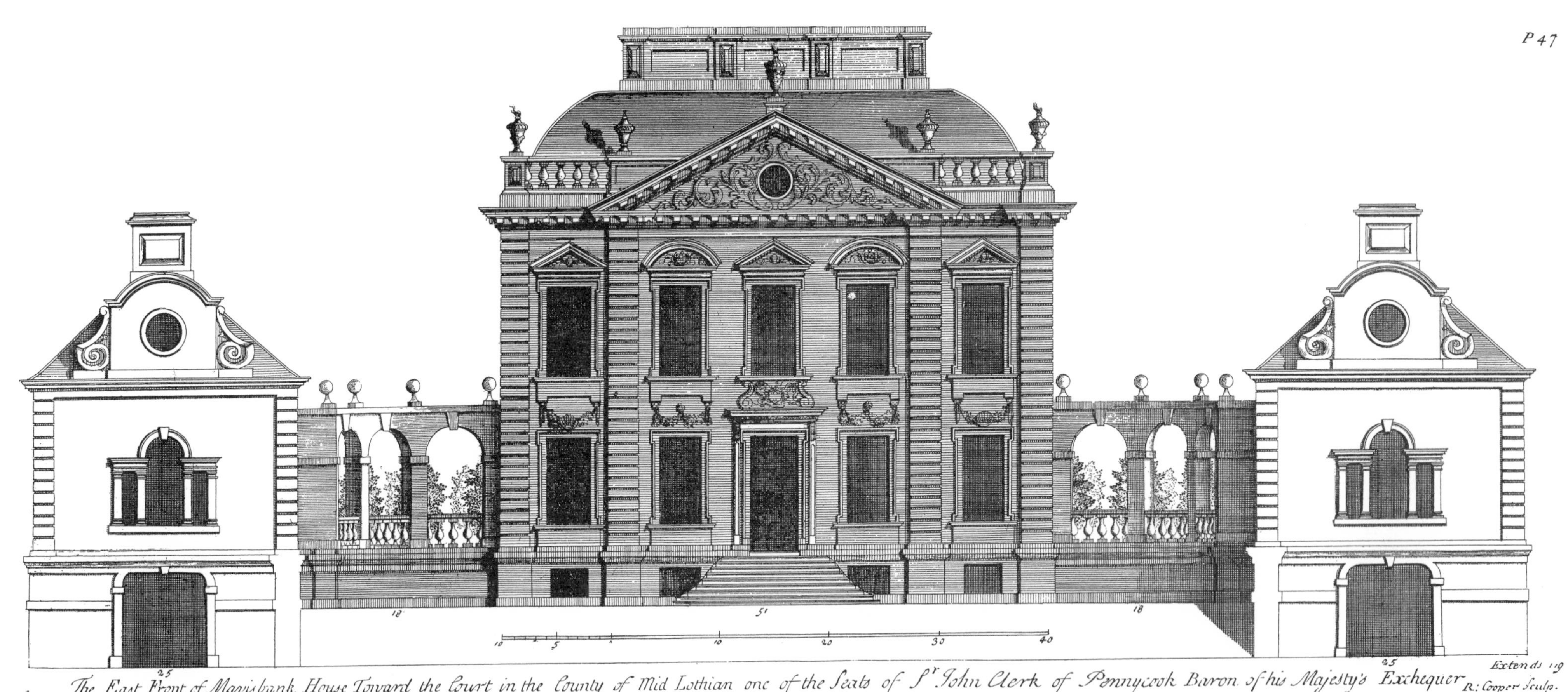

The East Front of Mavisbank House Toward the Court in the County of Mid Lothian one of the Seats of Sr. John Clerk of Pennycook Baron of his Majesty's Exchequer

Gul: Adam inv. delin   R: Cooper Sculp.

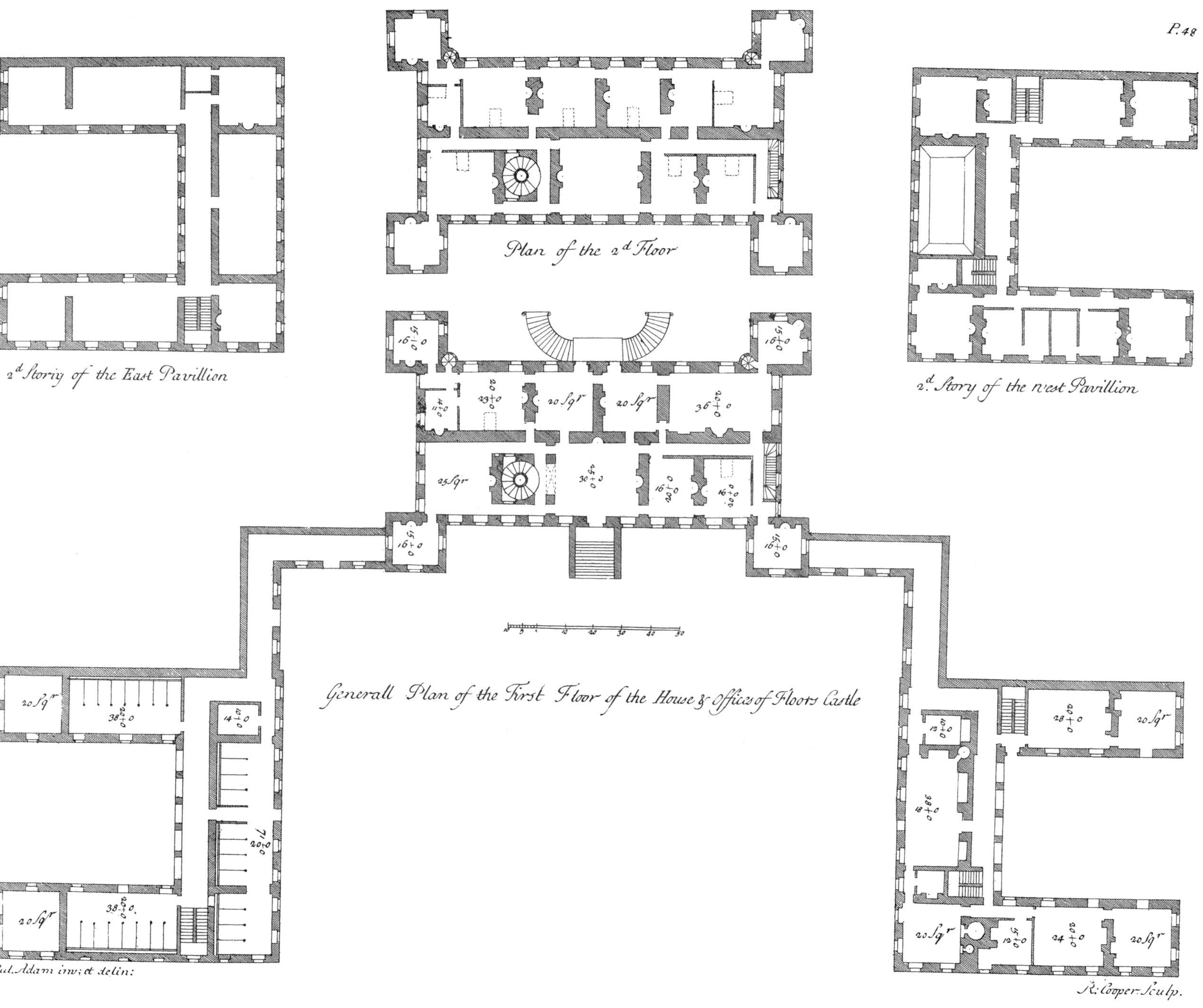
2d Storiy of the East Pavillion
Plan of the 2d Floor
2d. Story of the west Pavillion
Generall Plan of the First Floor of the House & Offices of Floors Castle
Gul. Adam inv: et delin:
R. Cooper Sculp.

The North Front of Floors Castle toward the Court one of the Seats of His Grace the Duke of Roxbrugh
In the County of Tiviotdale

Gul Adam inv: et delin:

R: Cooper Sculp

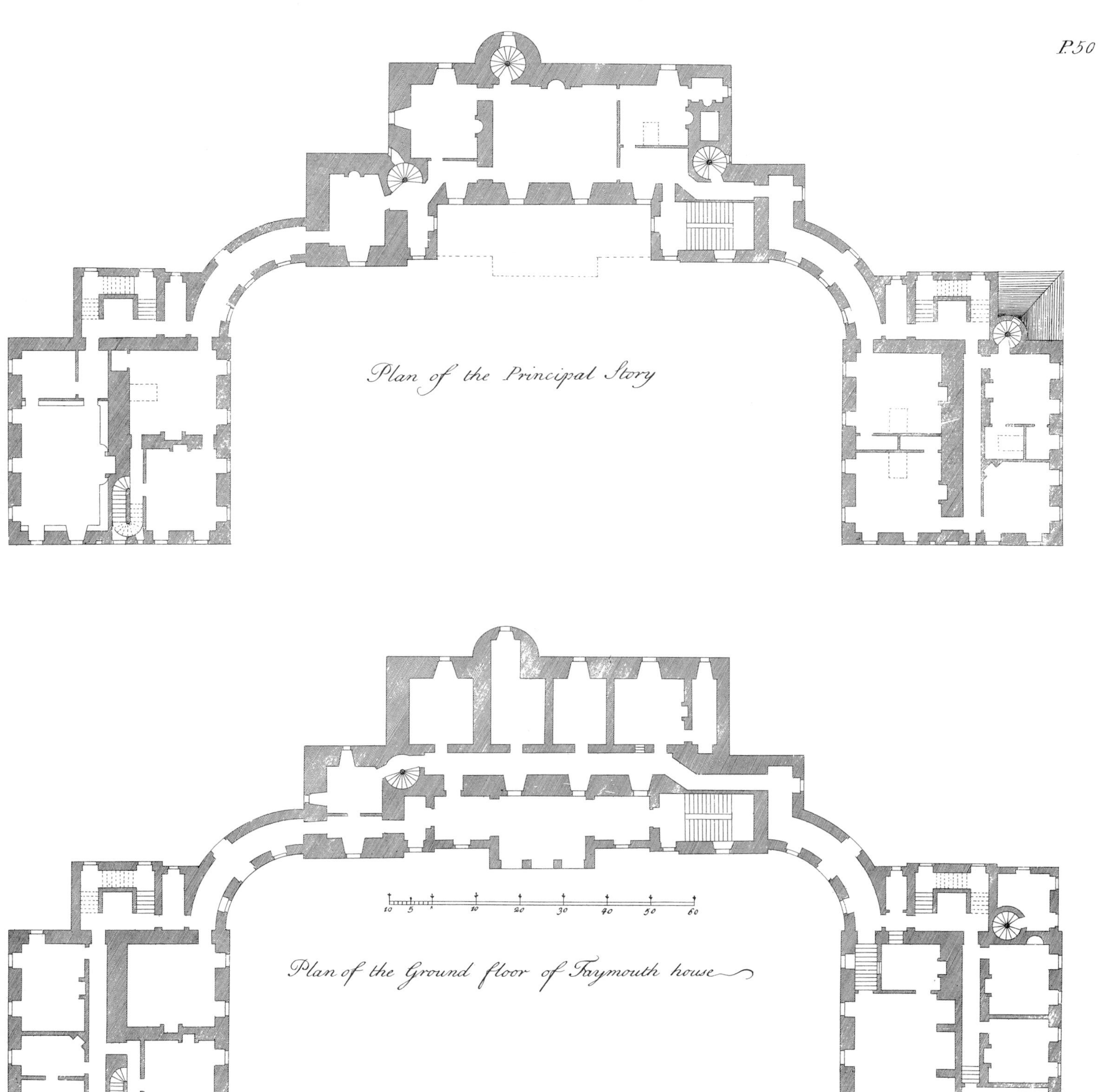

Gul Adam delin

R: Cooper Sculp

General Front of Taymouth house toward the Court The Seat of the Right Hon[ble] The Earl of BREDALBANE in the County of PERTH

The Pavilions & Collonades added by William Adam

R: Cooper Sculp

Extends 74 feet

One of the End Fronts of Castle Kenmore

West Front of Castle Kenmore facing the Loch

Extends 80 feet

The East Front of Castle Kenmore toward the Court

Gul: Adam inv:et delin

R: Cooper Sculp

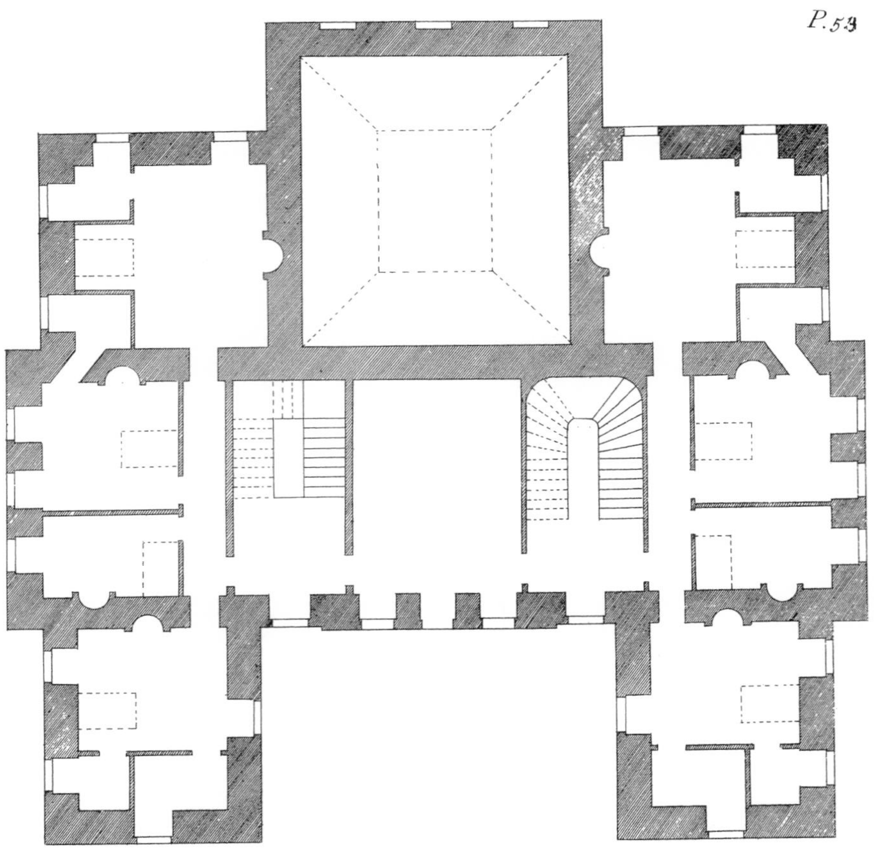

Plan of the Attick Story

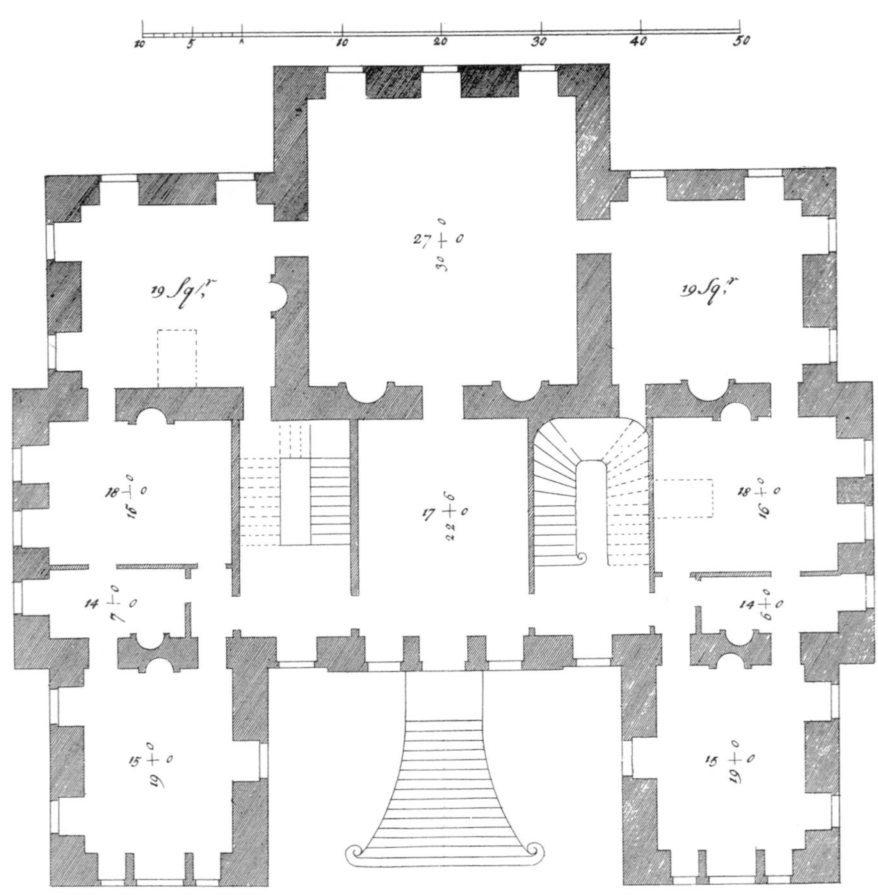

Plan of the Principal Floor of Castle Kenmore

Gul: Adam inv: et delin *R: Cooper Sculp*

Plan of the Ground Floor of Haddo house

A Common Hall
B Second Table room
C Ale Cellar
D Wine Cellar
E House keepers room & Closet
F Bed room
G Ladys Gentlewomans room
H Nursery
I Charter room
K Counting room
L Bed room & Closet
M Butlers room
N Potters Lodge
O Bottle room
P Pantry

Q Kitchen
R Scallery
S Cook room
T Milk house & Cheese room
U Bake house
V Latter Meat hall
W Meal Granary
X Ser.ts Bed rooms & Closets
Y Laundry
Z Meal Granary
a Hunters Stable
b Coach horse Stable
c Work hors Stable
d Room for horse furniture
e Grooms Bed room
f Victual Granary

Gul: Adam inv: et delin

R: Cooper Sculp.

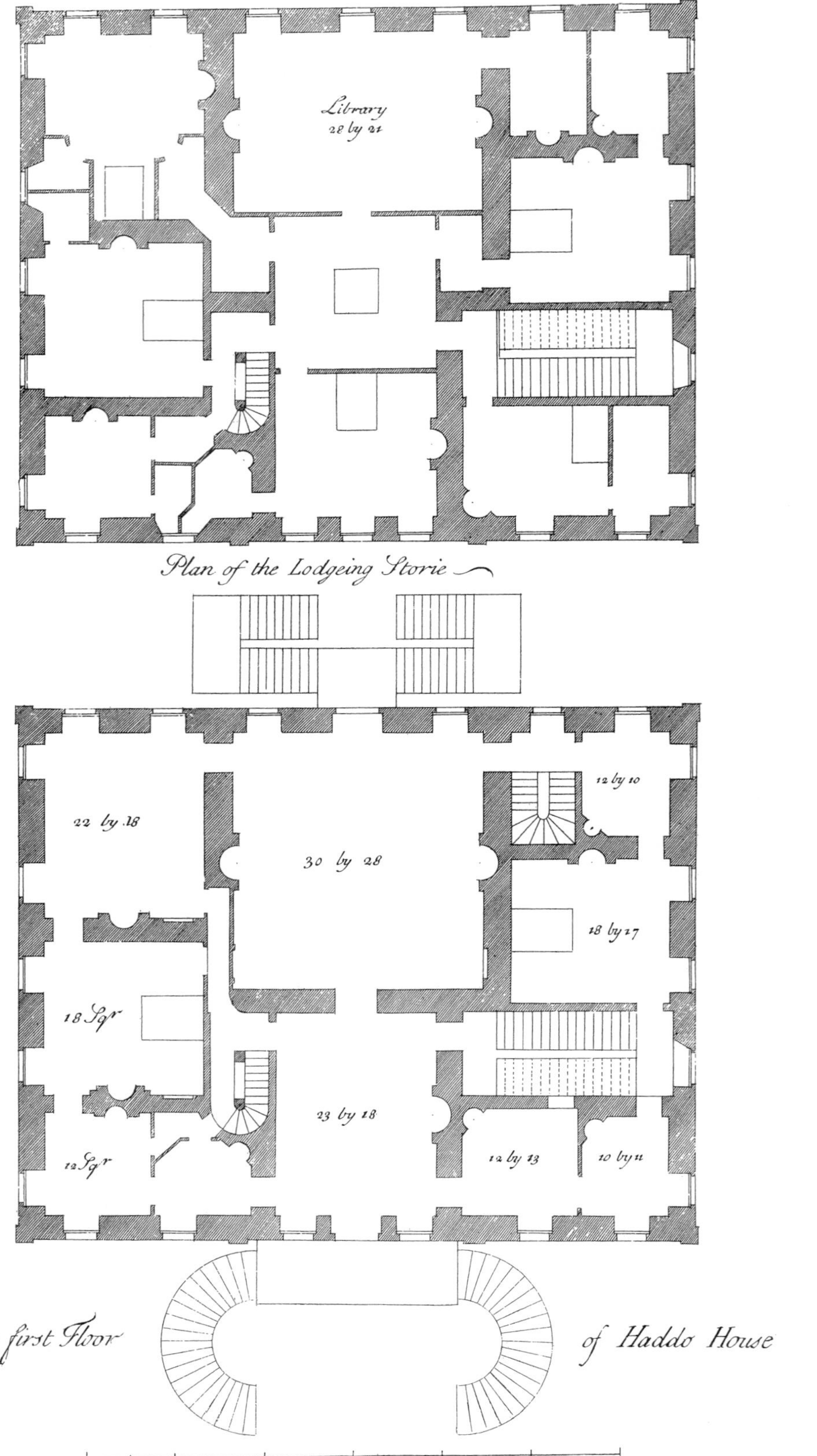

Plan of the first Floor of Haddo House

Gul: Adam Inv. & Delin

R. Cooper sculp:

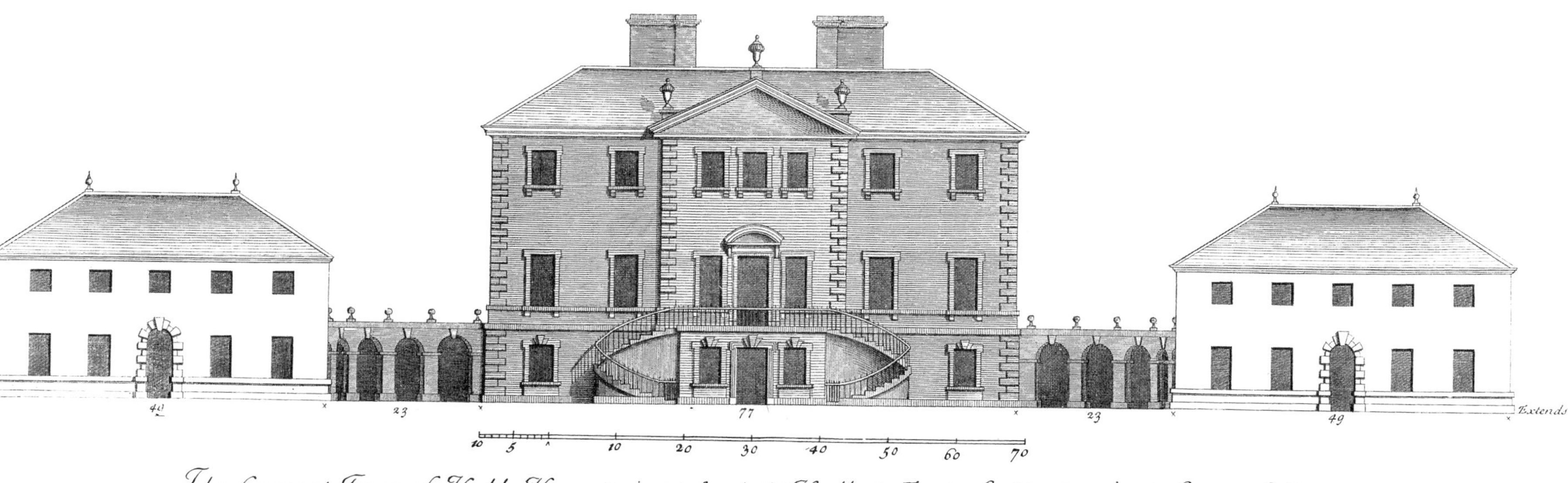

The General Front of Haddo House Design'd for the Rt. Honble. the Earl of Aberdeen in the County of Aberdeen

Gul. Adam Inv. et delin.

R. Cooper Sculp.

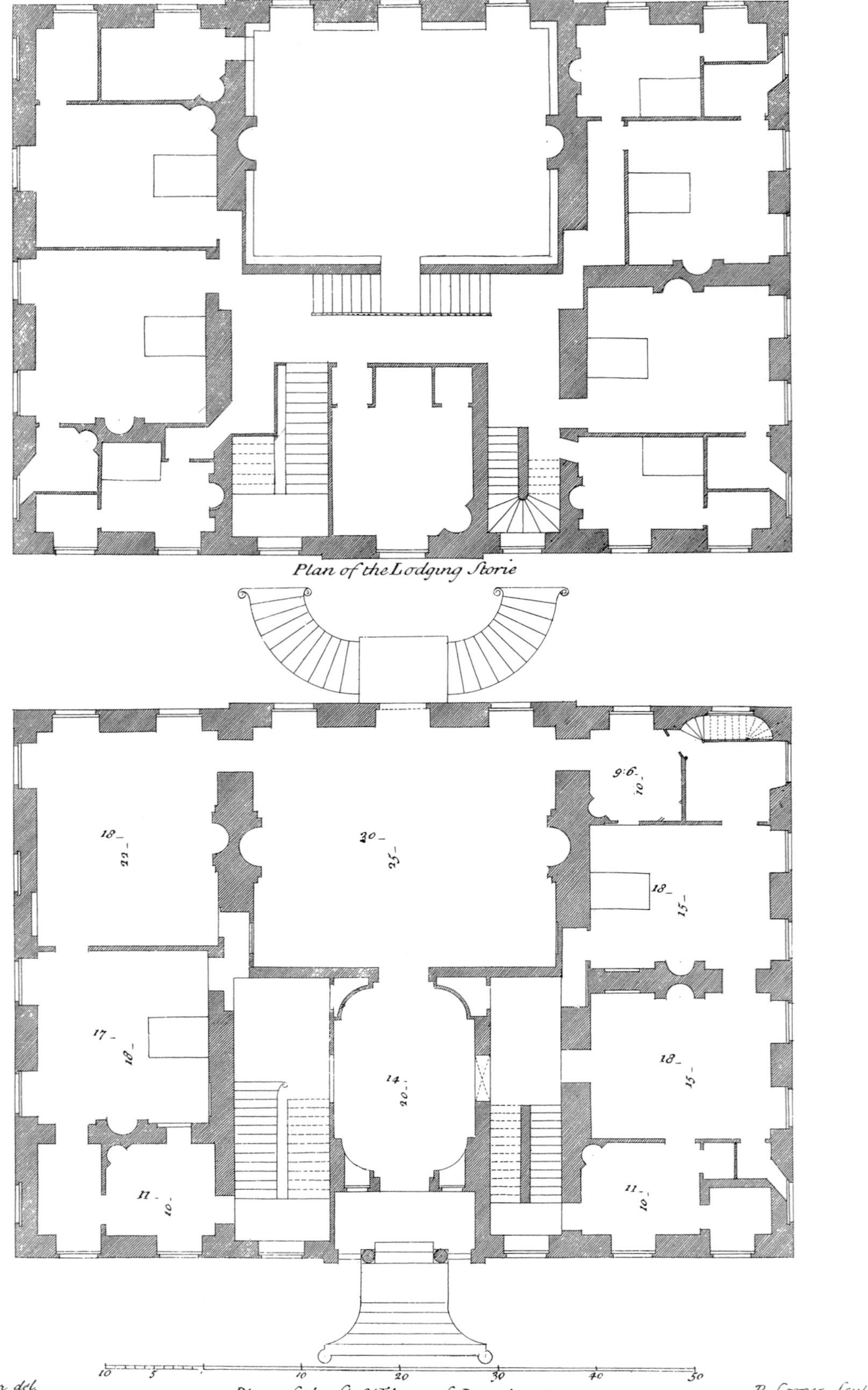

Gul. Adam del.

Plan of the first Floor of Dun house.

R. Cooper Sculp.

The Garden Front of Dun house
as first Design'd Extends 78 Feet

The Court Front of Dun House toward the North

10 5 10 20 30 40 50

A. The Laigh Hall
B The privat Kitchin & Scallerie under y^e Stair
C The Nursery
D Closets & Back Stair to the Ladys room above
E Cellars
F. Second Table room
G Litle bed room and Closets
H Woman House
I Larder
K Latter meat Hall
L Pantry
M. Milk room
N Potter lodge under y^e Stair

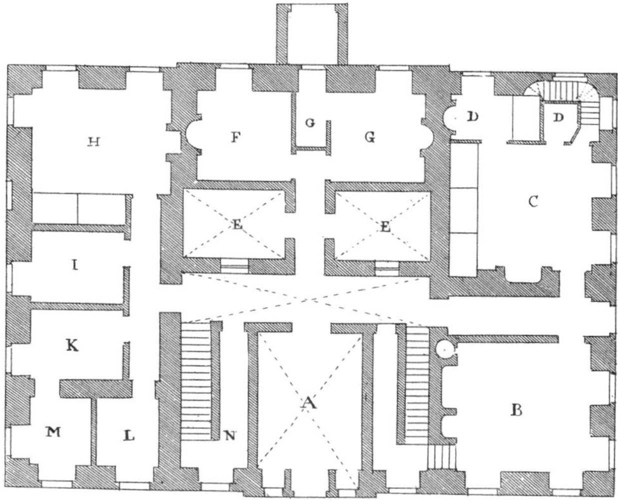

A Plan of the Ground Floor

Gul. Adam inv. et delin.

R. Cooper Sculp.

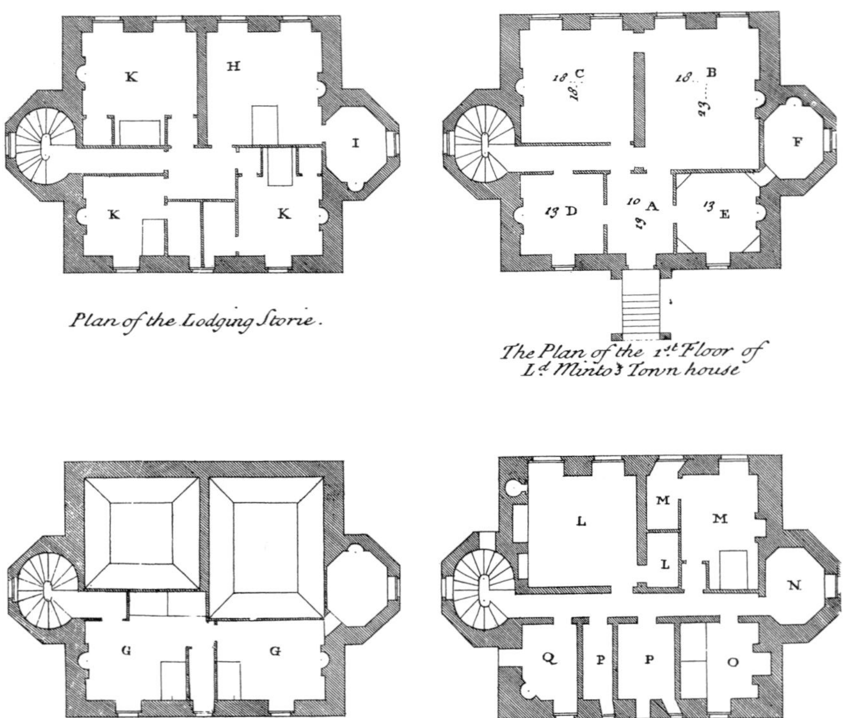

Plan of the Lodging Storie.

The Plan of the 1st Floor of Ld. Minto's Town house

Plan of the Mezzanin Storie

Plan of the Ground Floor

A *The Vestuble*
B *The Dinning Room*
C *The Drawing Room*
D *Parlour*
E *Lord's Dressing Room*
F *His Closet*
G *Nurserie & Landrie with two Closets in the Mezanin Story*
H *Lady's Bed Chamber*
I *Her Closet*
K *Three Bed Chambers more with Closets in the Lodging Story*
L *Kitchen and Scallerie*
M *B: Chamber & Closet for the Chaplain*
N *Pantrie*
O *Servants Room*
P *Cellars & Larder*
Q *Lobbie*

Gul Adam inv: et delin — *R. Cooper Sculp.*

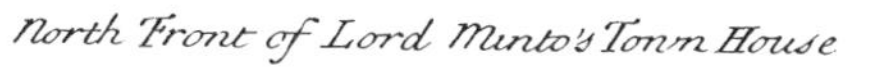

North Front of Lord Minto's Town House

Front of the South Side

Gull: Adam Archit:

R. Cooper sculp.

S.r John Bruce's House at KINROSS.

The Vaults

Third Floor

First Floor

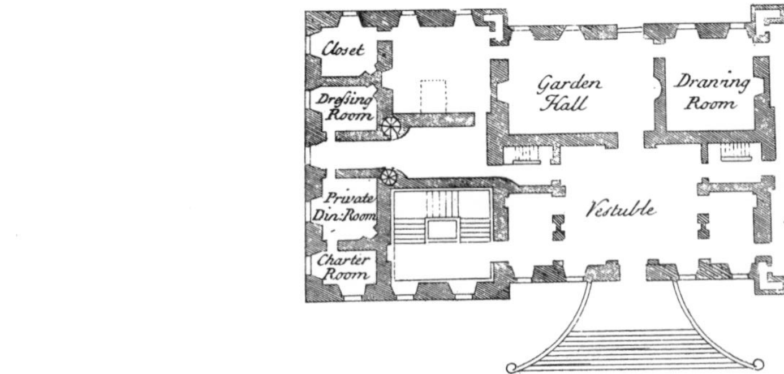

Second Floor

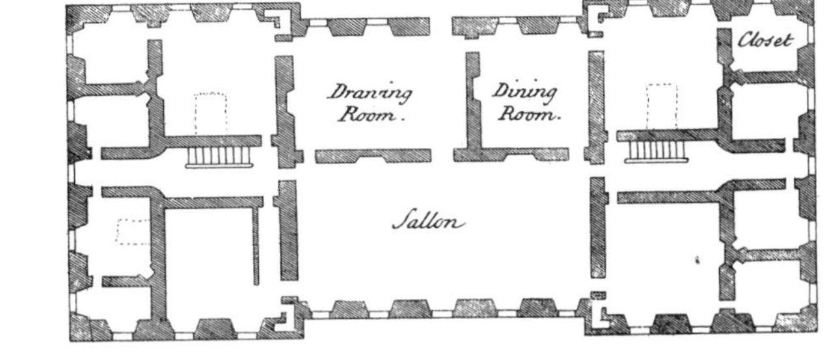

A Scale of Feet

0 20 40 60 80 100 120 140

KINROSS.

IRREVOCABILE

S.r W.m Bruce himself Arch.t 1685. The House of S.t John Bruce. G. Borlack delin.t R. Cooper sculp.

West Front of *BALLOCH MYLE HOUSE* The Seat of *ALLAN WHITEFOORD* Esqr.
in the County of Ayr.

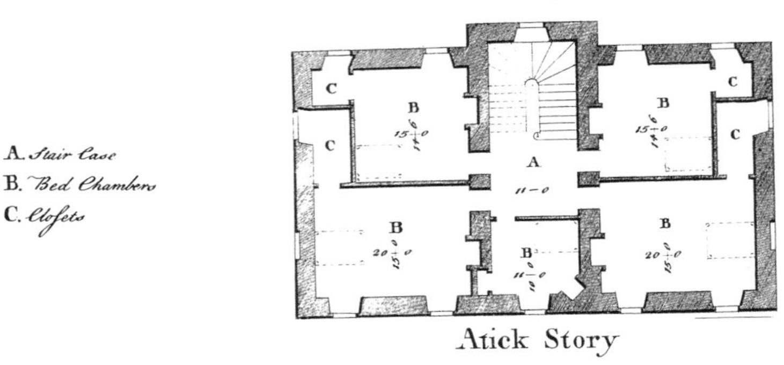

A. Stair Case
B. Bed Chambers
C. Closets

Atick Story

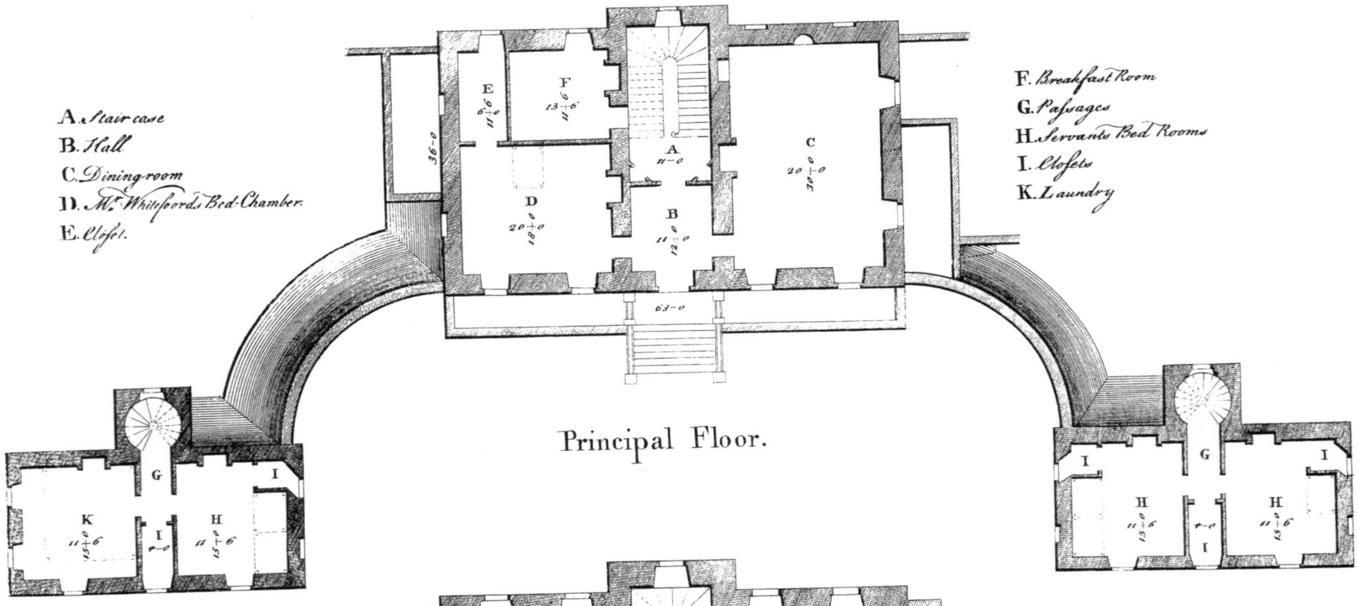

A. Stair case
B. Hall
C. Dining-room
D. Mrs. Whitefoord's Bed-Chamber
E. Closet.

F. Breakfast Room
G. Passages
H. Servants Bed Rooms
I. Closets
K. Laundry

Principal Floor.

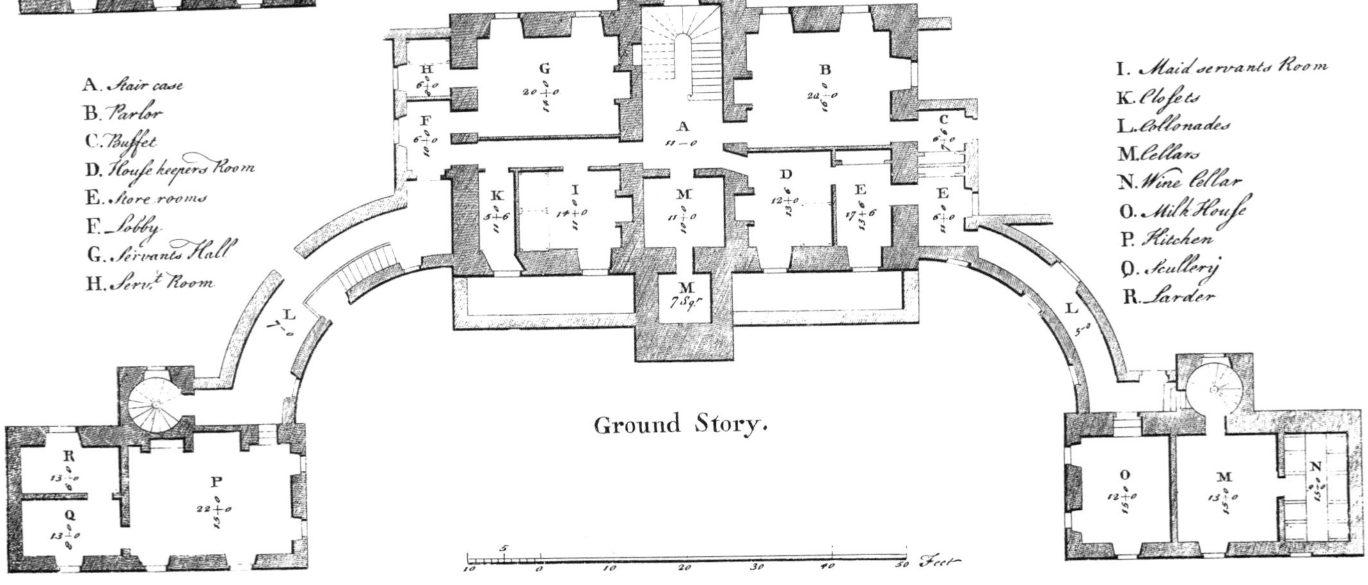

A. Stair case
B. Parlor
C. Buffet
D. House keepers Room
E. Store rooms
F. Lobby
G. Servants Hall
H. Servt. Room

I. Maid servants Room
K. Closets
L. Collonades
M. Cellars
N. Wine Cellar
O. Milk House
P. Kitchen
Q. Scullery
R. Larder

Ground Story.

5 10 0 10 20 30 40 50 Feet

Adams Archt. T. Smith Sculpt.

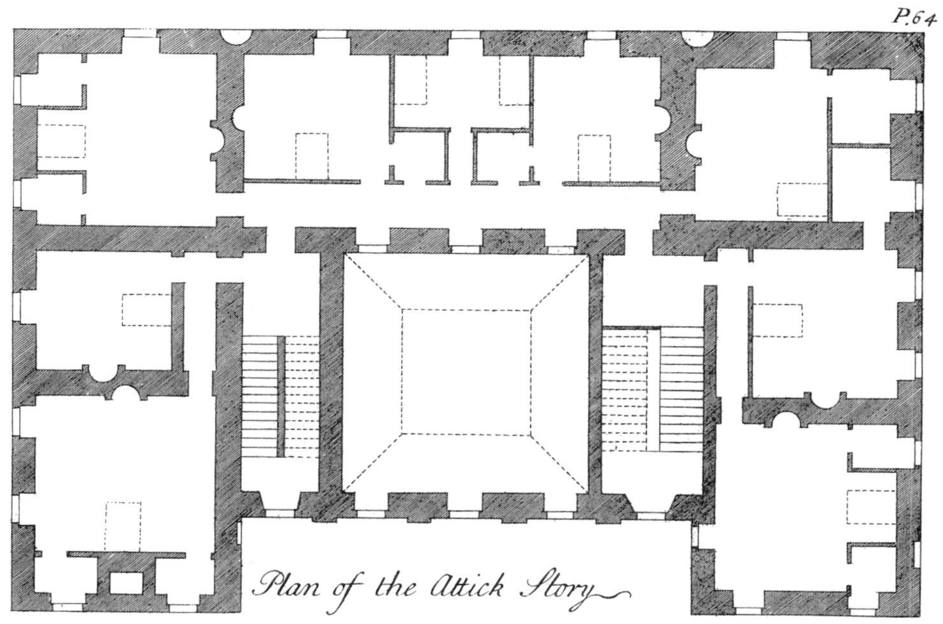

Plan of the Attick Story

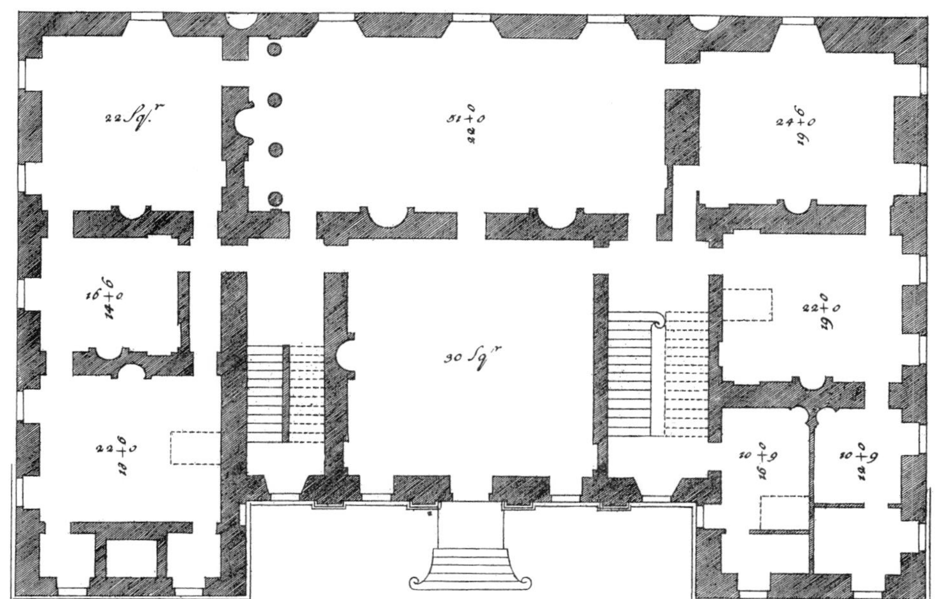

Plan of the first Floor of Airth House

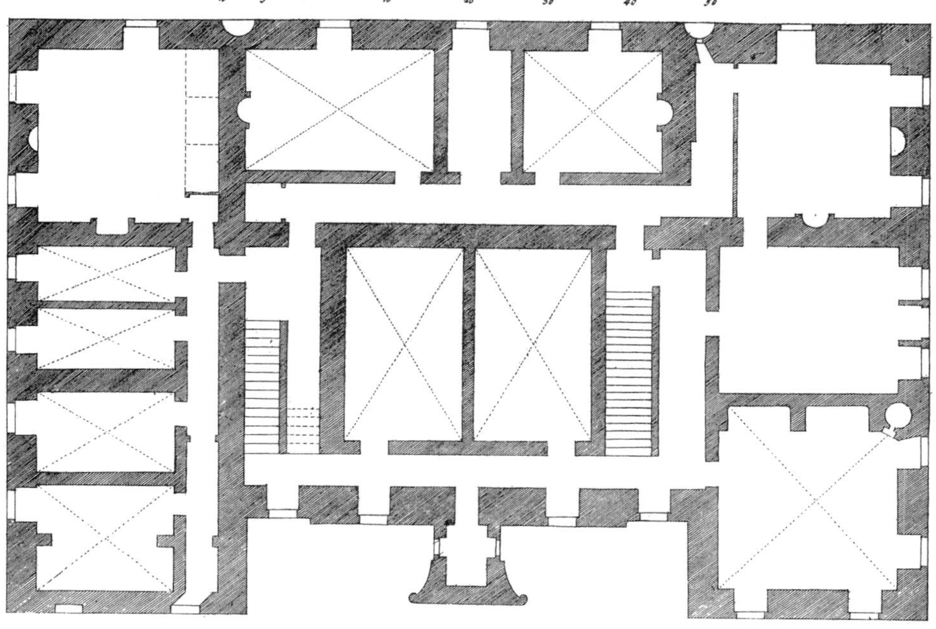

Plan of the Ground Floor

Gul: Adam Inv: et. delin R: Cooper Sculp.

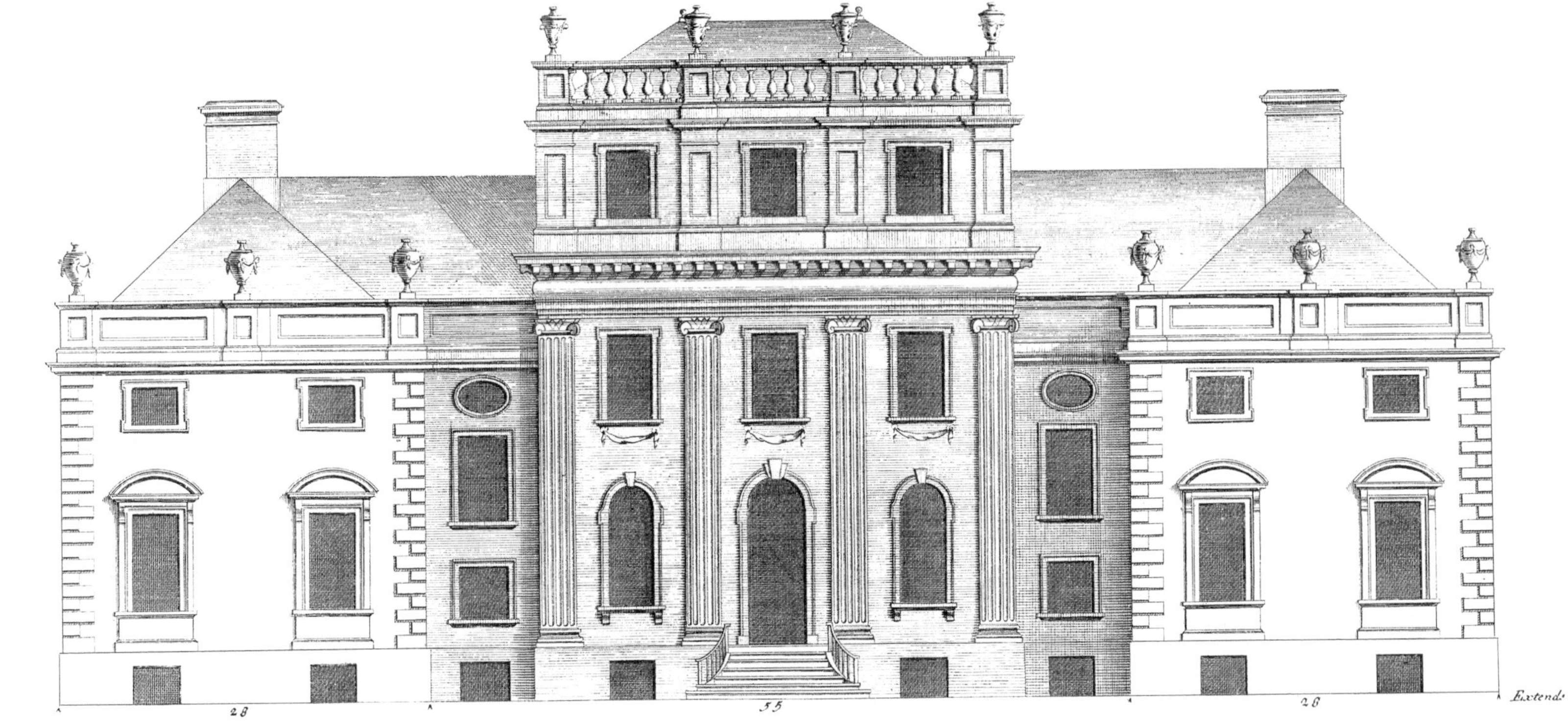

The North Front of Airth House towards the Court The Seat of Mr. James Graham of Airth Advocate in the County of Stirling

Gul: Adam Inv: et delin

R. Cooper Sculp

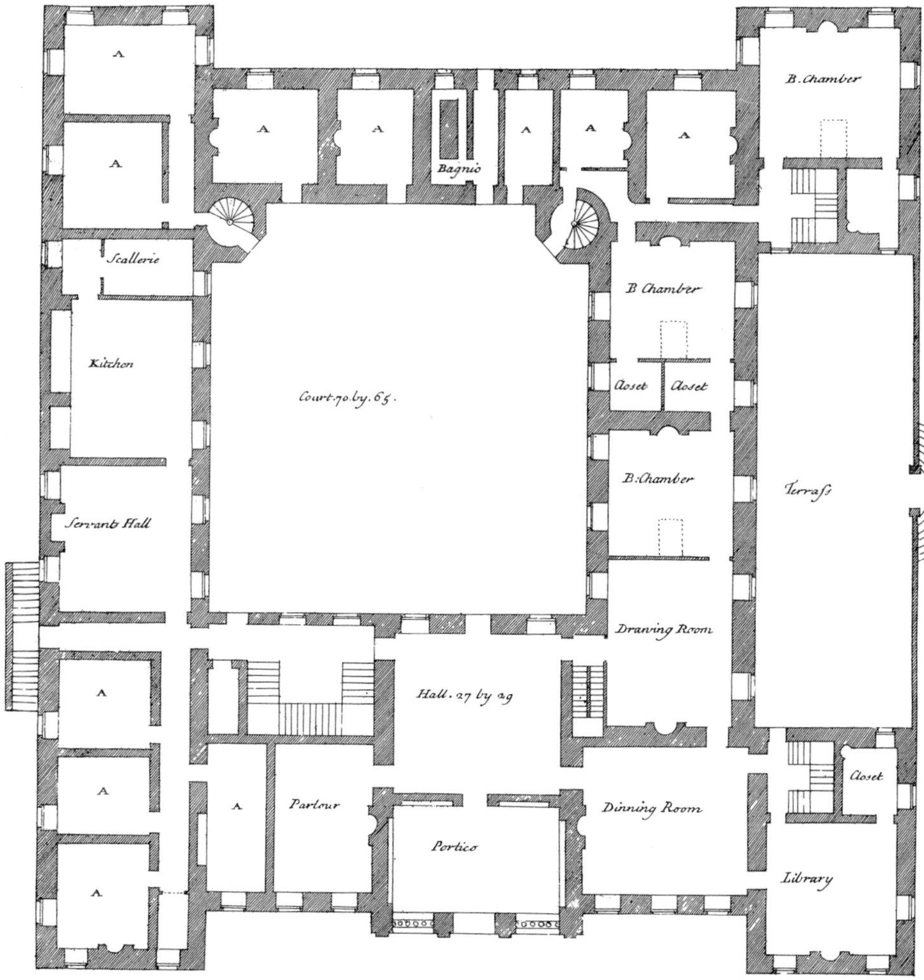

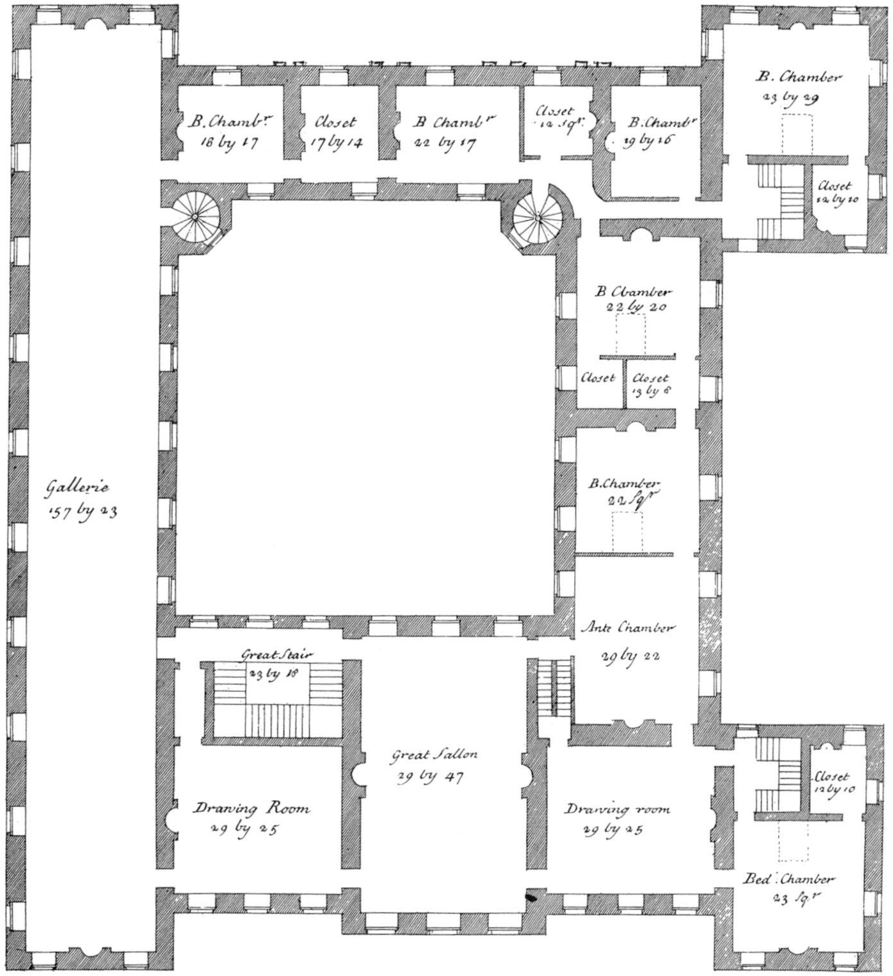

The Plan of the first Floor of Lesly

The different Rooms mark'd with Letter A are Servants rooms Larder, Milk House Pantry &c & the Cellars are in a Vaulted Story on the North side of the House

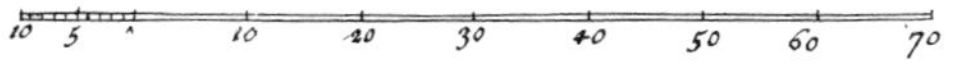

The Plan of the 2d Storie or State Floor

Gul Adam delin

R. Cooper sculp.

The West Front of Lesly House toward the Court the Seat of the Right Honourable the Earle of Rothess in the County of Fife

Gul. Adam del. R Cooper Sculp.

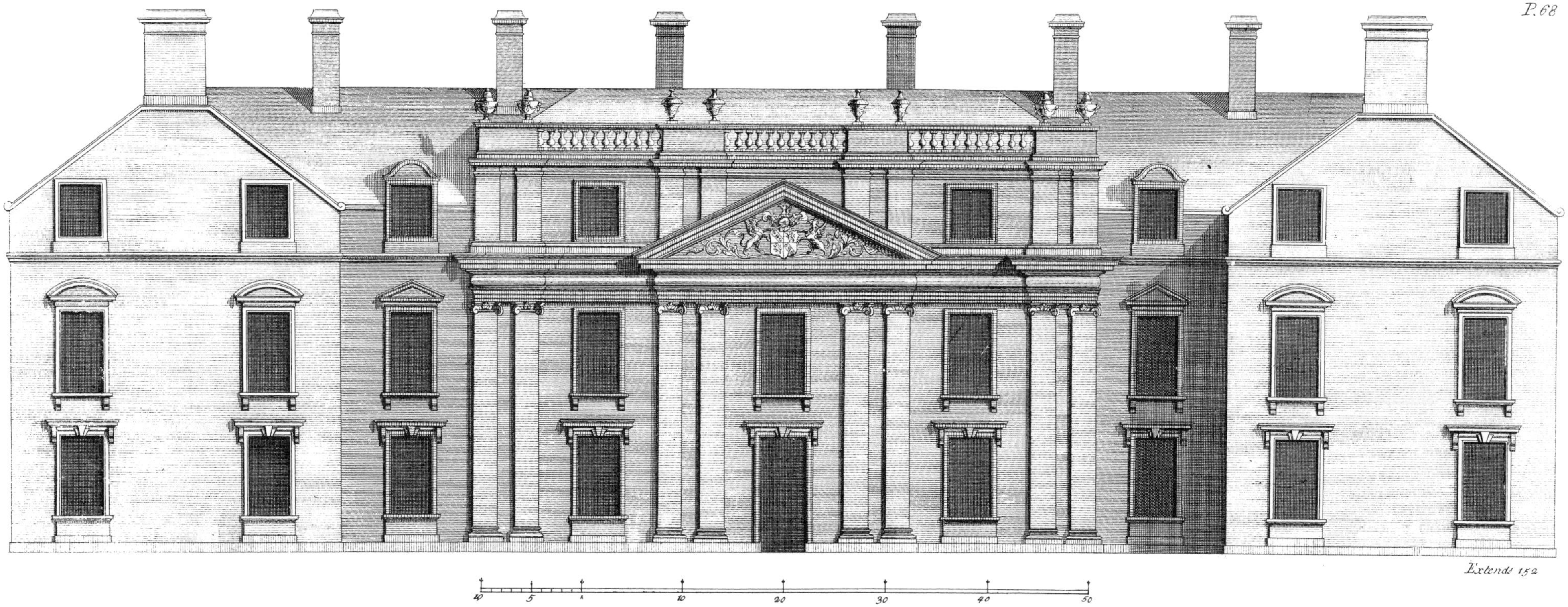

Extends 152

10 5 1 10 20 30 40 50

The East Front of Lesley House toward the Court the Seat of the Right Hon.ble the Earl of Rothess in the County of Fife

Gul Adam delin

R: Cooper Sculp

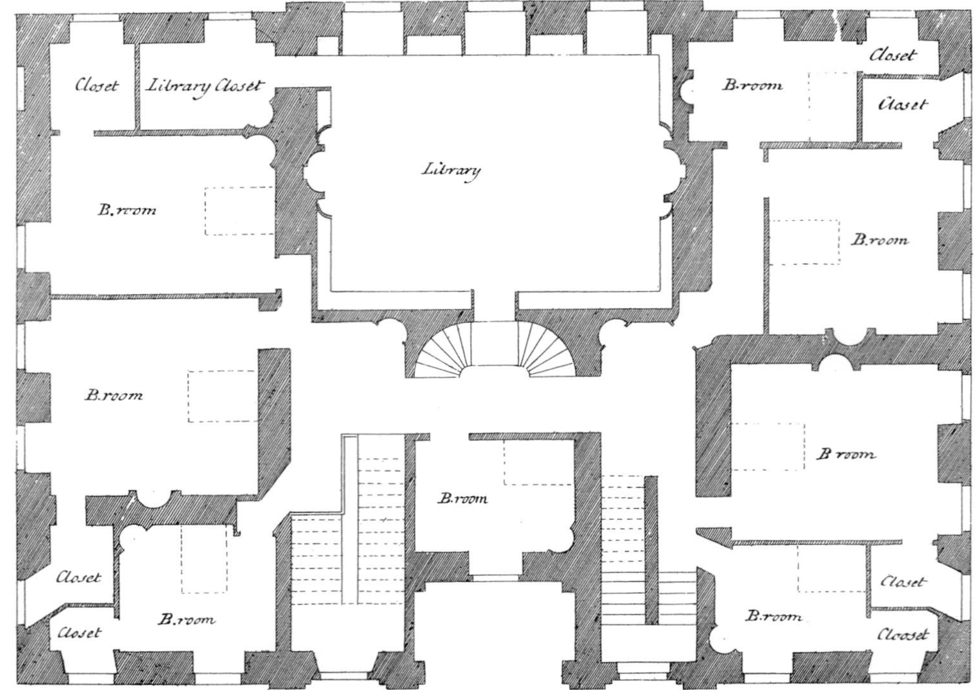

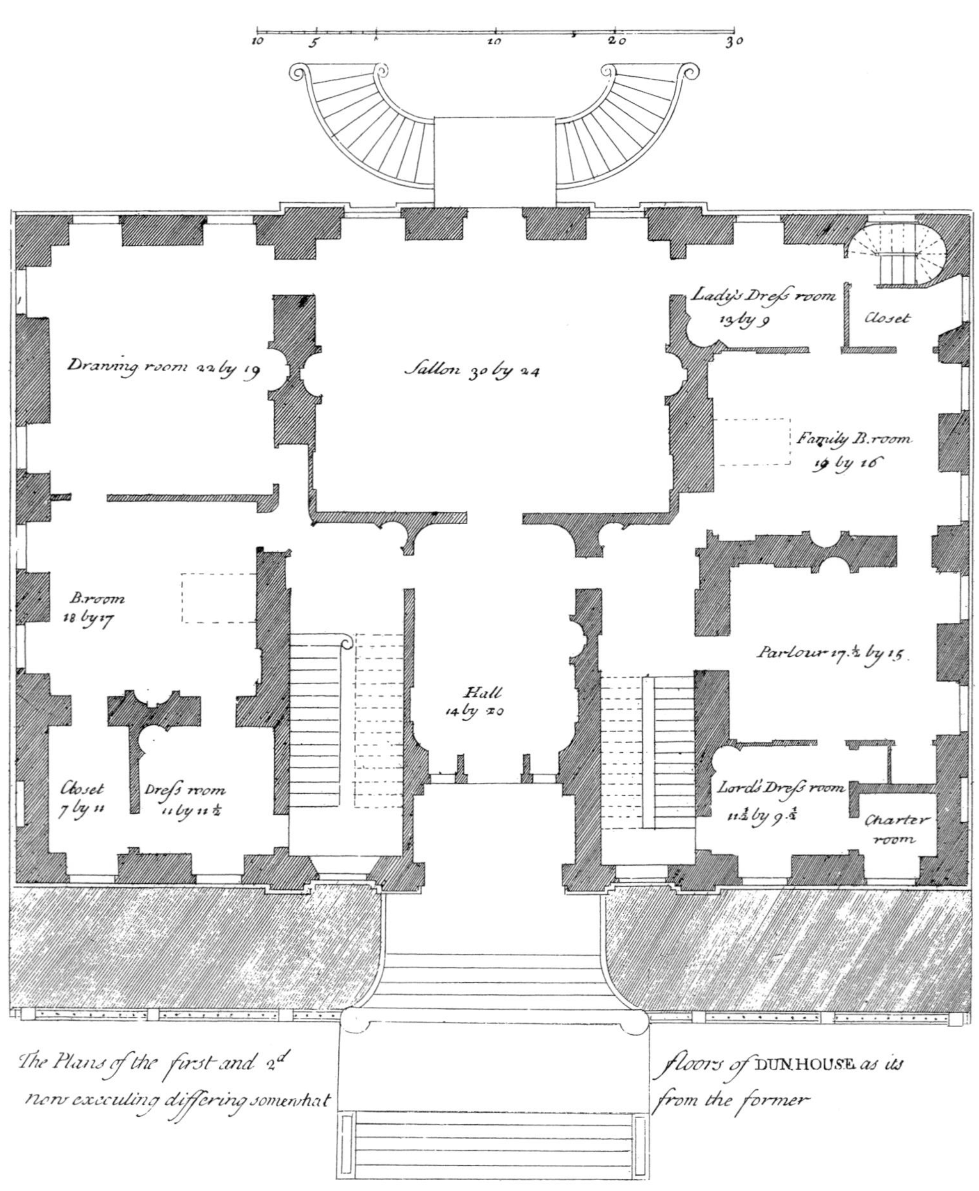

The Plans of the first and 2d floors of DUNHOUSE *as its now executing differing somewhat from the former*

Gul. Adam inv. et delin

The South Front towards the Garden

These Fronts of the 2d Design being more ornamented than the former are executing accordingly

The North Front of DUN House towards the Court in the County of ANGUS. The Seat of the Honourable DAVID ERSKINE of DUN one of the Senators of the Colidge of Justice

Gul. Adam inv. et Delin

R. Cooper Sculp.

GROUND STORY of INVERARAY CASTLE, with the FOSSEE & CASEMATES.

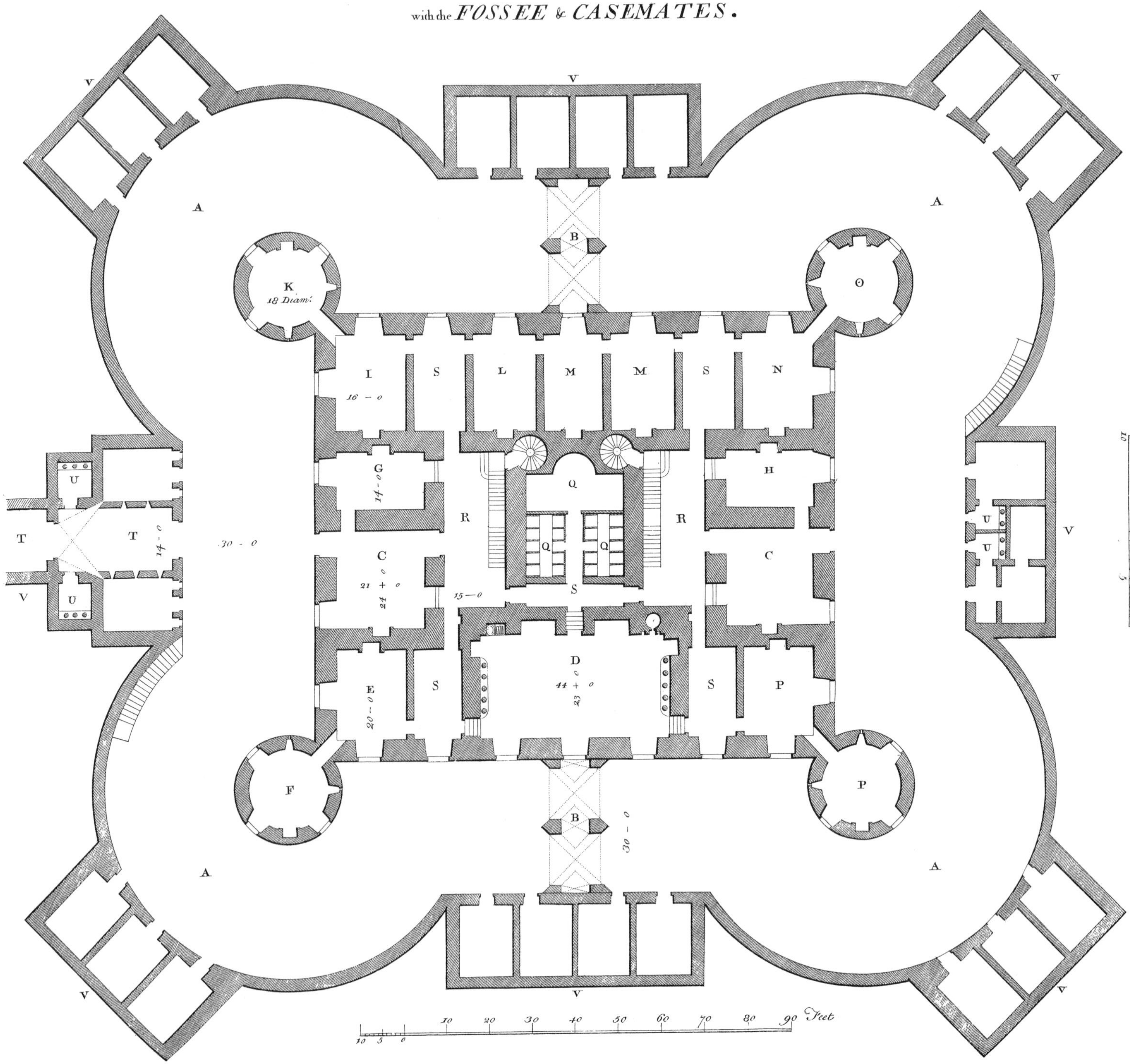

A. Fossee round the House.
B. Bridges across the Fossee.
C. Servts Halls.
D. Kitchen.
E. Scullery.
F. Pastry room.
G. Lattermeat room.
H. Porters Lodge.
I. Stewards Hall.
K. Butlers room.
L. Pantry.
M. Lardens.
N. Housekeepers room.
O. Store room.
P. Laboratorys.
Q. Cellers.
R. Stairs.
S. Passages.
T. Underground Passage to the Fossee.
U. Necessary Houses.
V. Casemates round the Fossee.

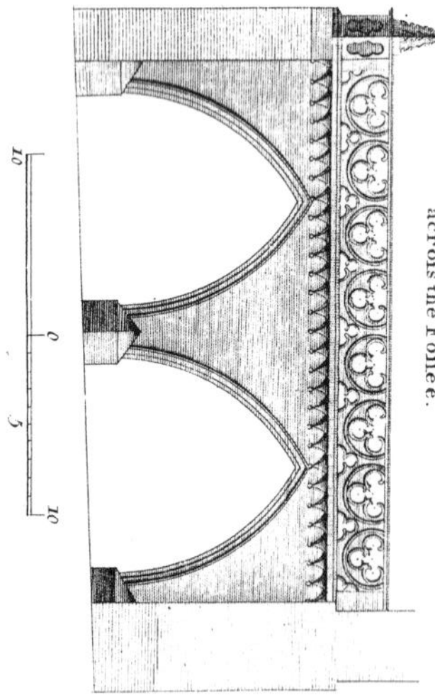

Elevation of One of the Bridges across the Fossee.

A. Bell Sculpt.

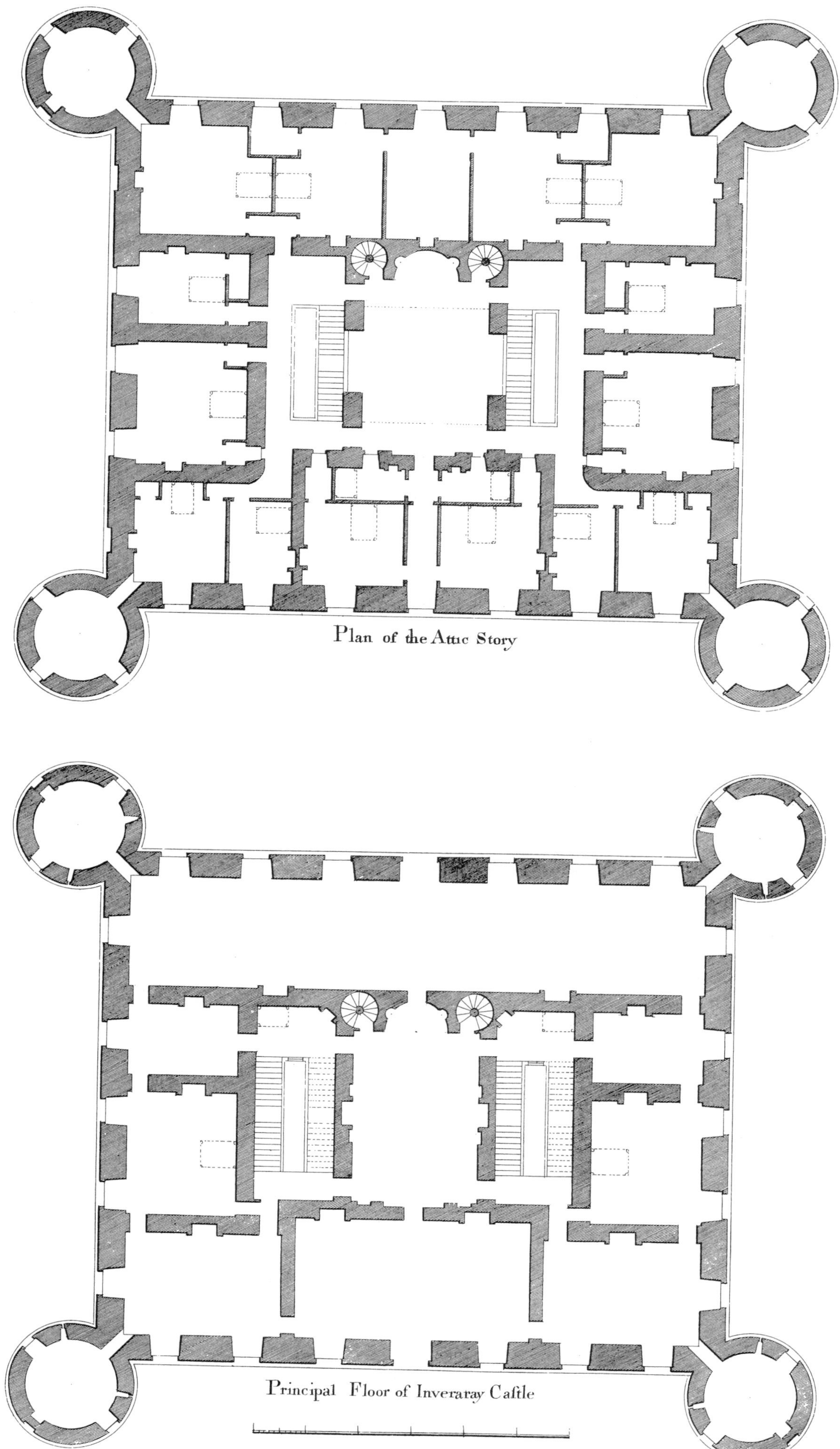

R. Morris Archt.

Generall Front of Belvidere toward the West the Seat of the Honourable George Dalrymple Esqr one of the Barons of His Majestys Exchequer

Gul Adam inv et delin

R. Cooper Sculp.

South Front of Inverary Castle, the Seat of His Grace the Duke of Argyll in the County of Argyll

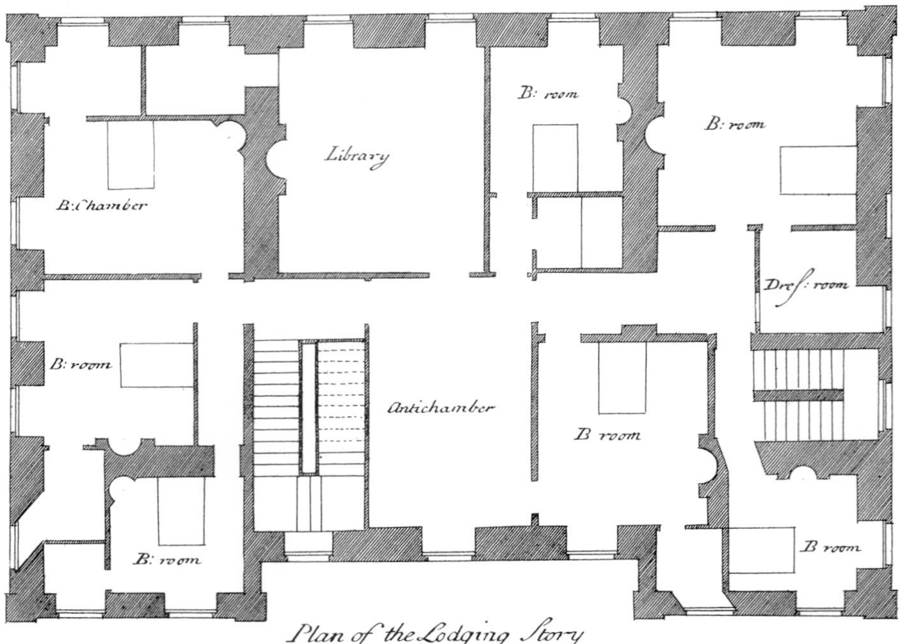

Plan of the Lodging Story

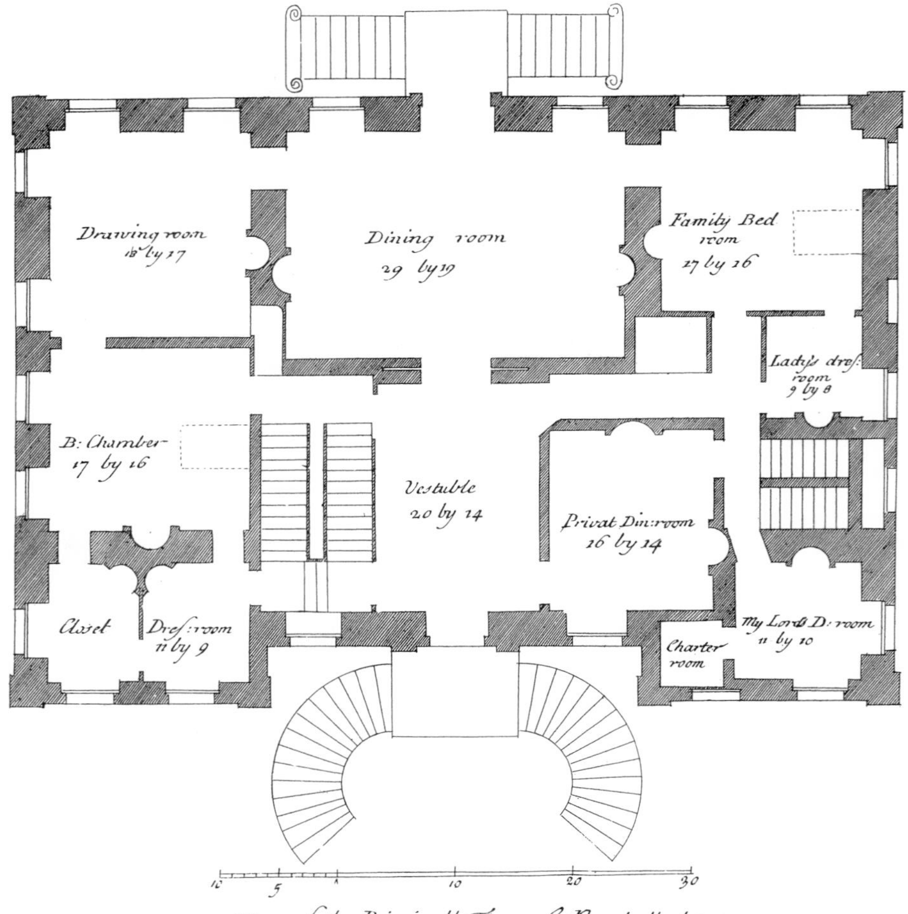

Plan of the Principall Floor of Newhall house

Gul: Adam inv: Delin

R: Cooper Sculp

East Front of Newhall House toward the Court the Seat of the Honourable John Hay of Newhall Esqr in the County of East Lothian

Gul: Adam inv: delin:

R: Cooper Sculp.

BRIDGES at INVERARAY

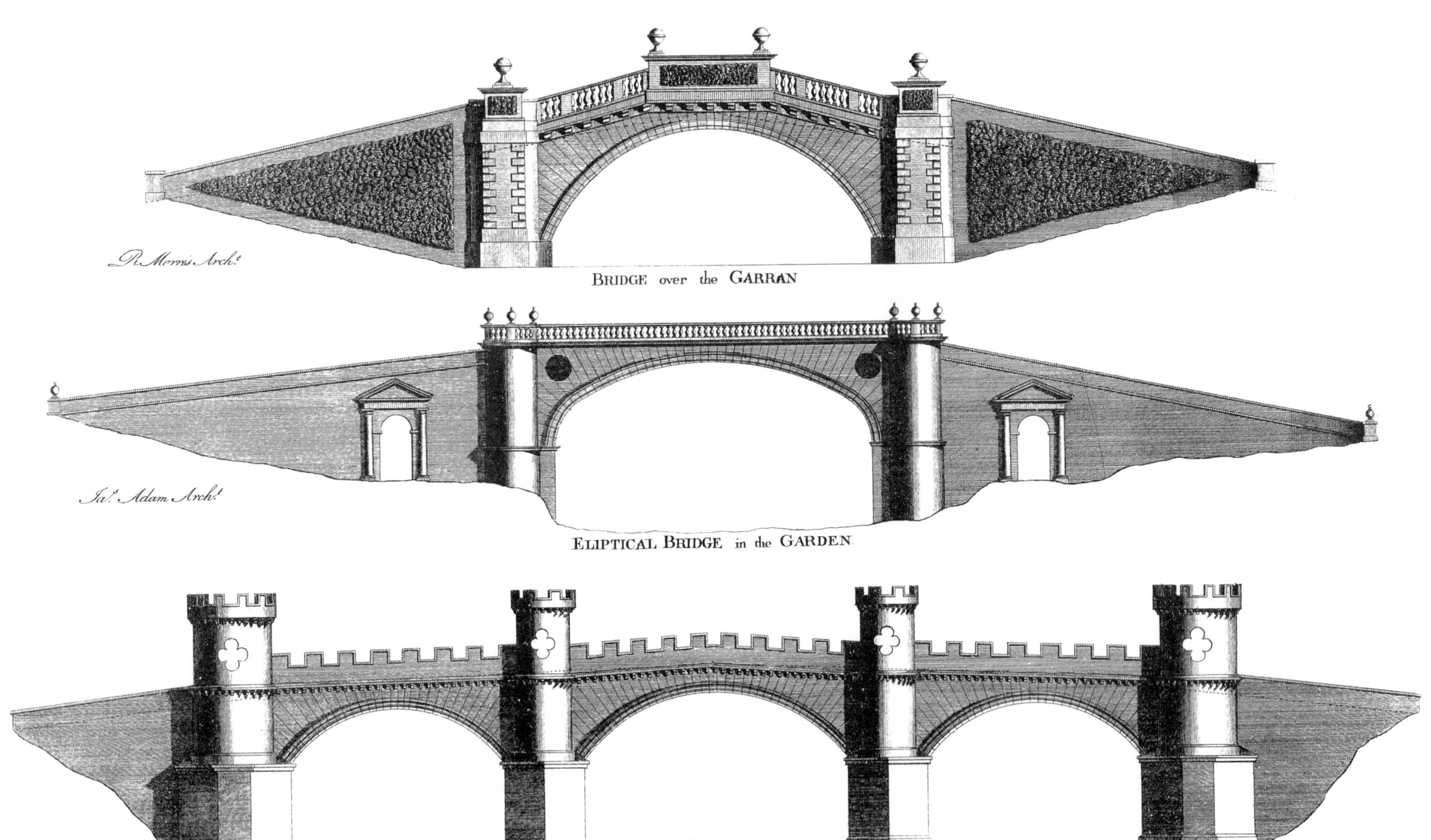

BRIDGE over the GARRAN

ELIPTICAL BRIDGE in the GARDEN

BRIDGE at the Mouth of the RIVER ARAY in the GOTHICK Stile

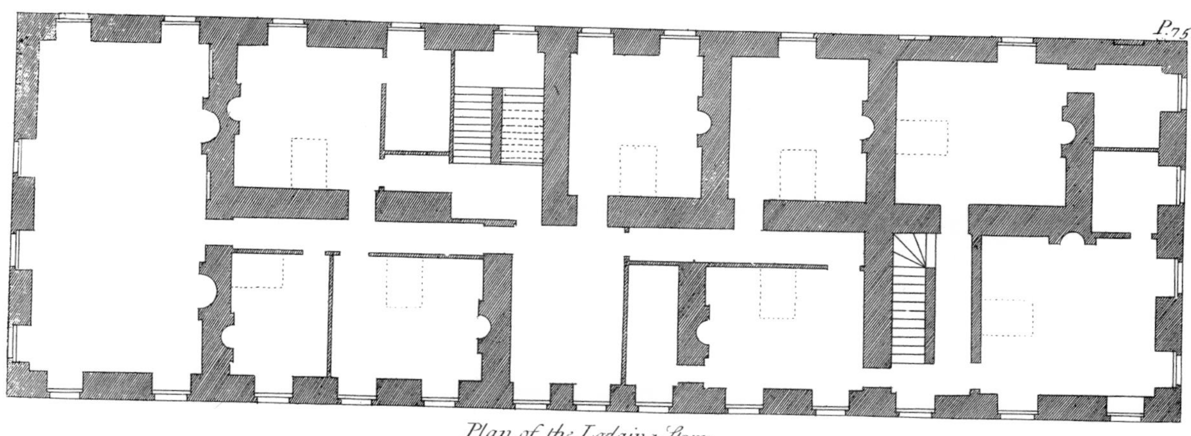

Plan of the Lodging Story

10 5 0 10 20 30 40 50

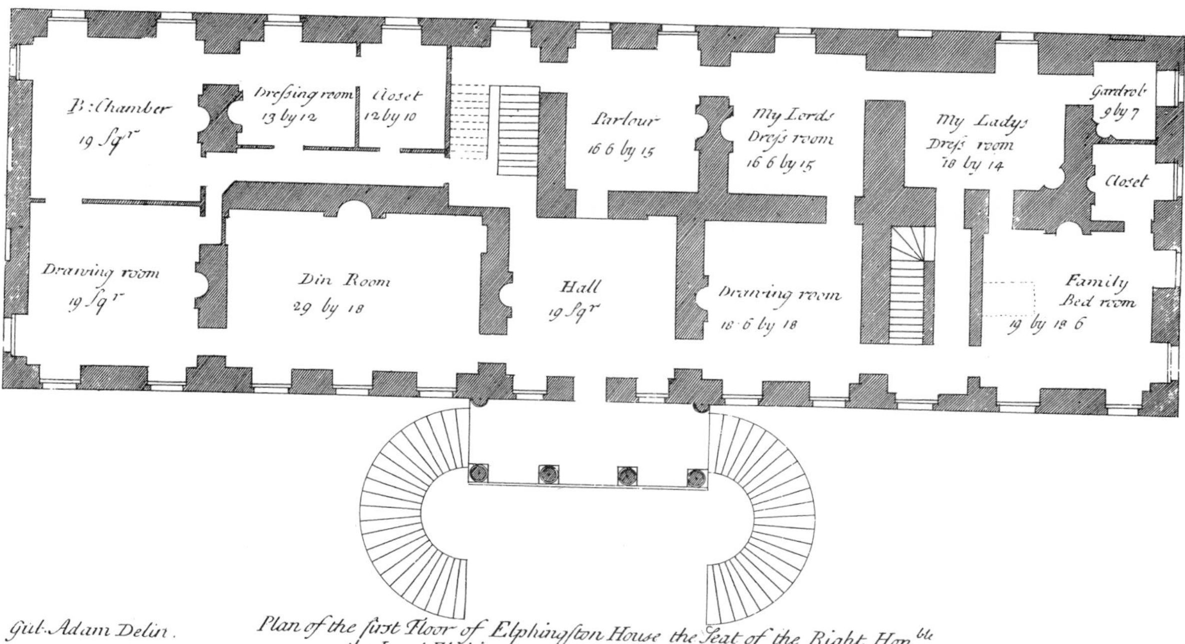

Gul. Adam Delin.

Plan of the first Floor of Elphingston House the Seat of the Right Hon.[ble] the Lord Elphingston in the County of Stirling

R. Cooper Sculp

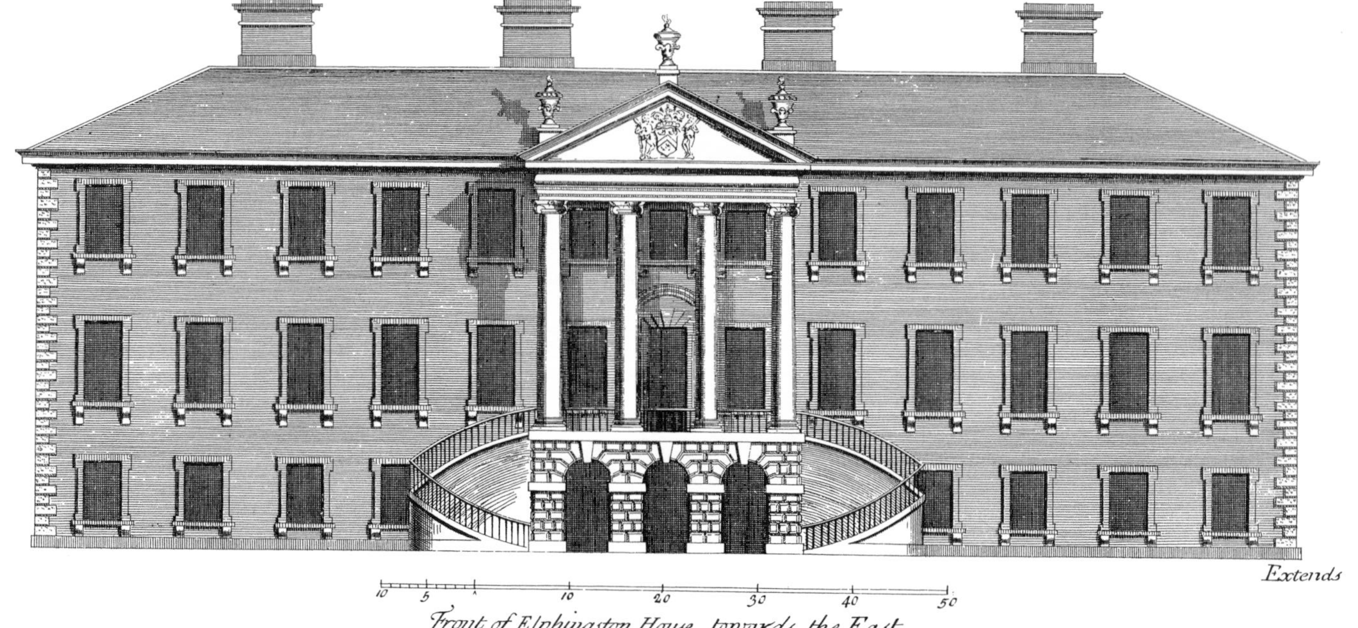

Front of Elphingston House towards the East

Gul Adam delin

R. Cooper Sculp

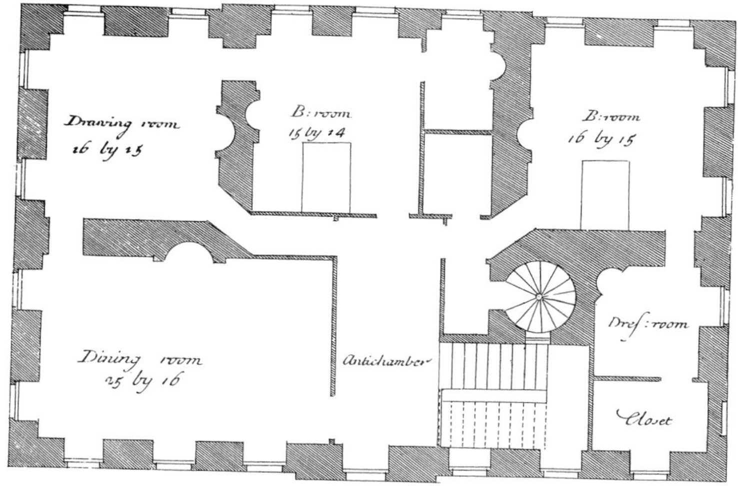

Plan of the Principal floor

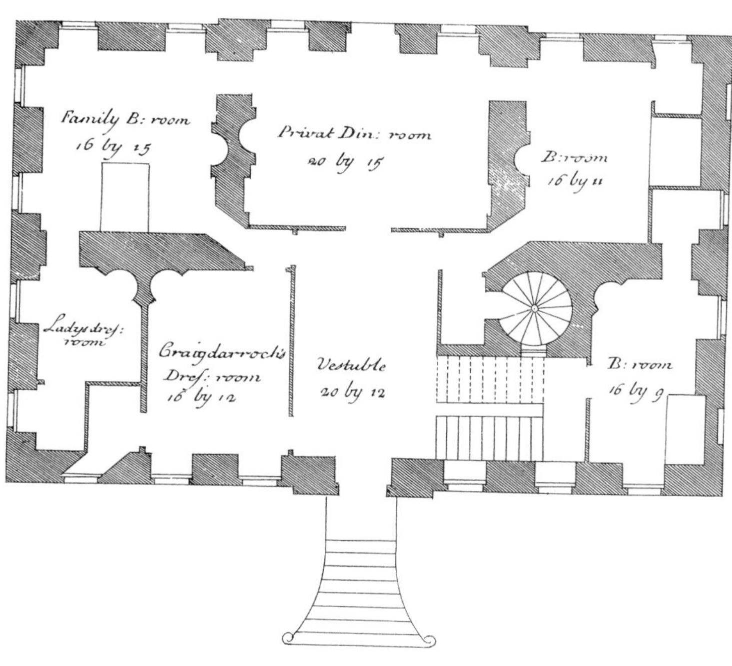

Plan of the Vestuble floor of Craigdarroch

Gul: Adam inv: delin

R Cooper Sculp

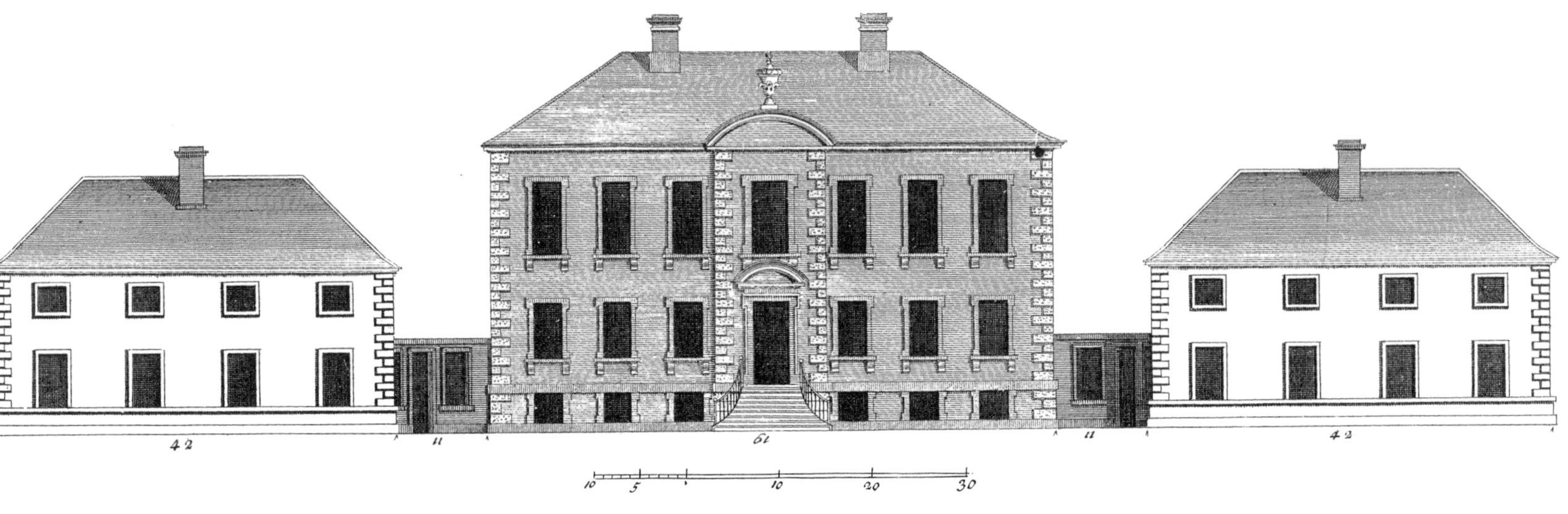

East Front of Craigdarroch toward the Court the Seat of Alexander Ferguson Esq.r in the County of Nithisdale — Extends 167

Gul. Adam. inv: delin

R: Cooper Sculp.

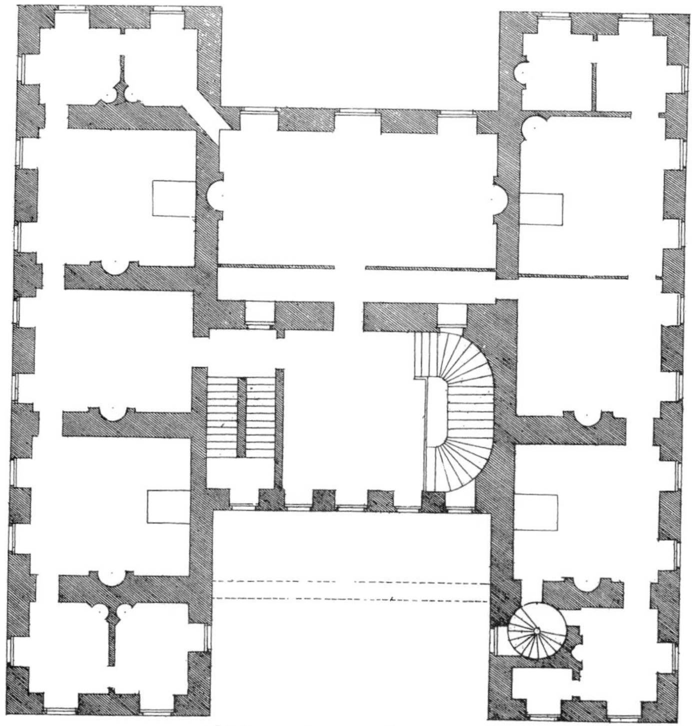

Plan of the Lodging Story

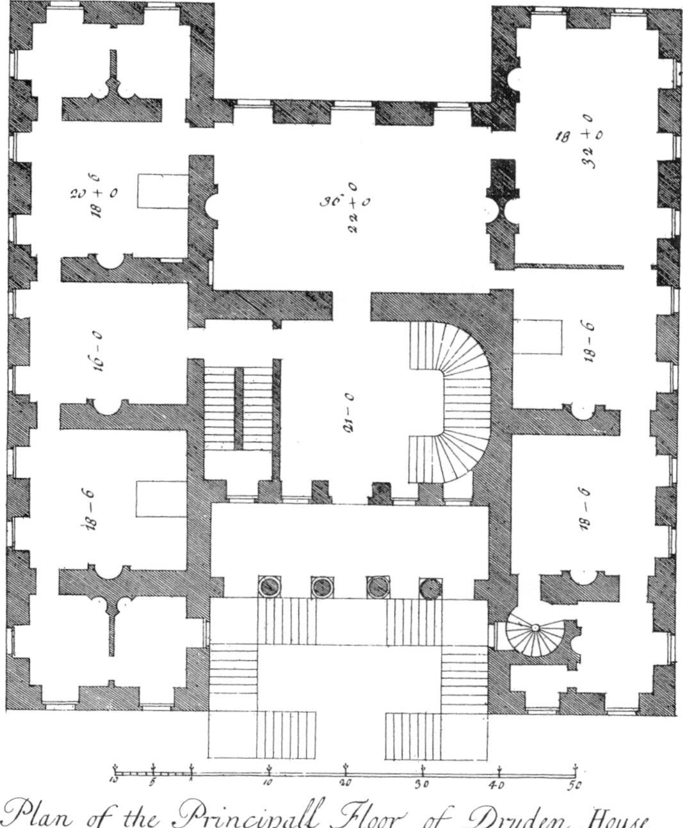

Plan of the Principall Floor of Dryden House

Gul: Adam delin:

R: Cooper Sculp

The West Front of Dryden House towards the Court the Seat of George Lockhart of Carnwath Esq.r in the County of Midd-Lothian

Gull: Adam delin

R Cooper Sculp

A Plan of the first Floor of East-Park one of the Seats of Her Grace the Dutchess of Bucleugh In the County of Mid-Lothian.

Gul. Adam del.

R. Cooper Sculp.

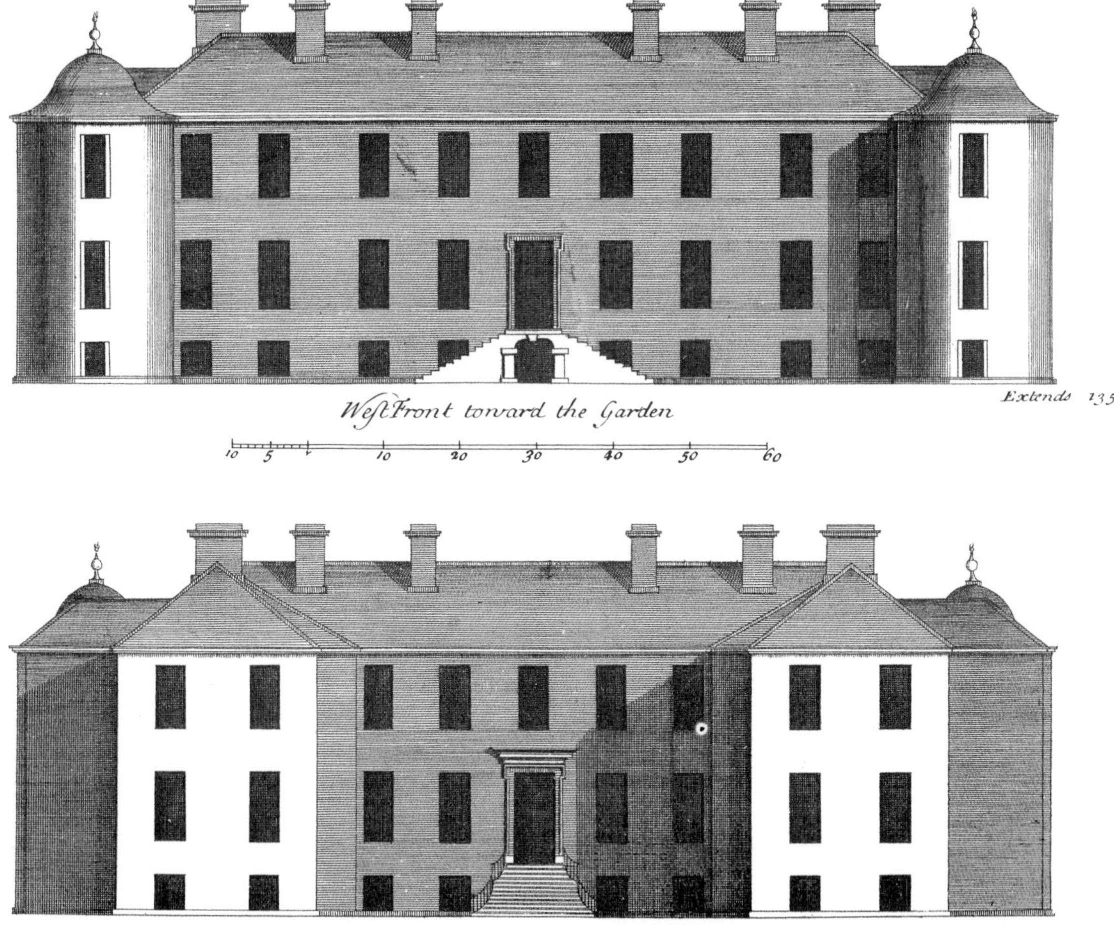

Front of East Park House toward the Court, one of the Seats of his Grace the Duke of Buccleugh in the County of Mid Lothian.

Gul: Adam delin.

R: Cooper Sculp.

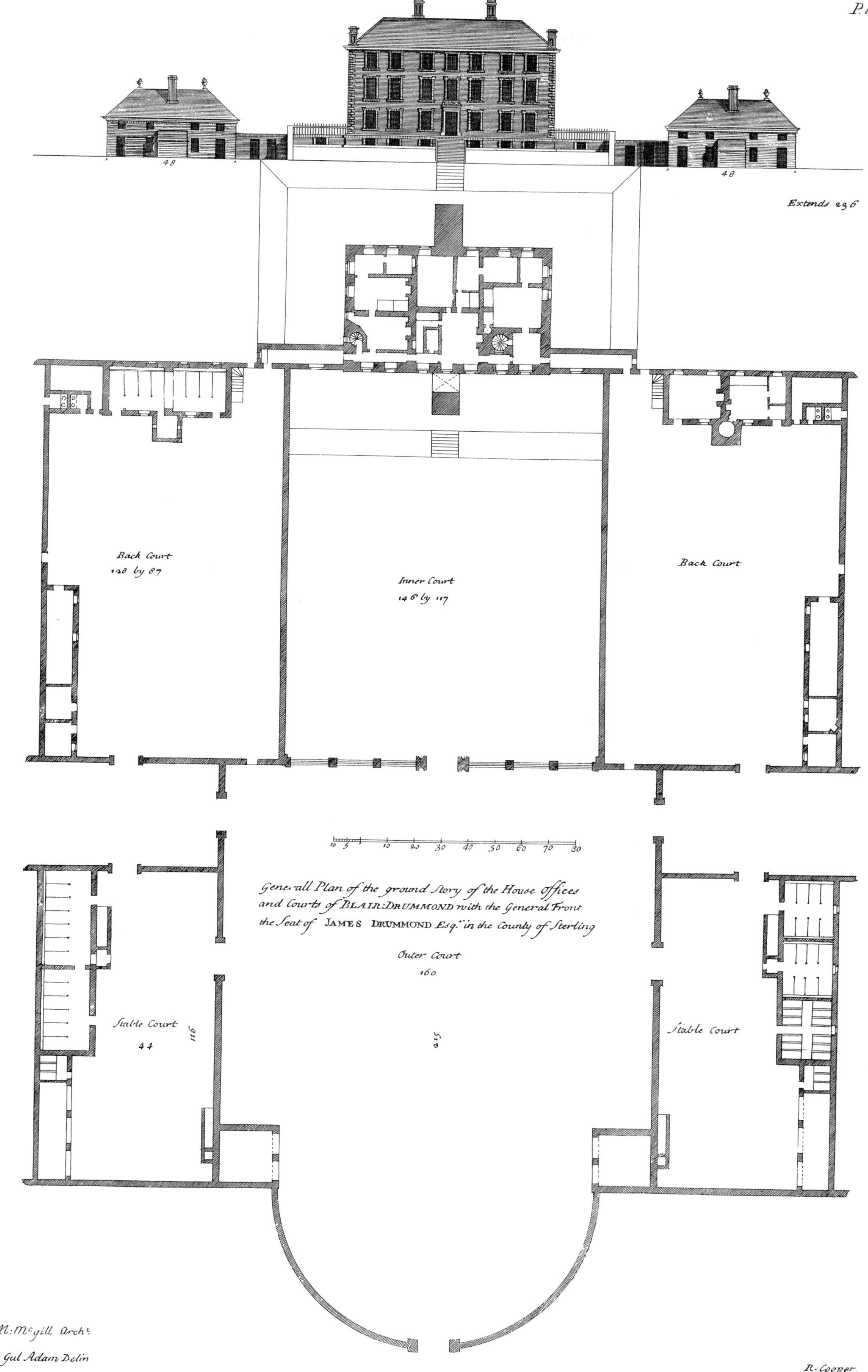

Mr. M: Mcgill Arch.t

Gul Adam Delin

R. Cooper

Elevation of *GARTMORE=HOUSE* The Seat of *NICHOLAS GRÆME* Esq.r
in the County of Stirling.

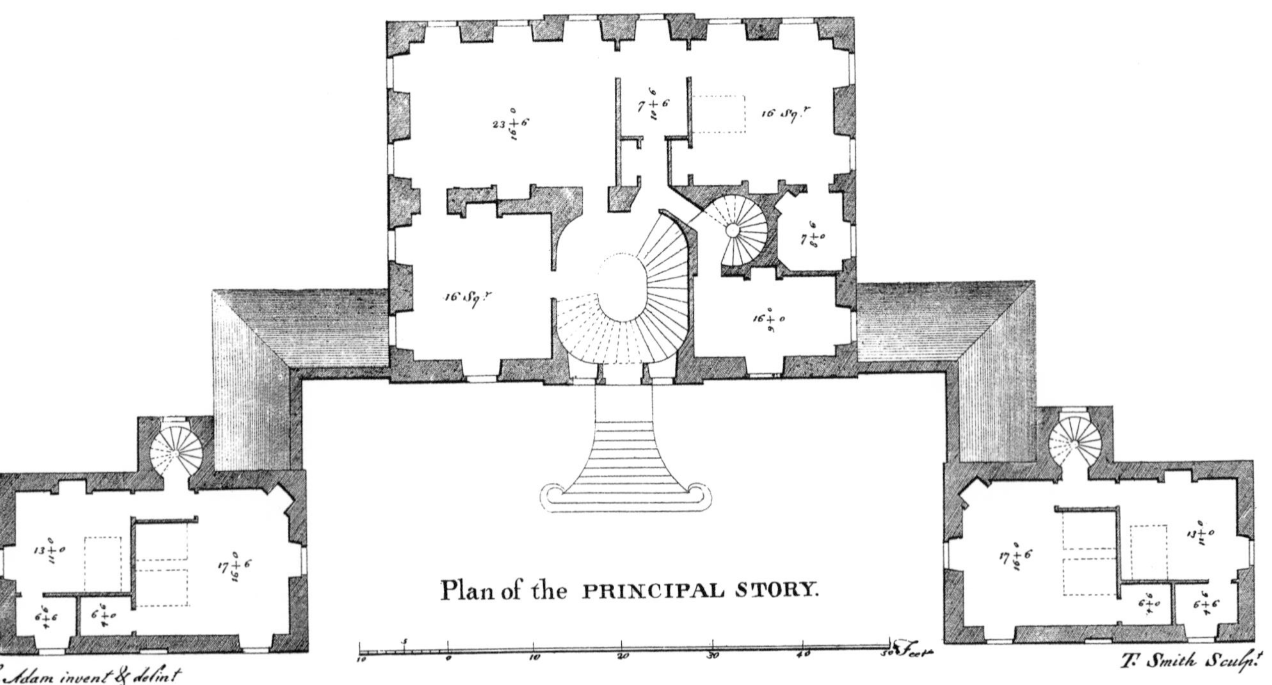

Plan of the PRINCIPAL STORY.

Gul. Adam invent & delin.t *T. Smith Sculp.t*

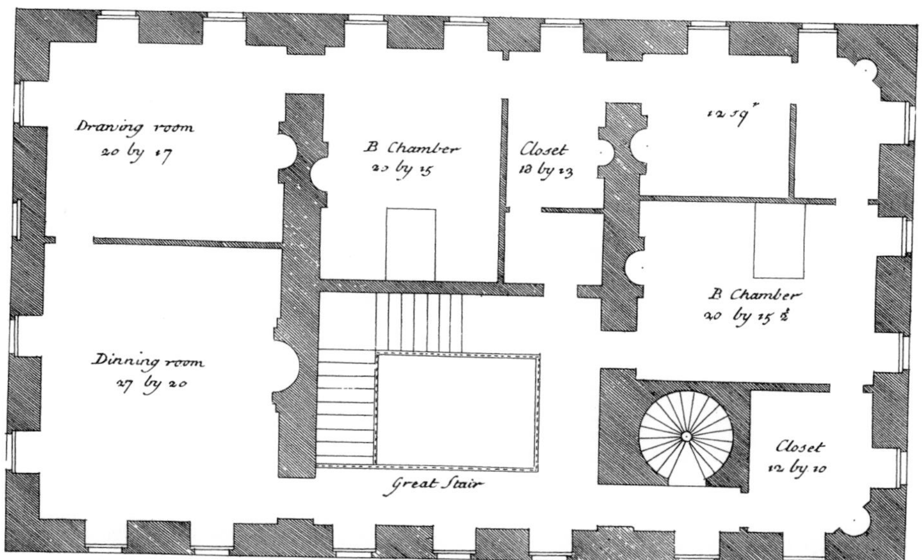

Plan of the 2^d Floor or principal Story

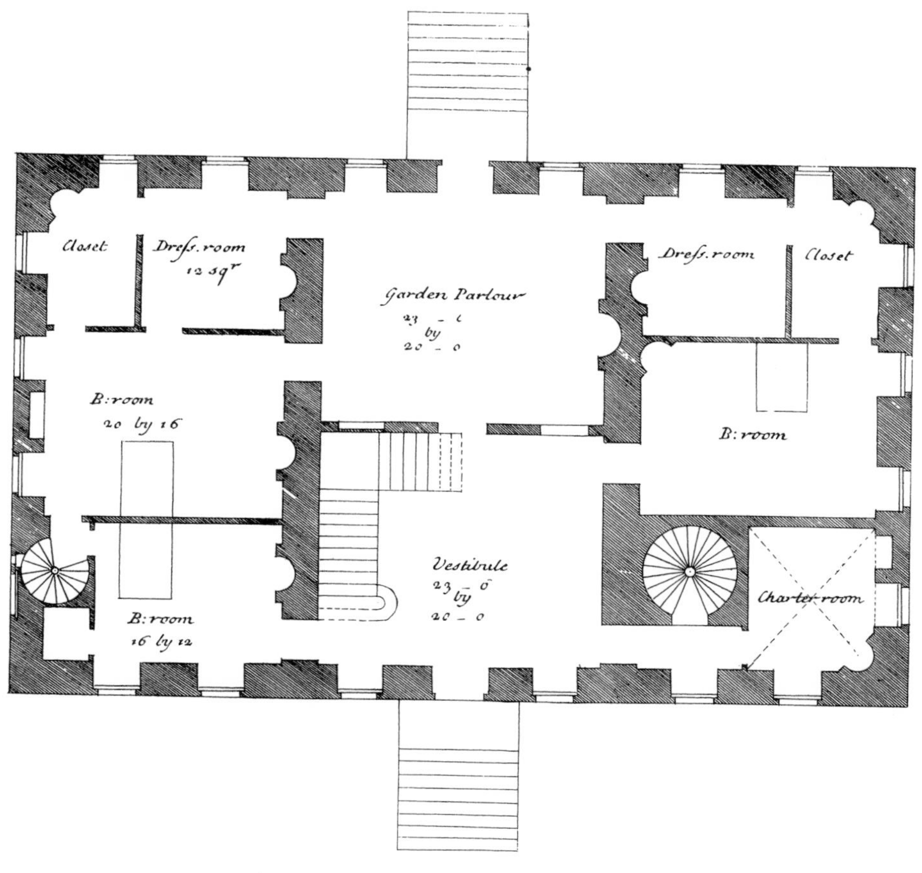

Plan of the first Floor of Blair Drummond House

10 5 10 20 30

Gul Adam delin

R Cooper Sculp

Court Front of the body of the House towards the East — Extends . 75 -

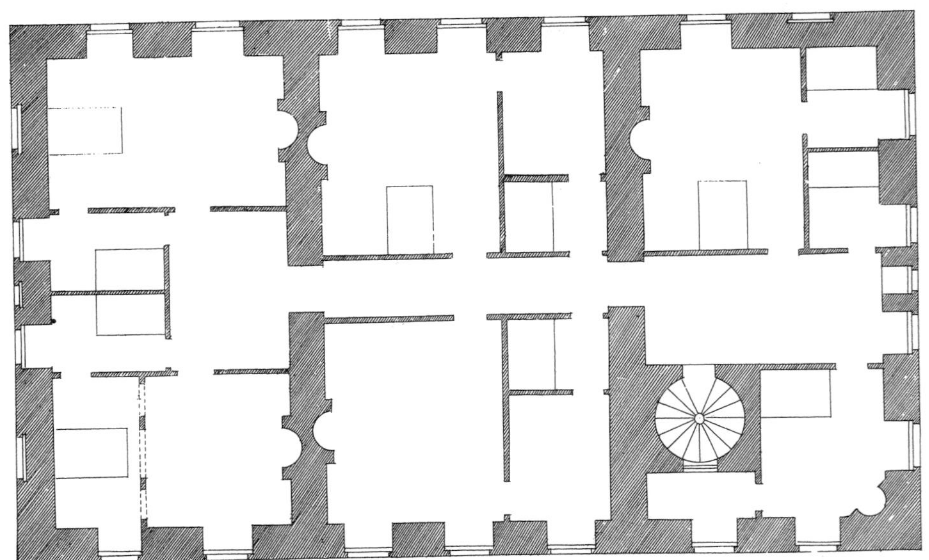

Plan of the Lodging Story

Gul Adam delin R. Cooper Sculp

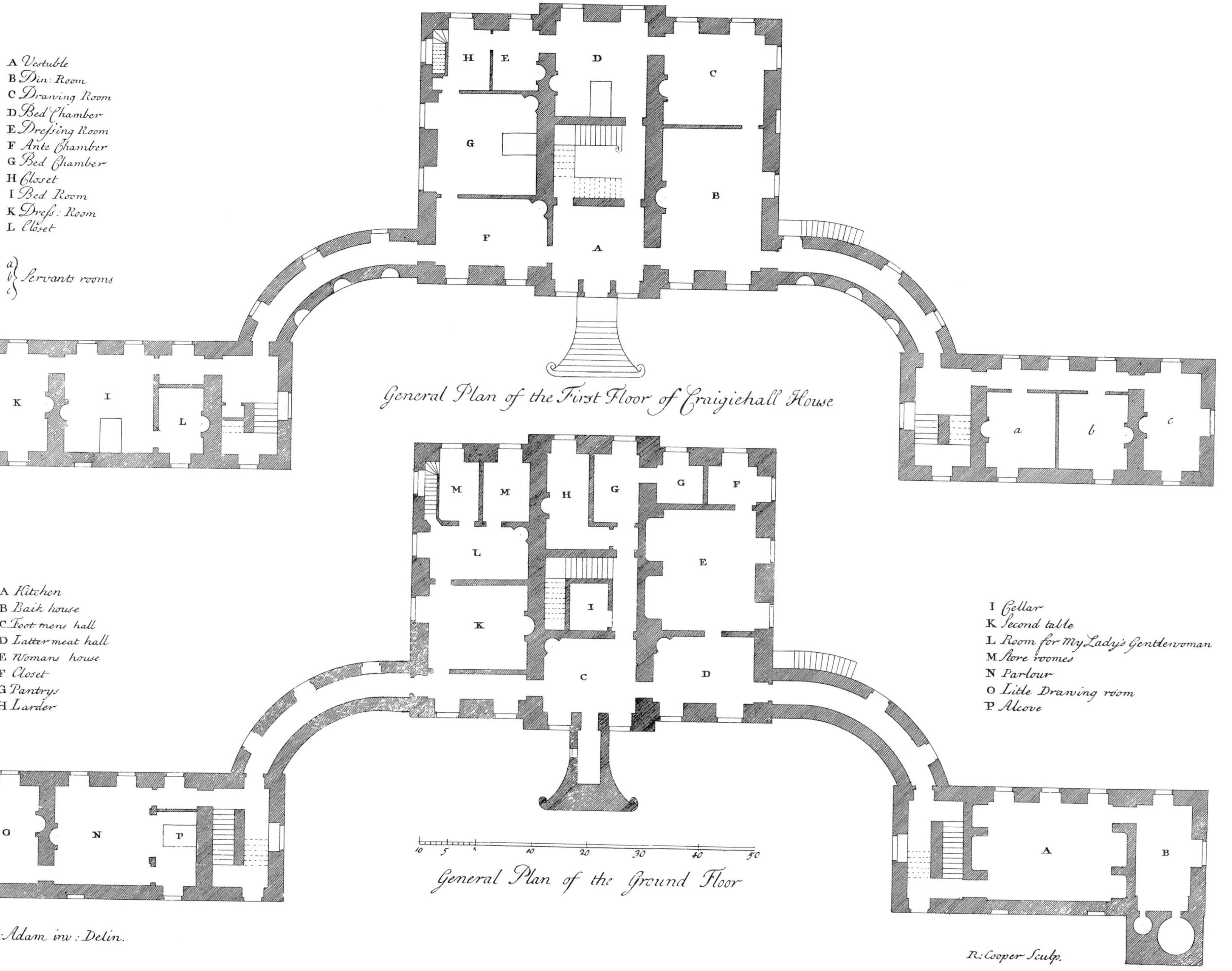
A Vestuble
B Din: Room
C Drawing Room
D Bed Chamber
E Dressing Room
F Ante Chamber
G Bed Chamber
H Closet
I Bed Room
K Dress: Room
L Closet
a b c Servants rooms
General Plan of the First Floor of Craigiehall House
A Kitchen
B Baik house
C Foot mens hall
D Latter meat hall
E Womans house
F Closet
G Pantrys
H Larder
I Cellar
K Second table
L Room for My Lady's Gentlewoman
M Store roomes
N Parlour
O Litle Drawing room
P Alcove
10 5 10 20 30 40 50
General Plan of the Ground Floor
Gul: Adam inv: Delin.
R: Cooper Sculp.

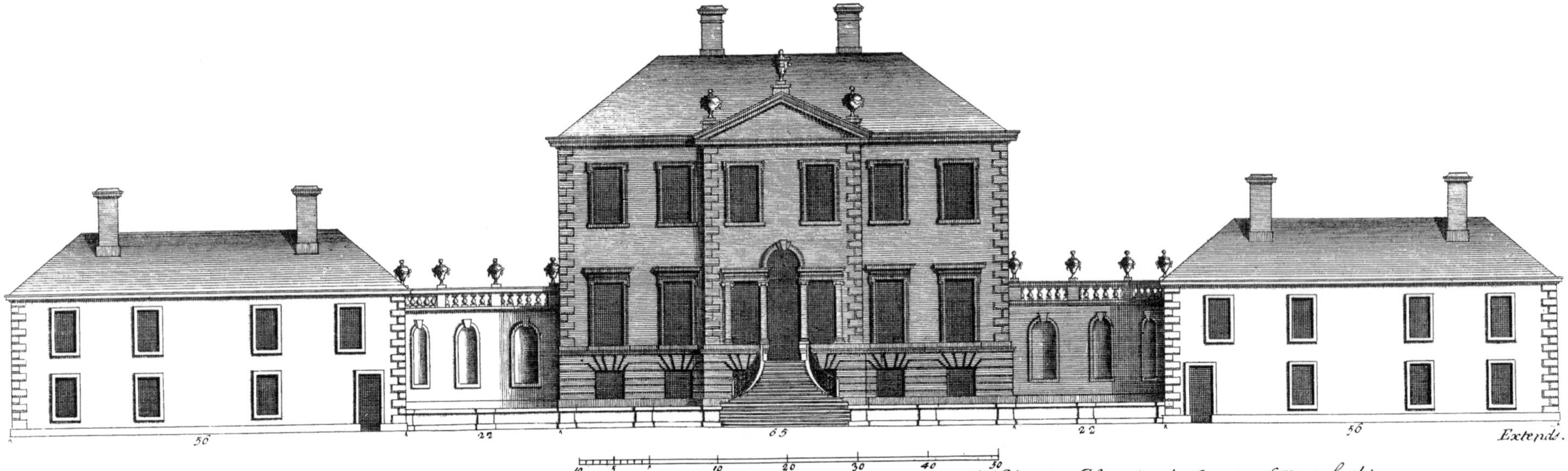

50 22 65 22 50 Extends. 221.

10 5 0 10 20 30 40 50

The General Front of Craigiehall House Toward the East The Seat of The Hon.ble Charles Hope in the County of West Lothian

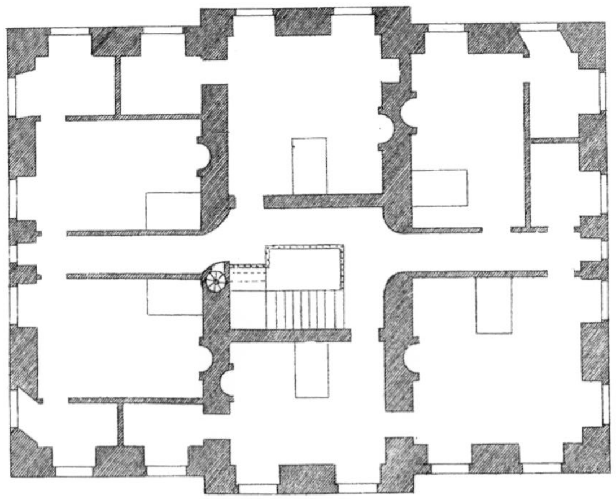

Plan of the Attick Storie

Gul. Adam delin.

R. Cooper Sculp.

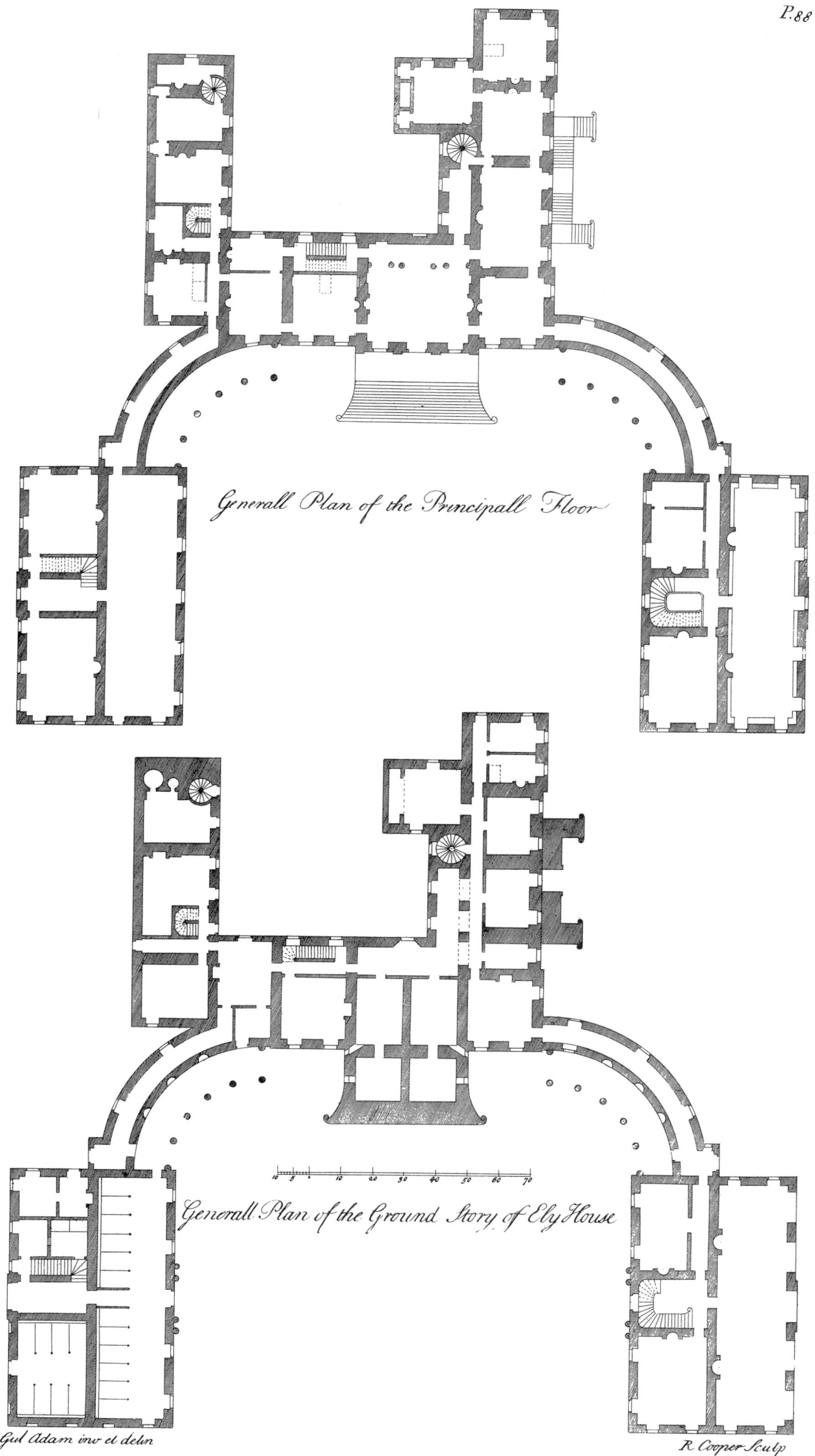

Generall Plan of the Principall Floor
10 5 0 10 20 30 40 50 60 70
Generall Plan of the Ground Story of Ely House
Gul Adam inv et delin
R Cooper Sculp

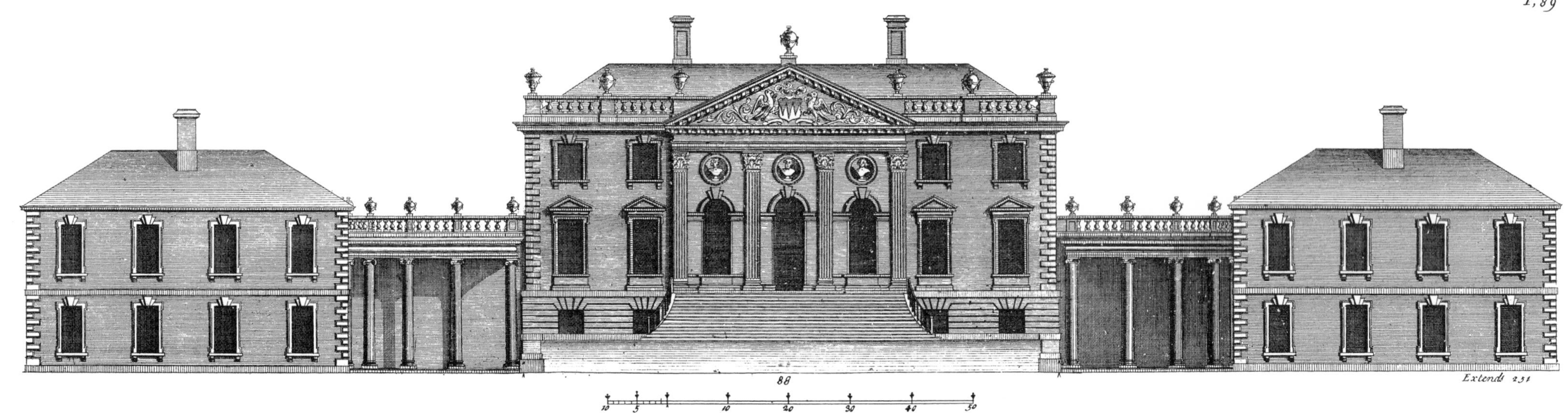

The West Front of Elie House toward the Court the Seat of the Honorable Sir John Anstruther of that Ilk Barronet in the County of Fife

Gul: Adam inv: et delin

R: Cooper Sculp.

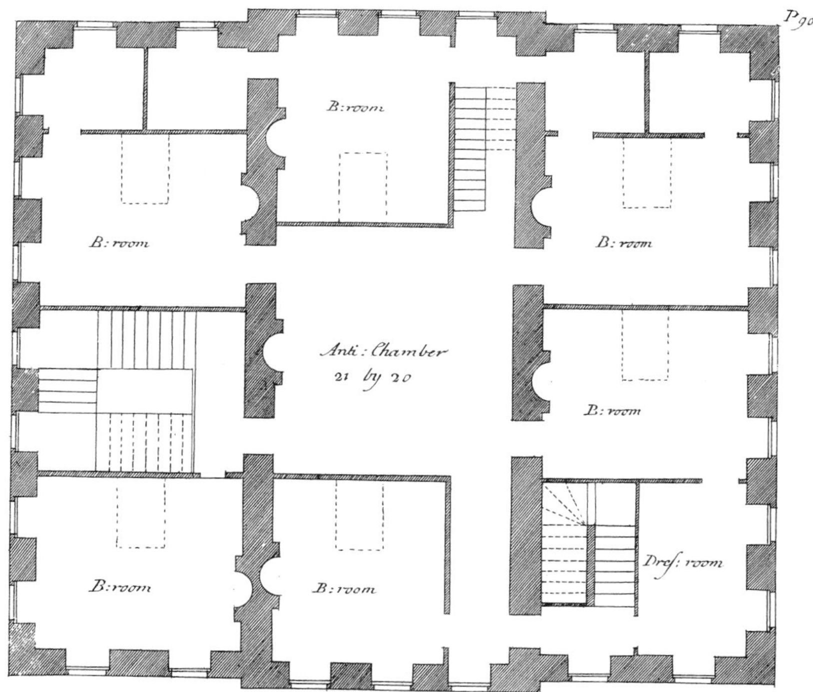

Plan of the Lodging Story

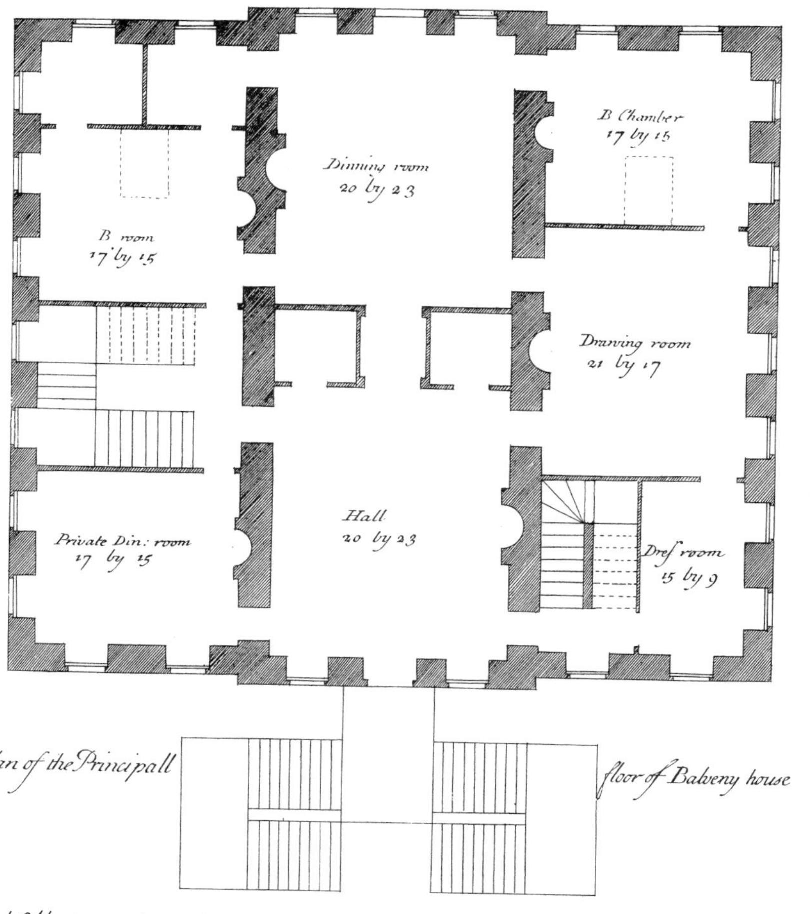

Plan of the Principall floor of Balveny house

Jacob Gibbs inv 10 5 10 20 30 R. Cooper Sculp

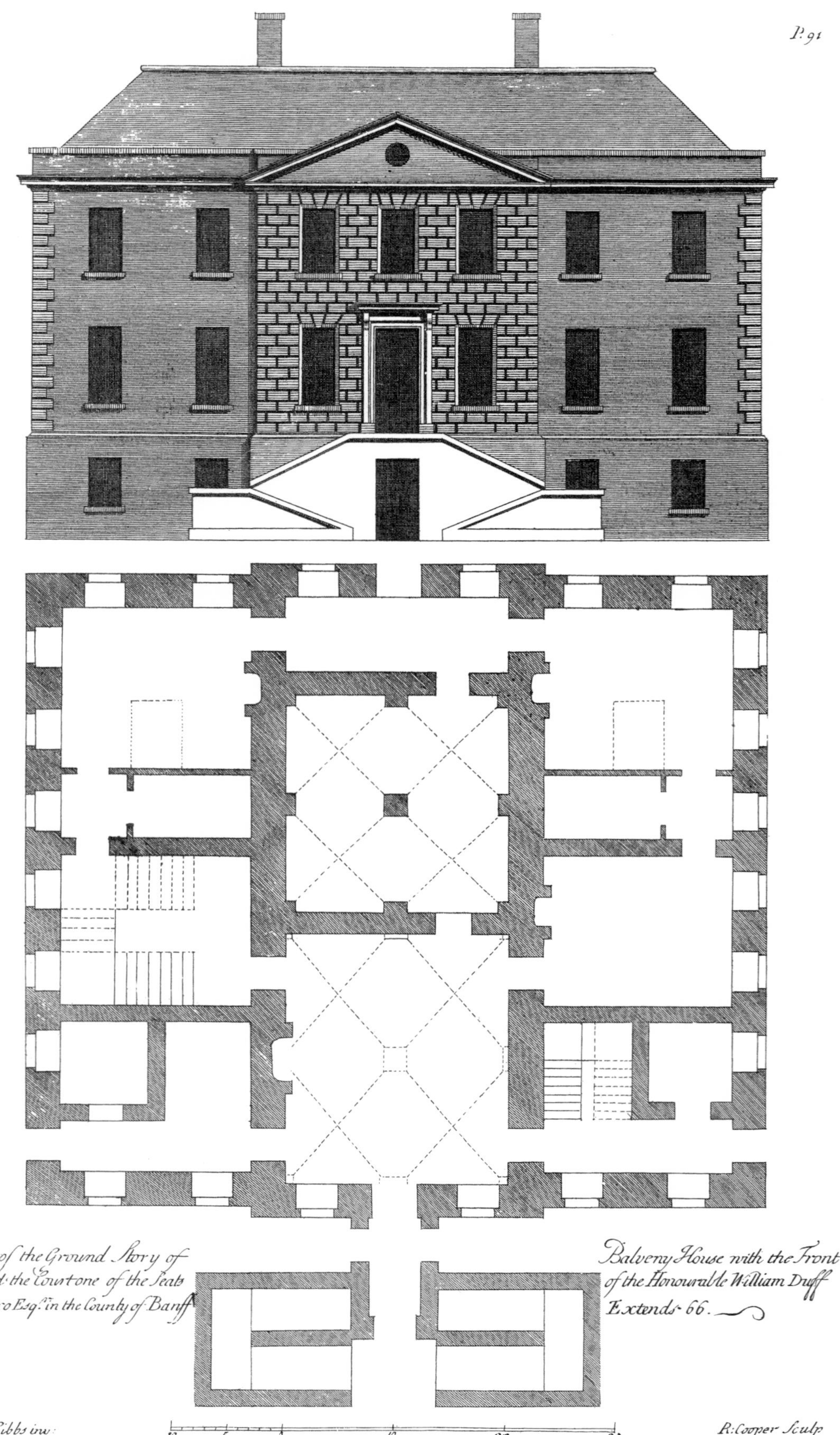

Plan of the Ground Story of Balveny House with the Front Toward the Court one of the Seats of the Honourable William Duff of Bracco Esq.r in the County of Banff Extends 66.

Jacob: Gibbs inv. R: Cooper Sculp.

Plan of the Principal floor up one pair of Stairs

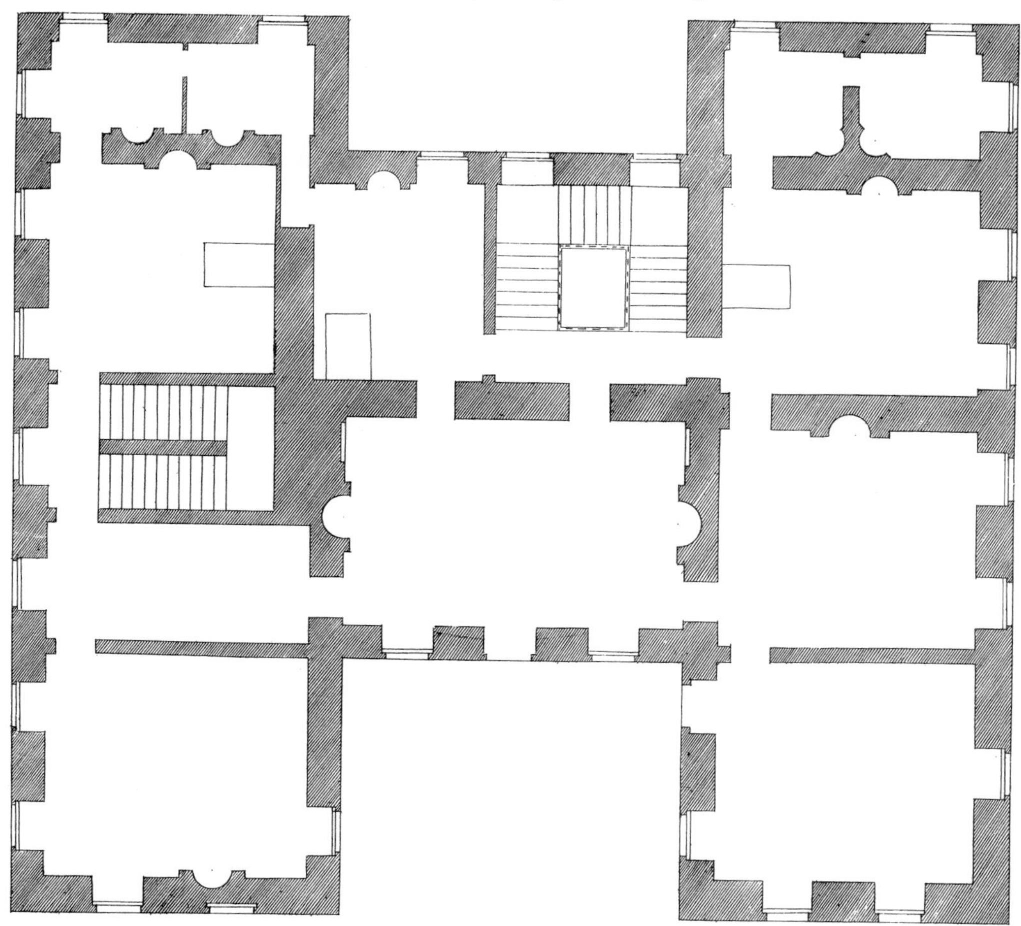

Plan of the First Story of Dunibirsle House

Gill Adam delin   R. Cooper Sculp.

South Front of Dunibirsle House

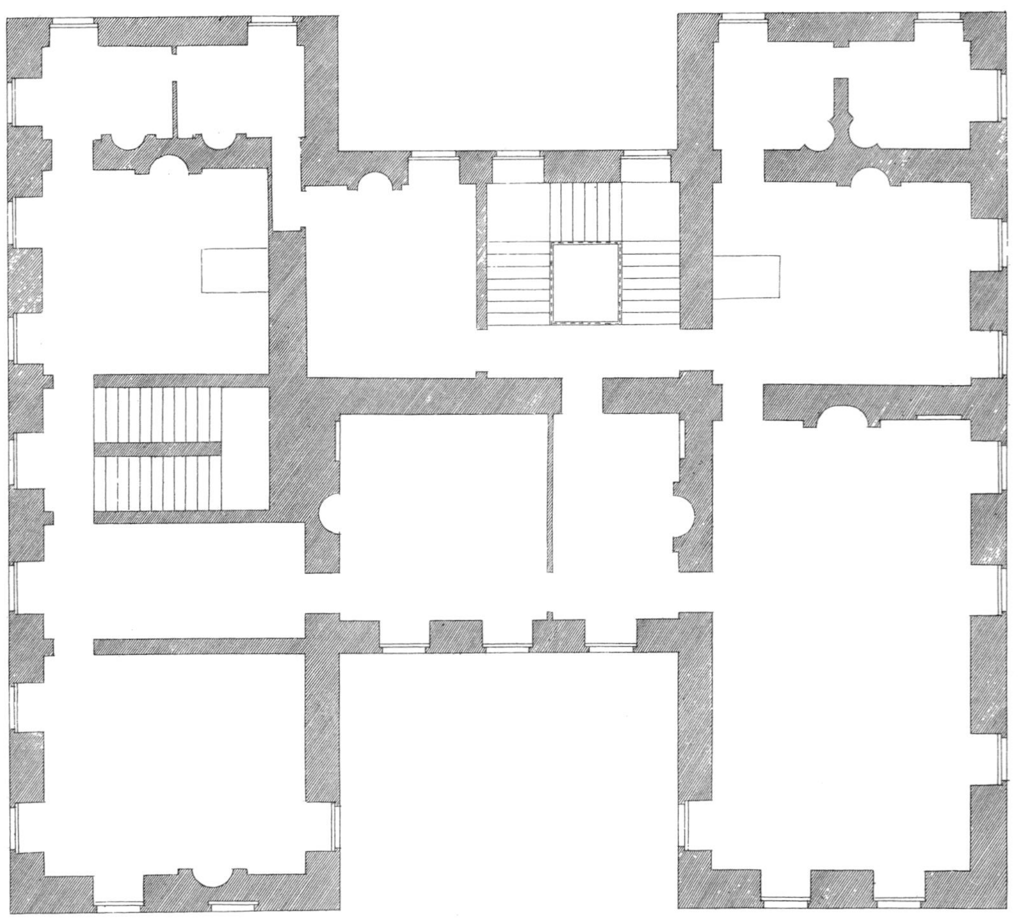

Plan of the 3d Storie

Gul Adam delin

R Cooper Sculp.

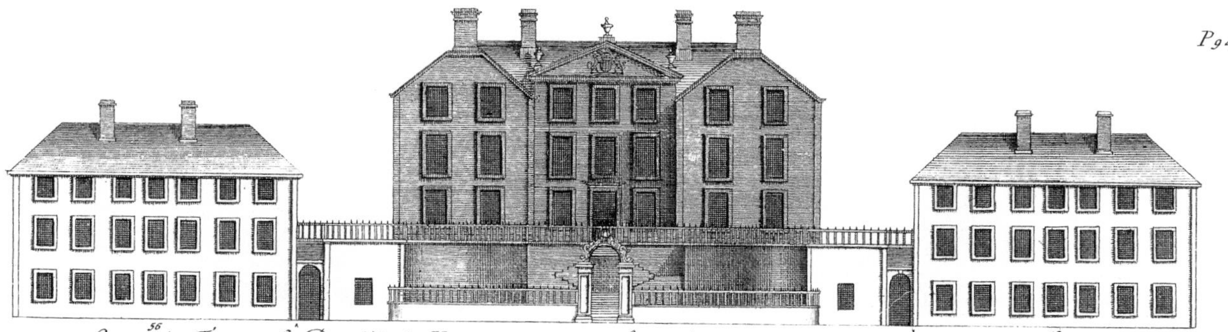

General Front of Dunibirsle House towards the South the Seat of the Right Honorable The Earl of Murray in the County of Fife

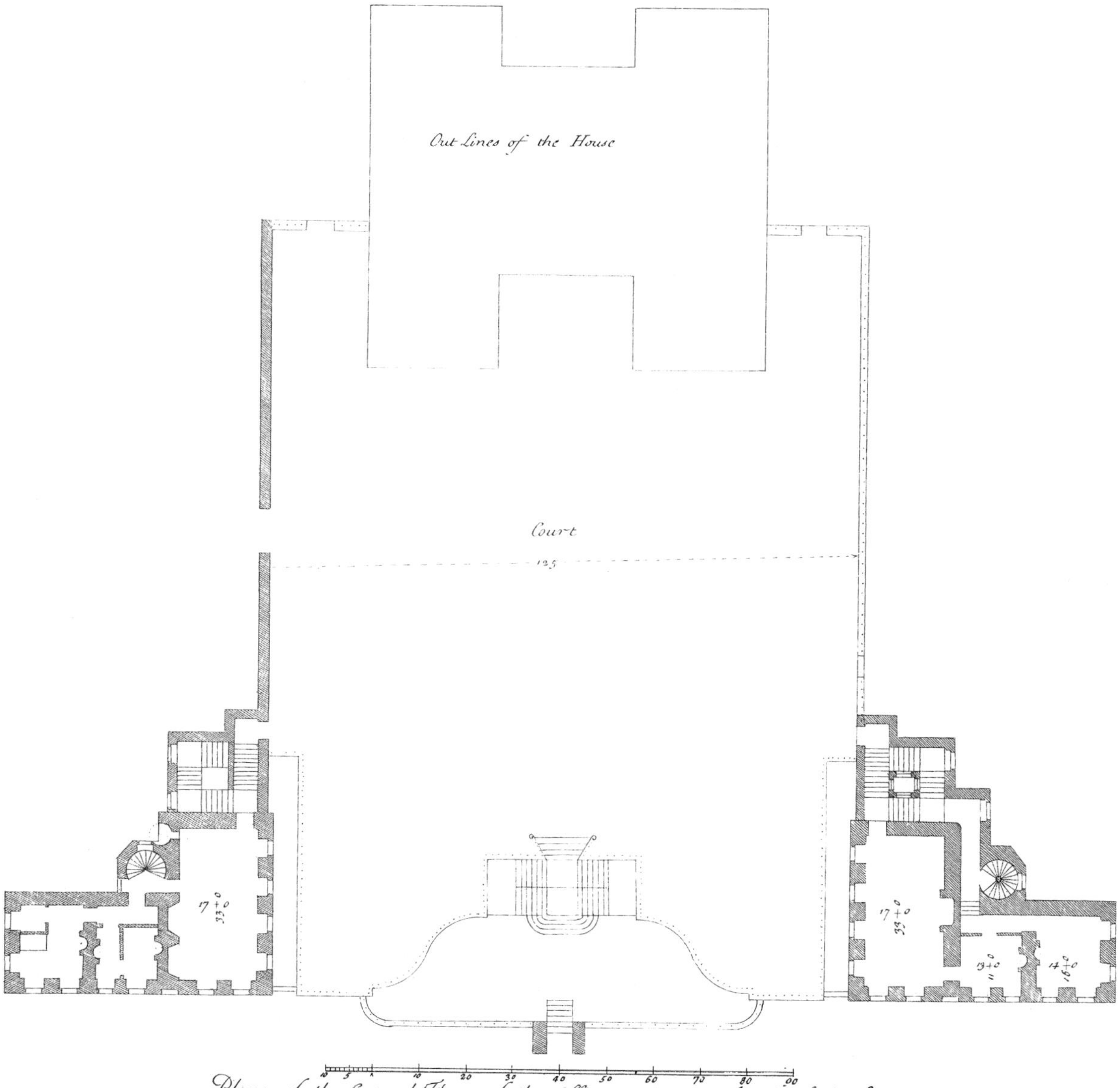

Out Lines of the House

Court

125

Plans of the Ground Floors of the Offices under the Levell of the Court

Mr. Al: Mcgill Archt

R. Cooper Sculp

Design of a House for John M.c Culloch Esq.r of Barholm in GALLOWAY

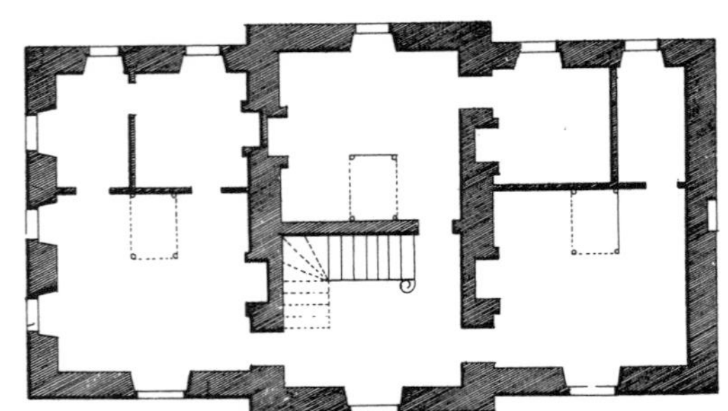

Plan of the Attic Story

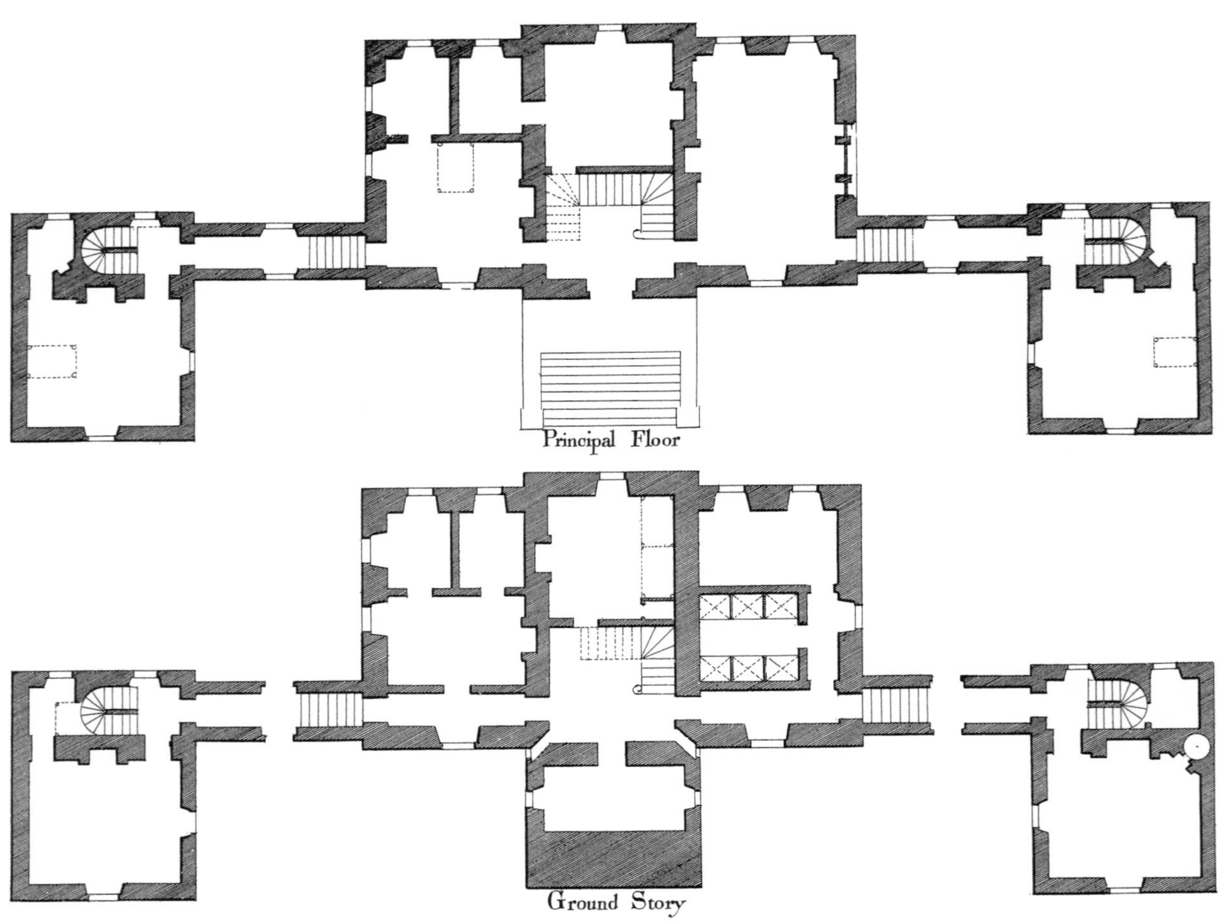

Adams Arch.t Mazell Sculp.t

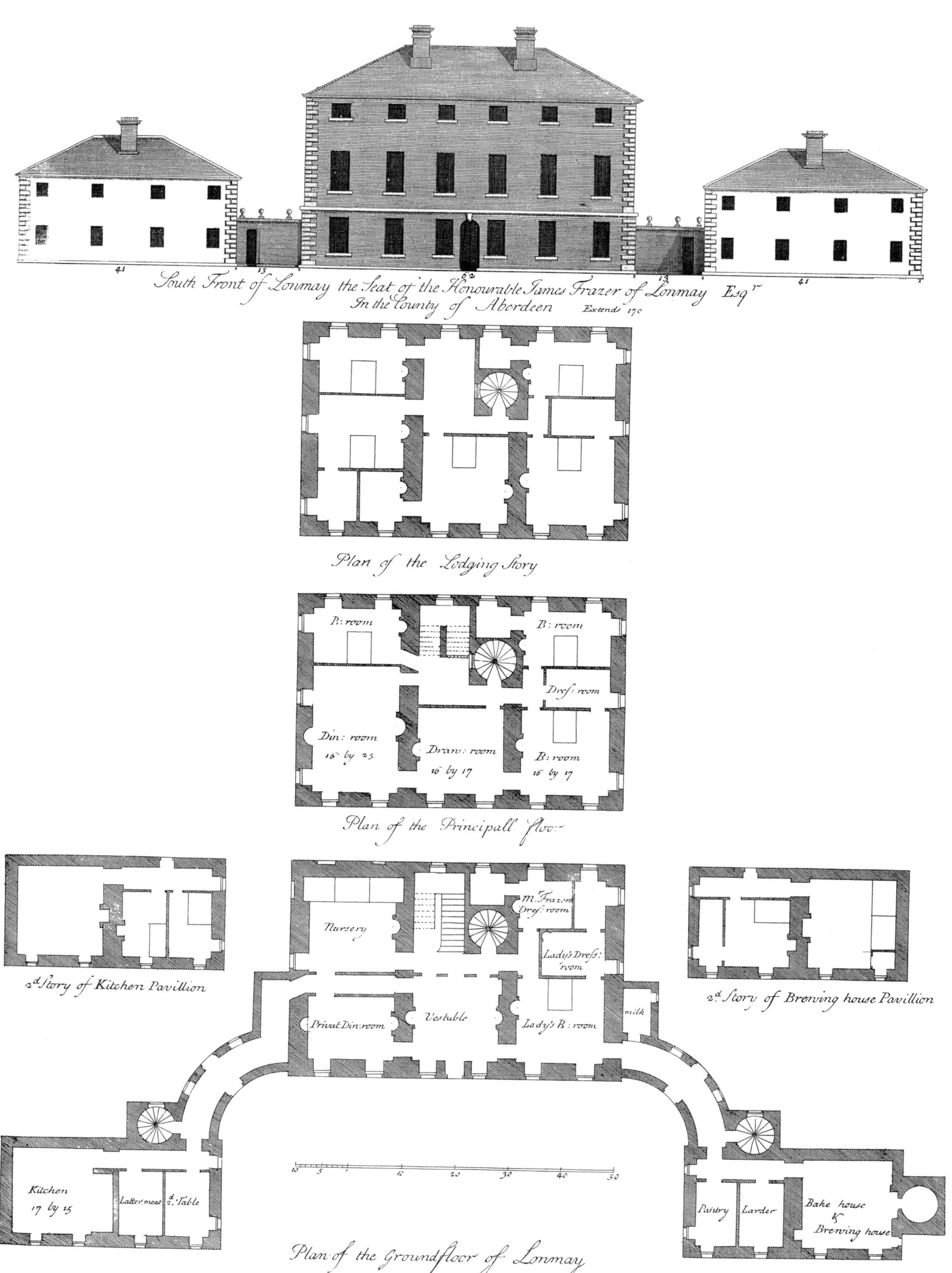
41
13
62
13
41
South Front of Lonmay the Seat of the Honourable James Frazer of Lonmay Esq.r
In the County of Aberdeen Extends 170
Plan of the Lodging Story
B: room
B: room
Dres: room
Din: room
16 by 25
Draw: room
16 by 17
B: room
16 by 17
Plan of the Principall floor
M.r Frazer
Dres: room
Nursery
Lady's Dress: room
Privat Din: room
Vestuble
Lady's B: room
milk
2.d Story of Kitchen Pavillion
2.d Story of Brewing house Pavillion
Kitchen
17 by 15
Latter meat
2.d Table
Pantry
Larder
Bake house
&
Brewing house
10 5 0 10 20 30 40 50
Plan of the Groundfloor of Lonmay
Gul. Adam inv: Delin
R: Cooper Sculp.

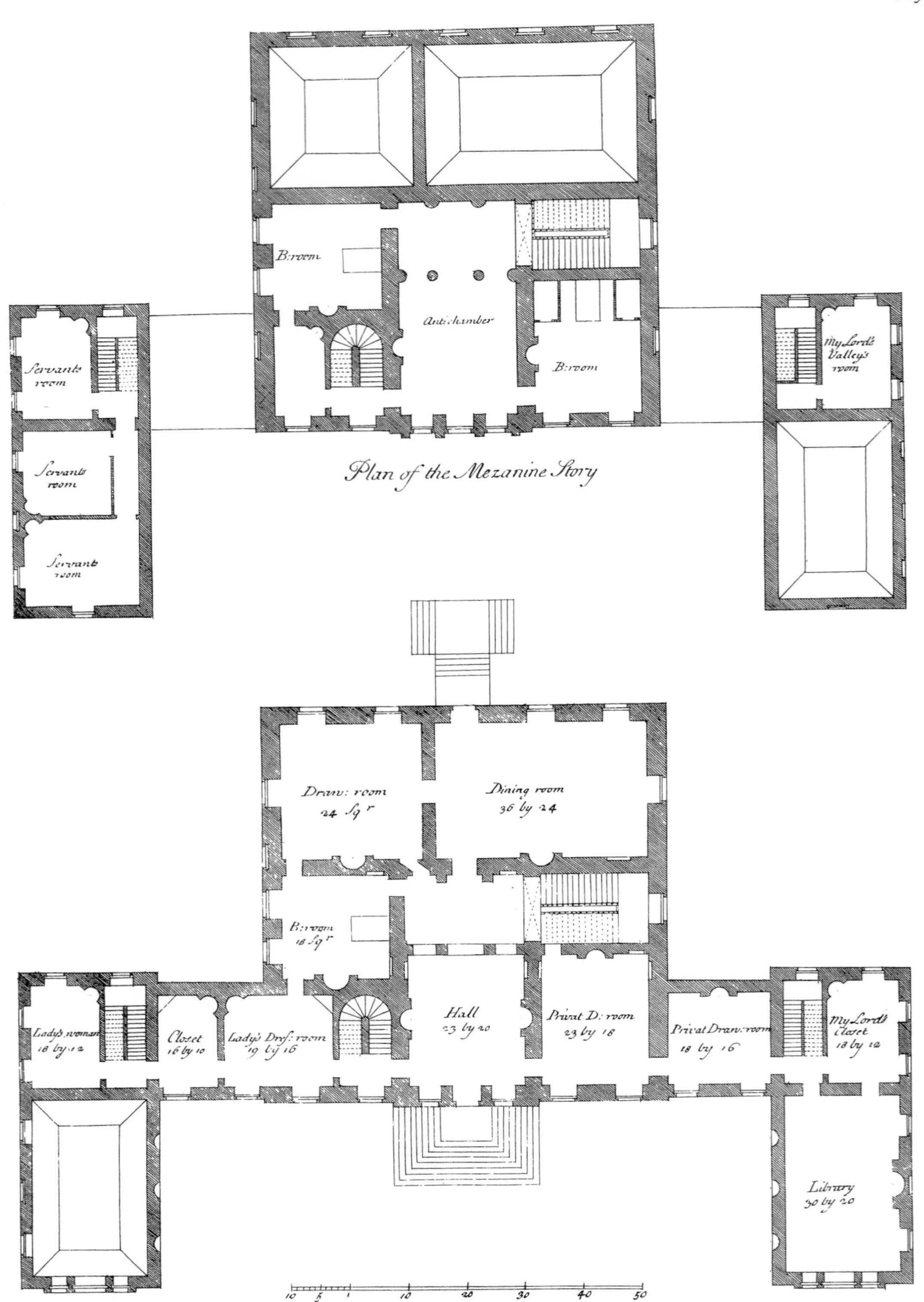

Plan of the Mezanine Story

Plan of the Principal floor design'd for a Person of Quality

Gul Adam inv: Delin

R: Cooper Sculp

South Front of a Design for a Person of Quality in Scotland not yet Built

Gul: Adam inv: delin.

R: Cooper Sculp.

48 | 9½ | 70 | 9½ | 48 | Extend: 188

10 5 10 20 30 40 50

The South Front of Gray House toward the Court

The Seat of The Rt. Honble. The Lord Gray in the County of Angus.

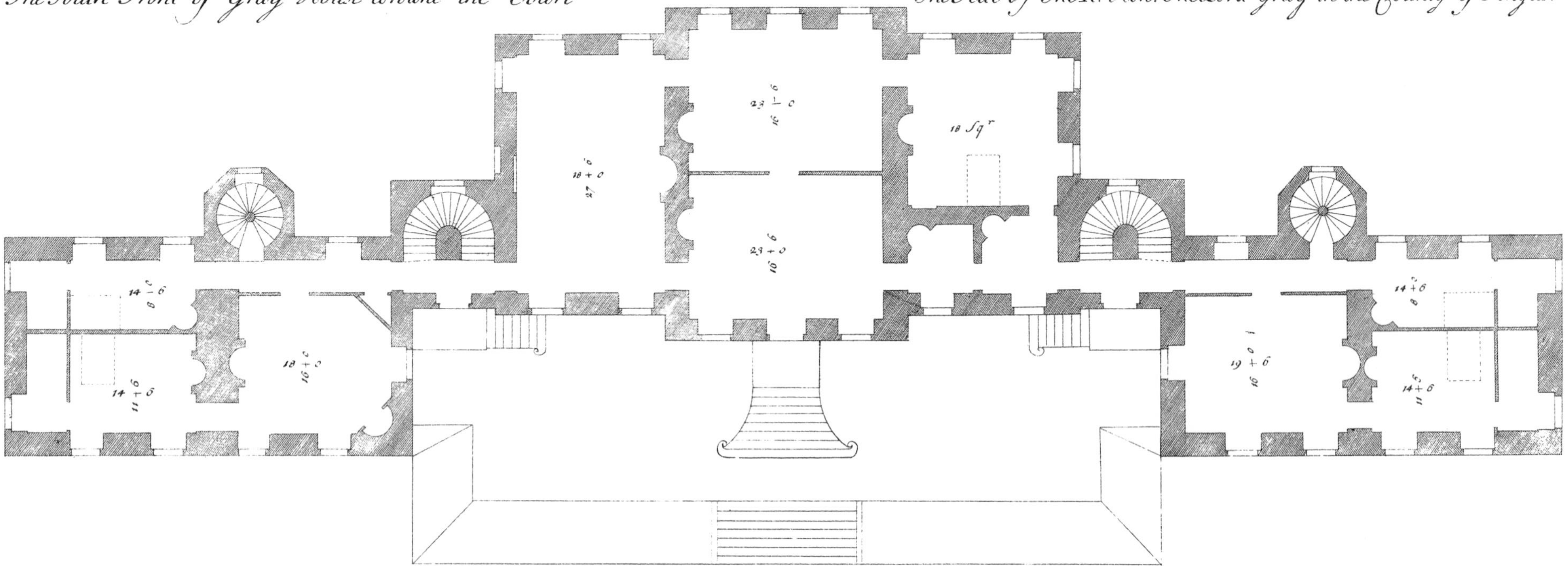

18 + 0
27 + 6

23 + 0
16 + 6

23 + 0
16 + 6

18 Sqr

14 + 6
8

14 + 6
11

18 + 0
16 + 0

19 + 6
16 + 0

14 + 6
8

14 + 6
11

Generall Plan of the First Floor

Gul: Adam delin

R: Cooper Sculp

The Elevation of Longformacus House The Seat of the Hon.ble S.r Rob.t Sinclair

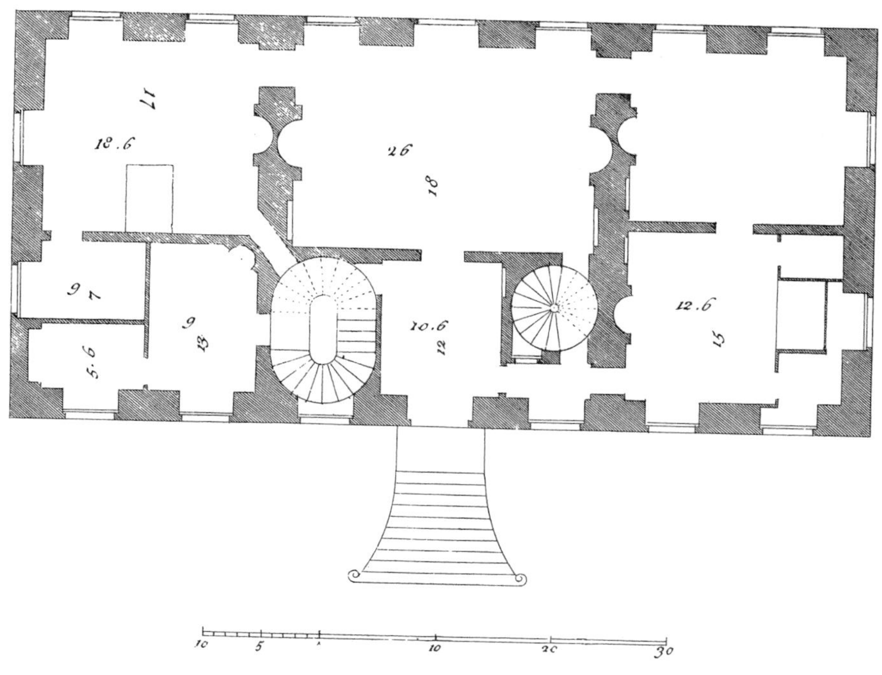

The Plan of the principal floor of Longformacus.

Gul. Adam delin.

R. Cooper sculp.

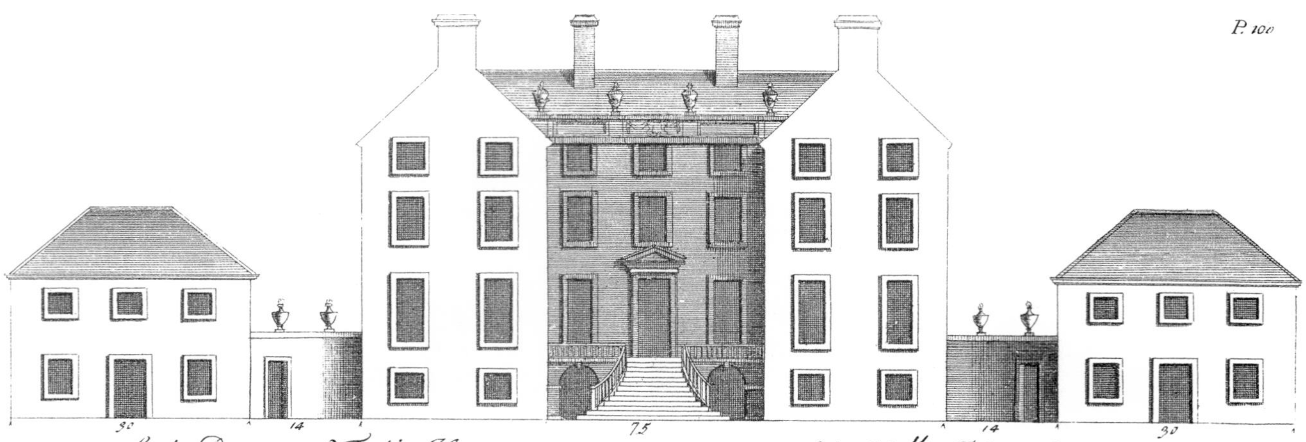

South Prospect of Faskie House toward the Court the Seat of the Hon.ble Sr. Alexr. Ramsay of Ballmain in the County of Mairns. Extends 163

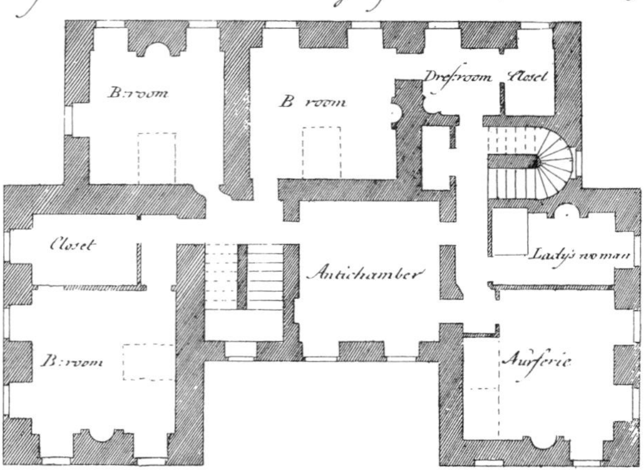

Plan of the Lodging floor

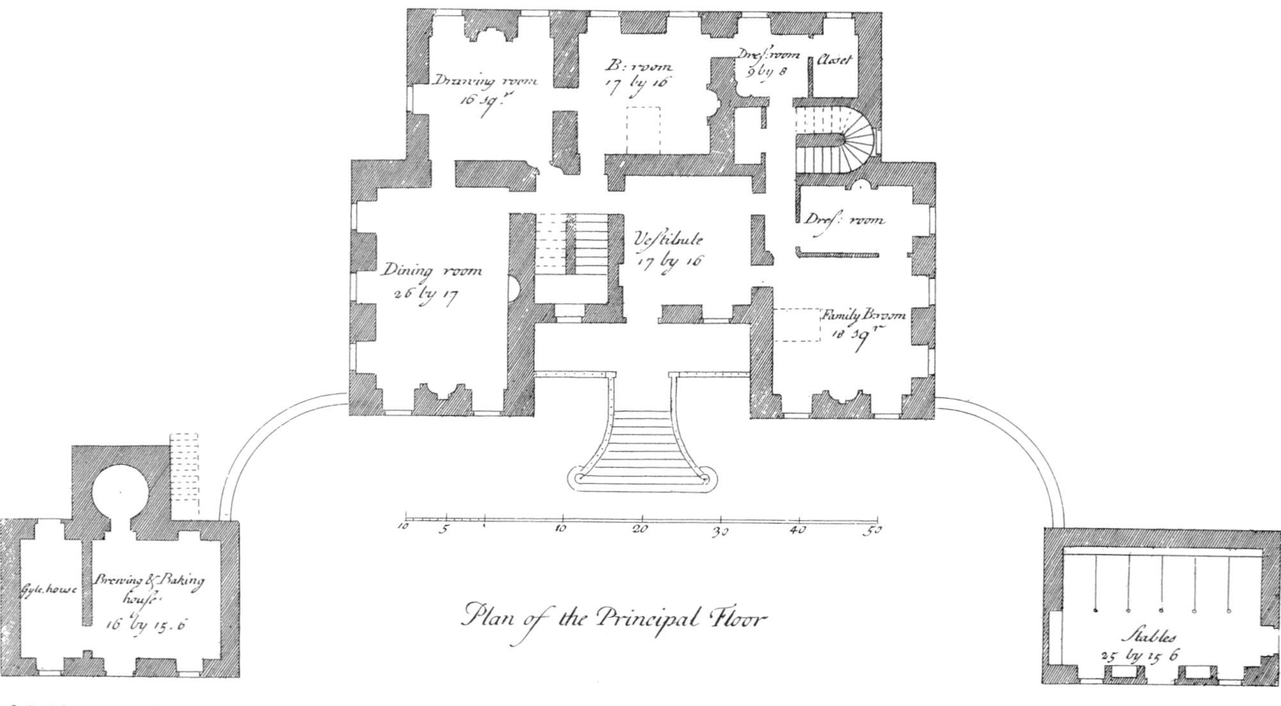

Plan of the Principal Floor

Gul: Adam inv: delin

R: Cooper Sculp

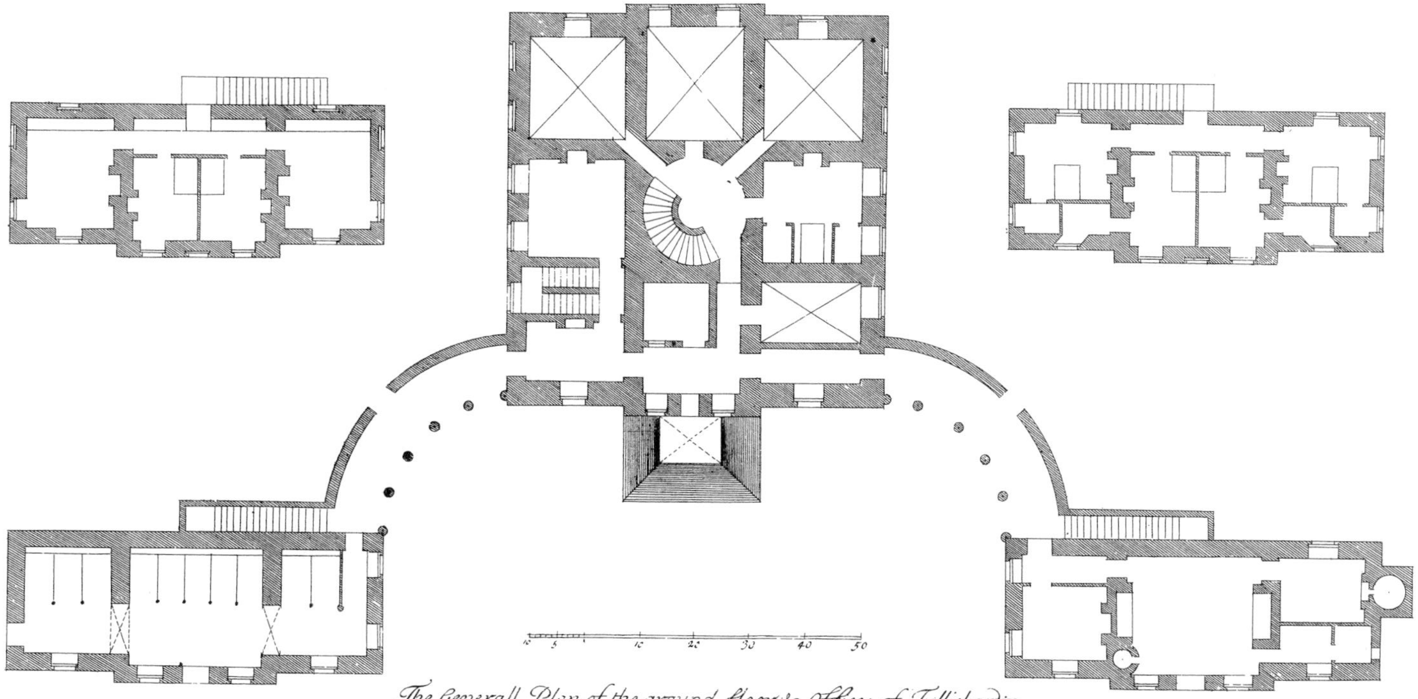

The Generall Plan of the ground floor & Offices of Tulliebardin

Gul. Adam inv: et delin

R. Cooper Sculp

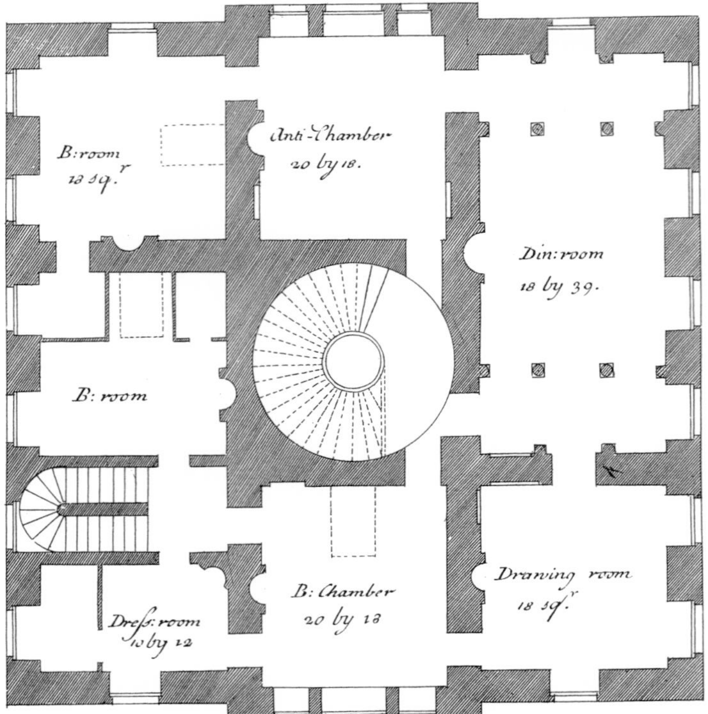

Plan of the Principall floor

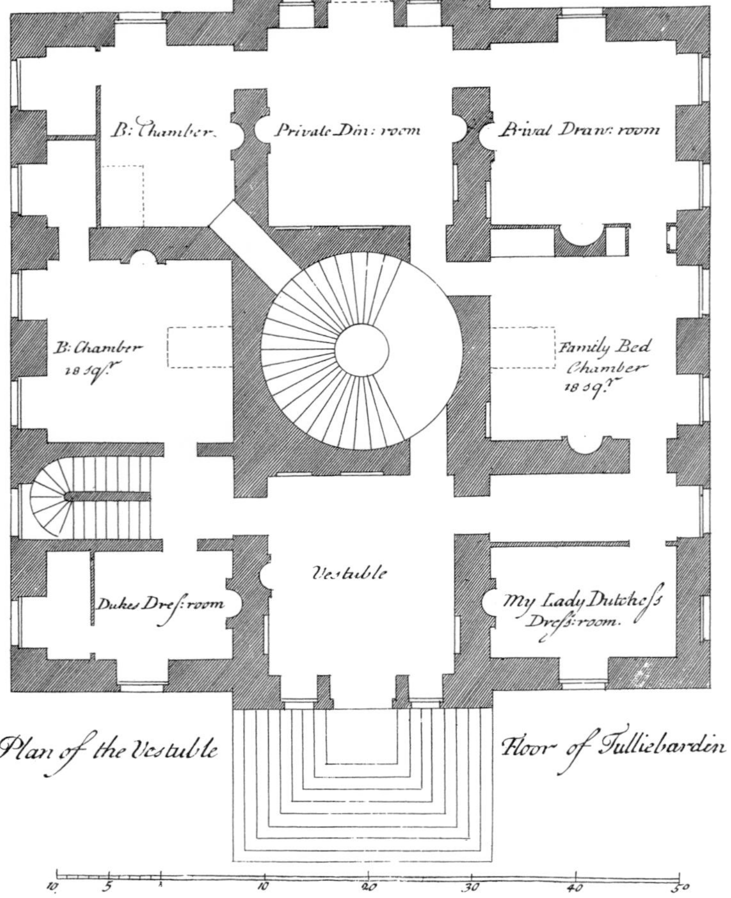

Plan of the Vestuble Floor of Tulliebardin

Gul Adam inv: et delin

R. Cooper Sculp.

The General Front of a new design for his Grace the Duke of Athol intended at Tullibardin in the County of Perth

Gul. Adam inv. et delin.

R. Cooper Sculp.

The Plan of the Principall Floor & Elevation of the Town House of Dundee Is most humbly Inscrib'd to Alexr. Robertson Esqr. Ld. Provest & the other Magistrates of the sd. Burgh.

Gul: Adam inv: et delin: *R. Cooper Sculp.*

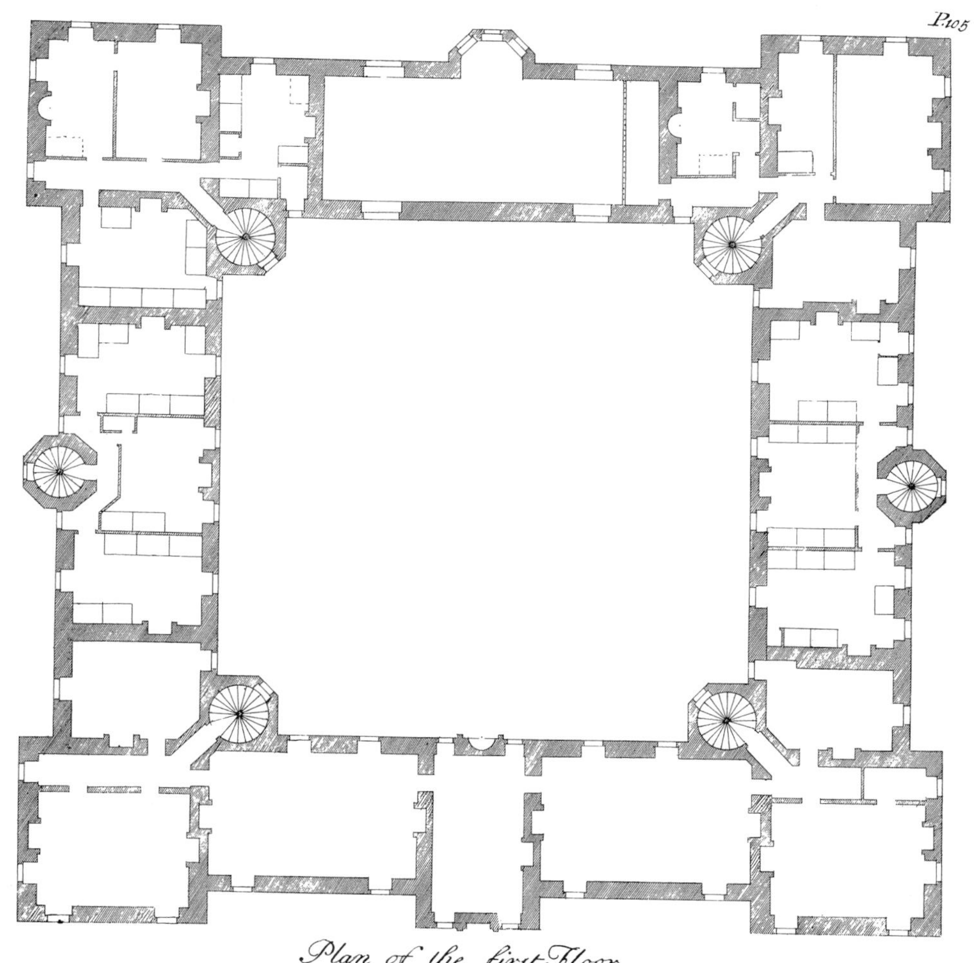

Plan of the first Floor

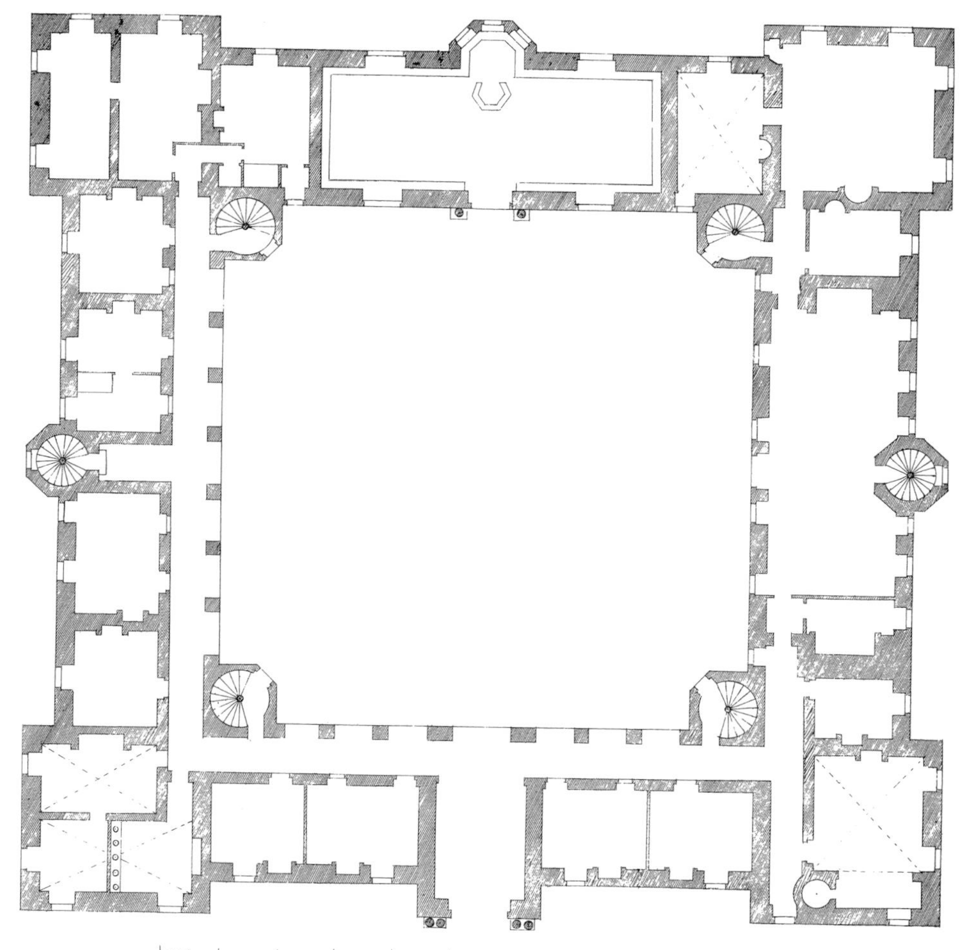

The Ground Plan of Heriots Hospitall

Gul: Adam delin

R: Cooper Sculp

The Elevation of the North Front of Heriot's Hospitall in the City of Edinburgh is most humbly Inscrib'd to Patrick Lindsay Esq.r Lord Provost of Edinburgh.

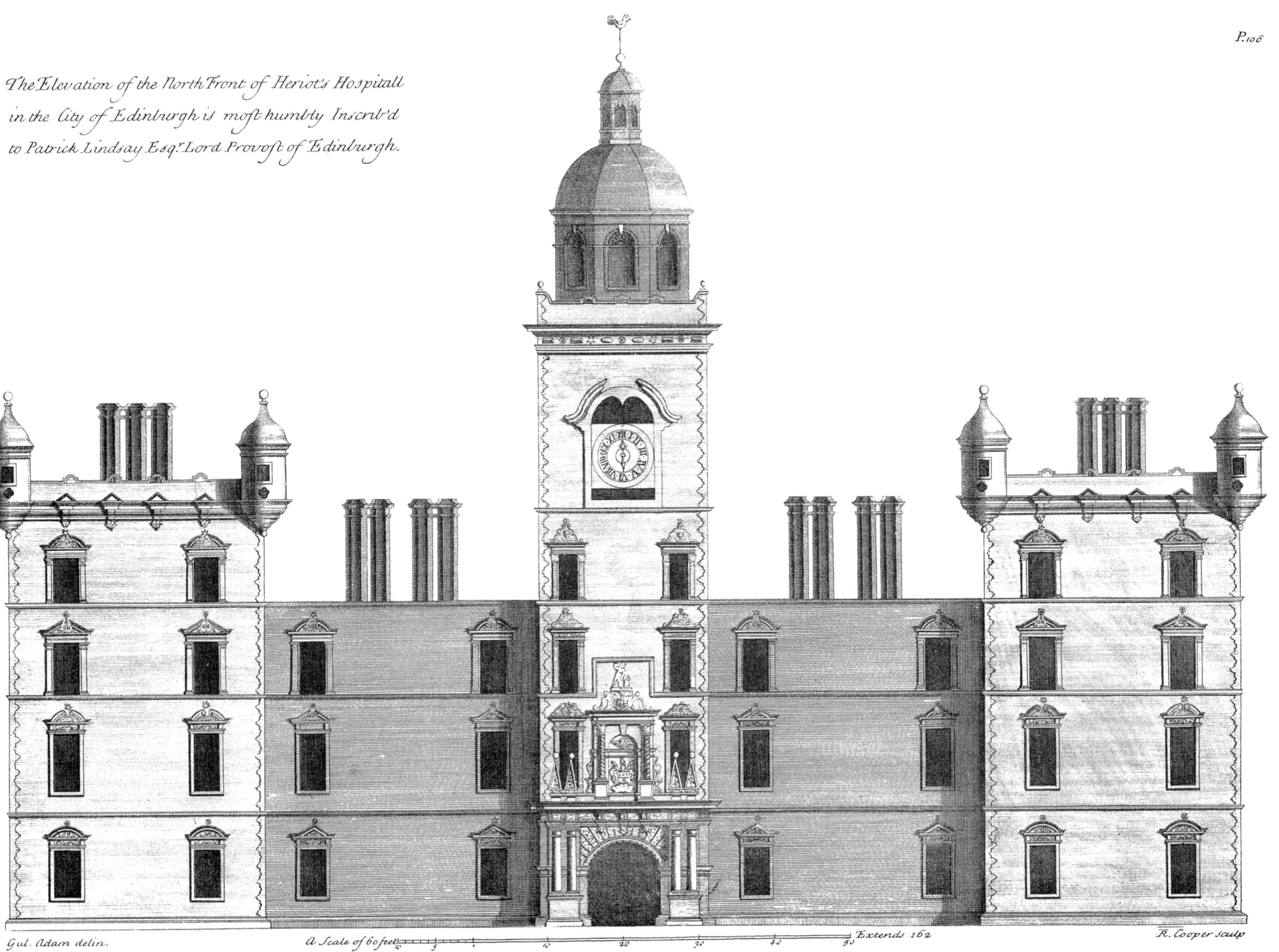

Gul. Adam delin.

R. Cooper sculp

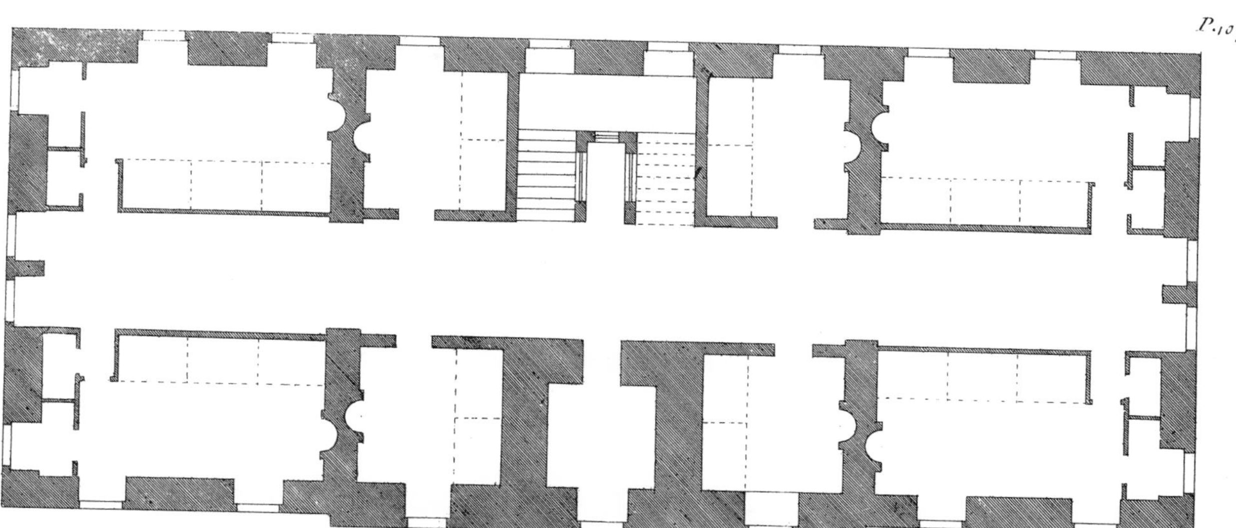

Plan of the 3d Story

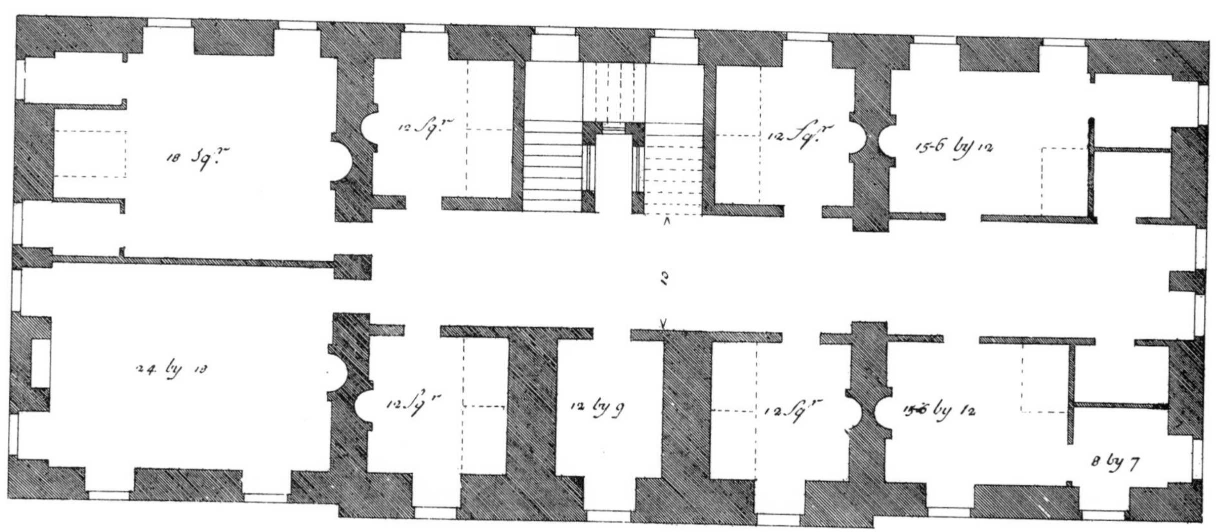

Plan of the Second Story

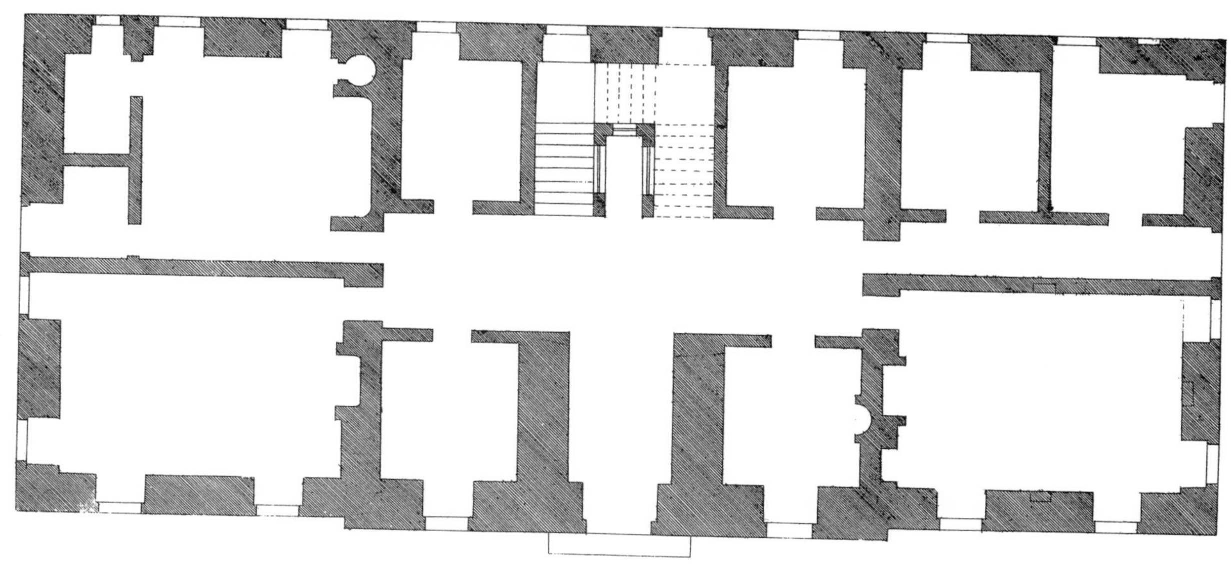

Plan of the Ground Story of Gordon's Hospitall att Aberdeen

Gul. Adam inv: delin.

R: Cooper Sculp.

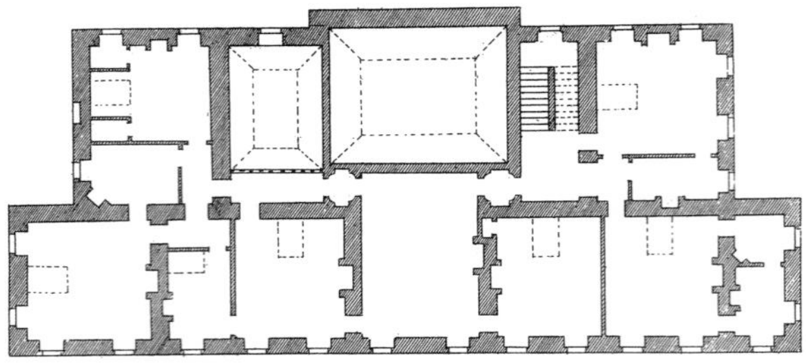

Plan of the Attick Story

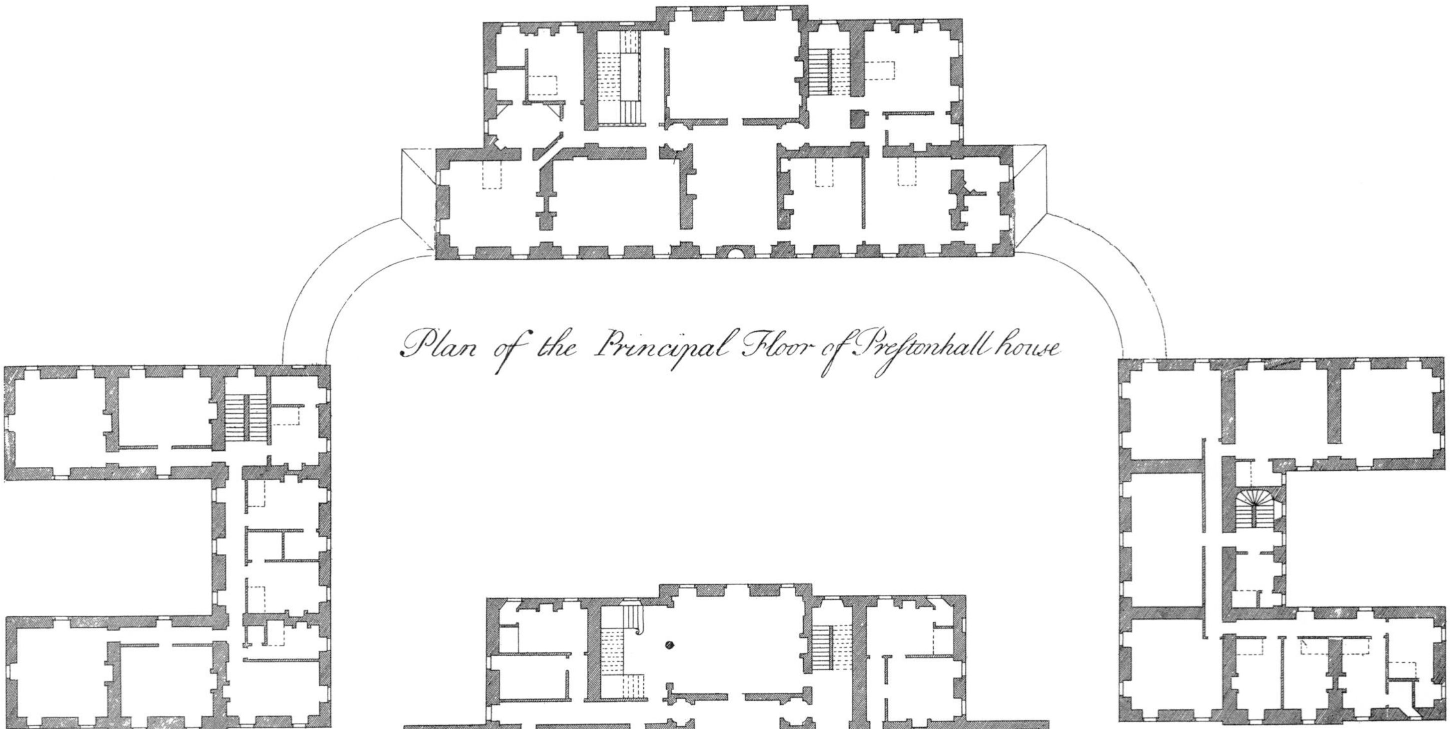

Plan of the Principal Floor of Prestonhall house

10 5 0 10 20 30 40 50 60 70

Plan of the Ground Story

Gul: Adam inv: et delin

R: Cooper Sculp.

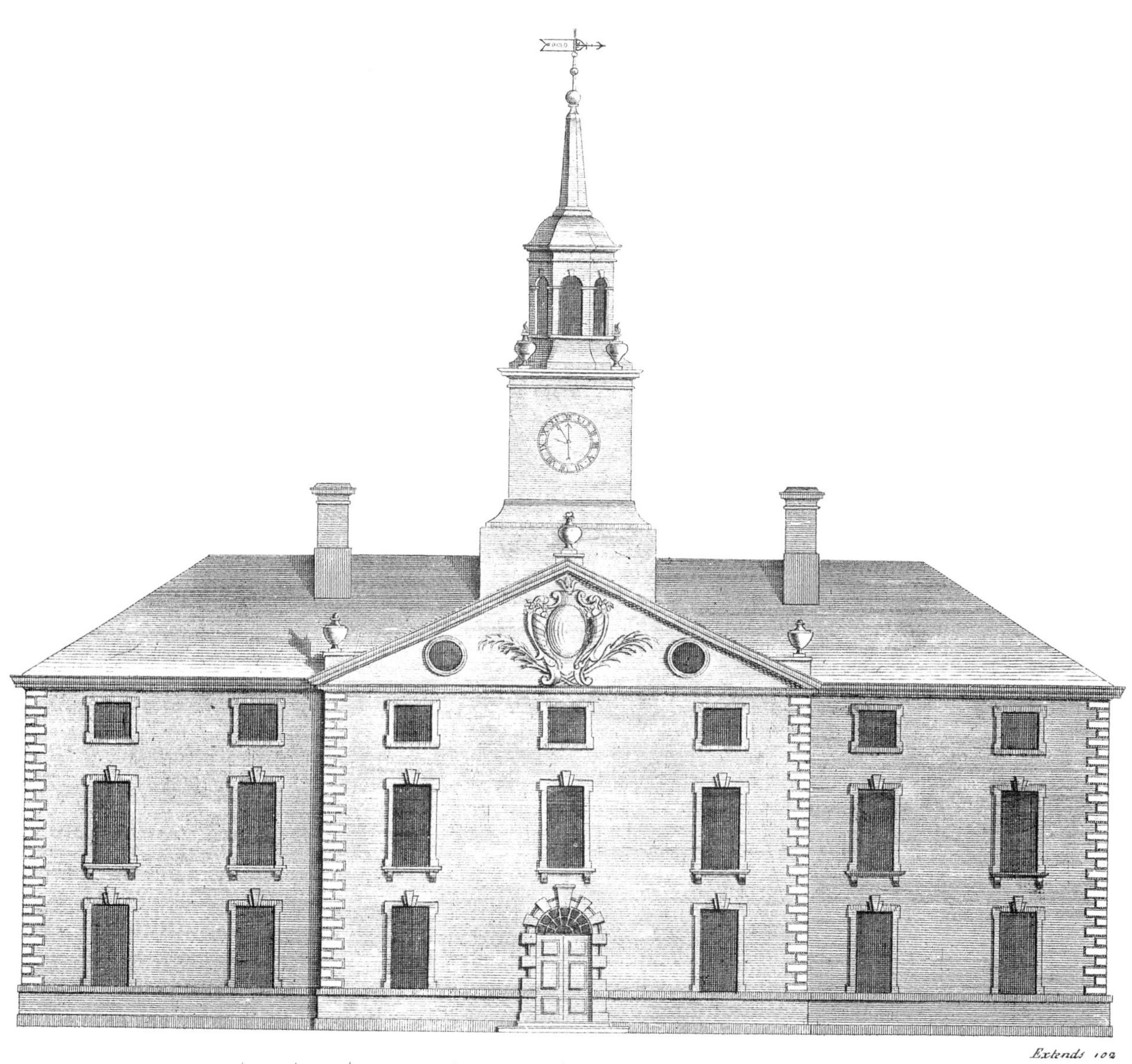

South Front of Gordons Hospital att Aberdeen

Gul. Adam inv. et delin *R: Cooper Sculp.*

The General Front of Prestonhall house toward the South the Seat of her Grace the DUTCHES of GORDON in the County of East Lothian

Gul Adam inv: et delin

R: Cooper Sculp.

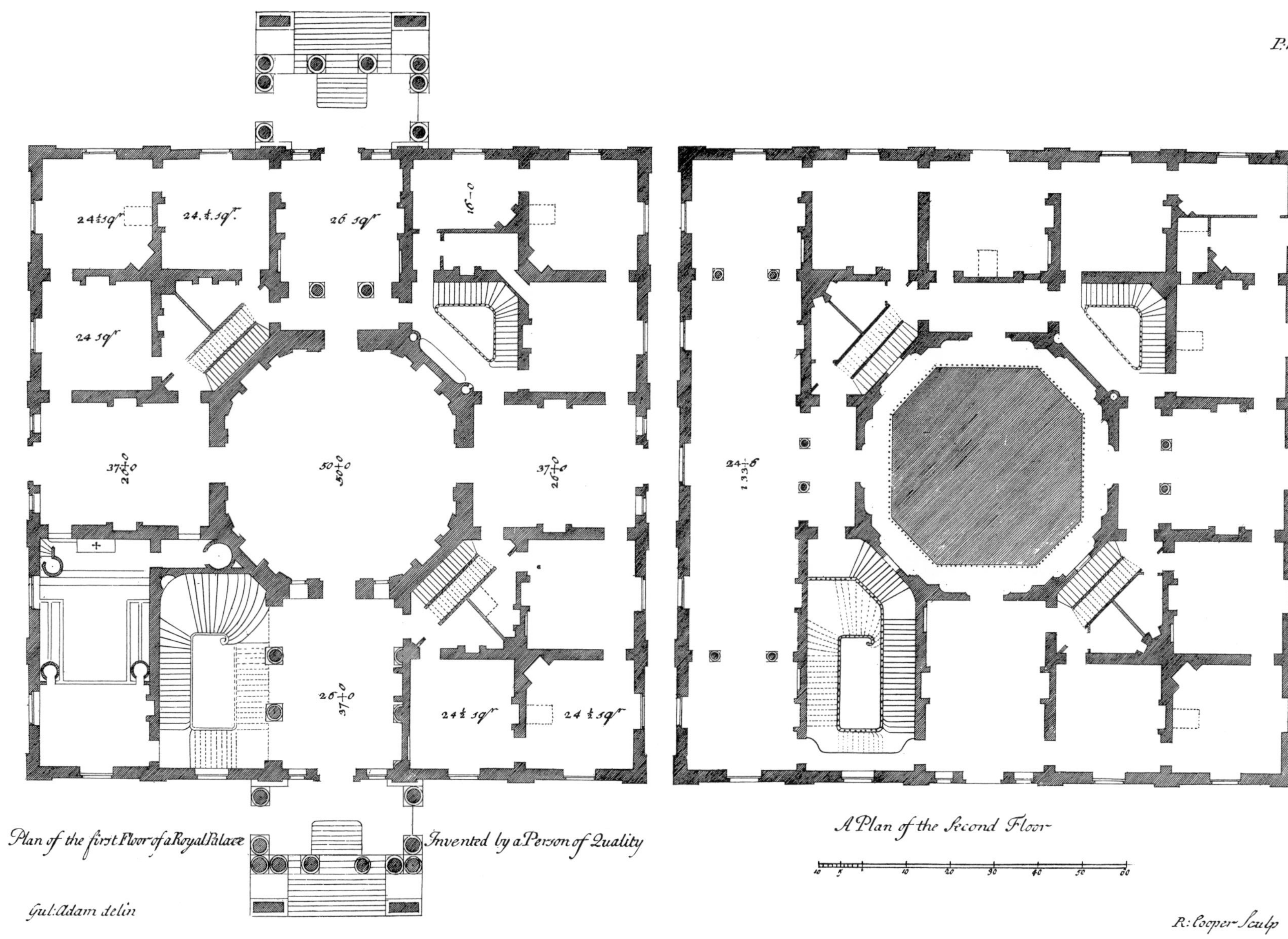

Plan of the first Floor of a Royal Palace Invented by a Person of Quality

A Plan of the Second Floor

Gul: Adam delin

R: Cooper Sculp

Extends. 144

10 5 0 10 20 30 40 50

One of the Fronts of the Royal Pallace as Design'd for the Preceeding Plans

Gul Adam delin — *R Cooper Sculp*

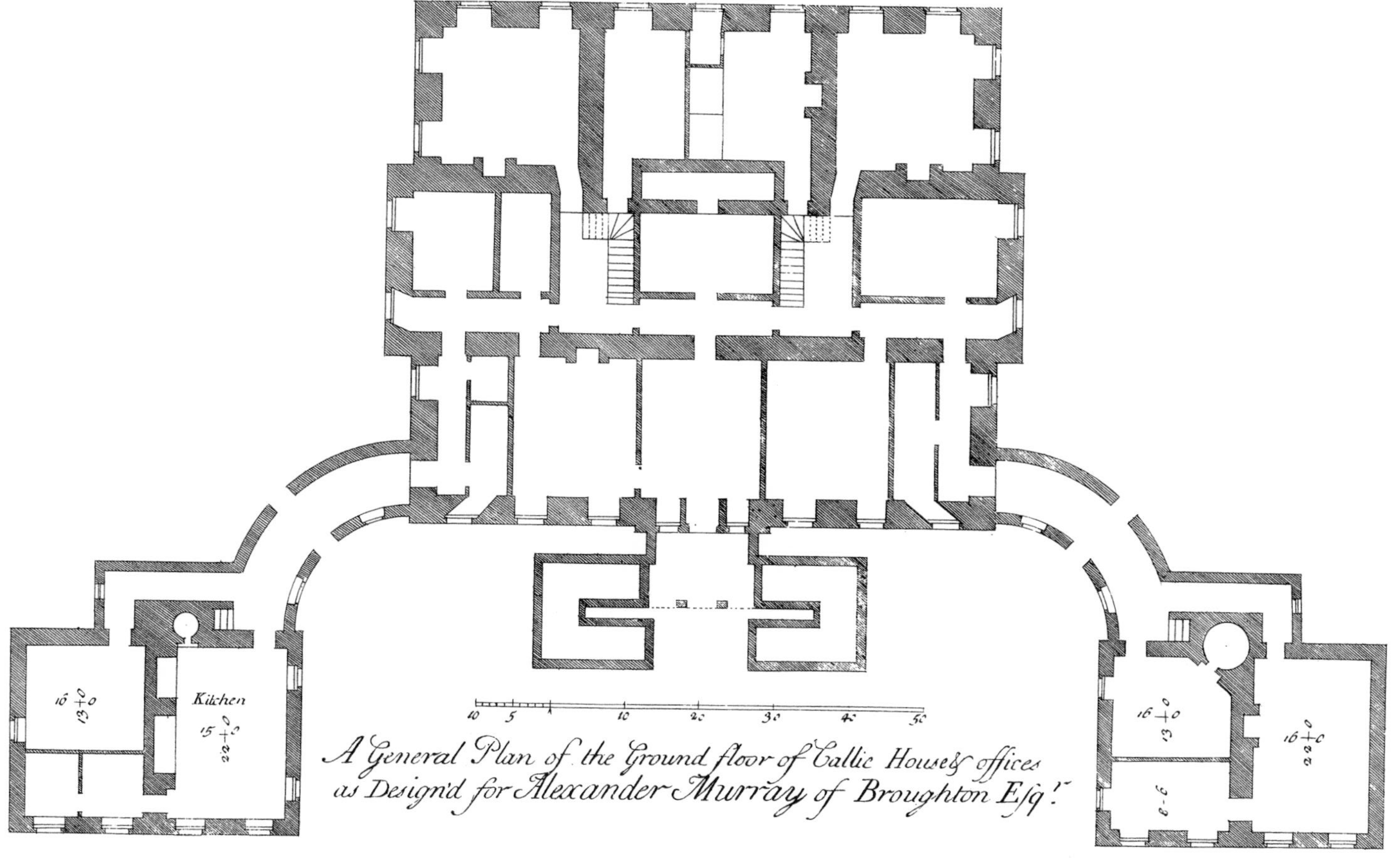

A General Plan of the Ground floor of Callic House & offices
as Design'd for Alexander Murray of Broughton Esq.r

Gul: Adam inv: & del:

R. Cooper Sculp.

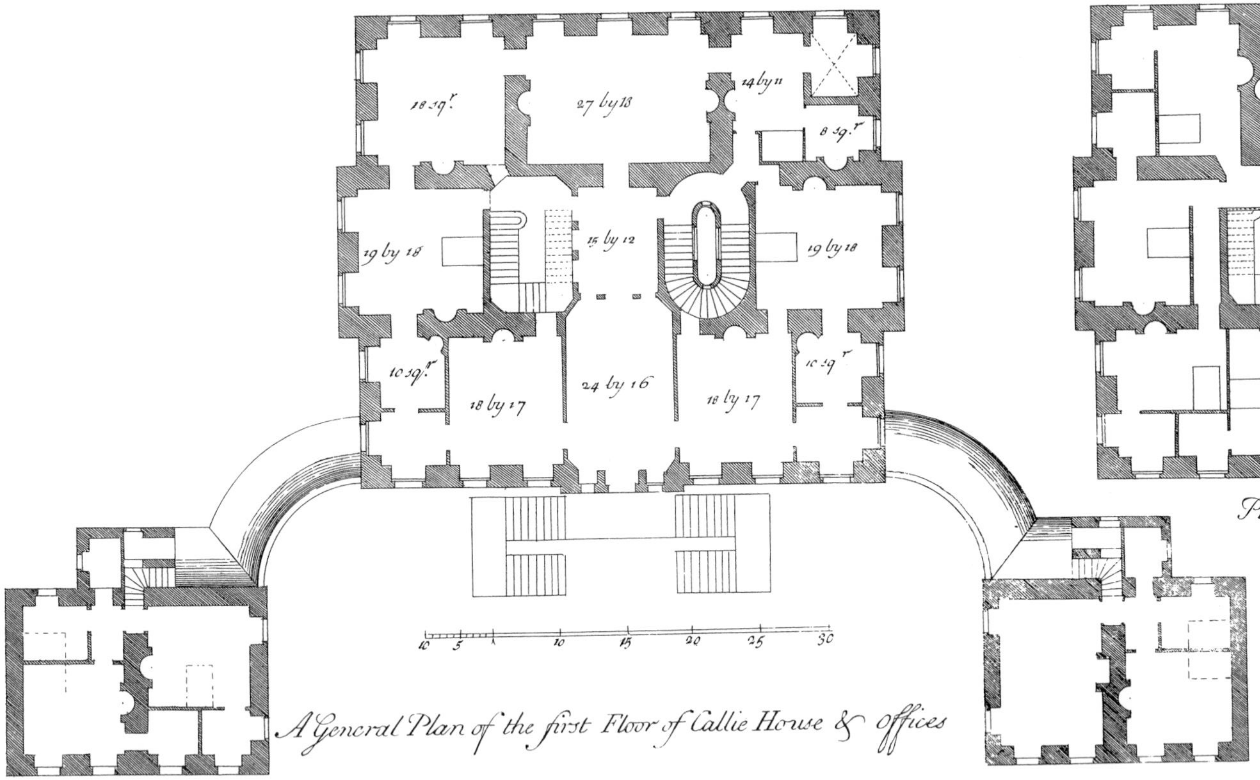

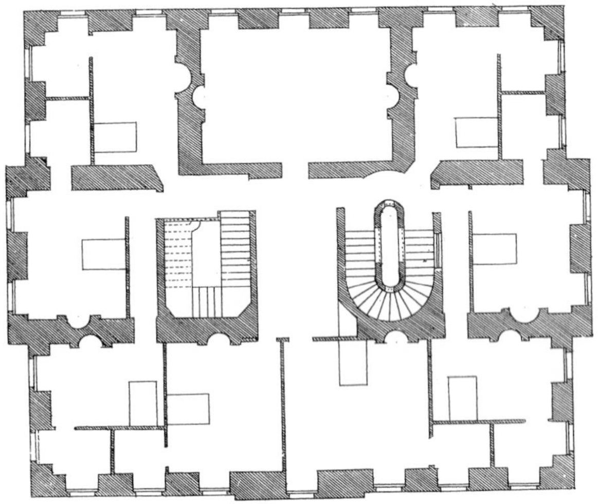

Plan of the Lodging Story

A General Plan of the first Floor of Callie House & Offices

Gul. Adam inv & Delin

R: Cooper Sculp

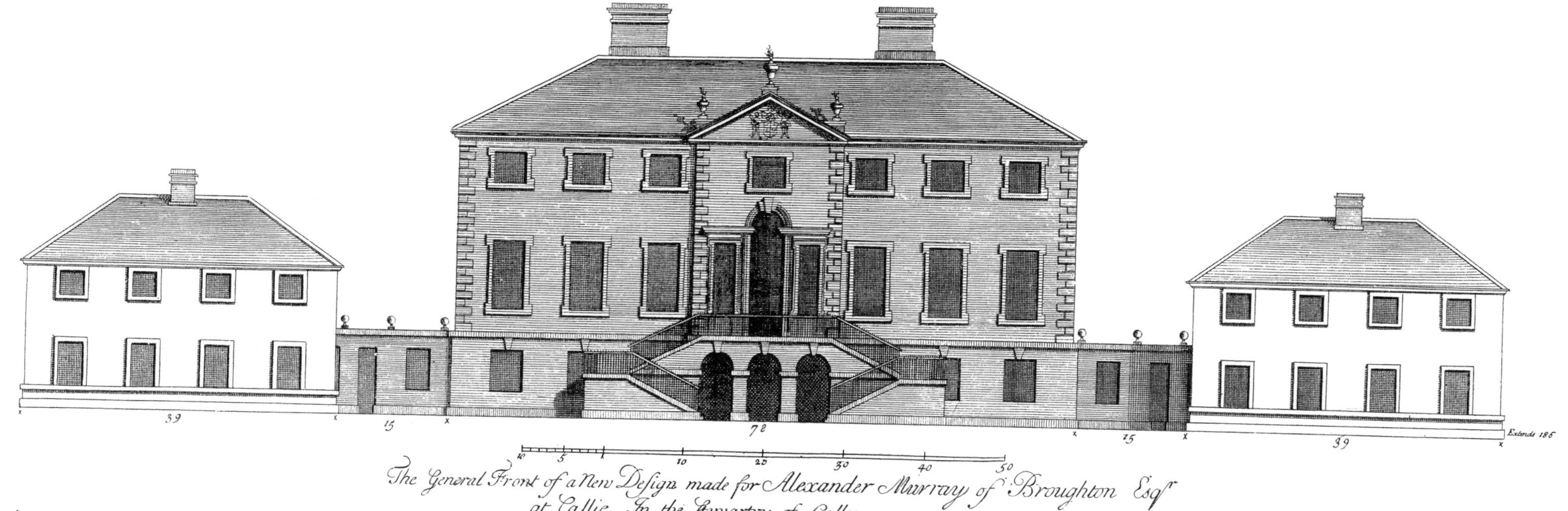

The General Front of a New Design made for Alexander Murray of Broughton Esqr
at Callie In the Stewartry of Galloway

Gul. Adam inv: et delin.

R. Cooper Sculp.

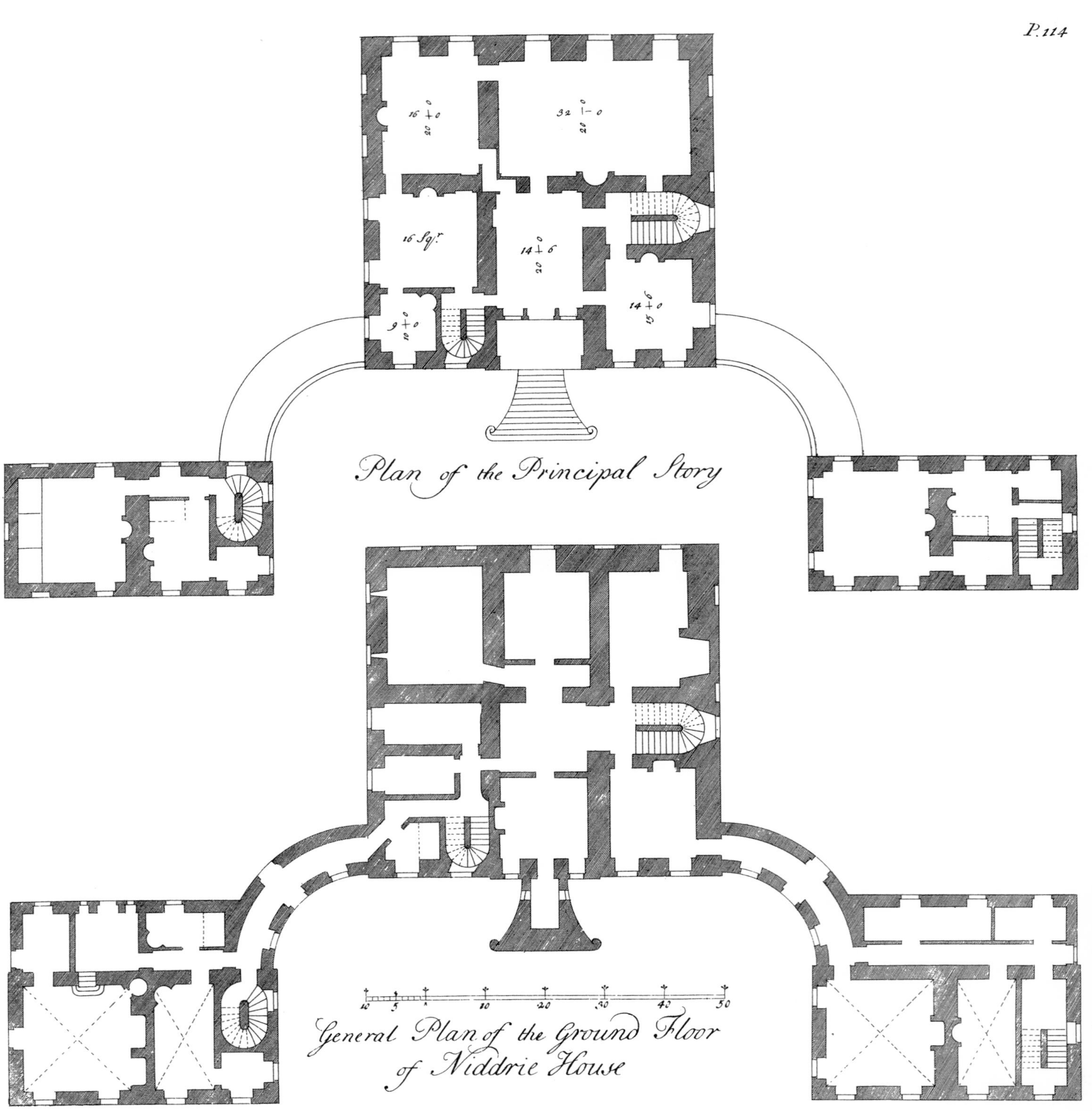

Gul: Adam inv: et delin

R: Cooper Sculp.

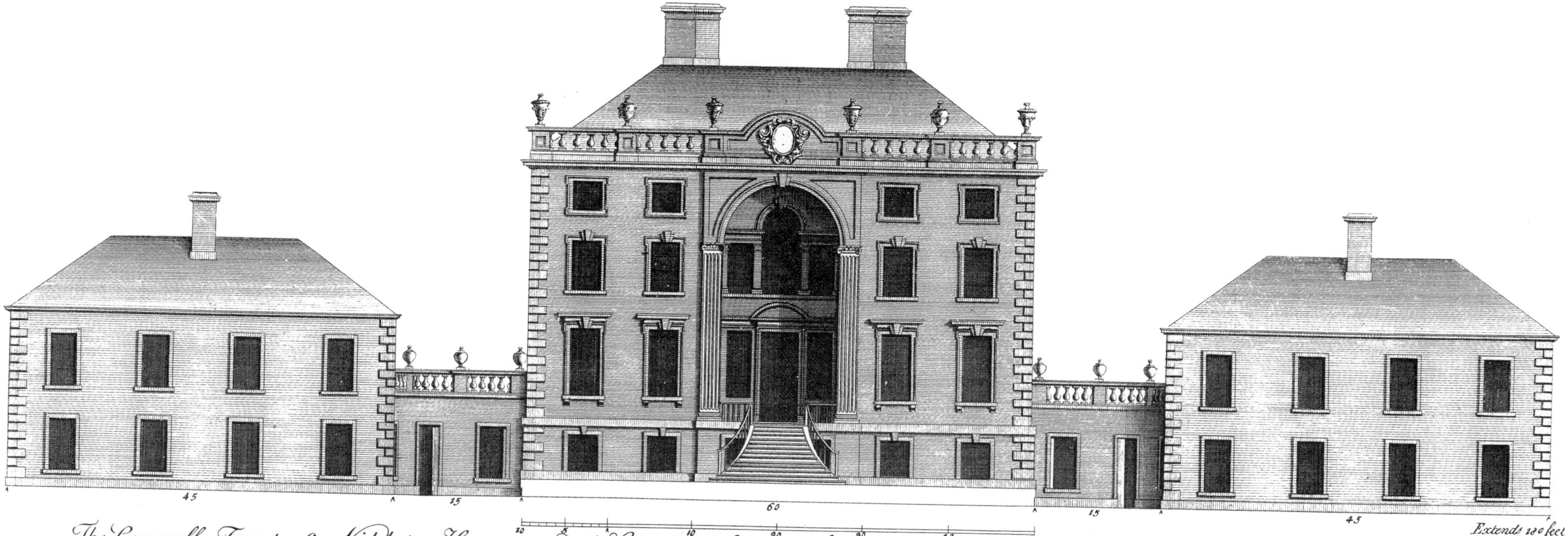

45 15 60 15 45

Extends 180 feet

The Generall Front of Niddrie House toward the Court the Seat of Andrew Wauchope of Niddrie Esq.r in the County of Mid Lothian

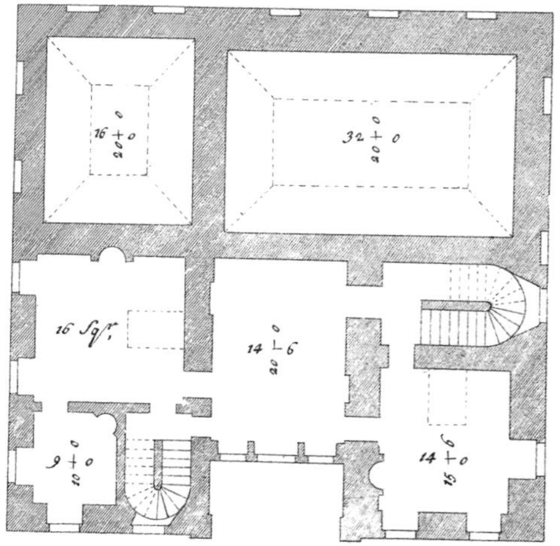

16 + 0 / 20 0

32 + 0 / 20 0

16 Sq.r

14 + 6 / 20 0

9 + 0 / 10 0

14 + 0 / 15 6

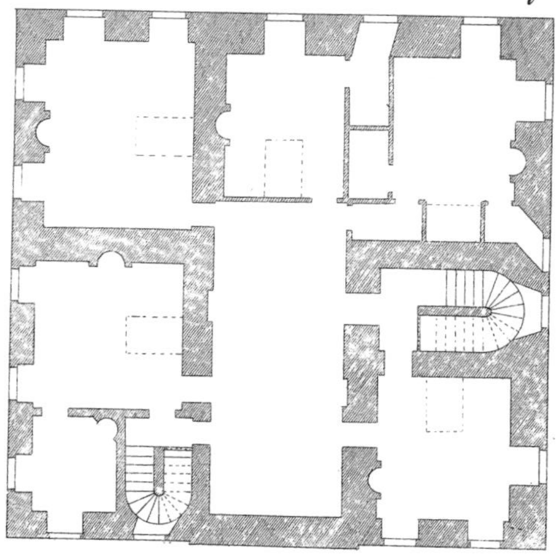

Plan of the Mezzanine Story

Plan of the Attick Story

Gul: Adam inv: et delin

R: Cooper Sculp:

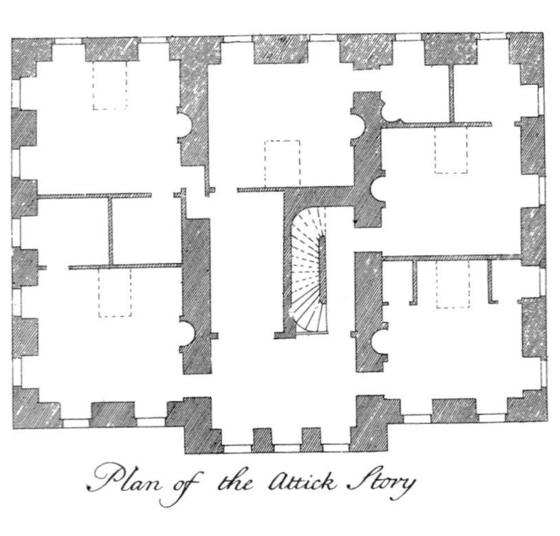

Plan of the Attick Story

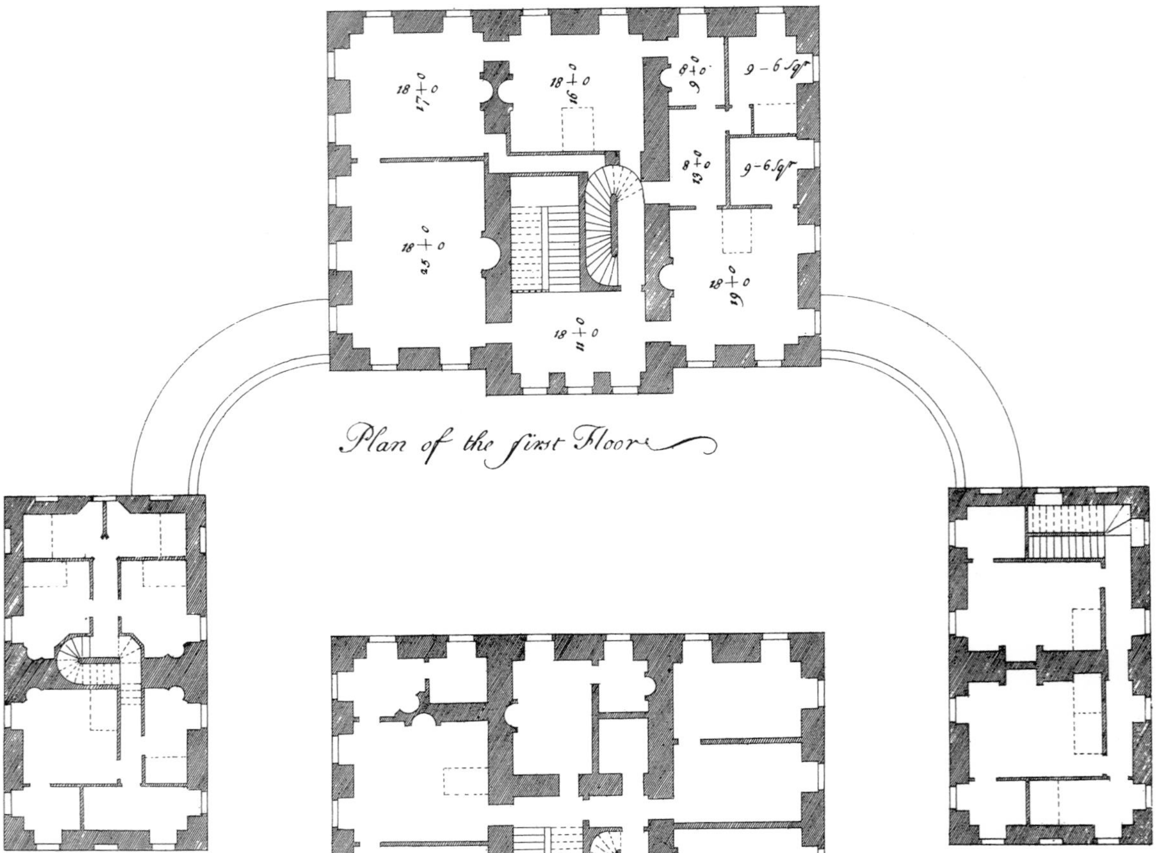

Plan of the first Floor

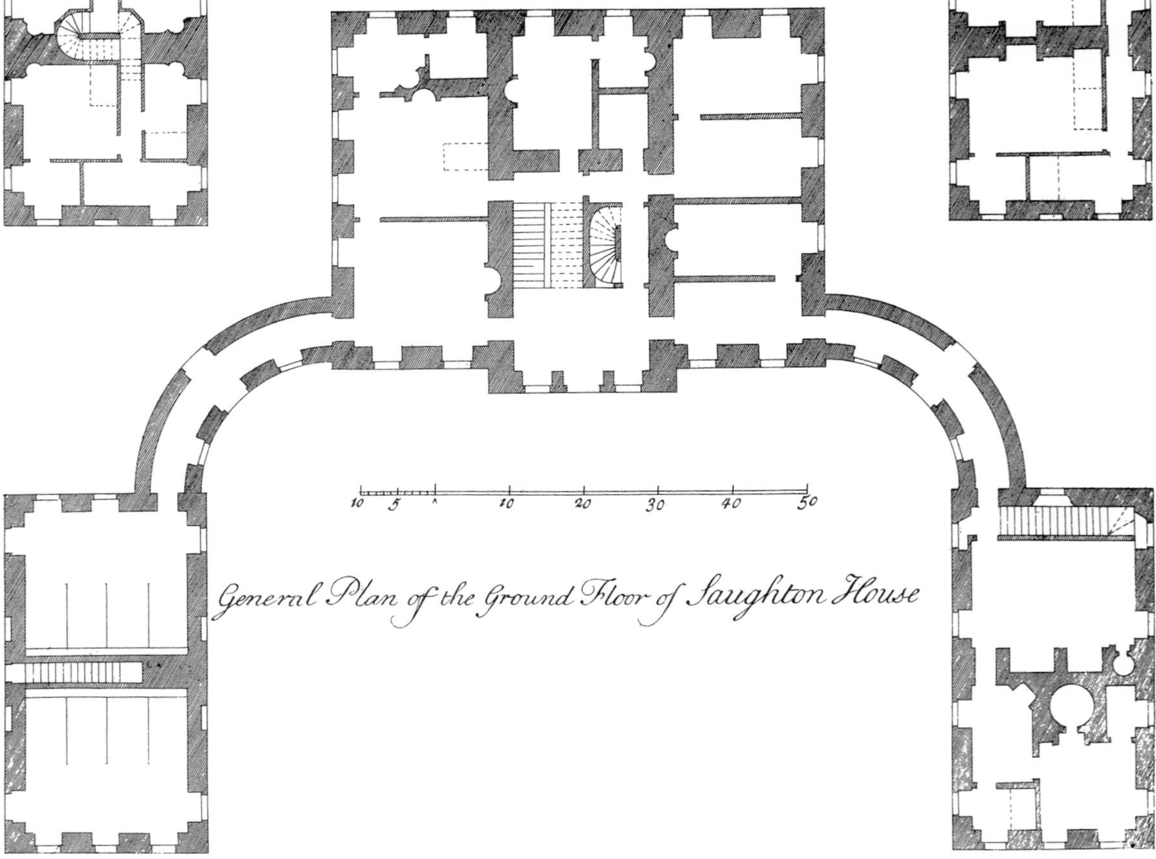

10 5 0 10 20 30 40 50

General Plan of the Ground Floor of Saughton House

Gul: Adam inv: et delin *R: Cooper Sculp:*

The East Front of Saughton House toward the Court the Seat of James Wattson of Saughton Esqr. in the County of Midd Lothian Extends 155 feet

Gul Adam inv: et delin

R: Cooper Sculp

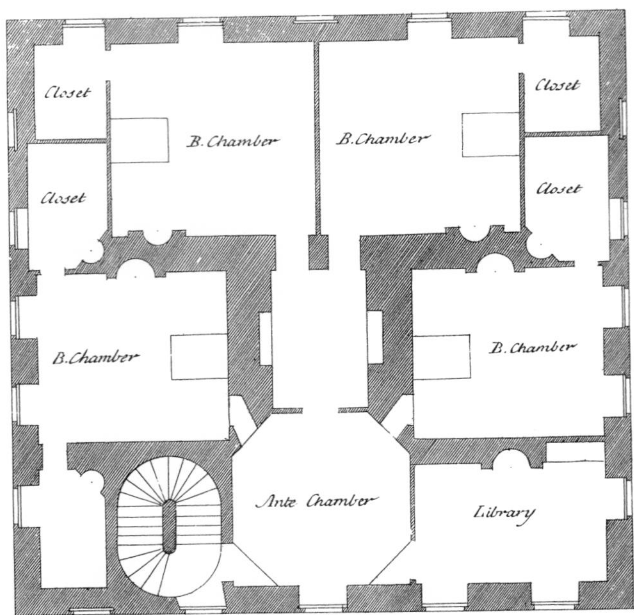

Plan of the Lodging Story

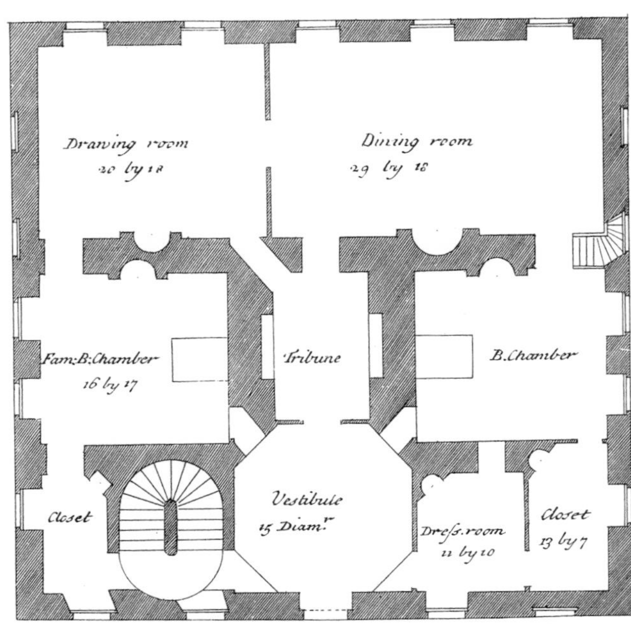

Plan of the Principal Floor above the Vaults of Broomland House

10 5 0 10 20 30

Gul Adam delin

R. Cooper Sculp

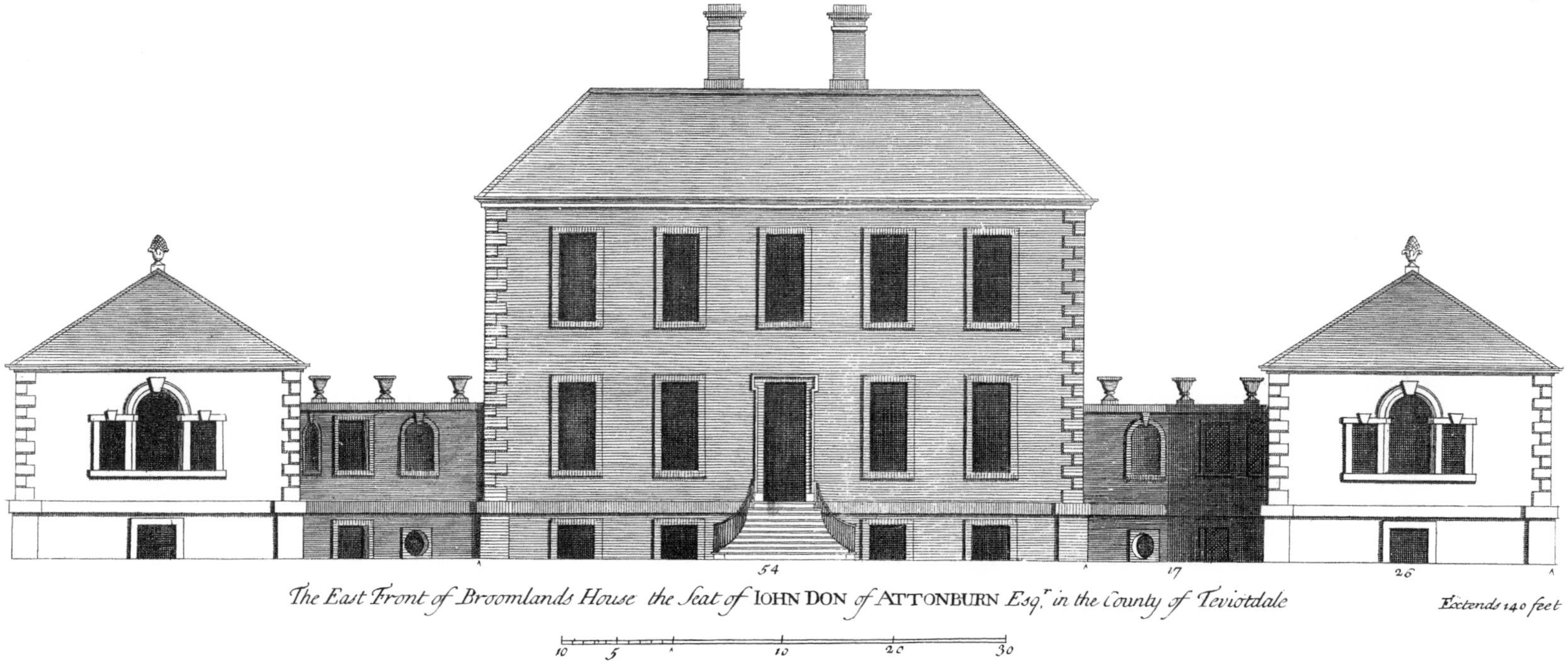

54 17 26

The East Front of Broomlands House the Seat of IOHN DON of ATTONBURN Esq.r in the County of Teviotdale

Extends 140 feet

10 5 10 20 30

Gul Adam Delin

R: Cooper Sculp.

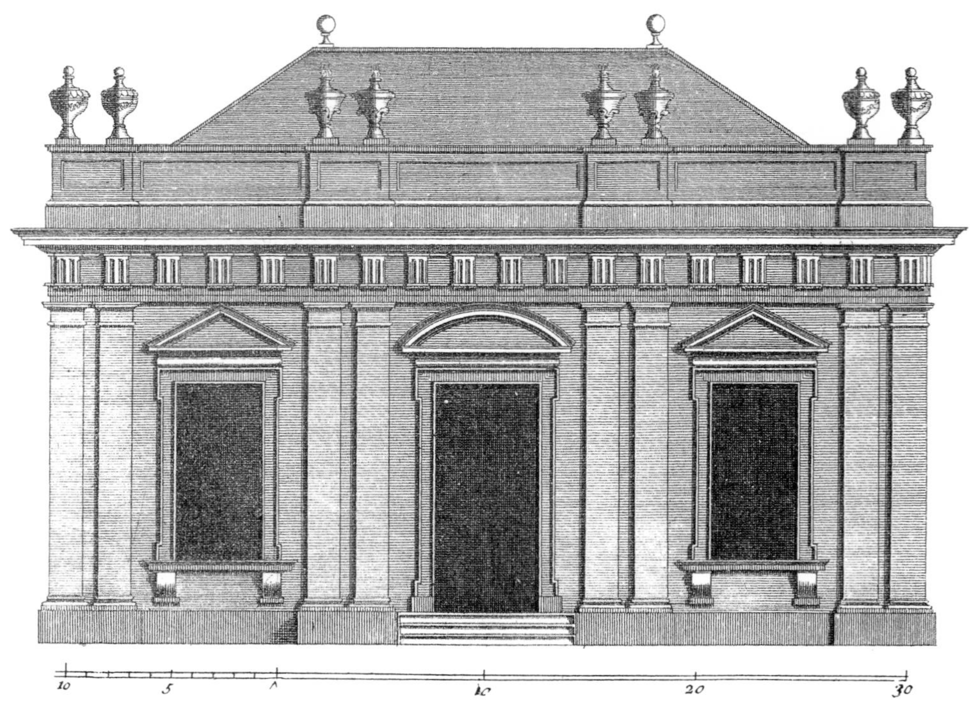

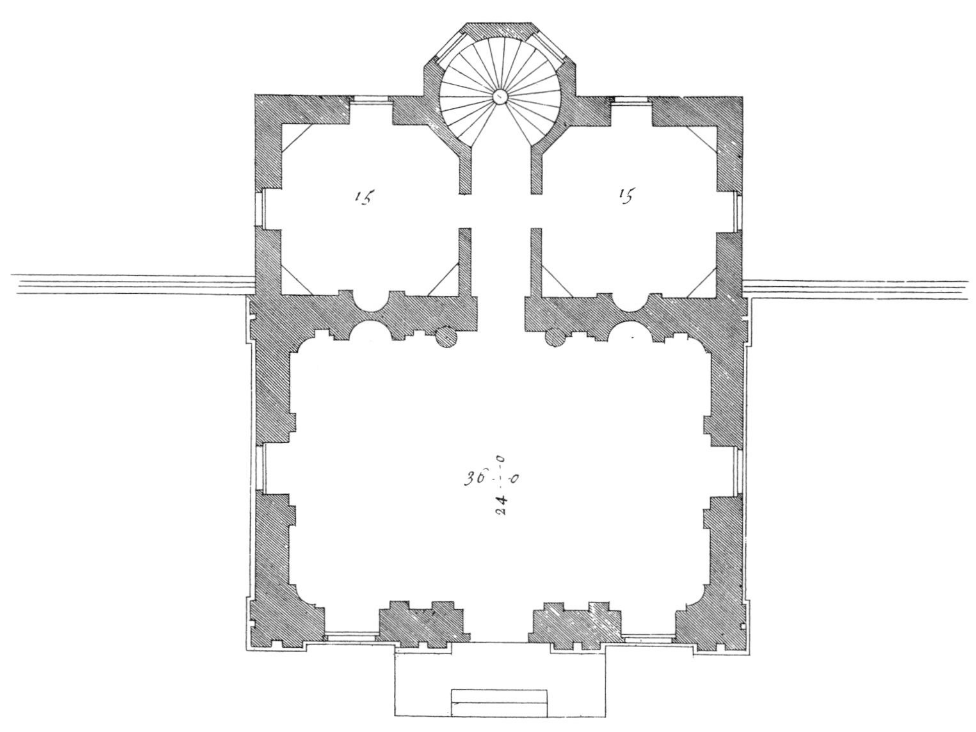

Plan & Front of a Temple Design'd att the end of the Bowling green of Castle Kennedy One of the Seats of the Right Hon.ble the Earl of Stair

Gul Adam inv. et Delin

R. Cooper Sculp

Elevation of *HAMILTON-HALL-HOUSE* The Seat of *THOMAS HAMILTON* of *FALLA* Esqr. in the County of Mid Lothian.

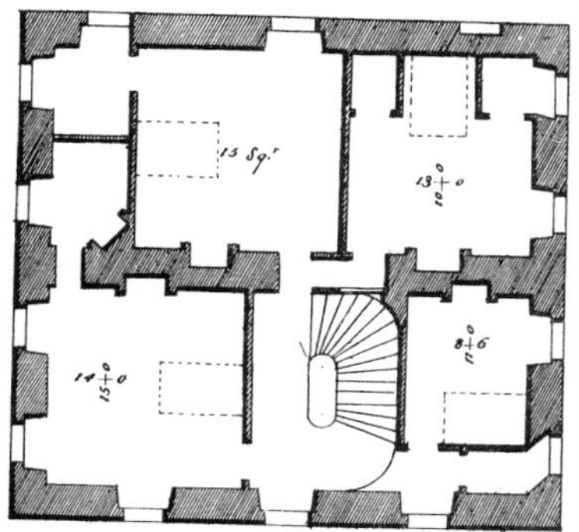

Attick Story.

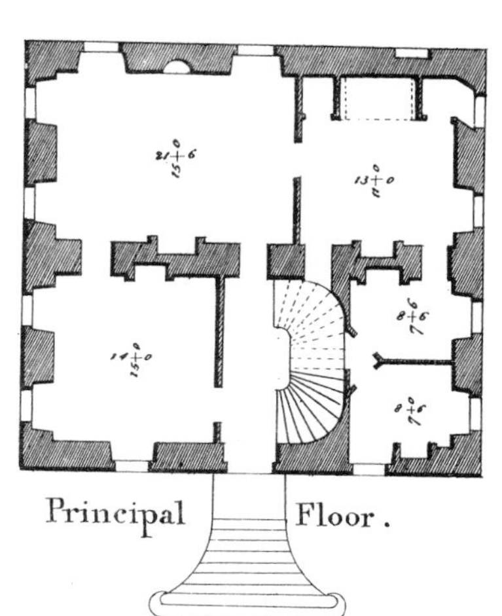

Principal Floor.

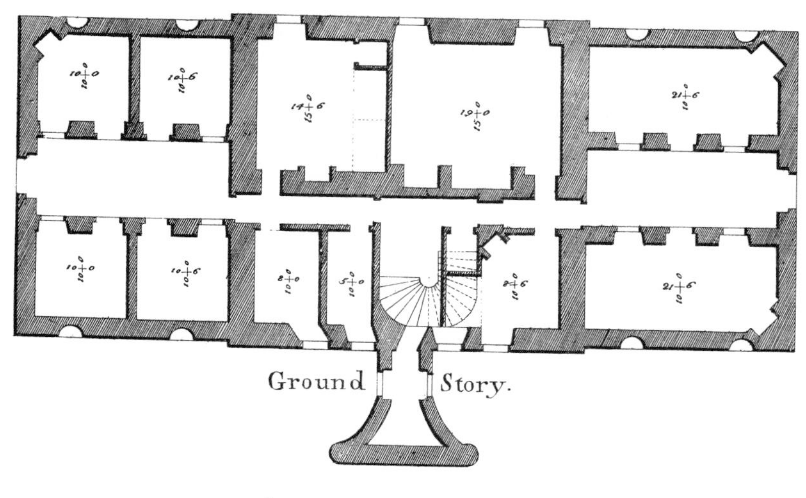

Ground Story.

Gul: Adam Invent. & Delint.

T. Smith Sculpt.

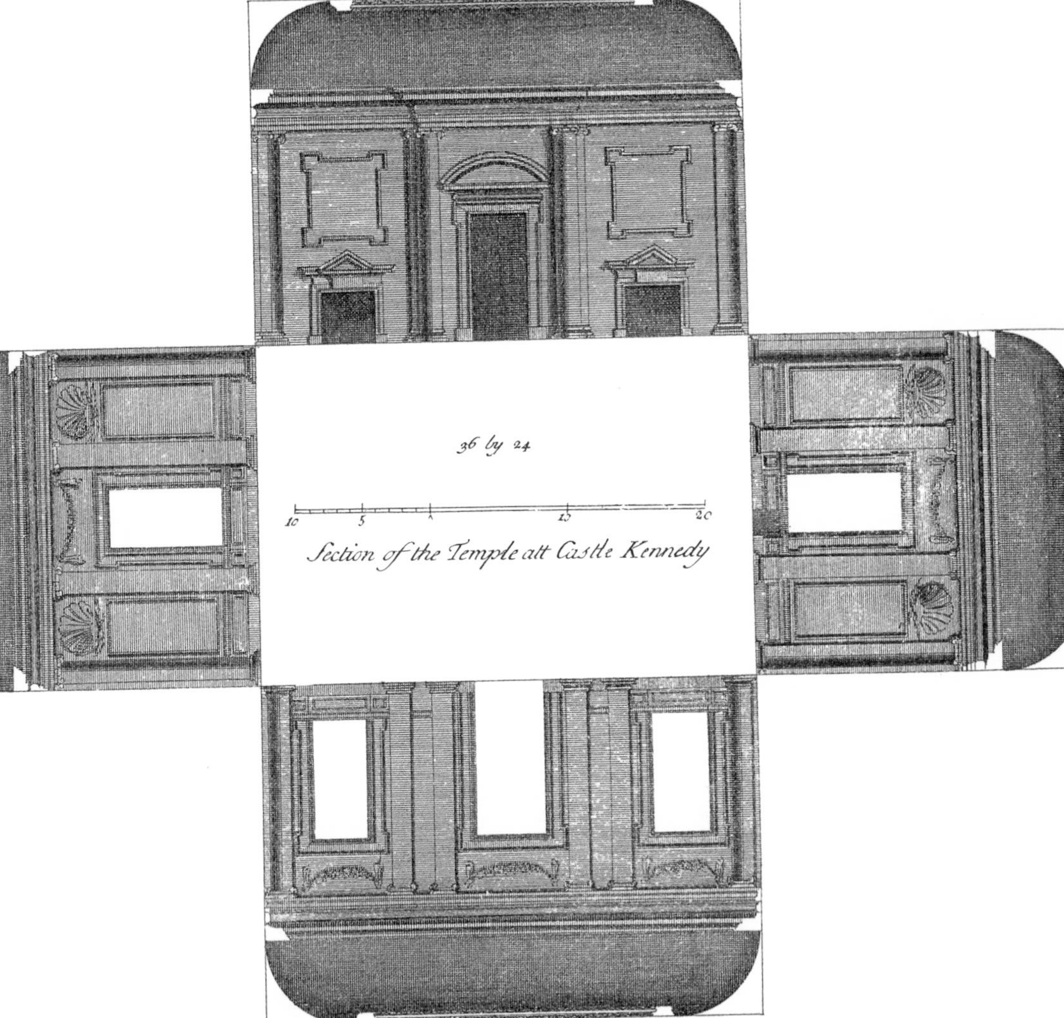

Section of the Temple att Castle Kennedy

Gul Adams inv.et delin

R. Cooper Sculp

The South Prospect, Plan of the Peers, and Cau

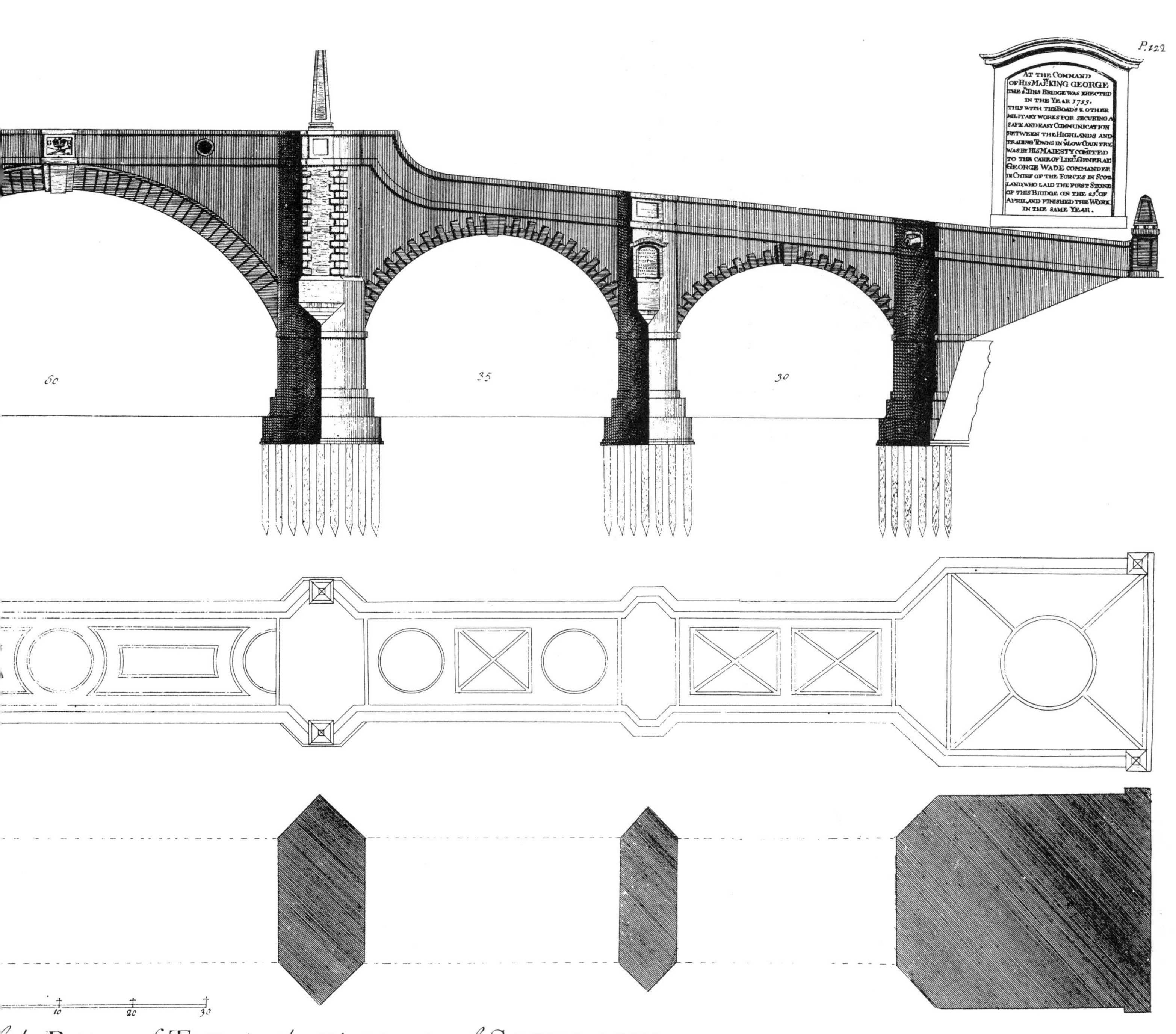

the Bridge of TAY, in the Highlands of SCOTLAND

R. Cooper Sculp.

Plan & Elevation of a Temple design'd for the Right Hon.ble the Countess of Eglintoune to be built in the Center of a Belvidere att Eglintoune

Gul. Adam inv. et delin. R. Cooper Sculp.

Lord Alemore's Villa at HAWKHILL near EDINBURGH

East Front

West Front

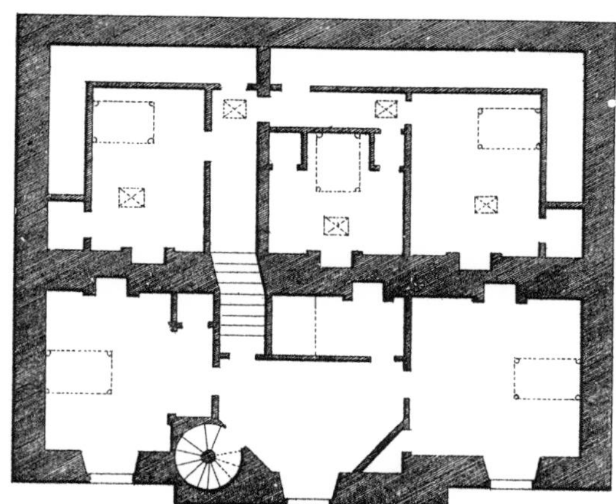

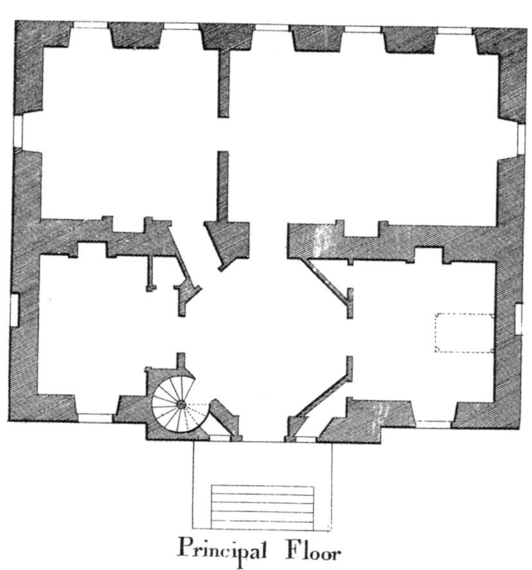

Principal Floor

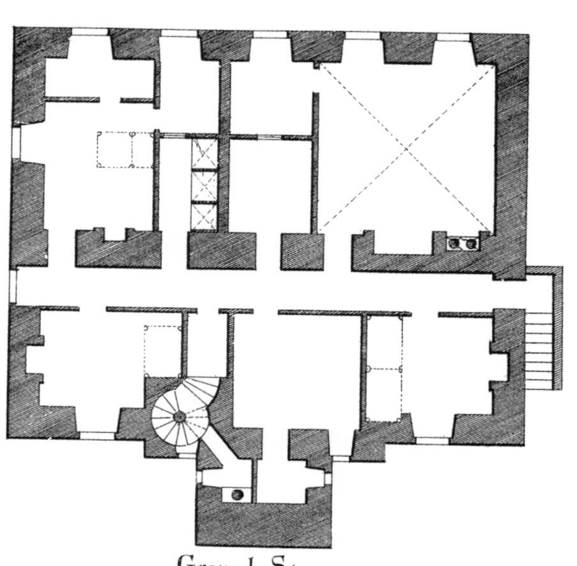

Ground Story

Jn.o Adam Arch.t

P. Mazell Sculp.t

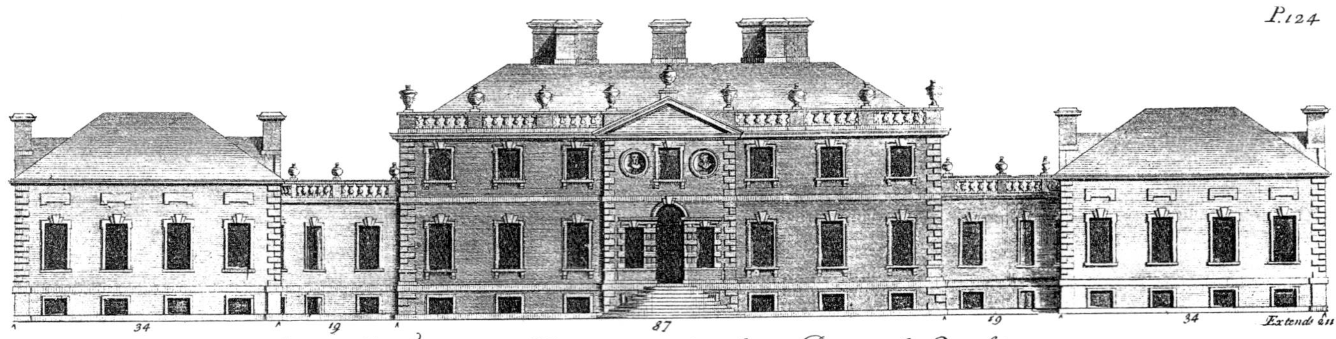

Generall Front of a House intended for a Person of Quality

A Kitchen
B Scallery
C Latter meat hall
D Cook room
E Footmens Hall
F Pantry
G Ladys Gentlewomans room
H Her Closet
I Nursery
K Second Table room
L House keepers room
M Her Closet
N Butlers room
O Powdering room
P Wine Celler
Q Ale Celler & Botle room
R Larder
S Outter milk house
T Inner milk house
U Brew house
V Gyle house
X Library
Y Woman house
Z Laundry

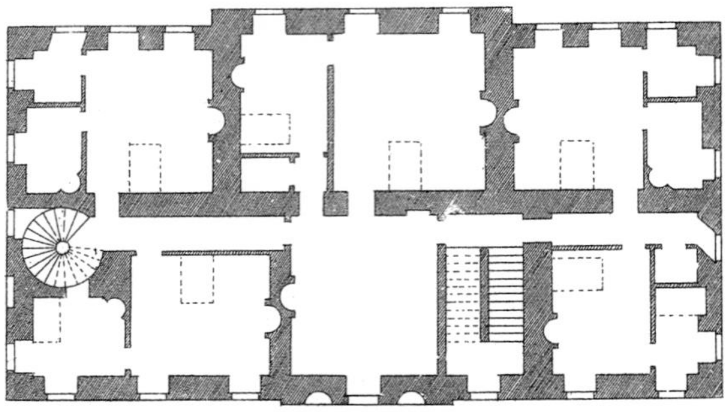

Plan of the Attick Story

Plan of the Principal Floor

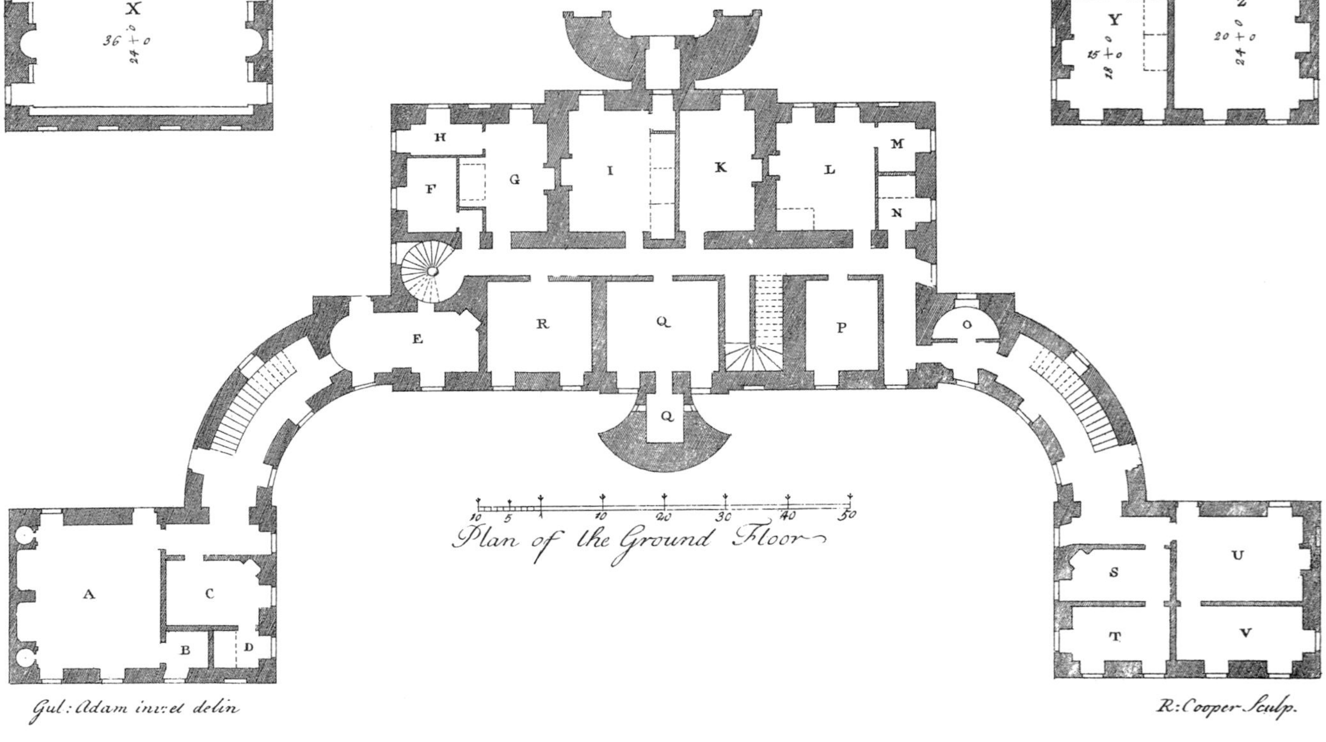

Plan of the Ground Floor

Gul: Adam inv. et delin

R: Cooper Sculp.

The Generall Front of Cumbernauld House Toward
in the

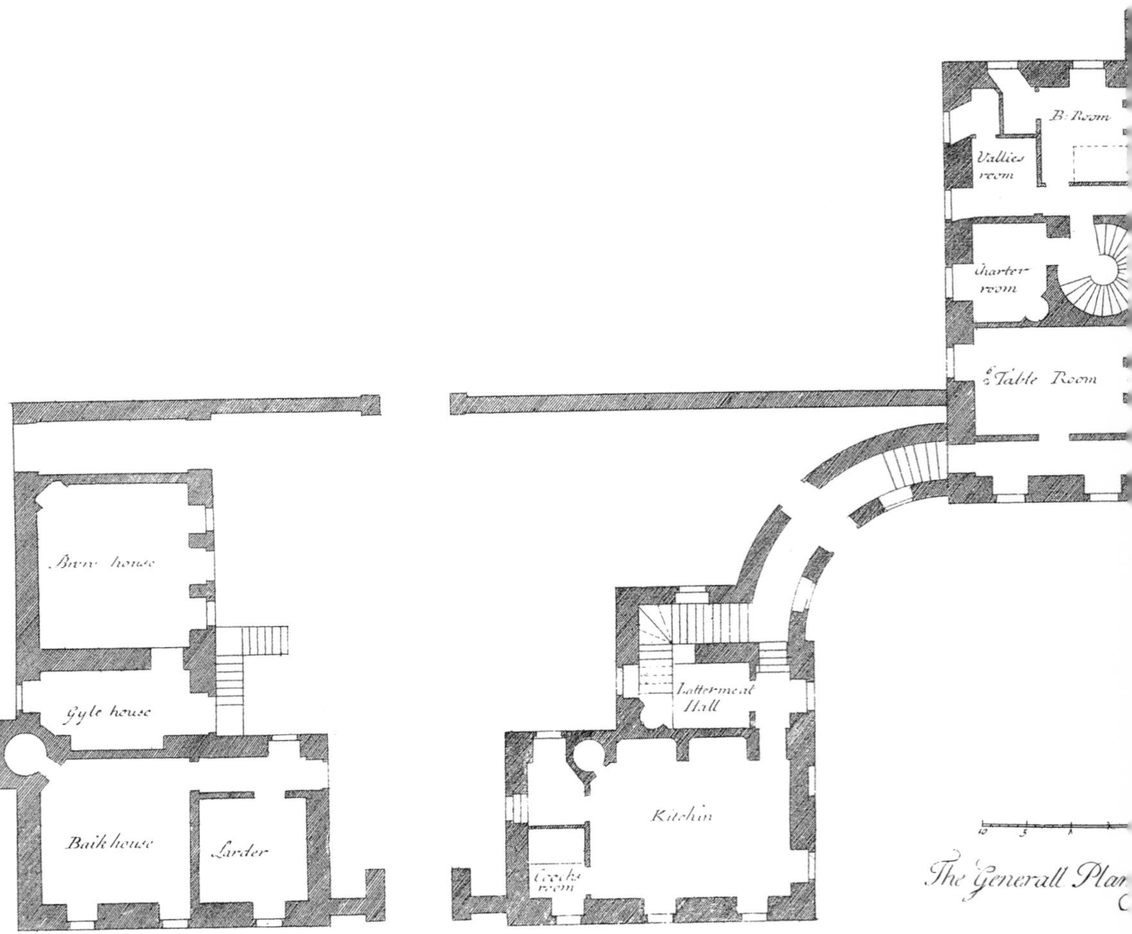

The Generall Plan

Gul: Adam Inv. & Delin

of the Right Honourable The Earl of Wigtoun
arton

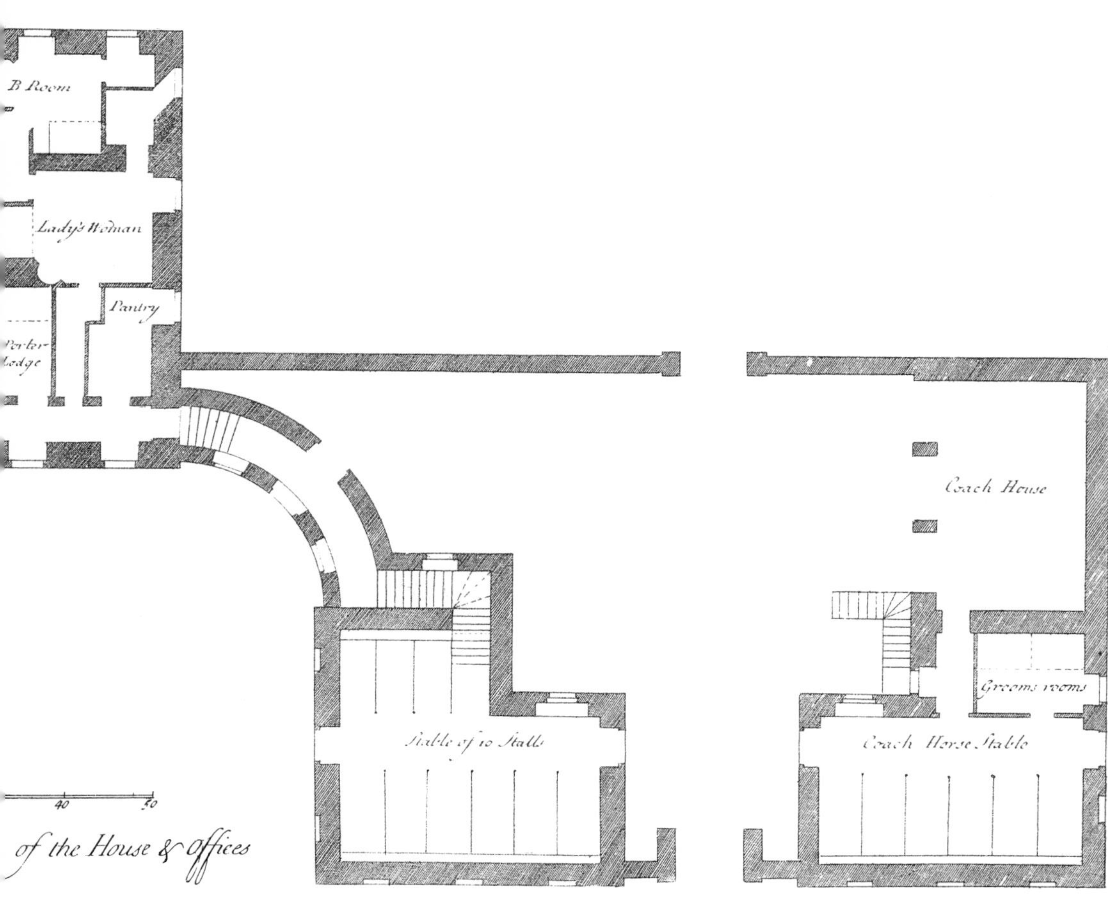

of the House & Offices

R: Cooper Sculp

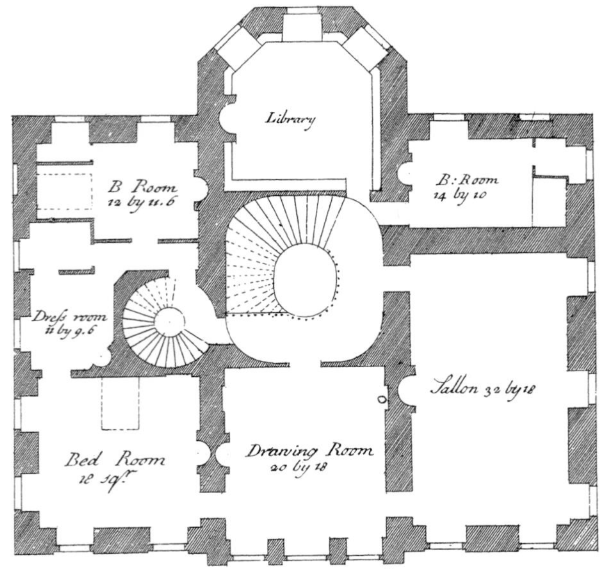

Plan of the 2d. Floor

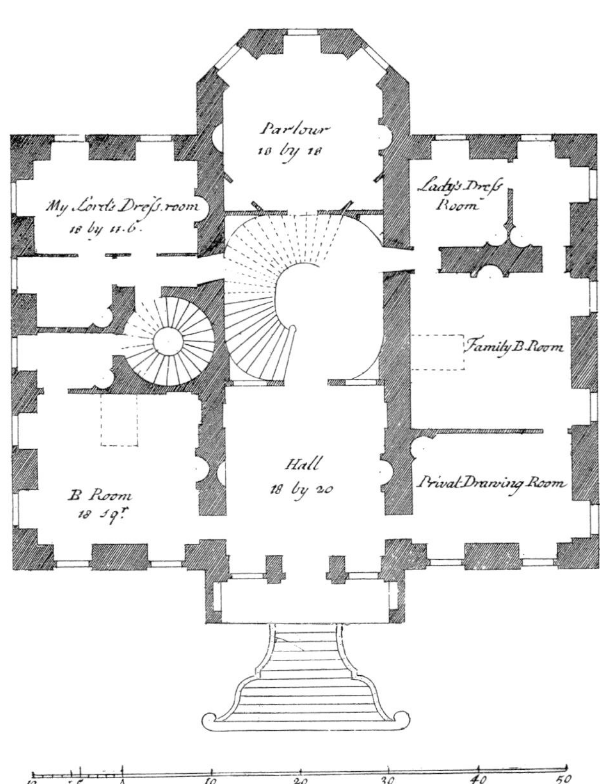

Plan of the first Floor of Cumbernauld House

Gul. Adam Inv. & Delin

R. Cooper Sculp

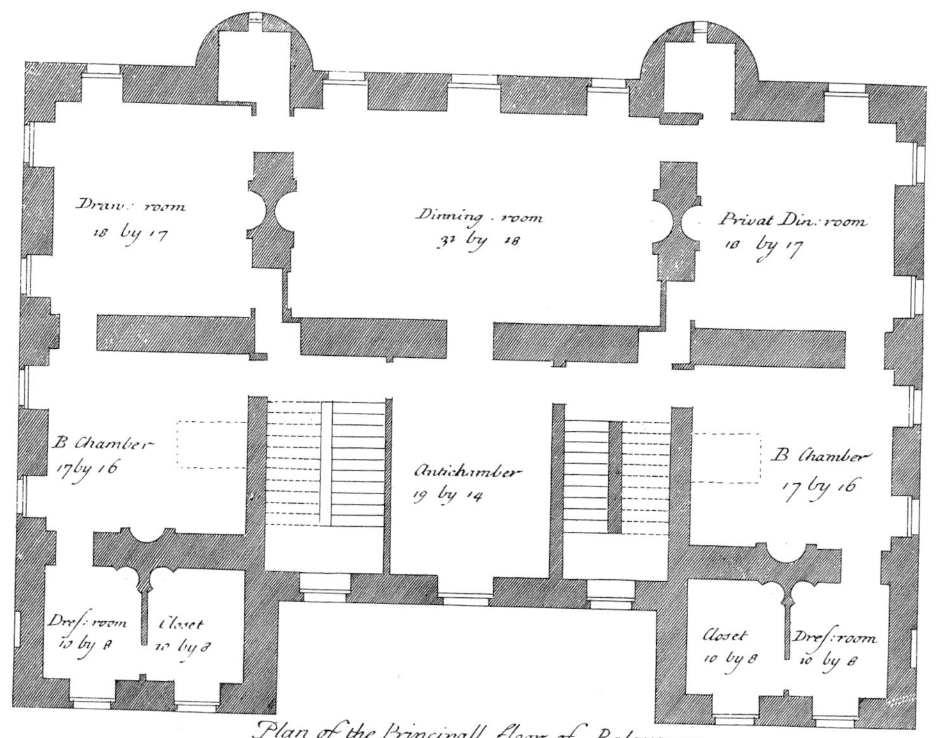

Plan of the Principall floor of Balgregan

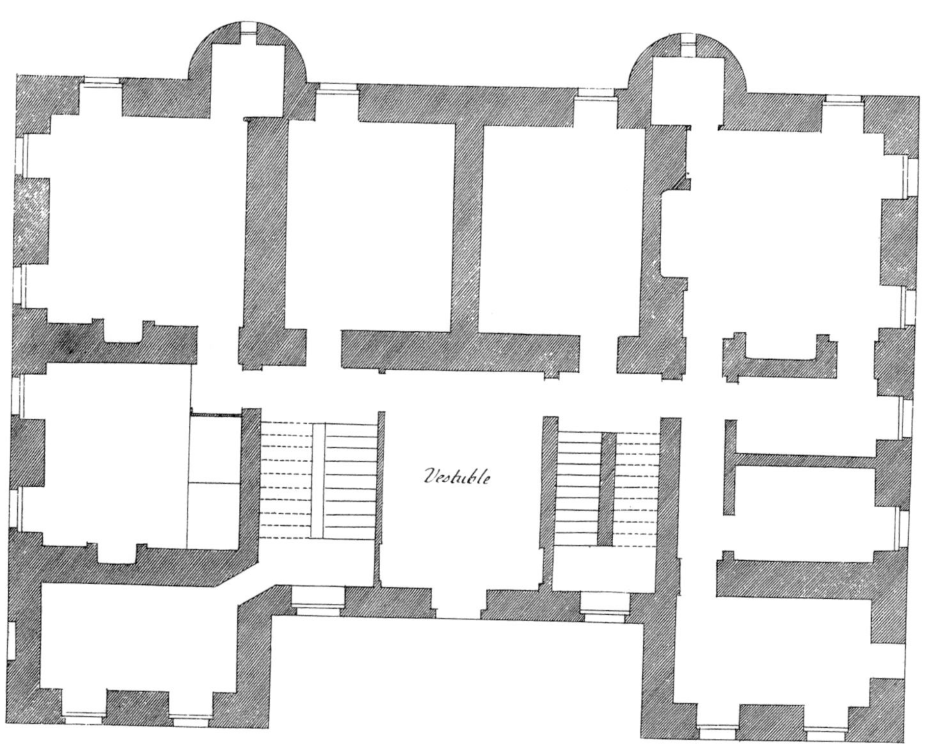

Plan of the Ground floor

Gul. Adam inv: delin

R Cooper Sculp

The Front of Balgregan House toward the Court the Seat of John Mc Dowal of Freuch Esqr in the County of Galloway. Extends 76

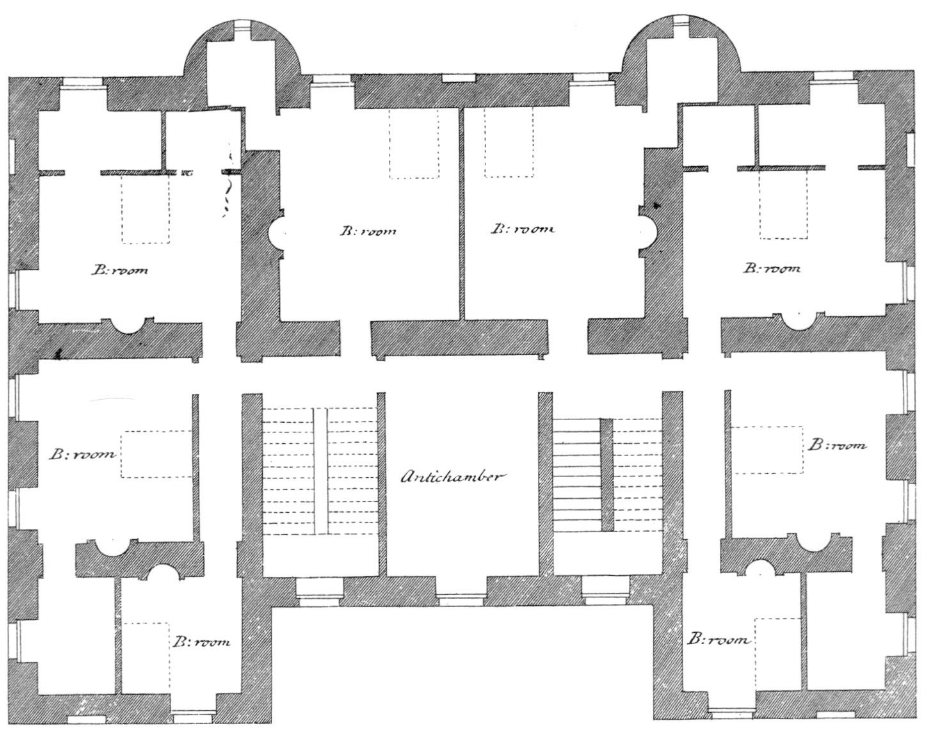

Plan of the Lodging Story

Gul: Adam inv: delin:

R: Cooper Sculp:

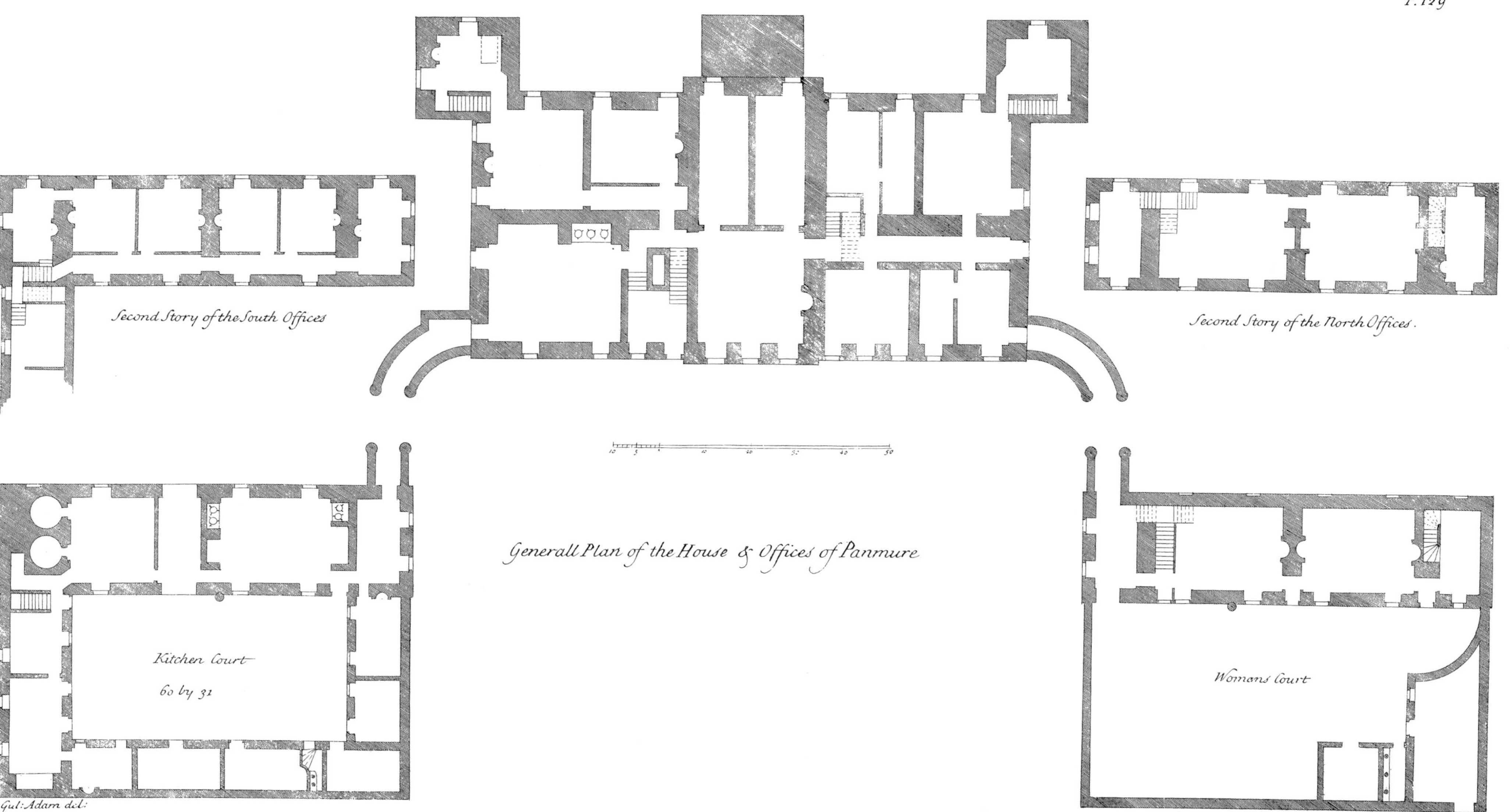

Generall Plan of the House & Offices of Panmure

Gul: Adam del:

R. Cooper Sc:

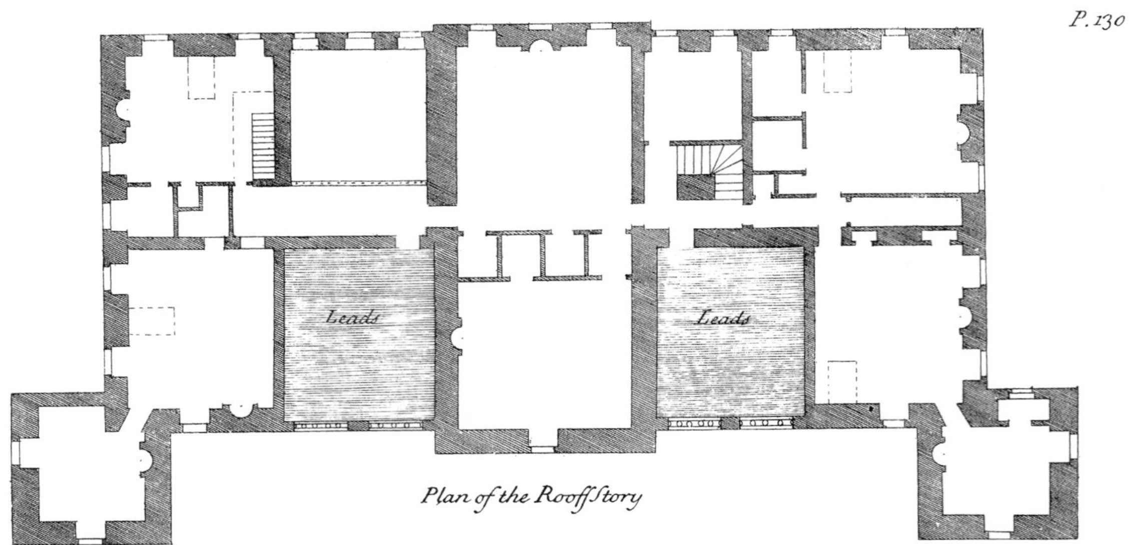

Plan of the Rooff Story

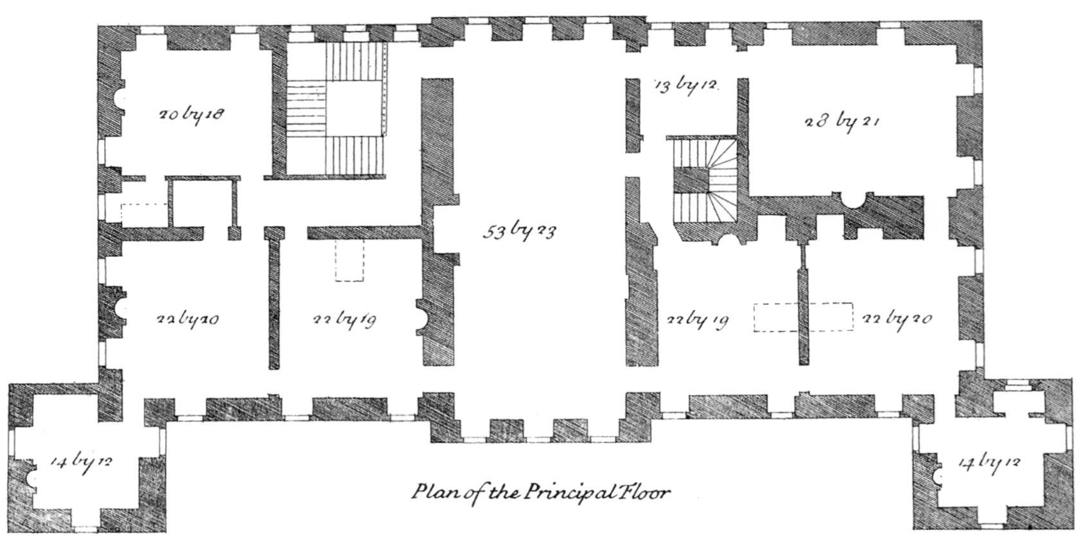

Plan of the Principal Floor

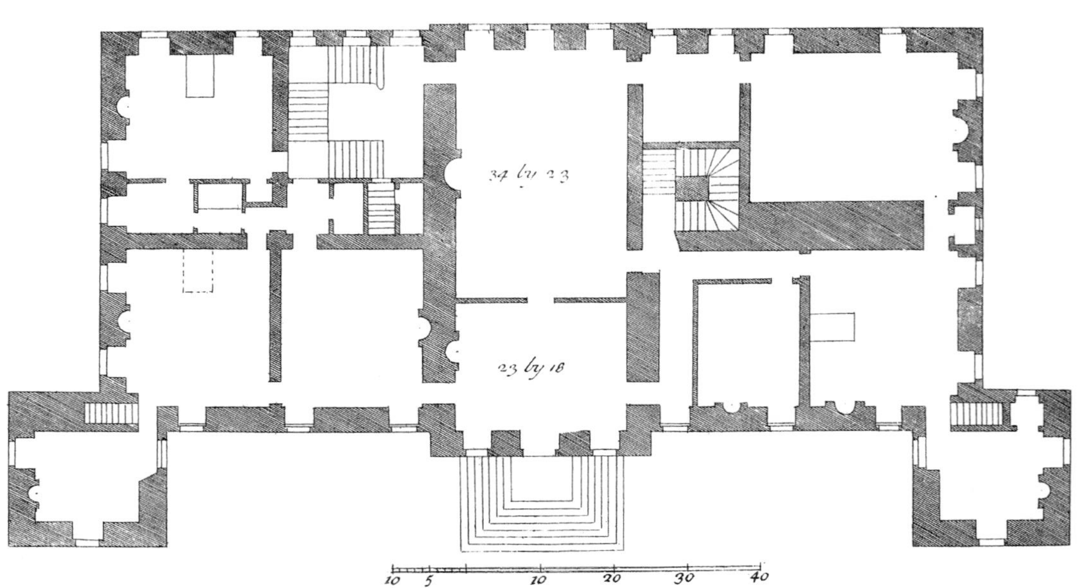

Plan of the First Floor of Panmure House.

Gul: Adam del. R. Cooper Sc.

90

145

0 5 10 20 30 40 50

90

Extends 325

Generall Front of Panmure House toward the West, The Seat of the Rt. Honble the late Earl of Panmure in the County of Angus.

Gul: Adam del:

R. Cooper Sc.

Genéral Front of Rosehall House toward the North The Seat of Sir James Hamilton of Rosehall in the County of Clydsdale

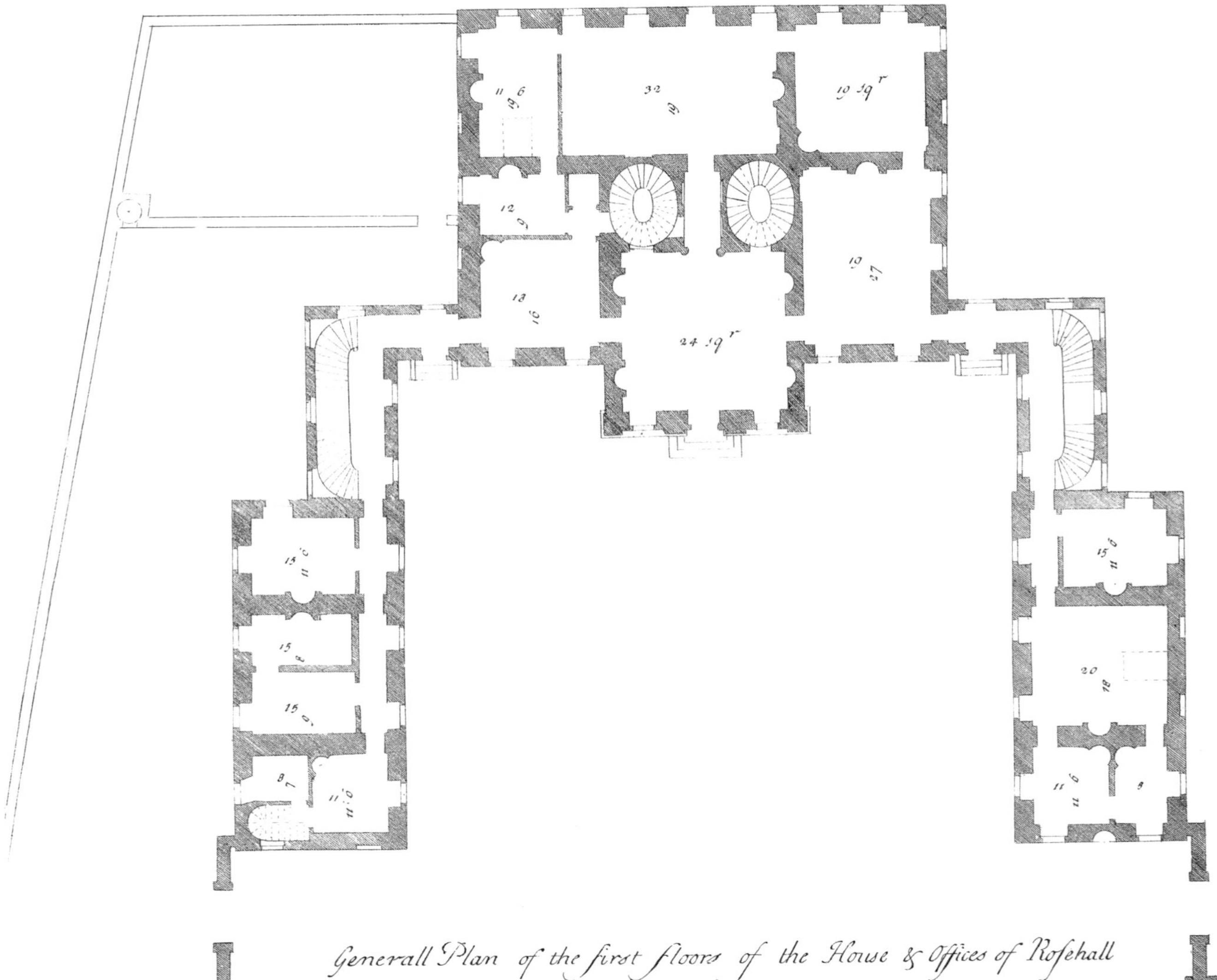

Generall Plan of the first floors of the House & Offices of Rosehall

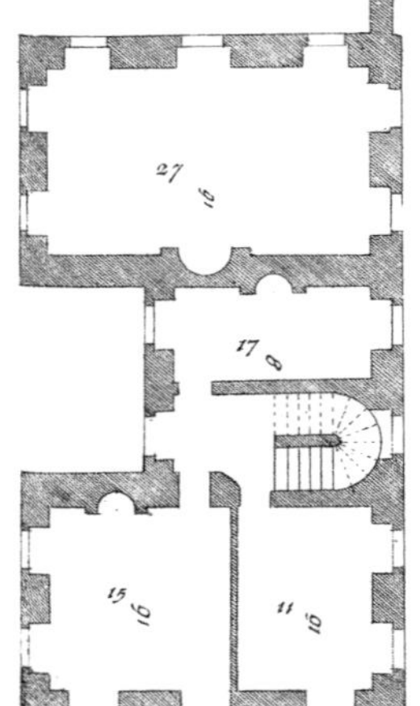

10 5 0 10 20 30 40 50

Gul: Adam Delin

R. Cooper Sculp.

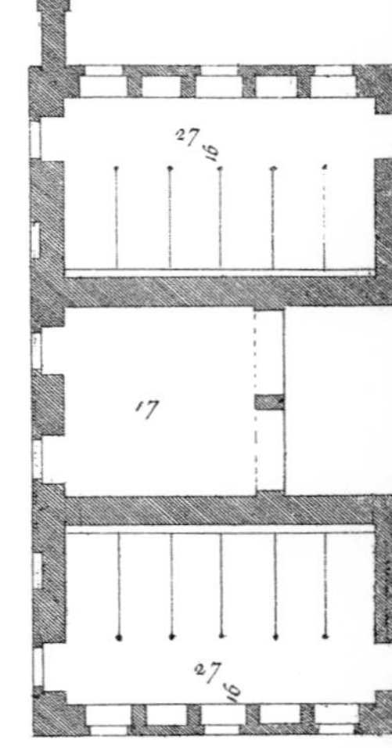

Plan of the Library above the Rooff

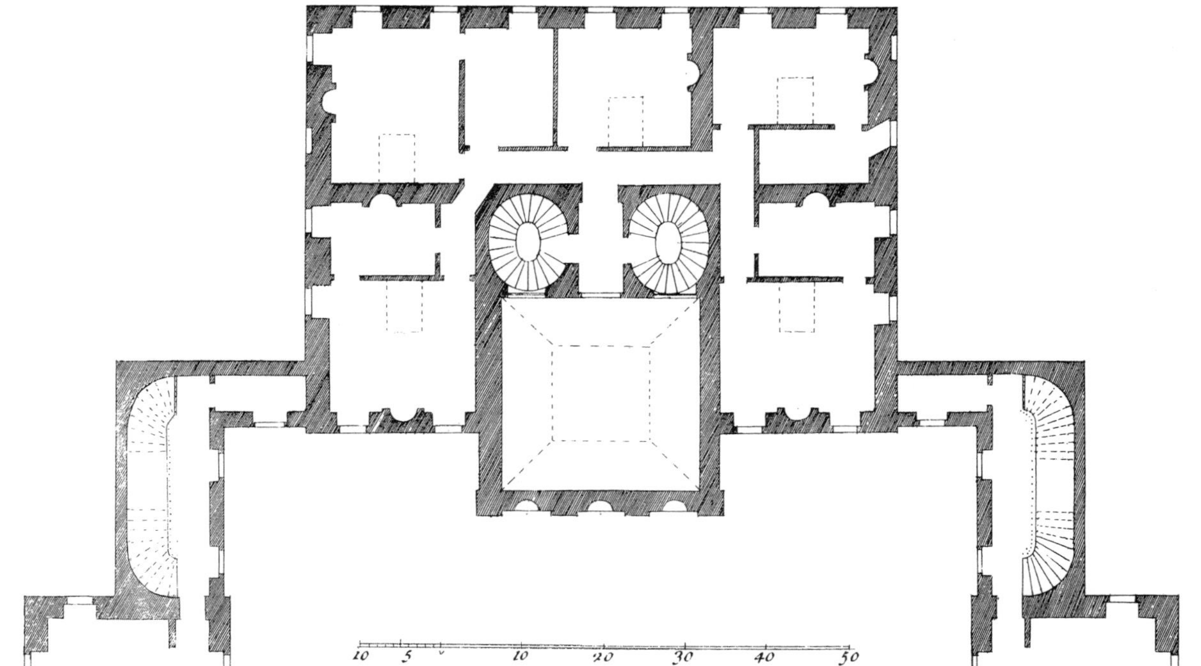

10 5 0 10 20 30 40 50

Plan of the Second Story of the House & Lodging Pavilions of Rosehall.

Gul: Adam del.

R. Cooper Sc.

Section of Rosehall with the Fronts of the two Pavilions towards the Court

Gul: Adam delin

R: Cooper Sculp.

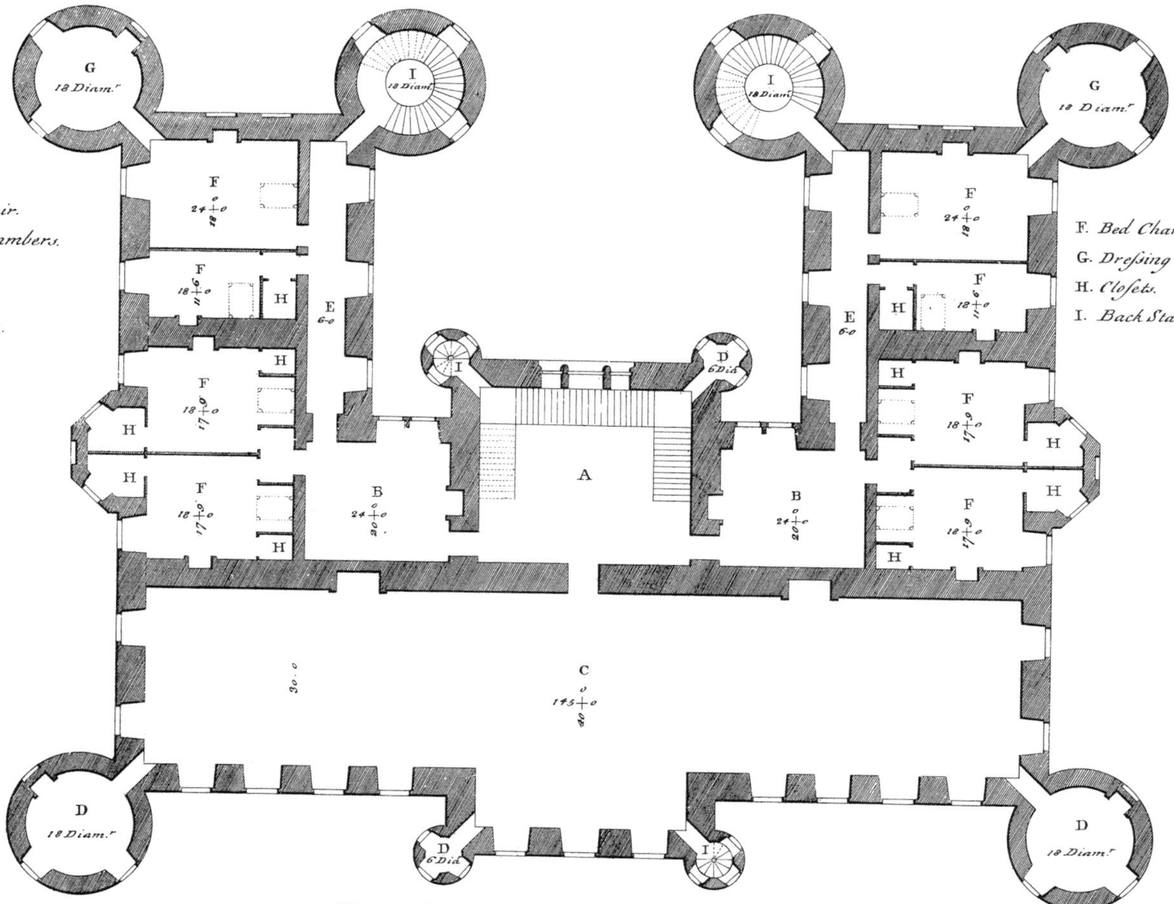

A. Great Stair.
B. Ante Chambers.
C. Gallery.
D. Closets.
E. Passages.

F. Bed Chambers.
G. Dressing rooms.
H. Closets.
I. Back Stairs.

Plan of the One pair of Stairs Story.

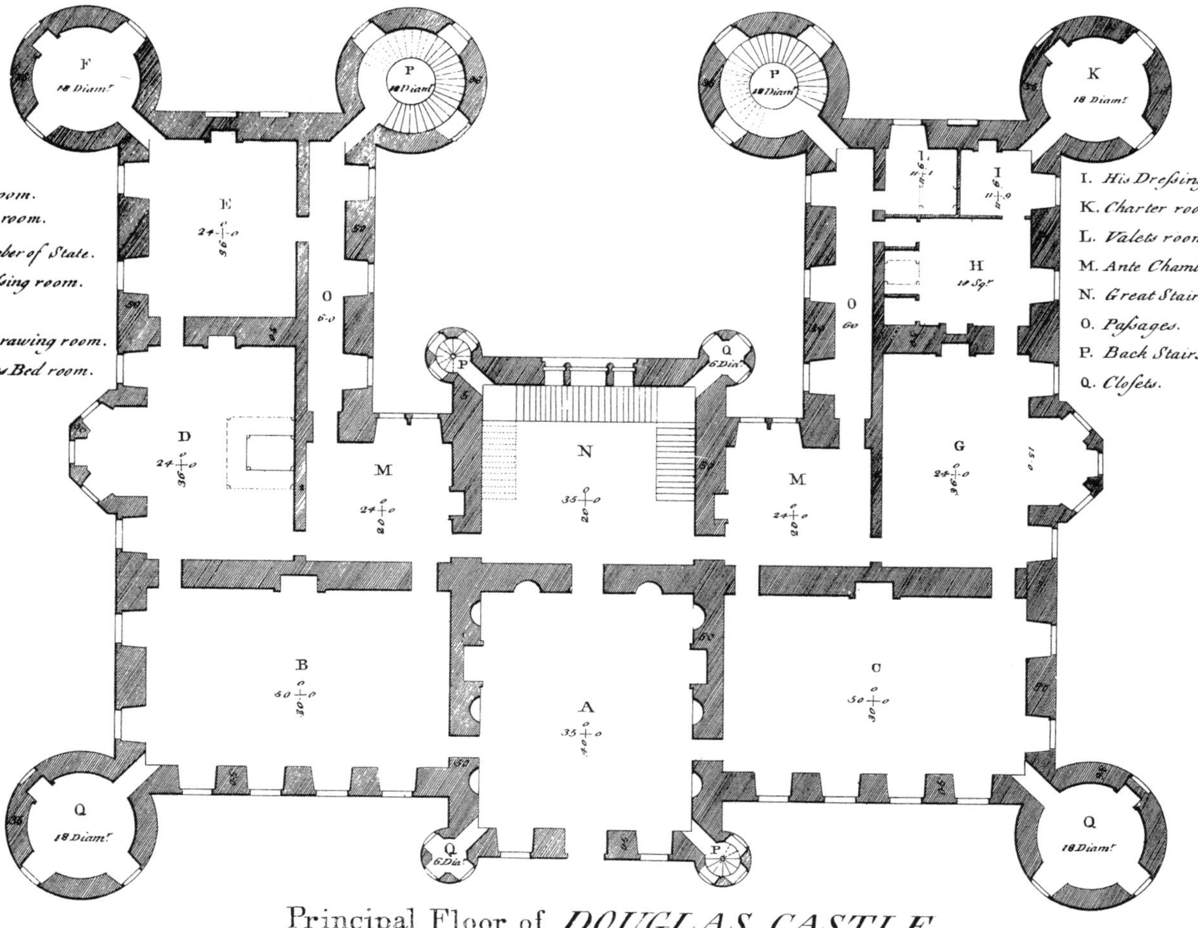

A. Hall.
B. Dining room.
C. Drawing room.
D. Bed Chamber of State.
E. Great Dressing room.
F. Closet.
G. Private Drawing room.
H. His Graces Bed room.

I. His Dressing room.
K. Charter room.
L. Valets room.
M. Ante Chambers.
N. Great Stair.
O. Passages.
P. Back Stairs.
Q. Closets.

Principal Floor of *DOUGLAS CASTLE.*

Adam's Archt.

J. Smith Sculp.

Generall Front of a House an

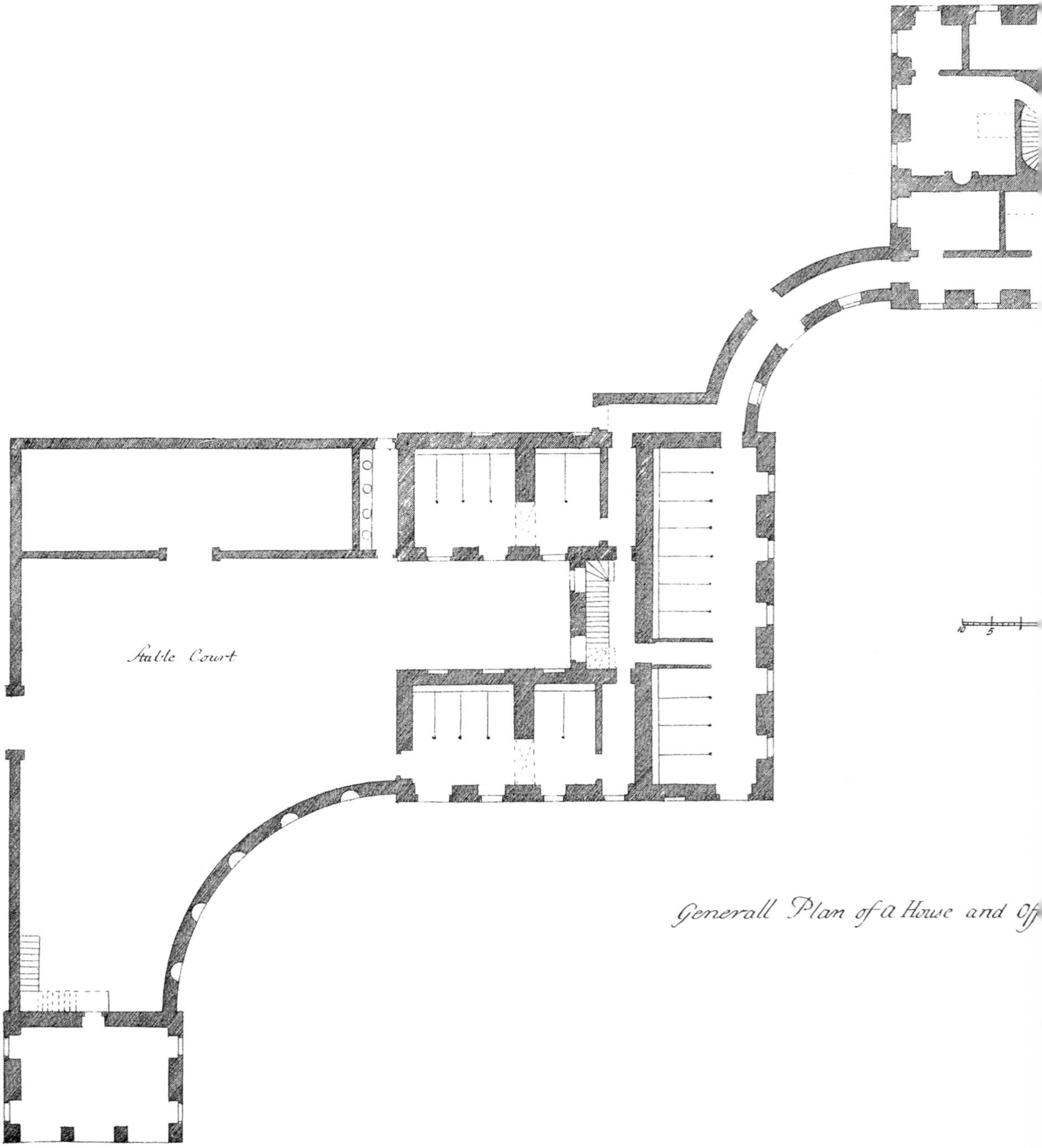

Stable Court

Generall Plan of a House and Off

Gul Adam inv delin

d, for his Grace the Duke of Montrose

Kitchen Court

40 50

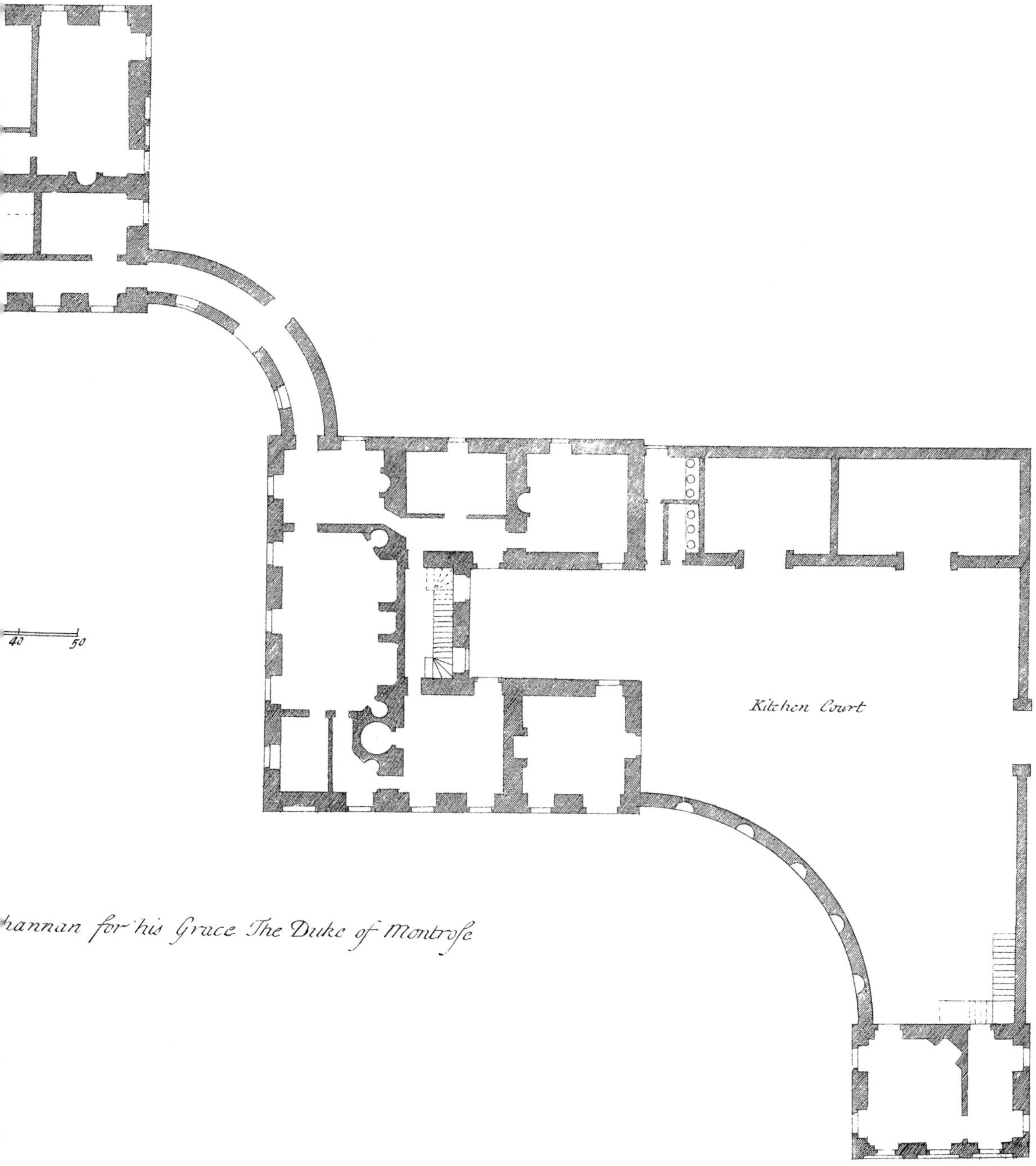

hannan for his Grace The Duke of Montrose

R: Cooper Sculp.

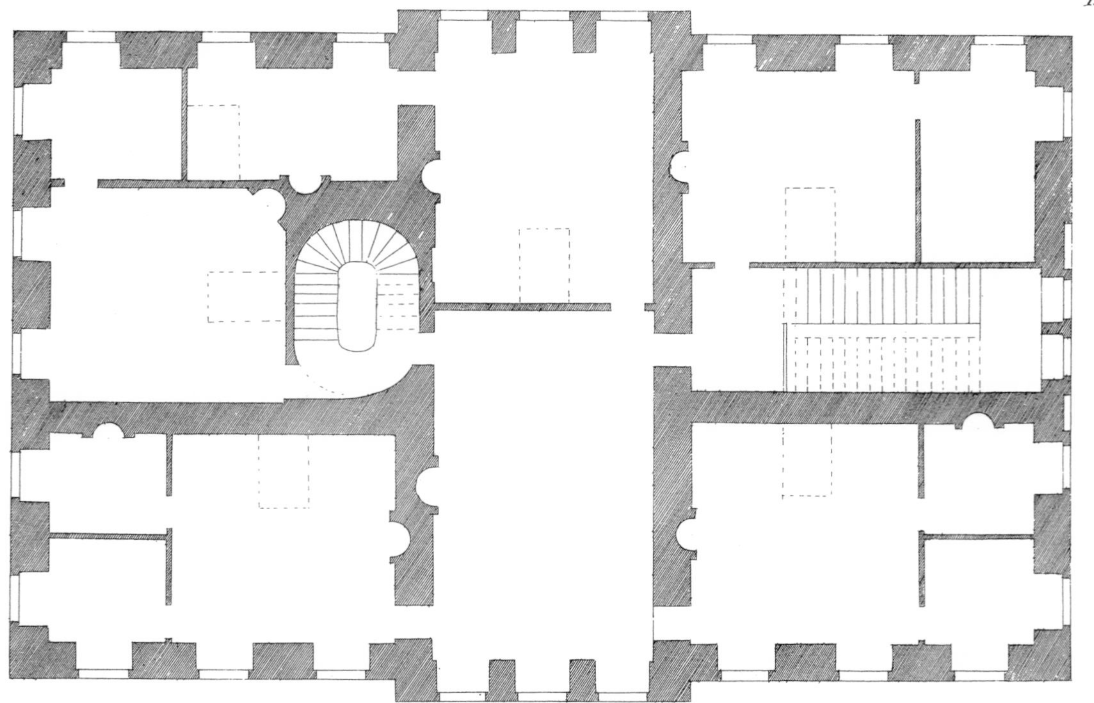

Plan of the Lodging Story

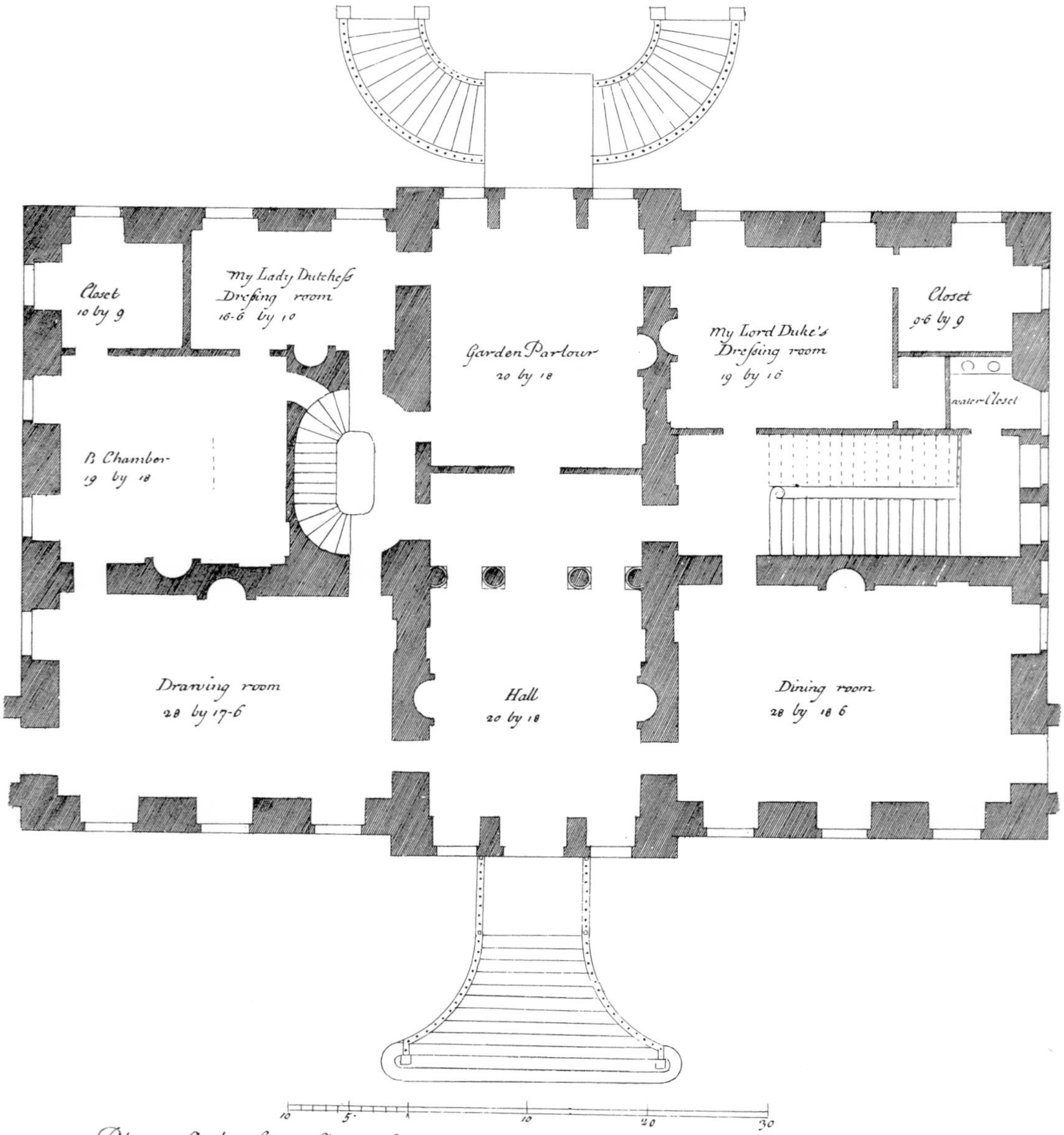

Closet
10 by 9

My Lady Dutchess Dressing room
16-6 by 10

Garden Parlour
20 by 18

My Lord Duke's Dressing room
19 by 16

Closet
9-6 by 9

water-Closet

B. Chamber
19 by 18

Drawing room
28 by 17-6

Hall
20 by 18

Dining room
28 by 18 6

10 5 0 10 20 30

Plan of the first floor of the House design'd for his Grace the Duke of Montrose

Gul. Adam inv: et delin

R. Cooper Sculp

West Front of DOUGLAS CASTLE The Seat of His Grace the Duke of Douglas in the County of Lanark.

Elevation of one end

T. Patton Sculp.

East Front

Adams Archt.

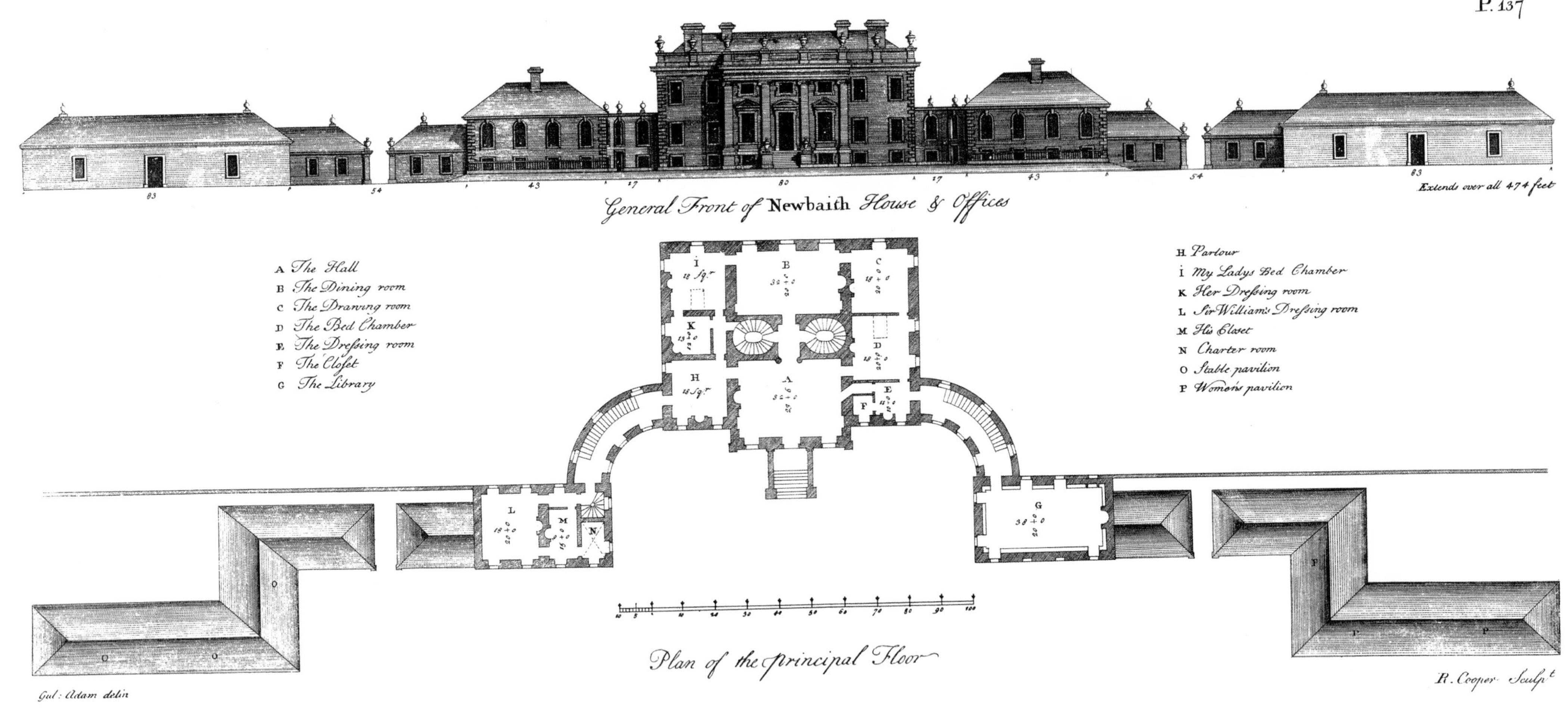
83
54
43
17
80
17
43
54
83
Extends over all 474 feet
General Front of Newbaith House & Offices
A The Hall
B The Dining room
C The Drawing room
D The Bed Chamber
E The Dressing room
F The Closet
G The Library
H. Parlour
I My Ladys Bed Chamber
K Her Dressing room
L Sir William's Dressing room
M His Closet
N Charter room
O Stable pavilion
P Women's pavilion
Plan of the principal Floor
Gul: Adam delin
R. Cooper Sculpt

North Front of Newbaith House towards the Court the Seat of Sir W.m Baird of Newbaith in the County of East Lothian

Gul: Adam delin

R: Cooper Sculp

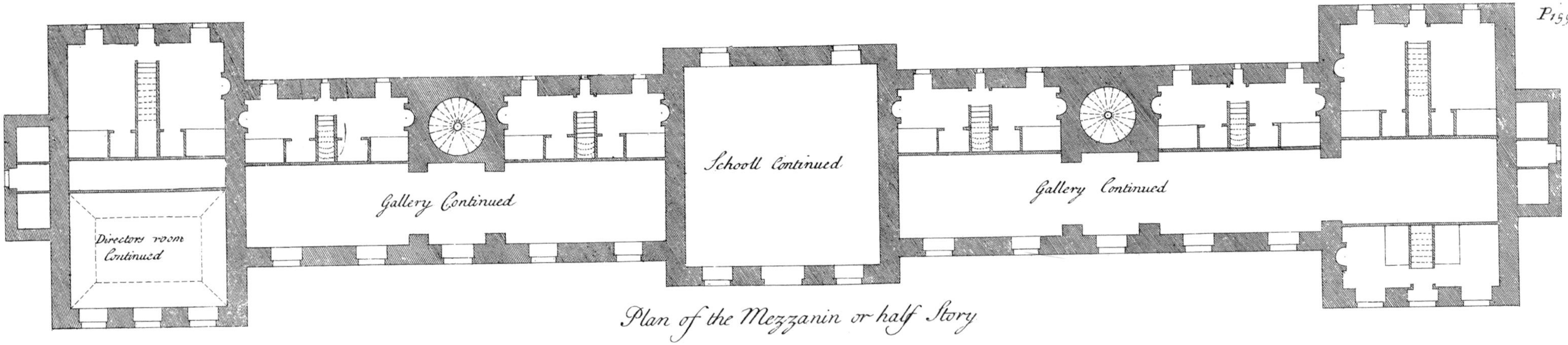

Plan of the Mezzanin or half Story

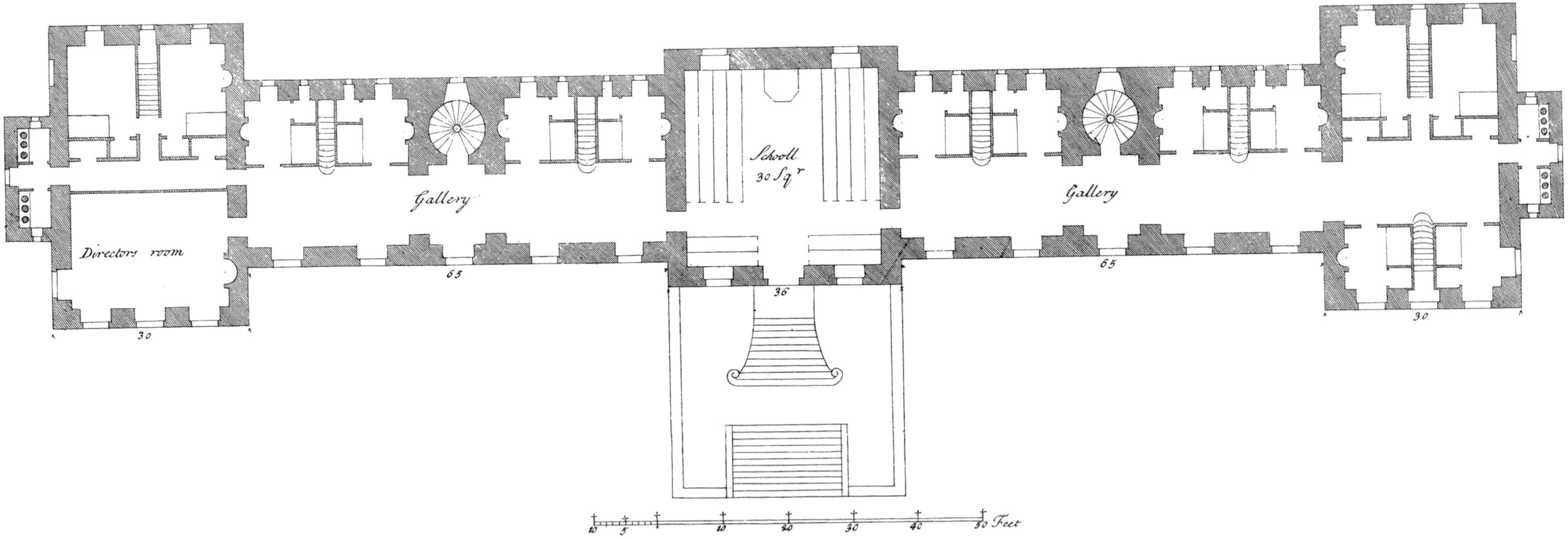

A Generall Plan of the First Floor of the **ORPHANS HOSPITALL at EDINBURGH** Begun in the Year 1754 and Carried on by the Charity of Well dispos'd Persons The Gallerys are 14 foot high and the Lodgeing Rooms 7 foot high with Mezzaninos over head for increasing the Lodgeing The whole Building Extends 226 feet

Gul: Adam inv: et delin

R: Cooper Sculp.

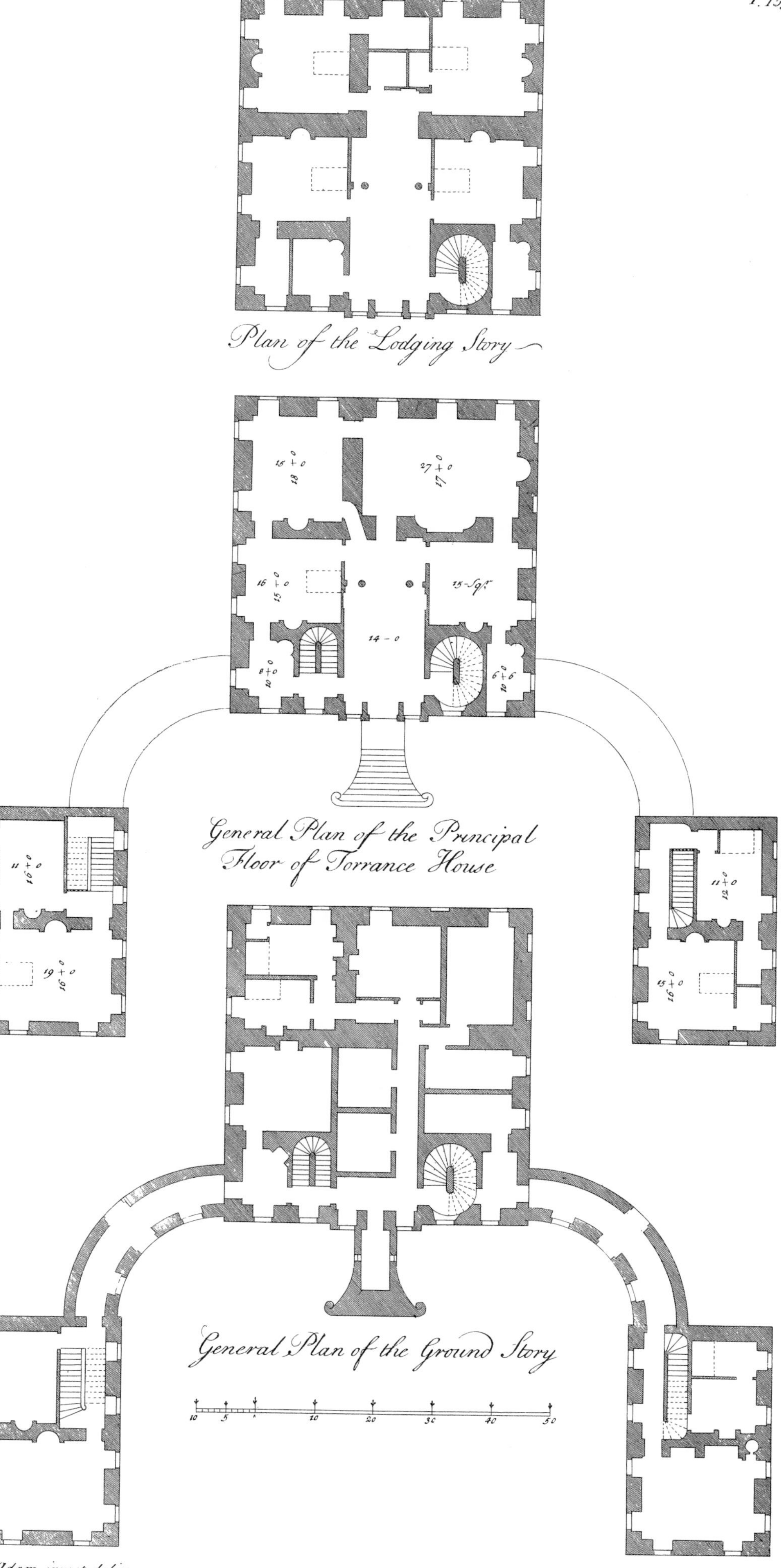

Gul: Adam inv: et delin

R: Cooper Sculp.

The Generall Front Designd for An Orphans Hospitall att Edinburgh

Gull. Adam inv: et delin

R: Cooper Sculp.

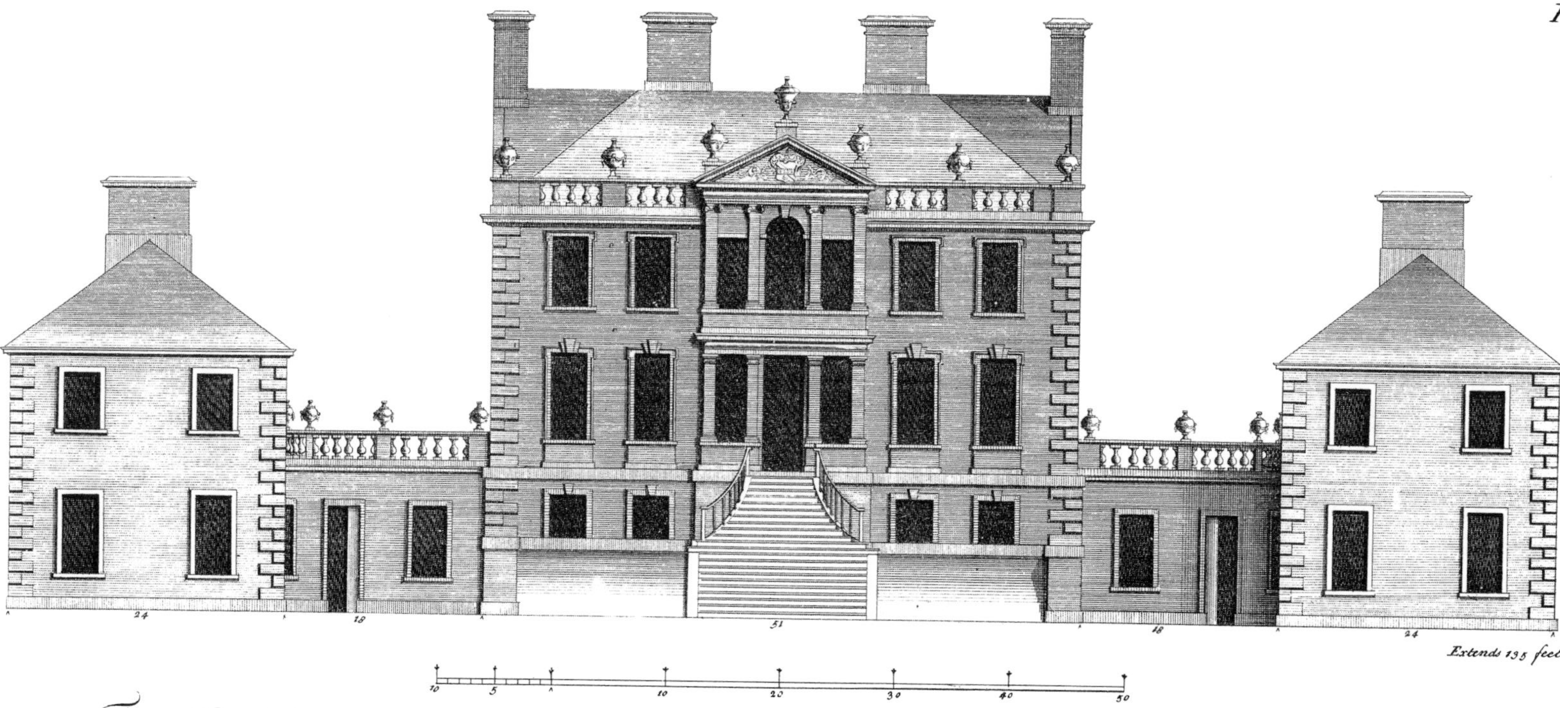

The North Front of Torrance House toward the Court, The Seat of the Hon.ble Collonel James Stewart of Torrance in the County of Clidsdale

Gul: Adam: inv: et delin

R: Cooper Sculp.

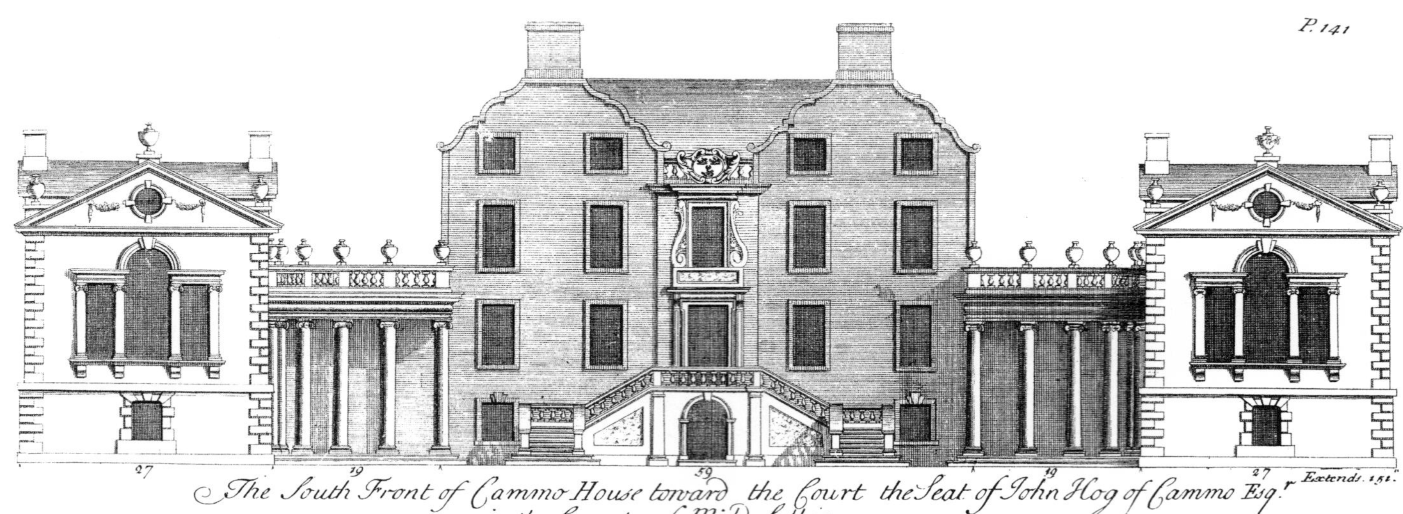

The South Front of Cammo House toward the Court the Seat of John Hog of Cammo Esq.r in the County of Midd Lothian

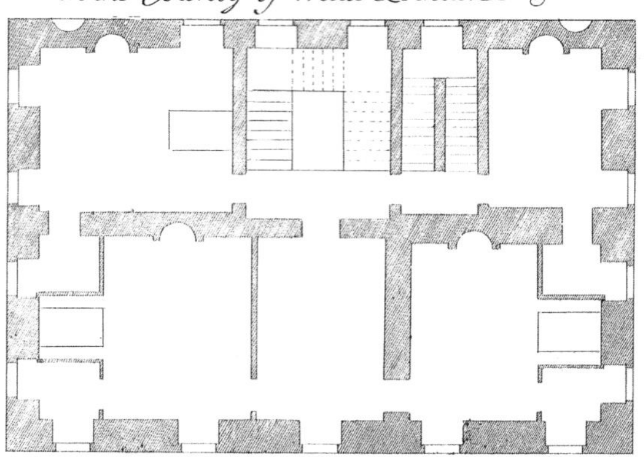

Plan of the Attick Story

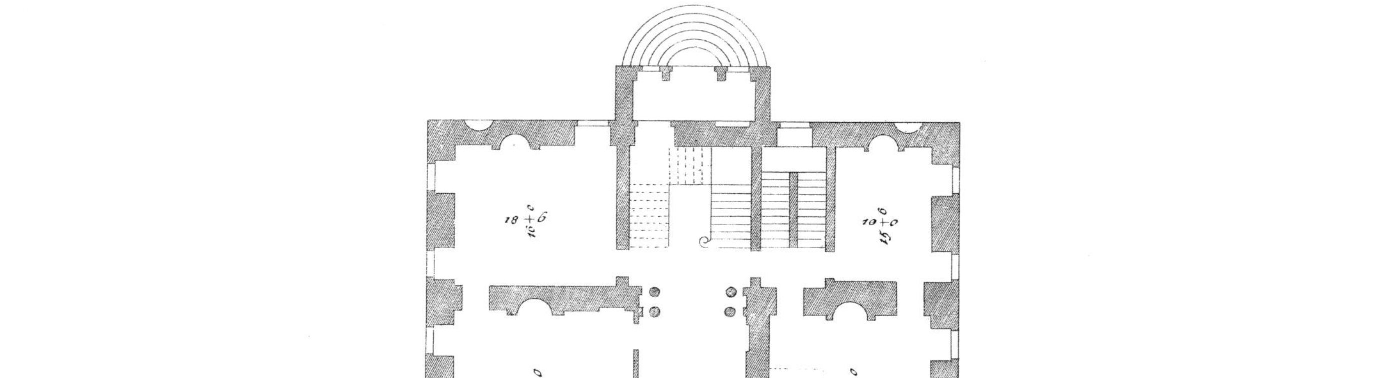

Generall Plan of the First Floor

10 5 0 10 20 30 40 50

Gul: Adam delin

R Cooper Sculp.

The Court Front of Harden House in the County of Teviotdale Extends 101 feet

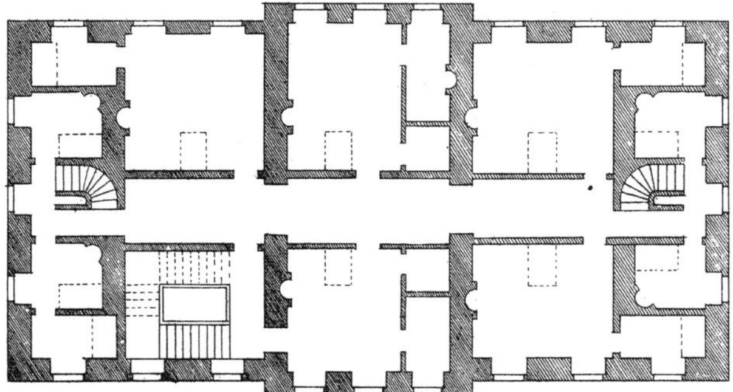

Plan of the Attick Story

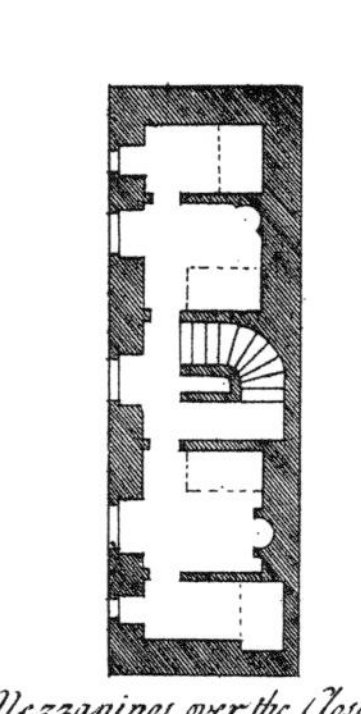

Mezzanines over the Closets

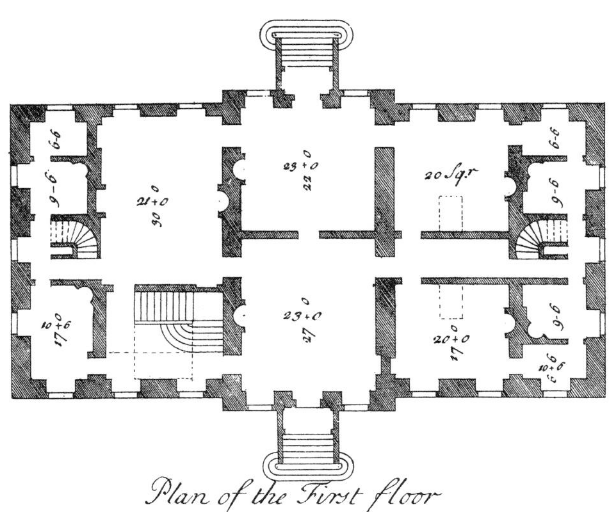

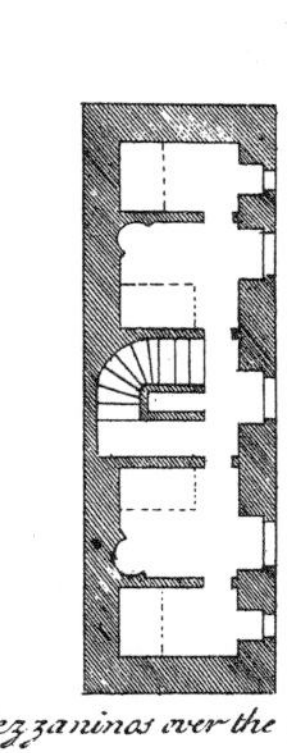

Mezzanines over the Closets

Plan of the First floor

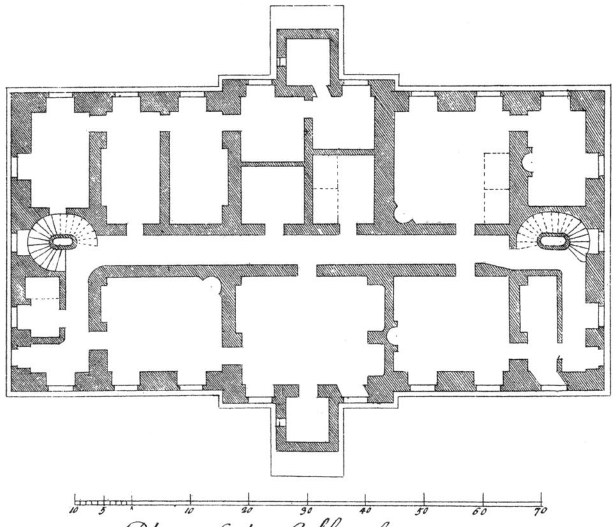

Plan of the Cellar Story

S.r W.m Bruce Inv.t
Gul Adam delin

R. Cooper Sculp.

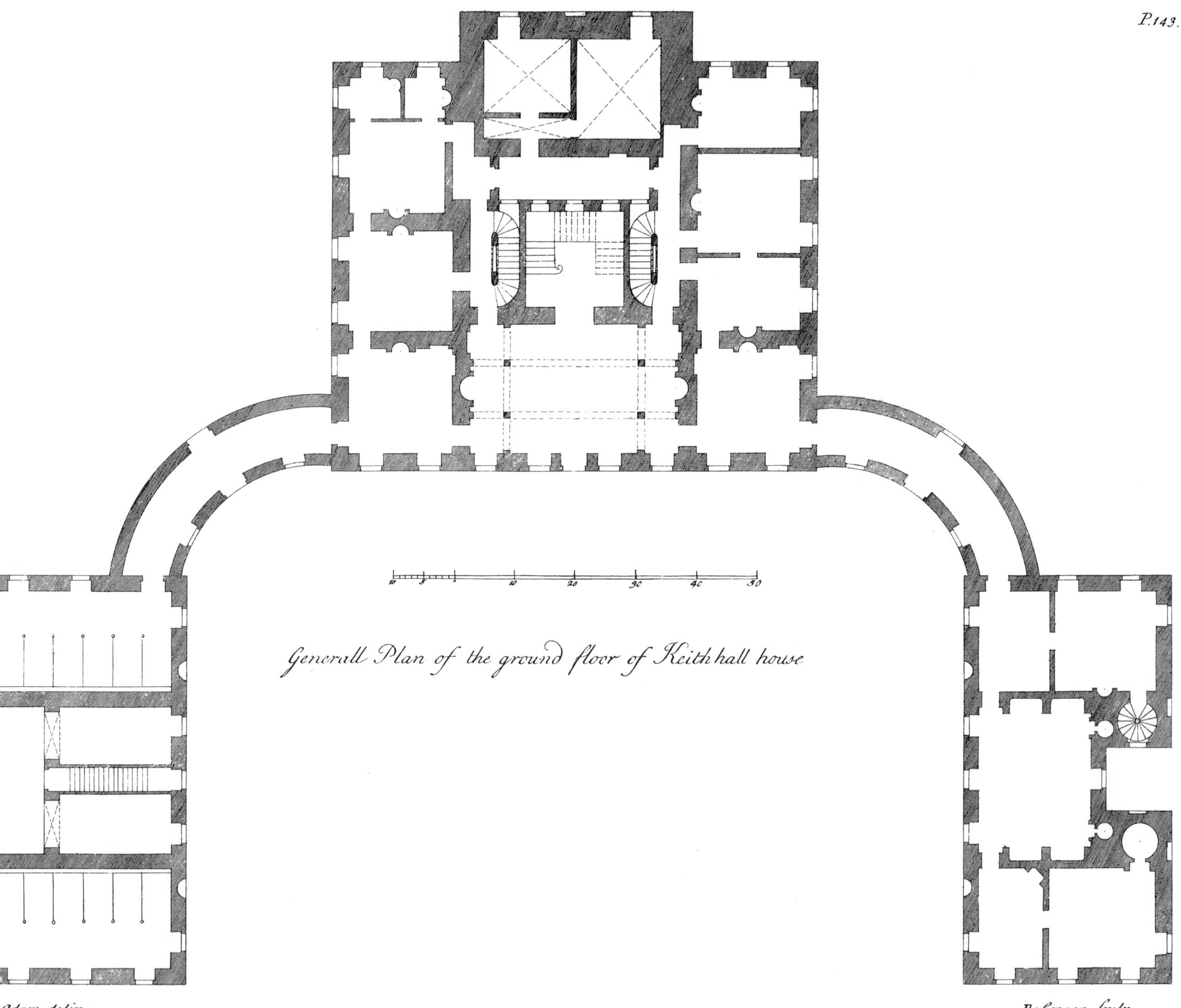

Generall Plan of the ground floor of Keith hall house

Gul: Adam delin.

R: Cooper Sculp.

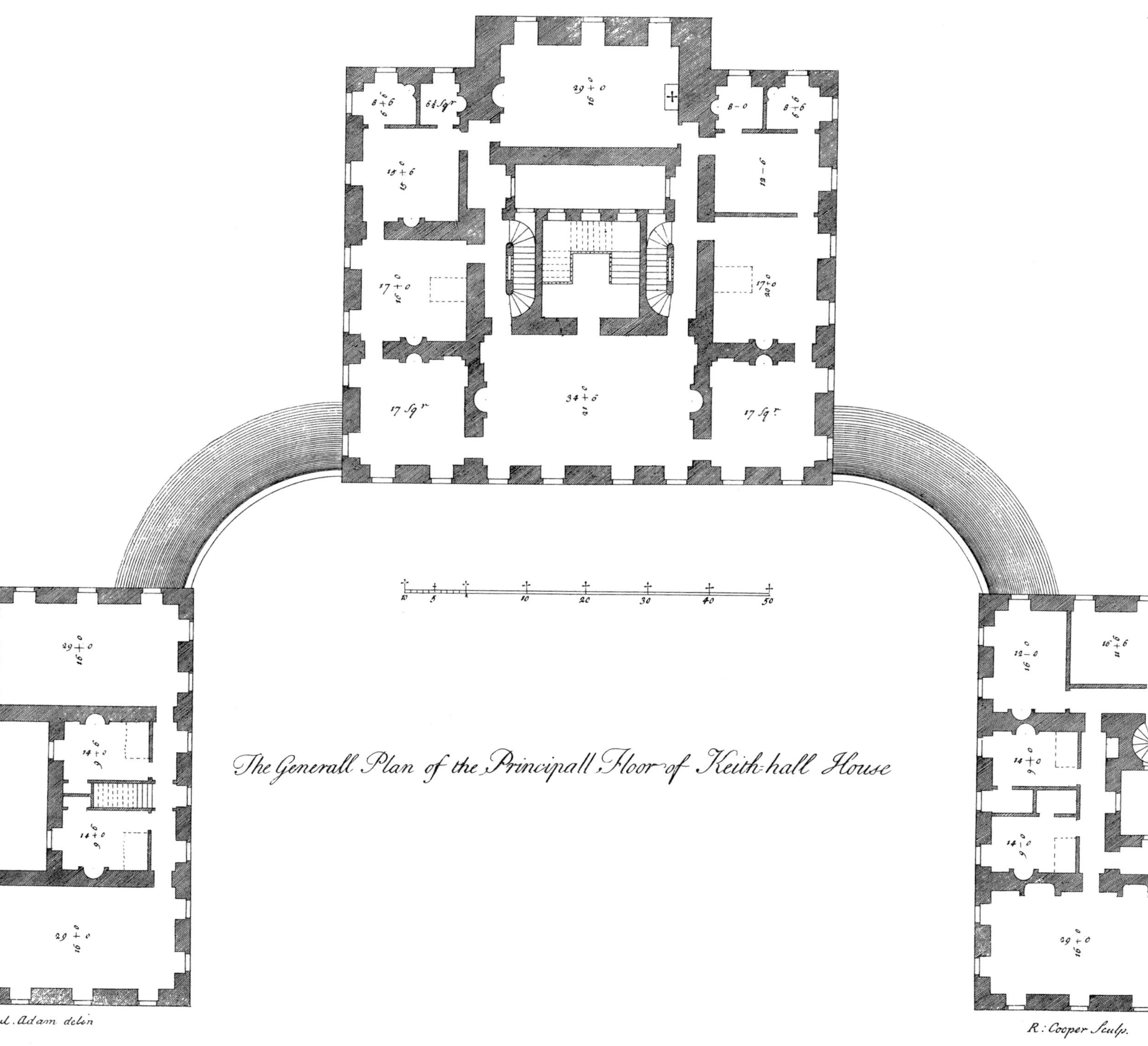

The Generall Plan of the Principall Floor of Keith-hall House

The South Front of Keithhall toward the Court The Seat of the Right Honorable The Earl of Kintore in the County of Aberdeen

Gul: Adam delin

R: Cooper Sculp.

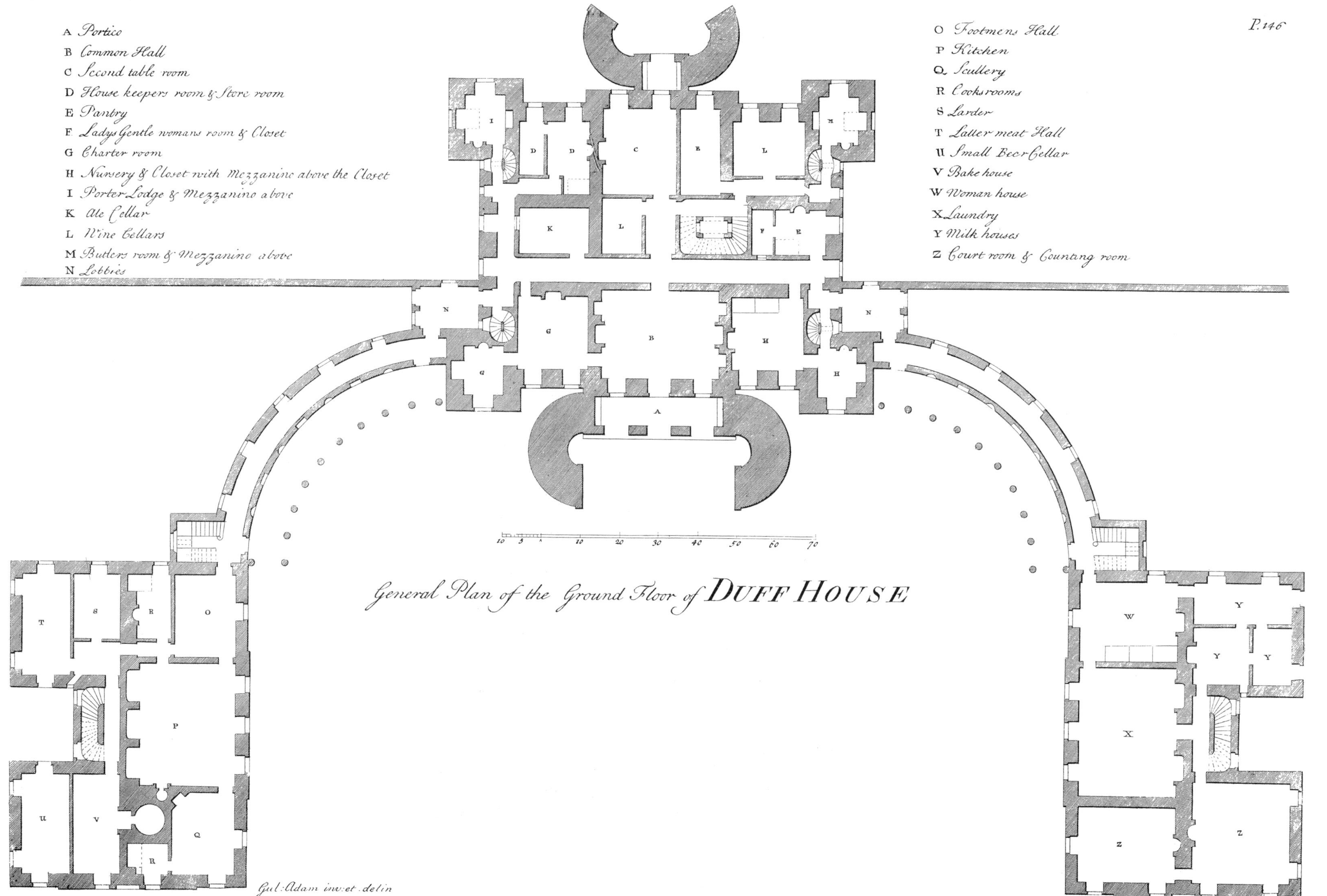

General Plan of the Ground Floor of DUFF HOUSE

A Vestuble
B Private Dineing room
C Private Drawing room
D Cabinet & Mezzanino above
E Bed Chamber
F Dressing room & Mezzanino above
G Family Bed Chamber
H Ladys Dressing room
I Her Closet & Mezzanino above
K My Lord Dressing room
L His Closet & Mezzanino above
M Libary
N Lodgeing for Servants

Generall Plan of the first Floor of DUFF HOUSE

Gul: Adam inv: et delin

R: Cooper Sculp

The Generall Front of DUFF HOUSE toward the Cou

A Sallon
B Anti=Chamber
C Great Drawing room
D Five Bed Chambers
E Four Dressing rooms with Mezzanino's overhead
F Four little Stool rooms

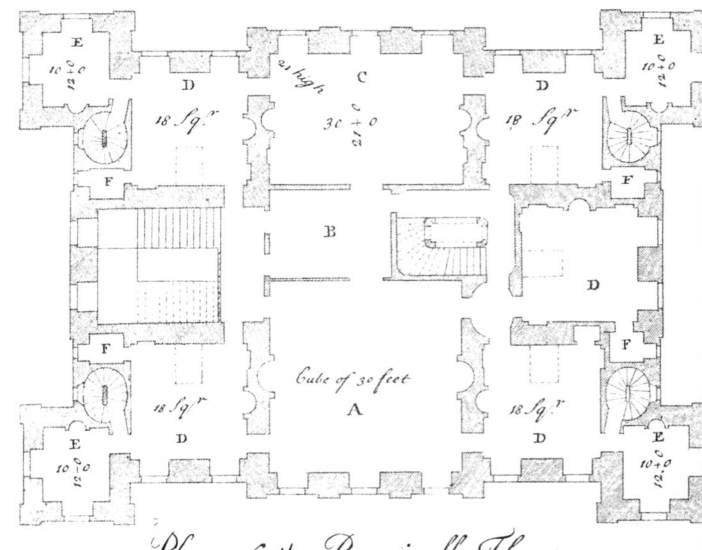

Plan of the Principall Floor

Gul. Adam inv: et delin

40 50 60 70

Extends 330 feet.

of the Right Honorable the EARL of FIFE in the County of Banff:

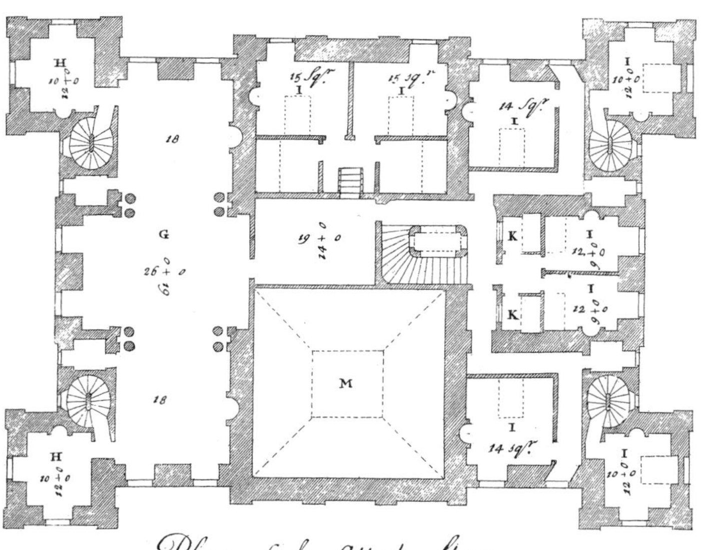

G Gallery
H Closets of it
I Bed Chambers
K Closets
L Ante Chamber
M Coving of the Sallon which is Carried up two full Storys

Plan of the Attick Story

40 50

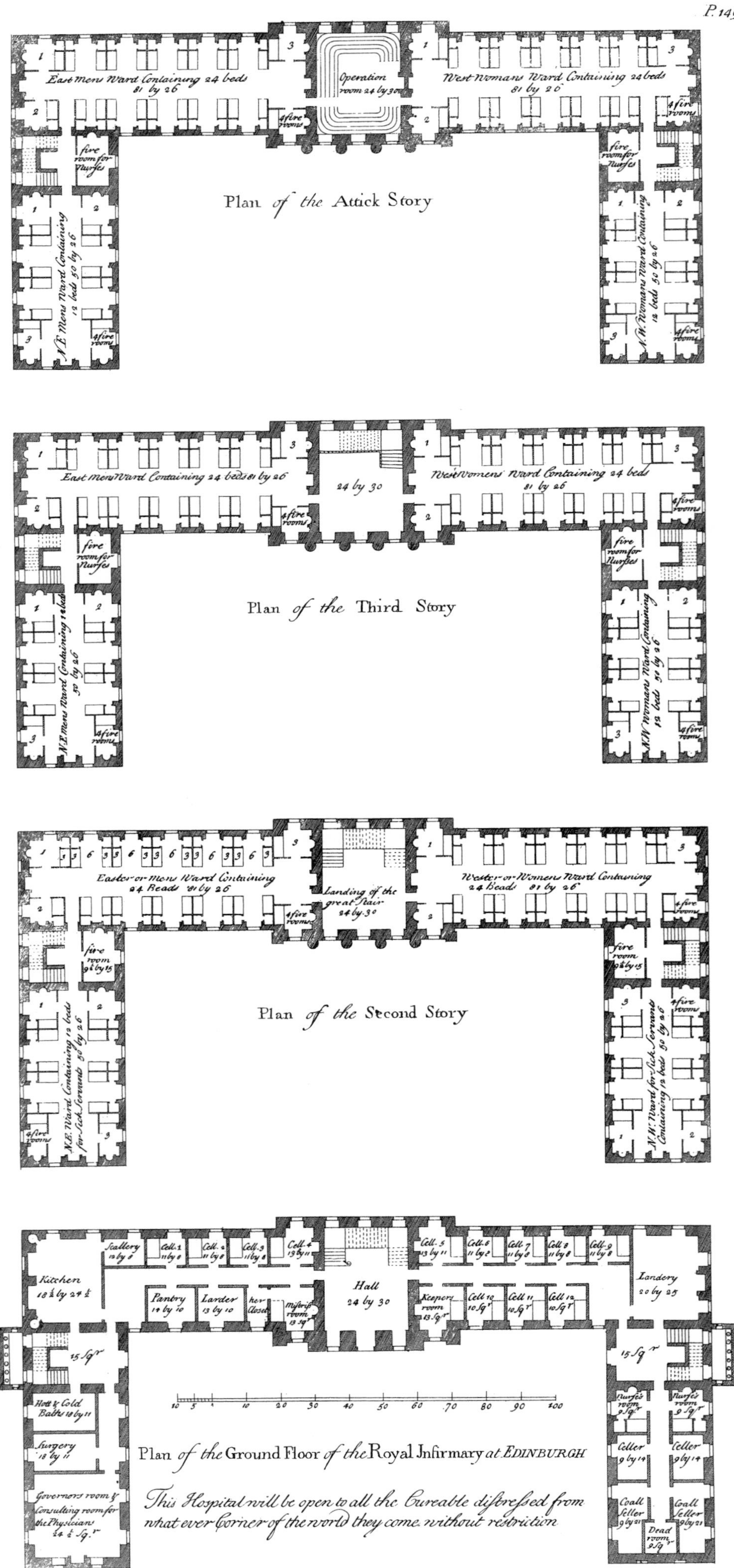

Plan of the Ground Floor of the Royal Infirmary at EDINBURGH

This Hospital will be open to all the Cureable distressed from what ever Corner of the world they come without restriction

Gul: Adam inv: et delin

R: Cooper Sculp.

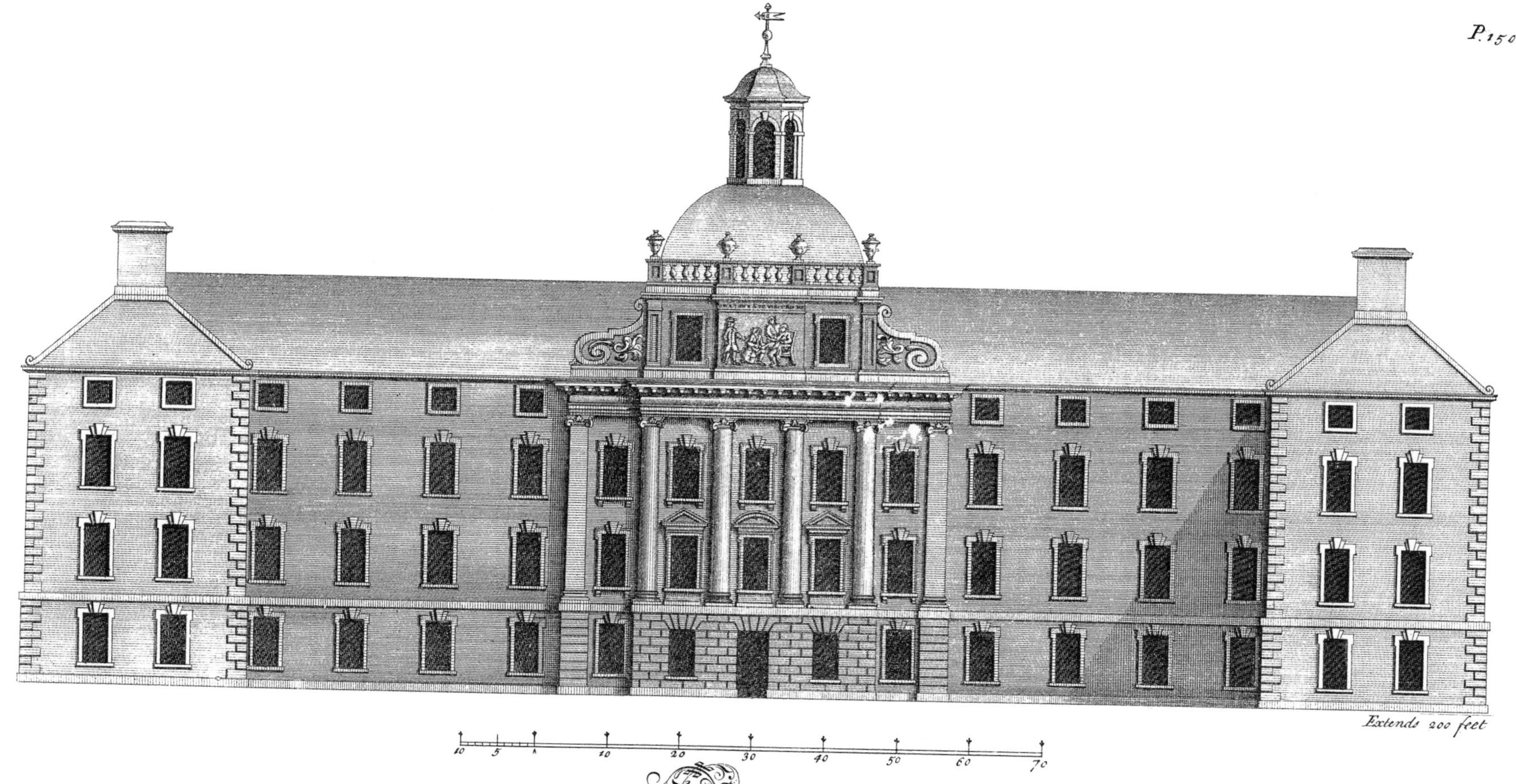

Gul: Adam inv: et delin

The North Front of the Royal Infirmary facing the City of Edinburgh

R. Cooper Sculp.

The North Front of Watsons Hospital at Edinburgh

Plan of the Lodging Story

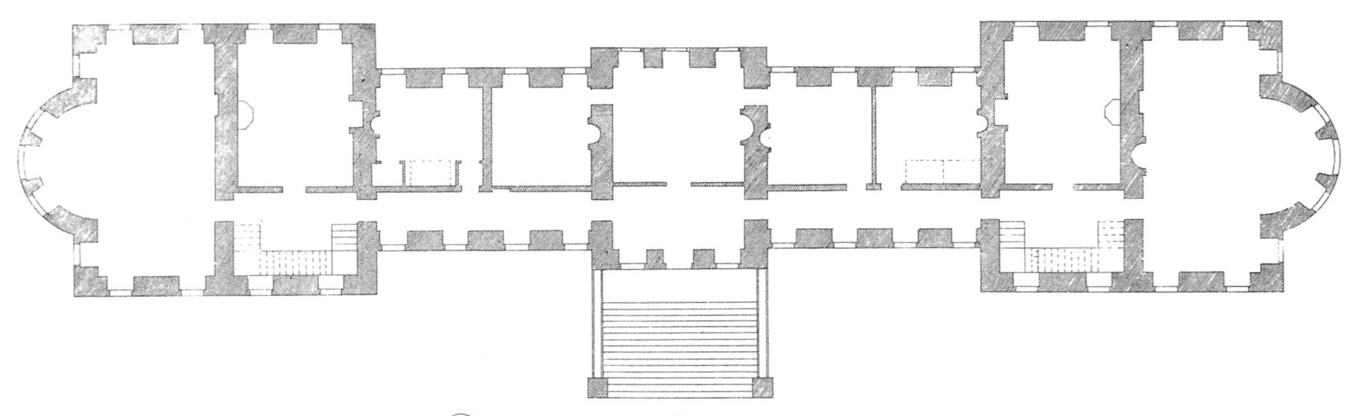

Plan of the Princip.l Floor

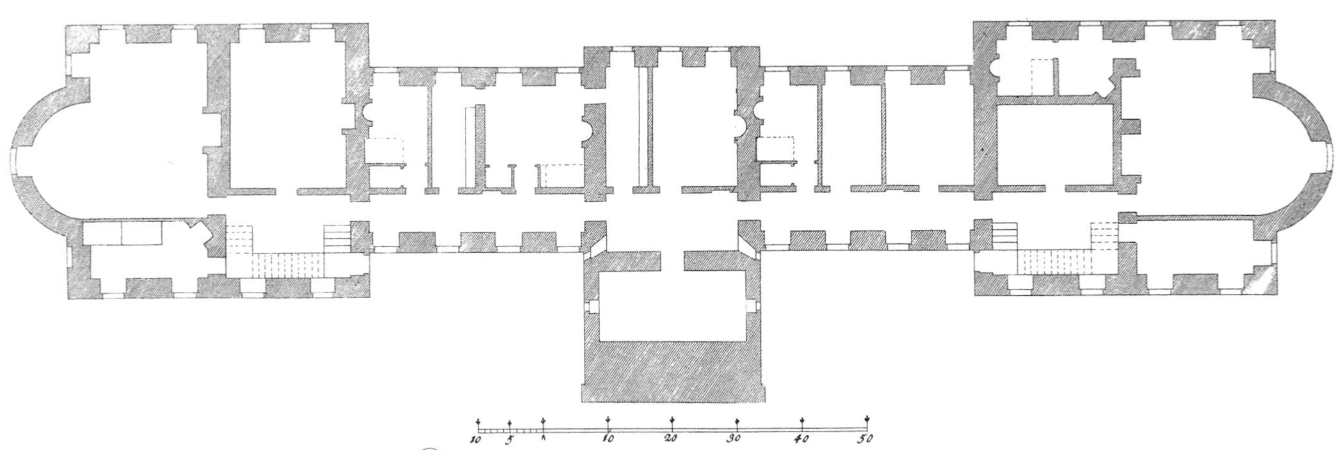

Plan of the Ground Floor

Gul: Adam inv: et delin

R. Cooper Sculp

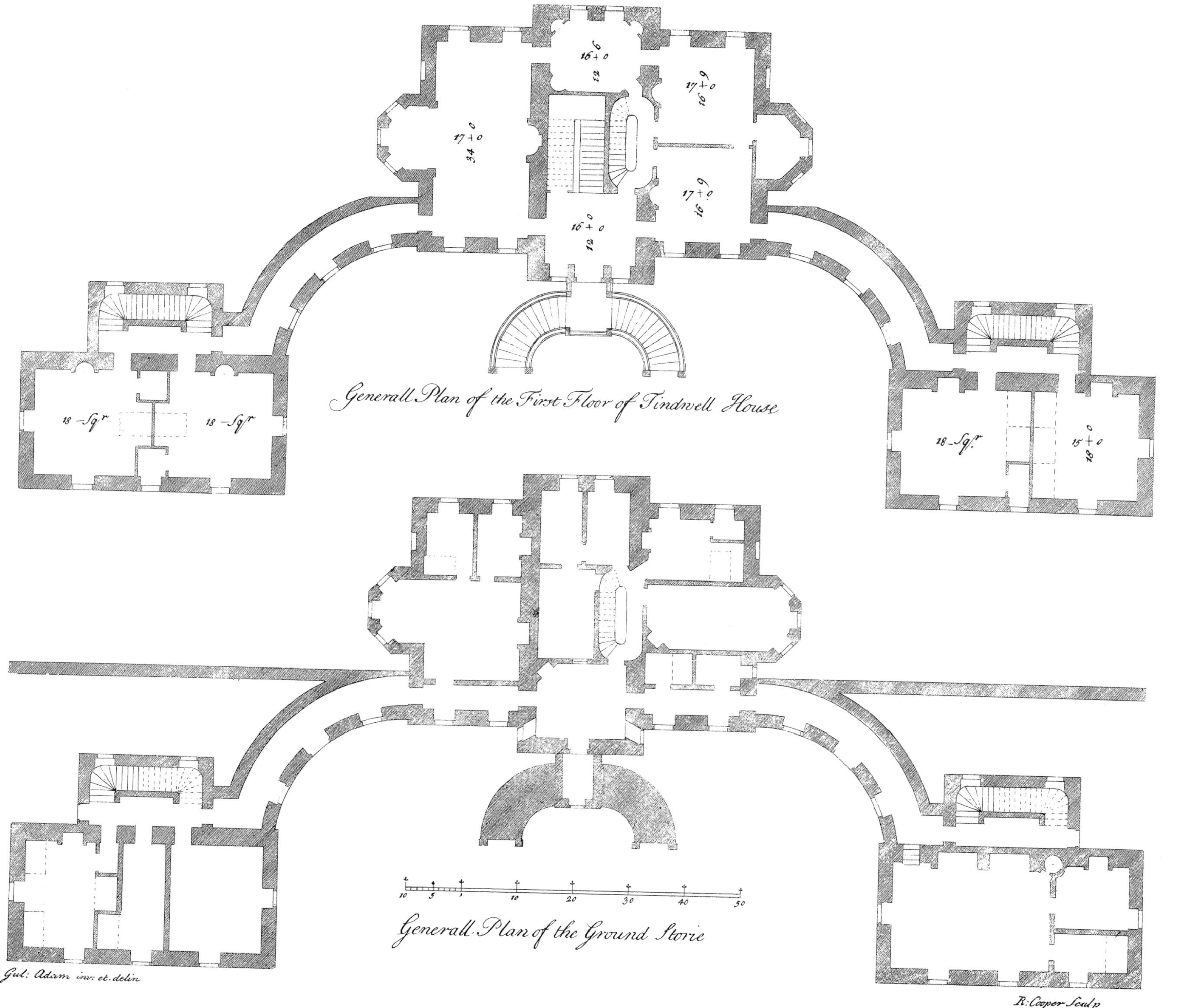

Generall Plan of the First Floor of Tindwell House
Generall Plan of the Ground Storie
Gul: Adam inv: et. delin
R: Cooper Sculp

The West Front of Tindwall House *toward the Court The Seat of the Right Honorable* Charles Areskine *of* Tindwall *Esqr*, *His* MAJESTYS Advocate *for* SCOTLAND *in the County of* Nithisdale

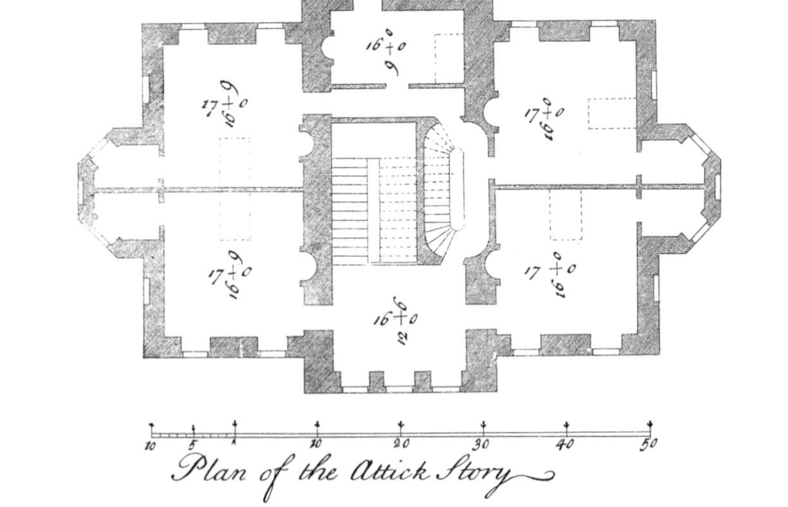

Plan of the Attick Story

Gul Adam inv et delin

R: Cooper Sculp.

The North Front of **Belhaven house** *toward the Court The Seat of the Right Honorable The Lord* **BELHAVEN** *in the County of East Lothian*

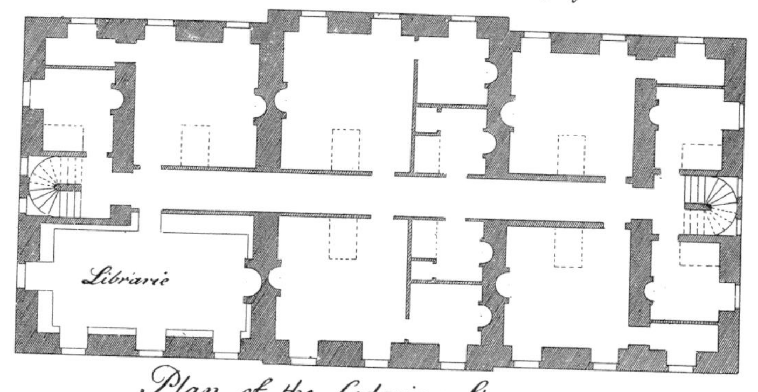

Plan of the Lodgeing Story

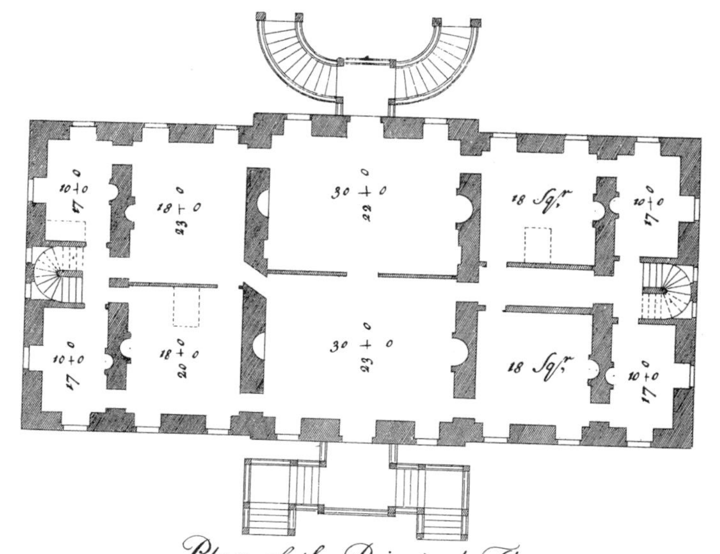

Plan of the Principal Floor

10 5 10 20 30 40 50 Feet

Plan of the Ground Story

Gul: Adam inv: et delin — *R: Cooper Sculp:*

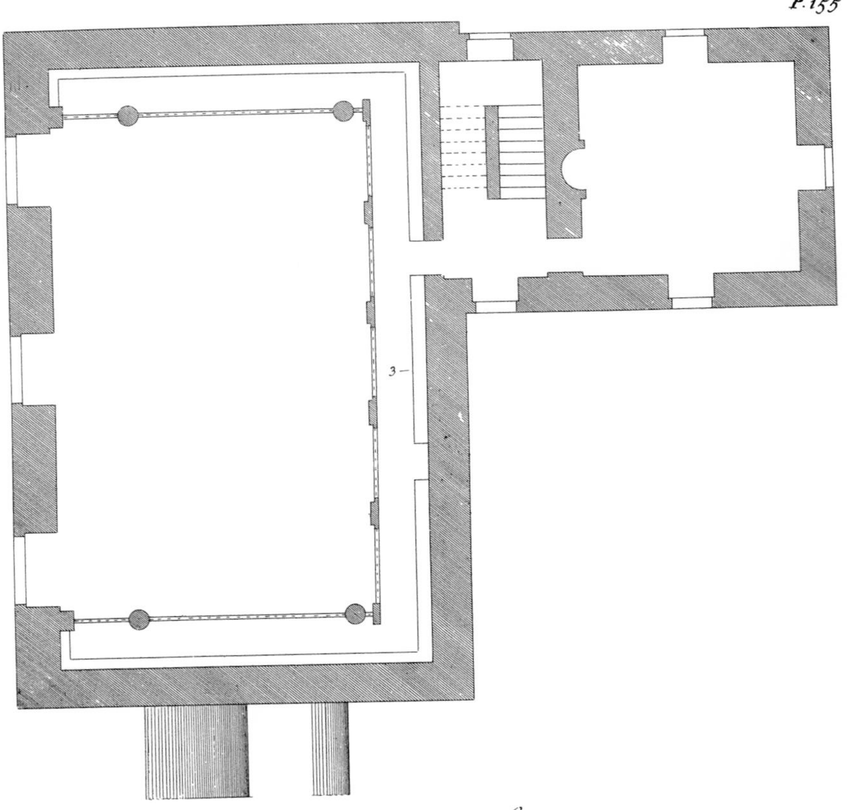

Plan of the Gallery Story

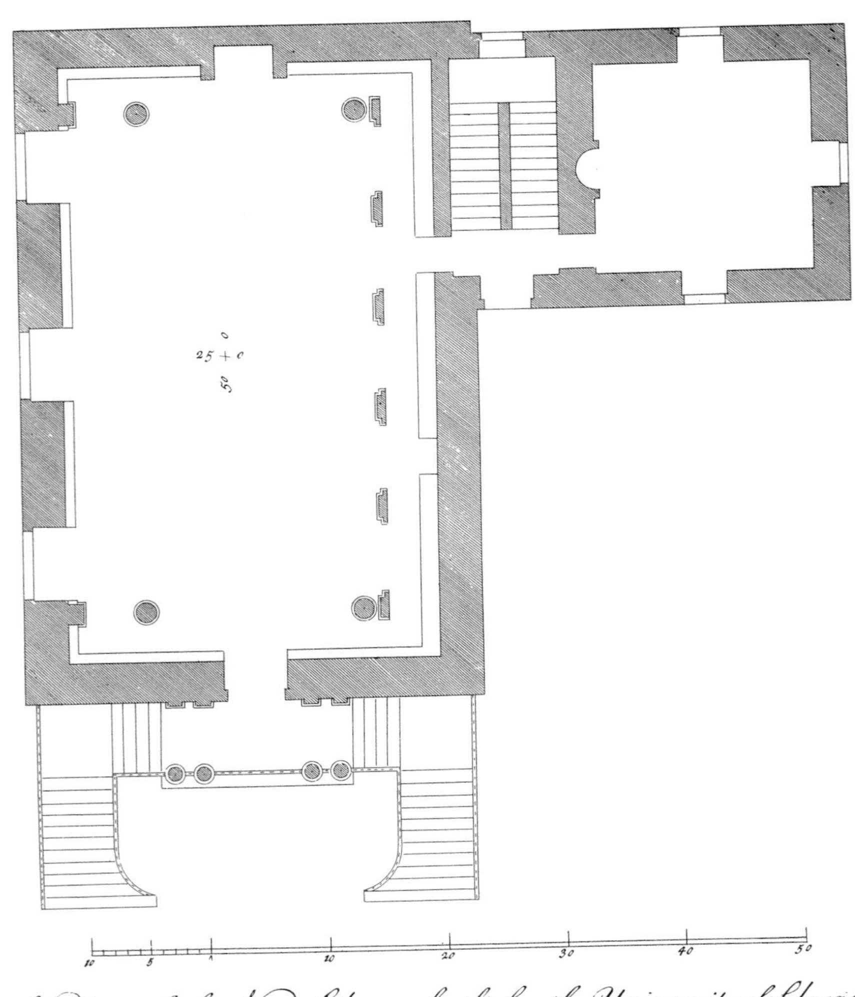

A Plan of the New Library built for the University of Glasgow

Gul Adam inv: et delin

R Cooper Sculp

North Front or Principal Entrance of the Colledge Library att GLASGOW

10 5 0 10 20 30

East Front toward the Garden

Gul: Adam inv: et delin

R: Cooper Sculp.

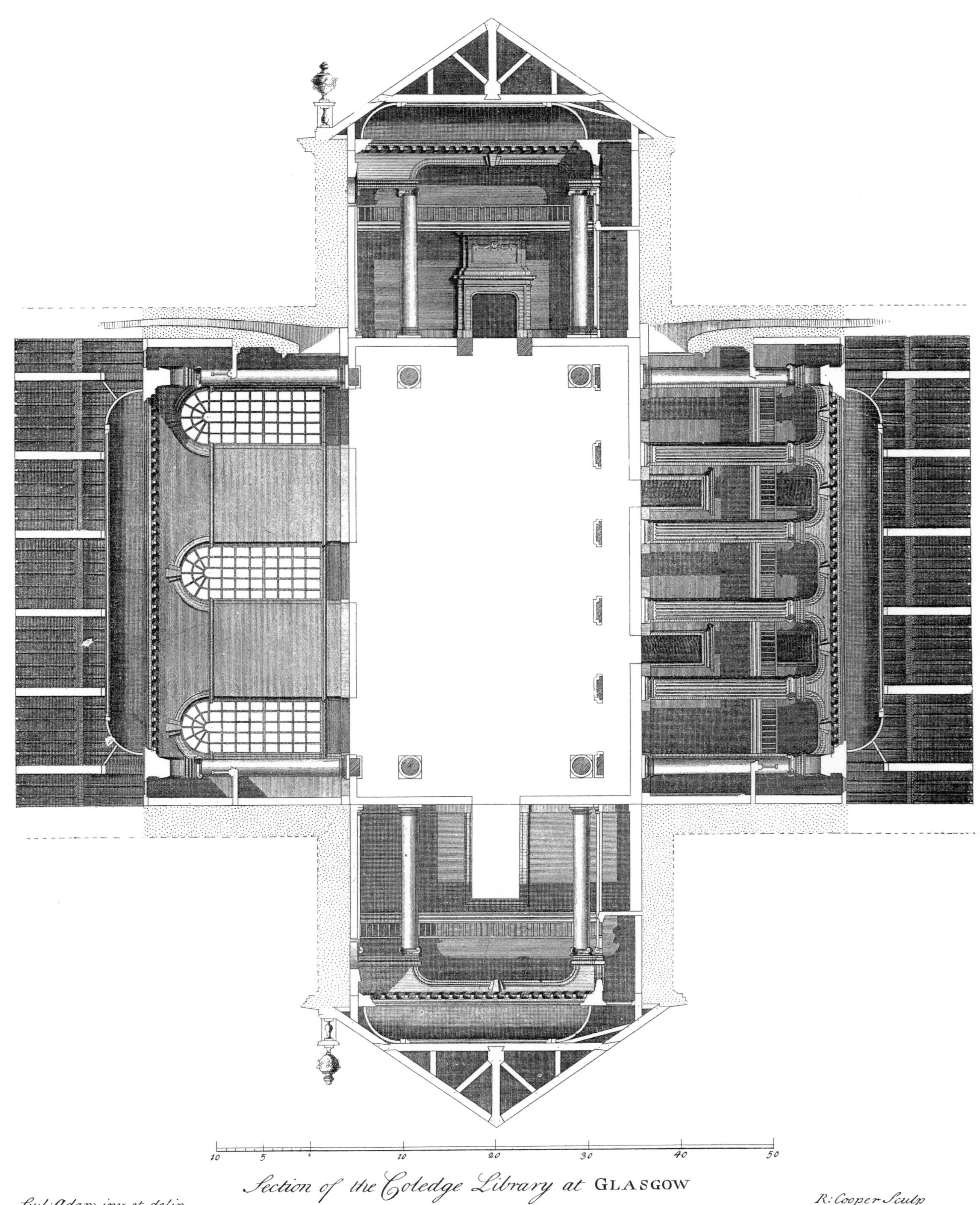

Section of the Coledge Library at GLASGOW

Gul: Adam inv et delin *R: Cooper Sculp*

The South Front of Lawers house toward the Court One of the Seats of the Hon.ble Brigadeer General James Campbell in the County of PEARTH

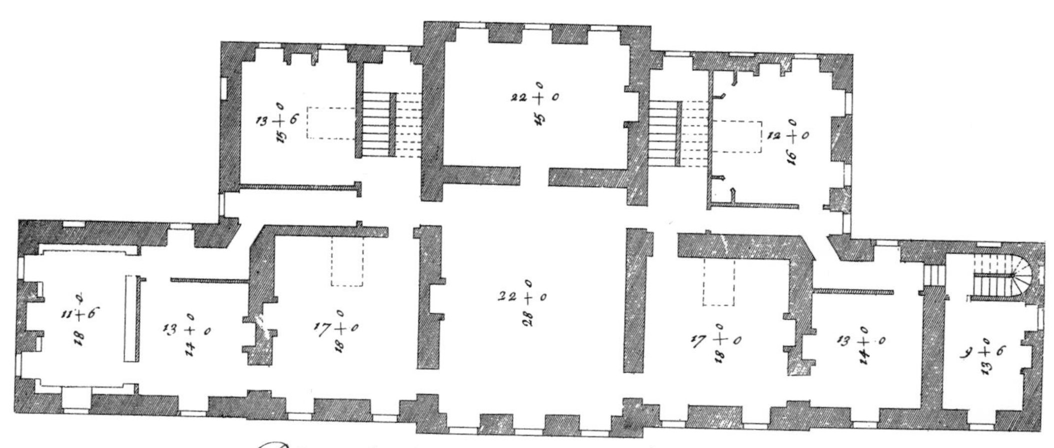

Plan of the Principal Floor

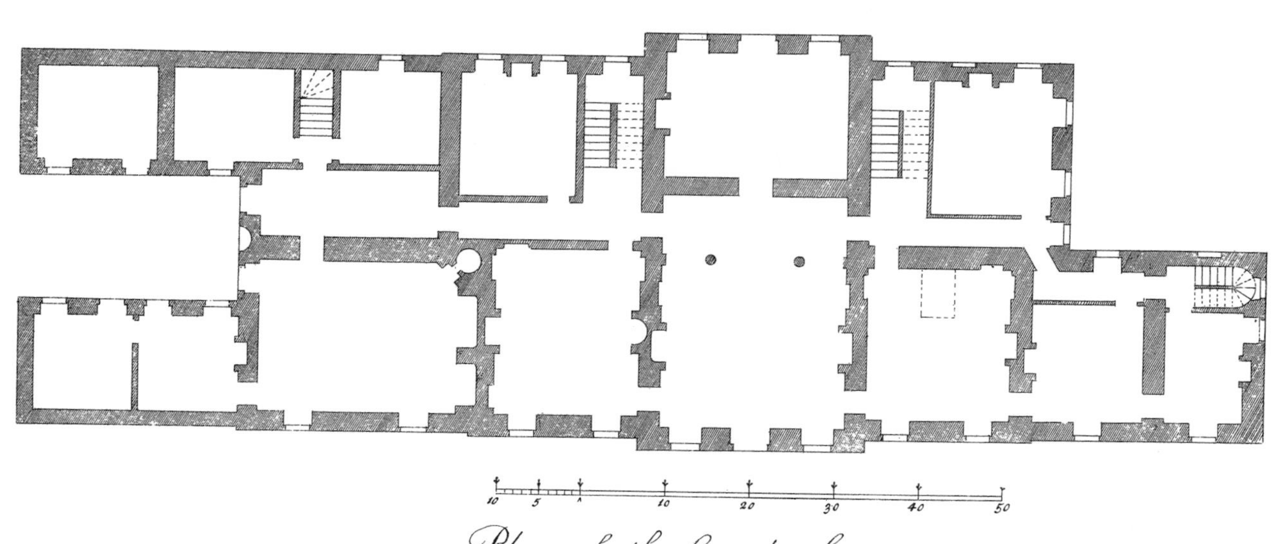

Plan of the Ground Story

Gul: Adam inv et delin

R: Cooper Sculp

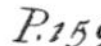

Section of the Sallon of Lavers house

28 by 22 & 19 feet high

10 5 0 10 20

Generall Front *toward the North of the Dogg Kennell att* Hamilton *Situate att the head of the South Avenue a mile Distant from, & Fronting the* Palace

Gul: Adam inv: et delin

R: Cooper Sculp